Using Evidence to Inform Policy

Using Evidence to Inform Policy

Pete Lunn & Frances Ruane

GILL & MACMILLAN

Gill & Macmillan
Hume Avenue
Park West
Dublin 12
with associated companies throughout the world
www.gillmacmillan.ie

© Pete Lunn & Frances Ruane 2013

978 07171 5972 7

Print origination by Carole Lynch
Printed by GraphyCems, Spain
Index by Grainne Farren

The paper used in this book comes from the wood pulp of managed forests.
For every tree felled, at least one tree is planted,
thereby renewing natural resources.

All rights reserved. No part of this publication may be copied,
reproduced or transmitted in any form or by any means,
without written permission of the publishers or else under
the terms of any licence permitting limited copying issued
by the Irish Copyright Licensing Agency.

A CIP catalogue record is available for this book
from the British Library

Acknowledgements

The editors are most grateful to their colleagues, and former colleagues, who authored the chapters in this book, having participated so enthusiastically in the *Renewal Project*. They also acted as referees for many of the chapters in the book, as did other colleagues in the Institute: Alan Barrett, John FitzGerald, Petra Gerlach, Richard Layte, Fran McGinnity, Laura Malaguzzi Valeri and Miriam Wiley.

Because of their particular policy focus, various chapters were also sent to policymakers for review. These external referee reports played an important role in the development of the papers, as presented at the Renewal Conferences. We thank the referees for their insightful comments and suggestions: Alan Ahearne, Donal Donovan, Eoin Gahan, Anne Looney, Muiris MacCarthaigh, Mary O'Dea, Declan Purcell, Orlaigh Quinn and Brendan Tuohy.

The chapters also benefited from the valuable comments and suggestions made by the participants at each of the four Renewal Conferences, and particularly by the formal respondents: John Cotter, Ann Fitzgerald, Cathal Guiomard, Deirdre Hanlon, Martin Lyes, Jonathan McMahon, Brigid McManus, Kieran Mulvey, Brid O'Brien, Paul Reid, Anne Vaughan and Liam Woods.

The development of this *Renewal Project* and the preparation of this volume would not have been possible without the administrative and editorial support of our colleagues. In relation to the project, we were ably assisted by Elaine Byrne, Eleanor Bannerton, Gillian Davidson and Regina Moore. The preparation of this volume benefited greatly from the careful work of Regina Moore and Dee Whitaker. Externally we received great support from Michael Gill, Marion O'Brien and Catherine Gough at Gill & Macmillan, and from Winifred Power, who pulled out all the stops to provide us with copy-editing for the first and final chapters at short notice.

Preface

In times of economic crisis, the importance of having evidence to help inform policymakers rises. At such times, the cost of policy errors is greater than ever. In the present global crisis, many of the key actions lie outside the controls of individual countries. While Ireland would favour greater emphasis on reducing employment and a slower adjustment to fiscal balance, it is not in a position to determine its own pathway to recovery. This does not mean that Ireland does not have policy levers, but rather that it has a limited range of policy levers.

In 2011 the Economic and Social Research Institute (ESRI) began a series of research studies to explore the evidence that might inform policy in a range of areas that would promote economic renewal and strengthen the economy against the types of failures that contributed to the scale of Ireland's crisis. A key feature of each of the projects was their focus on the evidence that the international literature could contribute to informing policymakers in Ireland about the relevant actions they might want to consider. Each project had a specific policy question which it sought to answer in a rigorous way based on the best available research evidence.

All of the research projects individually provided insights on exactly what research evidence can contribute to specific areas of policy. But the projects taken together present a picture for policymakers of the diverse range of research that can inform the policy process. In this book, we have developed a framework for the policy landscape to show where these papers interconnect with different types of policy actions. While the studies reflect the evidence at a point in time, they have a more timeless quality in demonstrating how evidence can be used inductively to inform policy.

We have brought the analyses of these projects together in book form because of their potential to give guidance to those engaged in policy analysis, to inform policymaking and to provide material for those engaged in teaching or studying the policymaking process what social science evidence can contribute.

As editors of the project, we are indebted to our colleagues who engaged so enthusiastically with the project and to the respondents and participants at the series of conferences where the initial papers were presented. We are also grateful to the generosity of the academics and policymakers who acted as referees for the papers, and to FBD Trust which provided seed funding for the project.

We dedicate this book to two individuals, Dr T.K. Whitaker and the late Dr R.C. Geary. As an individual, Dr Whitaker has, since the time he oversaw one of the largest changes in Irish policy, namely from protectionism to free trade, been a strong advocate for having more analysis within the policymaking arena. Dr Geary, the internationally renowned statistician, was the founder Director of the Central Statistics Office which has produced the data on which much empirical analysis is based. With the support of Dr Whitaker, Dr Geary became the founder Director of the Economic and Social Research Institute, where he set a high standard of how to undertake research that would produce the type of evidence that could be used for policy in Ireland.

To T.K. Whitaker and *in memoriam* R.C. Geary

Contents

Preface vii

1. When and How Can Evidence Inform Policy? 1
   Pete Lunn, Frances Ruane

2. Using Evidence to Improve Evaluation Methods for
   Public Infrastructure 23
   Edgar Morgenroth

3. Should Loan-to-Value Ratios be Limited? The International
   Evidence 39
   David Duffy

4. The Potential Role of Pay-for-Performance in Irish Healthcare:
   Lessons from the International Evidence 56
   Anne Nolan, Jacqueline O'Reilly, Samantha Smith, Aoife Brick

5. Learning from the Evidence: Using Educational Research
   to Inform Policy 77
   Emer Smyth, Selina McCoy

6. Boosting Innovation and Productivity in Enterprises:
   What Matters? What Works? 96
   Frances Ruane, Iulia Siedschlag

7. Do Active Labour Market Policies Activate? 118
   Elish Kelly, Seamus McGuinness, Philip J. O'Connell

8. Providing Economic Security Through Competition and
   Regulatory Policy: What Is the Evidence? 140
   Paul K. Gorecki

9. Protecting Consumers of Financial Services 162
   Pete Lunn

10. Fiscal Consolidation Strategies: Evidence from the
    International Experience 187
    Eddie Casey, Joseph Durkan, David Duffy

11. Evidence on the Pattern of Earnings and Labour Costs
    Over the Recession 217
    Adele Bergin, Elish Kelly, Seamus McGuinness

12. Quality of Public Services: Irish Public Perceptions and
    Implications for Public Service Reform 244
    Dorothy Watson

13. Increasing the Contribution of Evidence to Policy 266
    Frances Ruane, Pete Lunn

Index 275

CHAPTER 1

When and How Can Evidence Inform Policy?

Pete Lunn, Frances Ruane

> *'The most savage controversies are about matters as to which there is no good evidence either way.'*
> Bertrand Russell

INTRODUCTION

When and how can evidence inform policy? There is a sense in which the answer to this question is obvious. Whatever the policy domain, few would dispute that decision-makers are inclined to make better decisions when they have the relevant factual information, understand the main underlying processes involved, and possess reliable estimates of the likely outcomes associated with the options under consideration.

For example, health policy benefits from evidence that measures how many patients are treated in each healthcare centre (hospital, primary-care centre, GP practice, etc.), that explains how the patients come to be treated in these different centres, or that estimates the likely impact on the use of healthcare services of changing the way patients pay for their healthcare. Similarly, transport policy benefits from evidence that measures the demand for journeys, or that explains how people choose their mode of transport, or that estimates the impact on those decisions of a proposed change in service.

Furthermore, it is similarly uncontentious that ongoing policy development is likely to be improved by objective evaluation of the outcomes that policies generate. This is particularly the case if policies are readily open to alteration and if there is a willingness to absorb lessons for and from other policy areas.

This potential for evidence to inform policy and to help evaluate existing policies in order to drive improvements in policy design has long been recognised. Indeed, arguments about how evidence should relate to policy are at least 250 years old. Back in 1747, the Scottish physician James Lind conducted what is widely regarded as the first clinical trial, on the effects of citrus fruit as a cure for scurvy. Since naval power was vital to the creation and preservation of the British Empire and, at that time, more naval seamen were killed by scurvy than by enemy ships, the new form of evidence generated a vigorous policy debate, one which was not resolved for forty years (Bartholomew, 2002). The early application of evidence to health policy – and disease control in particular – has contributed significantly to the cessation of long-standing medical treatments that were damaging rather than beneficial to health.

This tradition continued to develop in the nineteenth century. In Ireland, for example, the Statistical and Social Inquiry Society of Ireland was founded in 1847 in the belief that statistics and economic analysis would provide scientific answers to the major problems of the time and in particular to the problems created by the 1840s' potato famine (Daly, 1997). The Society's journal provides a picture of the different kinds of empirical evidence that have been presented over the following sixteen decades, informing civil society and those with the power to react to the findings. For example, the papers that laid the background to T. K. Whitaker's *Economic Development* were presented to the society in the mid-1950s. Furthermore, Whitaker himself, together with other members of the society, was instrumental in establishing the Economic Research Institute in 1960, whose defined purpose was to provide evidence to inform policymaking in Ireland.[1] Ireland was not alone in this regard. Over the course of the twentieth century many governments in the developed world established organisations with the explicit aim of improving the quantity and quality of data (through their national statistical offices) and of analysis (through funding research institutes and research groups) across major policy areas. Thus, the concept of evidence-based policy is hardly new.

Yet the situation has changed since the 1990s. The digital revolution has transformed modern data systems, methods of analysis and access to domestic and international research output – greatly increasing the potential for more systematic use of evidence to inform the policy process. An identifiable movement towards evidence-based policymaking has emerged, the progress and potential benefits of which are analysed by scholars of political science and public administration. In addition, various conceptual frameworks have been developed that seek to analyse how knowledge is managed at the interface between researchers and policymakers, including the role of so-called 'knowledge brokers' (Mayer *et al.*, 2004; Magnuszewski *et al.*, 2010). Politicians, public servants, researchers, journalists, campaigning organisations and others with an interest in public affairs now place increasing emphasis on research evidence; the context is one where greater transparency and accountability are called for. Indeed, within a modern society, it is difficult to argue that the process of policymaking, together with the political and public debate that surrounds it, is not enhanced by the timely availability of relevant objective evidence.

---

1 The Economic Research Institute evolved over the following decade to incorporate social as well as economic domains, becoming the Economic and Social Research Institute in 1969.

What is new in the recent period is the greater availability of high quality scientific evidence to inform policymaking and decision-making. The production of scientific evidence has expanded greatly. Where previously selective pieces of data or analysis (sometimes of dubious quality) were used to make the case for or against a particular policy action, when we speak today of evidence, and especially research evidence, we mean careful and robust analysis based on established statistical methods applied to more comprehensive data. When we refer to evidence in this chapter, we have in our minds primarily peer reviewed, high quality research evidence. This is not to say that other evidence may not also be relevant to policymaking: rather, the intention is to focus on the particular form of evidence that lies at the heart of discussions of evidence-based or evidence-informed policy.[2] This includes both quantitative and qualitative evidence; the defining characteristic must be the rigour of the approach. The expectation is that researchers supplying policymakers with objective and high quality evidence, coupled with well-informed and experienced policymakers seeking and commissioning relevant objective research, should lead to better policy decisions and, hence, better outcomes for society.

Even so, this idealised picture of the contribution of evidence to policy in a modern society is, quite simply, at odds with reality. While many researchers and policymakers[3] might agree on the benefits of using evidence as a basis for policy in principle, in practice they find it much more difficult to engineer an effective meeting of minds. Moreover, there is great variation across policy domains. When the interface between researchers and policymakers works well, it amounts to a systematic, sophisticated and efficient exchange of information and perspectives – although rarely one that is entirely without tension. When the relationship works poorly, communication is one way, effective dialogue does not develop, or the relationship breaks down, with sharply differing perspectives on either side. Researchers sometimes perceive or find policymakers to be unreceptive to relevant research, ignorant of key findings and concepts, anti-intellectual, and more concerned with managing immediate political agendas than with developing policy that will best serve society. For their part, policymakers can perceive or find

---

2 We consider this distinction in greater detail later in this chapter. The key issue is whether policy can ever be truly based on evidence, or whether the evidence base must be just one factor among several that ultimately determine policy.

3 The term 'policymakers' is employed here in its broadest sense to cover all those with a responsibility for or direct influence on public policy. Those responsible include government ministers and politicians (on all sides of the House), political advisors, as well as civil servants and employees of government agencies that have a policy focus. Those who directly influence policymaking include members of government-appointed expert groups and private-sector consultants working directly for the public sector. Although the formulation 'politicians and policymakers' is often used, implying that politicians are somehow not policymakers, in our use of the term the politicians are included.

researchers to be excessively theoretical, ignorant of political realities and institutional details, aloof, driven by their own agendas and really more concerned with publishing papers than with helping to develop policy. Furthermore, professional researchers and experienced policymakers, despite being highly intelligent and very committed, frequently struggle to comprehend the view from the opposite side of this divide, let alone to benefit from adopting the alternative perspective offered.[4]

As we discuss further below, policymaking requires much more than research evidence and must take into account values, contexts (especially institutional factors), implementation challenges, risk and uncertainty. We recognise that decision-making involves balancing the findings of the research evidence with the many considerations that are ultimately outside the realm where research evidence can be of assistance.

THE AIMS OF THIS BOOK

Helping to bridge the divide between researchers and policymakers is the primary aim of this volume. Its chapters are written by researchers at the Economic and Social Research Institute (ESRI). They are based on a series of research papers that set out with the explicit intention of using research evidence to provide insight for policymakers in Ireland, as the country attempts to extricate itself from the wreckage left by a severe banking crisis and very deep recession. The eleven topics cover a range of research questions of clear relevance to Irish policymakers at this time. The studies are largely empirical, making only sparing use of theory. Policy implications are drawn with mindfulness of the constrained context in which policy decisions must be made.

Yet the purpose is not merely to inform policymakers and other stakeholders interested in the specific policy areas in question. The broader aim is to shed light on the relationship between research and policymaking, allowing themes and lessons to be drawn about the linkages between research evidence and policy. As noted above, we are concerned here with research evidence in particular; unless otherwise stated below, reference to evidence relates to research evidence. The intention, therefore, is that this collection of analyses should be instructive for policymakers, researchers and students irrespective of where their interests lie in the policy spectrum; the principles and practices discussed apply wherever bridges between research and policy need to be formed or strengthened. For policymakers, the chapters illustrate the variety of ways in which evidence can inform policy, in terms of the relevance of evidence at different stages of policy development and

---

4 The extent to which research has an impact on policymaking also depends on the importance of formal policy commitments in driving or corralling the policy agenda; as discussed in Ruane (2012), in the Irish case, the commitments in Programmes for Government, budgetary policies and social partnership agreements have strongly impacted on the capacity of the Irish policy system to respond to research findings.

the range of empirical and analytical techniques that can be exploited. For researchers and students, the chapters raise issues about how best to employ data, analytic methods and scientific literature to assist the policymaking process. For both researchers and policymakers, the various analyses reveal that, even where research questions are well defined and findings are of clear relevance, the precise policy implications of the evidence remain matters of debate. They are not obvious but require careful inference and judgement. In general, the evidence allows the decision-maker to be better informed and thus raises the possibility of better policy decisions, but it does not provide the final determination between the options facing the decision-maker.

By providing a set of example studies and associated discussion, the present volume also aims to make a contribution to the growing academic literature on the relationship between evidence and policy across a range of social and economic domains. In order to do this, we explore elements of the interface between researchers and policymakers, but our focus is primarily on demonstrating how different types of evidence can inform policy.[5] As described below, while the movement towards evidence-based policy is understandably popular among many researchers with an interest in policy, it has recently been subject to constructive criticism, most notably with respect to its regular failure to recognise the limits of evidence as a basis for policy and the inadequacy of government resources to respond in policy terms to the evidence. Since the studies presented here raise issues about how much can be inferred about policy from different types of evidence, they constitute examples that can help to inform this debate.

The remainder of this chapter sets the scene for the range of analyses that follow. It describes briefly the international movement towards evidence-based policy in recent decades and argues for a broader conception than is commonly adopted regarding when research evidence is of relevance. A new schema (Figure 1.1 below) is presented for conceptualising how and at what stage evidence can inform policy development. The studies presented in the chapters are ordered in keeping with the schema. However, while emphasising the breadth of the potential contribution of research evidence for policymaking, it is also important to consider its limitations. The different policy areas covered in this book vary also in the extent to which specific policy conclusions can be drawn.

THE MOVEMENT TOWARDS EVIDENCE-BASED POLICYMAKING

While governments have to varying degrees sought to use scientific evidence in the policymaking process for many decades, even centuries, since the 1990s there has been increased recognition in many countries of the desirability and potential

---

5 Coverage of the new and growing literatures on knowledge management and brokerage, and on implementation science lies beyond the scope of this chapter.

of using evidence in a more systematic way to inform policy (Nutley et al., 2010). Several drivers of this movement towards evidence-based policy have been suggested. One is the weakening of the traditional left–right divide in politics during the 1990s, which arguably reduced the extent to which ideology formed the basis of policy. This was exemplified by the centrist New Labour government in the UK, which became one of the international pioneers of the evidence-based approach. It stated explicitly after coming to power in 1997 that a core aim was to base more policy on evidence and to identify 'what worked' regardless of its genesis. A number of reforms of the UK civil service followed, including published guidelines on principles and practice to be followed when incorporating evidence into policy development (e.g., UK Treasury, 2011).

A second, and probably greater, factor is the vast increase in the availability of research micro-data and associated opportunities for statistical analysis that accompanied the acceleration of computing power. Right across the social sciences, the digital revolution is increasing access to data and boosting computing power for analysis dramatically. These trends have altered the balance between theory and empirics, in favour of the latter. The result has been not only greater possibilities for researchers to measure, model and estimate the magnitudes of economic and social phenomena, but also the development of the associated empirical skills within the research community. In at least some areas – where once the standard complaint was that data did not exist to test theories – data have become available before theory has developed precise hypotheses to test. Further, the digital revolution has also made it possible to access much of the latest research evidence across the globe at the click of a mouse, via search engines, databases and web portals specifically designed to organise and disseminate high quality, peer reviewed research.

A third factor behind the movement towards evidence-based policy is the success of the evidence-based approach in medicine, which has dramatically altered policymaking and practice in the health sector. In doing so, it has also highlighted some limitations of evidence and the danger when policy decisions respond to evidence that is not robust. This experience has had a knock-on effect for social science, both indirectly through the promotion of the practical benefits of applying scientific method rigorously and directly through the sharing of techniques such as randomised controlled trials and meta-analyses. It has also drawn attention to the need for multidisciplinary approaches to generating evidence in relation to major policy issues; for example, studies on child development or ageing typically involve a range of disciplines from medicine through to the social sciences.

Finally, the drive towards more open government in many liberal democracies, often coupled with legislation on freedom of information, has increased the demand for accountability and transparency. This demand has been reinforced by individual expectations of more and better use of evidence – a product of increased levels of education and greater knowledge of how governments work in other countries. Accountability and transparency place greater requirements on government to explain its expenditure and to shine light on how policy decisions are being (or have been) made. The focus on what factors were taken into account in decision-making has come to the fore following the global financial crisis when resources available for public expenditures have fallen and where governments need to make tough and unpopular decisions.

The rise of the movement for evidence-based policy is apparent from the setting up of organisations and events designed to promote it. The Economic and Social Research Council (ESRC) in the UK established the *ESRC Centre for Evidence Based Policy and Practice* in 2001. Also in 2001, the *Coalition for Evidence-Based Policy* was founded in Washington DC. In Ireland, the *National Economic and Social Forum* held a conference to promote evidence-based policymaking in 2005 and published an account of proceedings (NESF, 2007). The conference primarily addressed barriers to the adoption of a more systematic evidence-based approach and how these might be overcome. The view was expressed that Ireland was lagging behind the world leaders in integrating research and policy and that it needed to move on from what Gaffney and Harmon (2007, p. 7) referred to in their contribution to the conference as 'this increasingly isolated position'. Ruane (2012) contains proposals for improving the use of evidence in Ireland, which are discussed alongside some other relevant ideas in the final chapter of this volume.

Nevertheless, for all the praise and promotion of evidence-based policymaking, it is not without critics. Some have questioned the efficacy of the approach, arguing that it is naive in the face of political power (Pawson, 2006), or limited by the complexity and dynamic nature of real policy problems (Sanderson, 2009). These authors do not doubt the relevance of evidence for policy decisions, but do conclude that the evidence-based policy approach is much more limited in what it can achieve than many of its proponents claim.

Consideration of the developing international literature on the relationship between evidence and policy, coupled with the experience of putting together this volume, has led us to a balanced view of this debate. The next two sections outline this perspective and aim to provide a context for the chapters that follow. On the one hand, we contend that many interpretations of the role that evidence can play in policymaking are too narrow. They focus on the evaluation of policy but ignore research evidence's ability also to raise policy challenges and to improve the understanding of those who must develop policies designed to meet them. On the other hand, as we noted in the introduction, policymaking requires much more than research evidence. It must take into account priorities, values, contexts (especially institutional factors and legal constraints), costs and benefits, risk and uncertainty. While research evidence can sometimes contribute to a better understanding of these factors, others are beyond the reach of research evidence and involve normative considerations or subjective assessments where objective measures are not possible.

WHAT EVIDENCE CAN DO

Figure 1.1 presents a new schema designed to illustrate the range of ways that evidence can inform policy and a particular set of contexts in which evidence can be relevant.[6] We refer to our schema as the 'policy landscape'. It is not meant to represent a chronological process of policy development, nor do we claim that policy development is as orderly a process as this schema might imply. In addition, like all generalisable models, it is a greatly simplified framework, wherein complex, heterogeneous, multidimensional concepts are reduced to more straightforward unitary or unidimensional ones. For instance, policy areas such as education, taxation and criminal justice differ in many ways – not only on the dimension that we have chosen to single out (which relates specifically to how much change the policy area is currently undergoing). We highlight this dimension because it is potentially important for how evidence can and should be used to inform policy. The policy implications drawn may depend on whether a policy area consists of the oversight of a largely settled and embedded system, involves an ongoing reform process with a pre-established direction, or constitutes new territory for government. Overall, the aim of the policy landscape is to present a simplification that highlights those aspects of a complex system that are of particular interest for understanding the relationship between evidence and policy in the economic and social domains to which the chapters in this book relate.

Policy Challenges

Starting at the top of the schema, an issue for policy may develop from the recognition of a new challenge (or opportunity) that government might need or be expected to meet. Such policy challenges can arise either when something in our world changes or when our understanding of the world changes. Sometimes the change and the challenge it poses arise from an event that is plain for all to see. Other times it is researchers who are the first to identify, quantify and bring such challenges to the attention of policymakers, for example, through media articles, public lectures or submissions to Oireachtas Committees. It may be a global challenge, arising for all countries simultaneously (e.g., climate change), or a domestic challenge that is largely unique (e.g., an exceptionally high proportion of young households encumbered with unserviceable mortgage debt).

Alternatively, it may be a domestic challenge that is not new to the world but varies in its severity and timescale in individual countries (e.g., data protection, obesity), or may be led by an international driver (e.g., a European Commission policy target or actions taken by one country in respect of taxation or intellectual property policies that will affect other countries). In principle, and in these examples, evidence provided by researchers has a strong role to play in first

---

6 As noted above, we are not seeking here to set out a framework for the full researcher–policymaker interface.

tackling such policy challenges. Key facts must be established and the extent of the challenge assessed. Where the challenge is partly international, national policy and research communities need to stay abreast with and, where appropriate, engage with international research and policy formation. In this volume we concentrate on domestic challenges – issues that are currently important for Ireland but are not necessarily as important elsewhere. But even where challenges are primarily domestic rather than global, some lessons may be drawn from international as well as domestic evidence and experience. The key questions to be considered range from the positive to the normative: 'What is the extent of the problem?', 'What processes underpin it?', 'What happens if nothing is done?', 'Can something be done?', 'Should something be done?'

Figure 1.1: The Policy Landscape

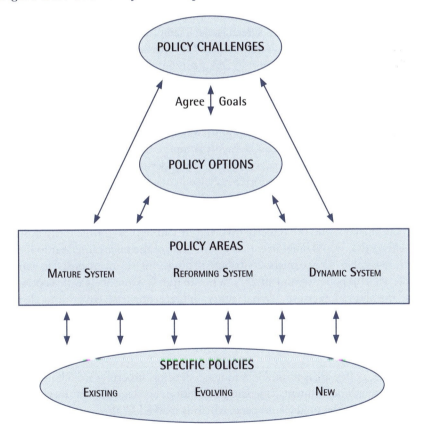

Policy Options

For policy challenges where it has been recognised that something should be done, there is often a period when the goal of policy has been broadly agreed but the policy mechanisms need to be developed. In this case, a range of alternative policy options is likely to be considered. In this part of the policy landscape there is sometimes a need for rapid decision-making, for example, when seeking to restore stability during a financial crisis. Other times, the time horizon is long and drawn out, as when dealing with a slowly developing problem such as the need to fund adequate and sustainable pensions in the face of demographic change. Ideally, research evidence can be used to estimate the likely outcomes of different policy options, including a critical assessment of the success or failure of such options (or similar approaches) where they have been implemented in other countries. More often, this ideal will be out of reach: only in certain policy areas are fully developed quantitative models specified that can be used to predict the success or otherwise of policy options in relation to agreed goals. Examples would be models of carbon emissions or tax-benefit simulation models. Nevertheless, valuable insight can be gained from research that categorises and quantifies who is likely to be affected by proposed policies, and from evidence in relation to the existence and/or strength of the causal mechanisms involved. To change outcomes, a policy must have a causal impact; an effective policy often provides additional support for a positive causal effect, or seeks to block or diminish a negative one. While in many policy areas the causal connections can be highly complex and involve many interacting effects, research has the capacity to increase understanding of the mechanisms involved and hence to make positive policy outcomes more likely. Understanding the mechanisms can be particularly important in helping to identify the possible risk of unintended negative side effects, especially where these are not the focus of the policymakers who are directly involved. It can also help to identify positive side effects that would draw attention to the value of the policy intervention. As a result, research evidence might contribute to answering the questions: 'How many people will this policy option affect?', 'Who are they?', 'How likely is this option to have the desired impact?', 'What other indirect impacts, either intended or unintended, may occur?'

Policy Areas

Over time, policy areas form. Governments develop structures for administering policy, through departments, agencies, legislation, agreements, contracts, and so on. This part of the policy landscape, which is marked by the rectangular box in Figure 1.1, differs from those marked by ovals in that it does not involve abstract ideas or processes, such as policy challenges, options or specific policies. Some debate surrounds the issue of how a public 'policy' is defined, but it is generally considered to be a guide for action at the level of principles and is hence a more abstract and potentially fluid notion than the concrete entities that characterise a policy area. Large or powerful institutions may play a particularly important role in shaping a policy area, as may specific pieces of legislation, but other characteristics will be influential too in determining the potential scope for change. These can include people, infrastructure, jobs, reports, available expertise, data sources, and even influential historical events. Here, we emphasise a dimension on which policy areas differ that we believe to be important for the relationship between evidence and policy. Figure 1.1 distinguishes different policy areas in terms of the extent to which the area is currently undergoing change.

Some policy areas are **mature** (e.g., defence, schools). While policy changes do occur, mature policy areas for the most part rely on settled systems that have evolved over time and bear the hallmarks of how the system originally developed and perhaps previous periods of more vigorous reform. At any given time, some policy areas are likely to be less settled and instead undergoing a period of more **systematic reform**, often with a prescribed overall direction. Present examples in Ireland include public service reform and tax policy. These are long-standing policy areas that are currently dynamic because they are in pursuit of agreed overall aims – cost reduction, increased accountability and the broadening of the tax base respectively. Lastly, there are policy areas that have only been in existence for a few decades and are therefore, in historical terms, relatively new. These **dynamic** areas are often associated with advances in technology (e.g., promotion of renewable energy, roll-out of broadband infrastructure), but may also reflect changing social trends (e.g., equality policy) or significant historical events (e.g., bank-restructuring).

The distinctions drawn above are not absolute and are, in many cases, debatable. But they nevertheless assist in understanding the variety of ways that evidence and policy relate. When engaging with a mature policy area, researchers and policymakers must be particularly mindful of the fact that the canvas is not blank. Measurements of the performance of the current system and understanding of its pre-existing underlying processes (some of which themselves may be due to previous policies) constitute both essential evidence and precursors for new policies or reforms. Institutions and practices become embedded, with positive effects for learning-by-doing, for building institutional memory, for developing administrative data systems and minimising operational risk. However, this can bring negative consequences in terms of a lack of flexibility or a lack of willingness or ability to absorb new ideas. Mature systems often evolve effective ways of achieving ends that are not centrally planned or monitored, such that aspects of the system may work well without much recognition and without being fully understood. Furthermore, a more mature policy area is more likely, in practice, to involve a genuine 'system' – a whole made up of interrelated parts.

Failure to recognise this systemic dimension can have serious consequences if elements of the system are considered in isolation when examining specific policy changes. For example, a specific policy, even if backed by good evidence of benefits, may have a negative or positive knock-on effect for other aspects of the system's performance, which may not have been considered by the researchers who produced the evidence on which the specific policy was formulated. Complex systems can also display 'path dependency', such that previous decisions alter or constrain present ones. For instance, policy on teachers' pay needs to consider not only comparative evidence regarding how pay rates and outputs/outcomes align with those in other countries, with jobs elsewhere in the public sector or with jobs in the private sector requiring similar skill levels and responsibilities, but needs also to take into account existing and historical aspects of the system. These might include historic remuneration agreements, the pattern of engagement in voluntary extra-curricular activity, measures of teacher performance, or incentives surrounding posts of responsibility or retirement. In a mature policy area, researchers' and policymakers' understandings of existing systems and their potential responses to change matter and need to be taken into account.

A policy area already undergoing reform is in some senses an easier environment for evidence to enter, provided it does not contradict a predetermined overall direction of reform (e.g., greater deregulation, increased preventative care, sustainable waste management, etc.). In such an area, there may be greater receptiveness to new information and ideas, some acceptance that the system concerned is underperforming and needs to change, and less need to tread carefully for fear of damaging the system's better features. Nevertheless, even in an already reforming area, researchers and policymakers must be mindful of unintended consequences. Accordingly, useful evidence may consist not only of research that is relevant to the pros and cons associated with specific parts of the system, but to the emergent properties of the system as a whole and how they change over the longer term. Such whole-system measures would include literacy and numeracy (education), life expectancy and quality of life (health), water quality (environment), among others. Furthermore, the process of reform itself usually requires that resources be temporarily devoted to making change happen, until the new system becomes sustainable. There is only so much reform a system can cope with simultaneously, so priorities and sequencing matter.

While some of the issues associated with changing established systems still apply, spreading policy on to a new canvas generates its own challenges, especially because of the unknowns involved. Researchers in newly developing policy areas can assist by assembling and analysing available data and studying systems in other countries, or perhaps in analogous policy areas, aiming to bring evidence of relevant successes and failures to the attention of policymakers. This requires a thorough understanding of systems in these other countries and how readily and reliably they might be successfully transplanted. Moreover, in many developing policy areas, it may be too early to evaluate the success or failure of policies introduced elsewhere. It can be dangerous to presume success merely because a more developed economy country, such as the United States or one of the Nordic countries, has taken a particular approach – countries do make policy mistakes and policy successes can reflect cultural factors that simply do not translate.

Emulation without careful contextualisation is also a potential hazard of the open method of coordination in the EU, which encourages comparative reference points as a basis for policy. There is therefore a need for caution and it is advisable to seek out independent evaluations or commentaries on the policy in the exemplar country.

A particular challenge that may arise in new policy areas is the need to communicate the rationale behind and operation of the policy to those affected, so that they understand the policy's purpose and as a result are willing to abide by new restrictions or to take advantage of new opportunities. Traditional analyses of how people respond to incentives may need to be supplemented by research that explores people's perceptions. Consequently, piloting of schemes, early evaluations and rapid evidence-gathering may bring substantial rewards in these particular areas.

Specific Policies

The final oval of Figure 1.1 relates to specific policies. Long-standing individual laws, regulations, systems and services are often subject to change, many as once-off changes rather than as part of far-reaching reform agendas. Yet apparently small changes to specific policies can nevertheless have lasting benefits or incur irritating costs, sometimes of surprising magnitude. They can also generate major reputational risks for the departments and agencies involved when they are unsuccessful. For example, the same government department that introduced Ireland's plastic bag levy, widely regarded as a successful policy, also attempted to introduce electronic voting machines, widely regarded as what might be politely called a policy fiasco. Research that can more accurately indicate the likelihood of success or failure of specific policies is obviously an attractive concept.

Again we think it useful to distinguish broad policy-intervention types: existing, evolving and new. In the case of the former, research can be undertaken to evaluate the existing policy's performance and, with appropriate methods, to identify where changes might be introduced. The analysis should identify a control group[7] to ensure that the benefits of the policy are not being over/underestimated. Rigorous evaluation of an existing policy can be difficult where the policy is widely used and where it interacts with other policies; for example, it is not possible to evaluate one element of enterprise policy without taking into account the other policies in place and the relationships between them.

At the other end of the spectrum, where a new policy is under consideration, research can help to inform the design of the intervention and to predict the likely outcomes of different policy designs. Best practice is to design an evaluation process at the time the policy itself is being developed, as set out in the UK Treasury Magenta Book (UK Treasury, 2011). This takes the analysis beyond the

---

7 The control group is one that is similar in characteristics to the group that has experienced the new policy changes but that has not been subject to these changes.

application of the simple logic model[8] in use in Ireland today to evaluate the effectiveness of programmes, by identifying a control group against which it is possible to measure rigorously the impact of the policy.

Specific policies or policy proposals are perhaps those most often considered in the context of the movement towards evidence-based policy, in the hunt for 'what works'. Thus, the *Coalition for Evidence-Based Policy* (CEBP, 2012) in the US describes its mission as 'to increase government effectiveness through the use of rigorous evidence about what works'. Better data and improved analysis methods have greatly increased the potential for researching the likely success of specific policies and policy proposals. The CEBP draws the parallel with advances in medical research through proper scientific evaluations, including via randomised controlled trials and 'natural experiments'. The idea is to measure agreed outcomes in equivalent areas with and without the policy intervention, or where that is not possible to compare outcomes before and after the intervention, trying to control for any other time-varying factors to the greatest extent possible. The increased availability of longitudinal data sets, collected by surveys or drawn from administrative records, provides the type of panel data needed for such analyses. In short, the aim is to subject specific policies to rigorous pre-testing and evaluation.

The Policy Landscape

However, the benefits of rigorous policy evaluation notwithstanding, part of the aim of this section and the policy landscape presented in Figure 1.1 is to show that the potential contribution of research evidence to policy is much broader than this. Establishing 'what works' is but one, narrow, channel through which evidence can inform policy. Returning to the top of the schema, evidence can highlight an issue hitherto unnoticed or underestimated. It can quantify and categorise the numbers and types of people affected. Research can help decision-makers to understand the most important causal mechanisms underpinning a policy area. It can therefore improve judgements of likely outcomes associated with different policy options. Good evidence can increase our understanding of systems in mature policy areas, contributing to more judicious reforms. It can inform policymakers as to the potential success of a policy that has been successful in another location but might interact with unique domestic contextual factors if introduced. Research can locate obstacles and opportunities associated with newly developing policy areas. While rigorous pre-testing and evaluation of specific policies are important, they are only part of what evidence can do for policy – and applicable to just one stage (the bottom oval) of policy development identified in Figure 1.1. Thus, the strong focus on policy evaluation should not be allowed to constrain the contribution that evidence can make to policy.

---

8   The logic model is a simple framework used to evaluate the effectiveness of a programme. It links the logical relationships between the resources, activities, outputs and outcomes of a programme to assess the causal relationships between the elements of the programme.

The order of the chapters that follow is designed in accordance with the schema presented. We begin at the bottom with studies that analyse the evidence relating to specific policies and end with studies that show how evidence raises new challenges for policy and which invite a policy response. Before fitting the analyses into the schema more precisely, however, it is worth considering not only what evidence can do but also what it cannot do.

WHAT EVIDENCE CANNOT DO

Policymaking requires more than evidence, as we noted at the outset. To policymakers, this statement is obvious; to researchers it can sometimes be less so. Social scientists have long distinguished between positive and normative analysis – how things work versus how they should work. For many normative issues, there is no amount of evidence that can be decisive for policy decisions. While evidence might be available that indicates likely outcomes of policies, in terms of impact and cost as well as winners and losers, it cannot determine whether these outcomes should be regarded as fair. Even in unusual circumstances where, for example, survey evidence reveals that the large majority regard a given policy as fair or unfair, the evidence cannot tell you whether that large majority are right to do so. More generally, however, research into perceptions of fairness (e.g., Charness and Rabin, 2002) reveals considerable heterogeneity – individuals reach different conclusions from each other about what is and what is not fair. Even where there is agreement about the fairness of a given policy, normative judgements may be required regarding the priority it should be accorded relative to other prospective policies. This judgement can be assisted by objective evidence, which might estimate the scale of expected benefits and identify the people affected, but policy-makers cannot escape normative considerations, which are not the responsibility of researchers.

Similarly, no amount of evidence can determine how much risk to take. Yet it is a rare policy change that does not involve some risk. How accurate is the assessment of risk? How can even the best-researched policy insulate itself from unintended and unforeseen consequences? What is the likelihood of such consequences? Even where risk can be assessed, a significant amount of uncertainty will remain. Uncertainty is inherent in policymaking and, consequently, so is subjective judgement about what constitutes a risk that should be borne and what constitutes a risk that should be avoided. Furthermore (and this is perhaps one of the recurring tensions between researchers and policymakers), while the researcher may be in a better position than the policymaker to understand the evidence in terms of soundness of method and validity of statistical inference, the policymaker may often be better able to judge the risk of implementing the policy to which the evidence lends support. The success of a policy may depend crucially on the context into which it is launched. Policymakers will often have a better awareness of stakeholders' and the public's likely response, greater familiarity with the communication and managerial abilities of those tasked with implementing the change, and more imagination when it comes to envisaging potential pitfalls. To understand whether a policy is implementable and to gauge the likelihood of successful implementation requires knowledge of multiple aspects of the given policy area and judgement as to how it might respond to change. Note, however, that this unavoidable uncertainty underlines the advantages of an open and systematic process of policy review, combined with a willingness to alter policy if it does not deliver as expected. So, while the reasoning suggests that policy cannot be inferred from evidence alone, it does suggest a further need for additional evidence regarding how the chosen policy performs.

These considerations matter even where evidence is of a very high scientific standard, such as from repeated randomised controlled trials. Inductive logic is not foolproof. Even a policy that has proven to be successful everywhere it has been tried may fail for the first time in a new setting. Cartwright and Hardie (2012) delve deeper into the issue of when it is and when it is not valid to infer that a policy shown to work in one context is likely to work in another. These scholars expose the complex logical conditions required for this specific form of inference from evidence to policy to be valid. For example, a policy that has been shown to work well in some contexts may be unsuccessful in another because a key causal effect differs between the contexts. More subtly, a condition for success may be necessary but not sufficient, leading a policy to fail because of the absence of one or more necessary support factors. Research evidence can help to make the causal mechanisms involved better understood, making a sound inference from evidence to policy more probable, but any assessment of the likelihood that a causal mechanism has been misunderstood or a key support factor missed is always going to be a matter of subjective judgement.

The issues raised so far in this section (fairness, priorities, risk, uncertainty, and the complexity of the inferences from evidence to policy) introduce both normative and subjective aspects to the decisions policymakers are required to make. Thus, they limit the extent to which research evidence can be decisive for a policy decision. They arise over and above the two factors that are perhaps more often raised in this context, namely political and financial realities. Policymakers may of course be unwilling to pursue a policy backed by evidence because it is politically unpalatable or because they are not willing (or able) to fund it, regardless of the estimated return. Even so, in trying to comprehend the relationship between evidence and policy, and between researchers and policymakers, it is vital to understand that these are far from the only considerations when assessing the implications of research evidence for policy.

Some scholars who have addressed the issue go further, arguing that in the relationship between policymakers and researchers, political considerations are not the preserve of the former. This more fundamental critique of evidence-based policymaking posits that researchers are incapable of the objectivity that is, theoretically, the cornerstone of the evidence-based approach. For instance,

Boden and Epstein (2006) argue that researchers in higher education have been subject to a 'neo-liberal colonisation', which biases their thinking and restricts their imagination. Boden and Epstein use the phrase 'policy-based evidence' to describe the phenomenon of how researchers themselves can become constrained or captured by prevailing political philosophies. This criticism is not without force, as researchers need constantly to question the assumptions they bring to their analysis, but nor does it mean that researchers who strive for objectivity cannot produce evidence that is genuinely objective and informs policy. This interpretation challenges researchers to be sufficiently questioning and reflective and is far from the other interpretation of 'policy-based evidence' often employed by researchers themselves, when referring to the cherry-picking of evidence by policymakers to support predetermined policies (e.g., Tombs and Whyte, 2003).

Still, the uncertainty and subjectivity inherent in the process of inferring policy conclusions from evidence has arguably become more apparent as the movement towards evidence-based policy has progressed and lessons have been learned along the way. William Solesbury, Senior Visiting Research Fellow at the *ESRC Centre for Evidence Based Policy and Practice*, told the UK House of Commons Science and Technology Committee in 2006:

> *I think the concept that policy should be based on evidence is something that I would rail against quite fiercely. It implies first of all that it is the sole thing that you should consider. Secondly, it implies the metaphor 'base' and implies a kind of solidity, which [...] is often not there, certainly in the social sciences although I think to a great degree, [...] not always in the natural and biological sciences.*
> (House of Commons Science and Technology Committee, 2006, p. 45)

This report, which investigated the use of science in policymaking via interviews with a selection of professionals at the interface of research and policy in the UK, considered a range of criticisms of the evidence-based approach. It concluded that it was possible to overplay the mantra of evidence-based policy, preferring instead the notion of 'evidence-informed policy'. Despite recognising these limitations, the report nevertheless went on to make the case for greater public investment in research to assist policymaking. The committee also called for transparency regarding when policy is based on evidence, when it is the product of other considerations, and when it ignores or contradicts available evidence.

We return to the issue of how best evidence can be incorporated into policymaking and whether evidence can realistically be considered a 'base' for policy in the final chapter, since the analyses we present in the intervening chapters shed light on this very issue. For the time being, given the discussion above regarding what evidence can and cannot do, we advocate a balanced conclusion: good evidence is likely to result in better policy decisions, but good policy cannot be deduced from evidence alone.

THE RESEARCHER–POLICYMAKER RELATIONSHIP

The complexity of the issues discussed above, when research evidence is produced, policy implications are derived, and policymakers must infer how best to employ the evidence for policy, is such that the nature of the relationship between researchers and policymakers has also been subject to greater scrutiny as the movement for evidence-based policy has progressed. Various theoretical frameworks for understanding this relationship have been proposed (e.g., Levin, 2004; European Commission, 2007; Best and Holmes, 2010). Space does not permit a thorough review of these frameworks here, but the Knowledge-to-Action framework developed by Allan Best and various colleagues (and described in Best and Holmes, 2010) merits brief discussion.

These analysts distinguish three models of increased effectiveness that characterise the relationship between researchers and policymakers (or in some cases also practitioners such as teachers, health workers, regulators etc.). The most basic 'linear' model is one that views knowledge as a product. Researchers supply it; policymakers demand and consume it. Under such a model, the communication is largely one way and the focus is on the dissemination or diffusion of the research findings. In contrast, the 'relationship' model is one where knowledge comes not only from research, but from policy and practice too. That is, the relationship between researchers and policymakers is just that: a relationship. Ideas and information flow in both directions when researchers and policymakers engage in collaboration. Lastly, the 'systems' model is one where researchers and policymakers are embedded in a dynamic system that involves not only them, but other stakeholders too. The system has opportunities for communication in all directions and multiple feedback loops. Best and Holmes argue that the systems model has the capacity to be transformative and to result in what they call 'engaged scholarship'. By embedding research and researchers into the key systems of the policy area, it is argued that the likelihood of effective transference of knowledge into action is greater.[9]

Based on our own experience, these models of the relationship between researchers and policymakers represent helpful ways of thinking about the relationship and how it might be improved. Embedding good, objective, research in systems is likely to bring benefits from better use of knowledge. The emphasis on the word 'objective' is key, however. Researchers are likely to learn more and to be more influential when regularly engaged with policymakers and stakeholders, but must ensure that the relationships generated do not compromise their

---

9   This 'systems view' in a policy space mirrors approaches developed by Lundvall (1992), Nelson (1993) and Freeman (1995) to conceptualise the innovation process, wherein the concept of a 'national innovation system' was developed to describe the relationship between scientific discovery and economic growth through the process of innovation. It highlighted the context in which scientific researchers and businesses operate and the institutional structures that link them.

objectivity. In other words, the researchers must not suffer 'capture' by the policy process. Independence, as well as high quality analysis, is crucial for good research (Ruane, 2012). One way to enhance independence and objectivity is for researchers to maintain close professional links with national and international research networks as well as with national policymakers and other stakeholders.

THE STRUCTURE OF THIS BOOK

This introductory chapter provides a context for the chapters that follow. While the contribution that evidence can make to policy is much broader than is often envisaged, perhaps especially by those who beat the constant drum of policy evaluation, that contribution is nevertheless limited. This needs to be recognised at the interface between the policy system and the research community. In each of the chapters to follow, ESRI researchers have specified a clear research question of relevance to Irish policy. The context for the questions addressed is one where fiscal resources are in decline and where there is great emphasis on efficient policy delivery. The researchers have sought to apply appropriate methods, ranging from a comprehensive review of international and domestic findings to fresh analysis of newly obtained Irish data. Each chapter considers the policy implications of the evidence it presents. In some cases this goes as far as to suggest entirely untried policy options. In many cases the discussion involves an evaluation of potential policy options tried or considered elsewhere, while in still others it seeks only to ensure that policymakers take decisions with awareness of relevant evidence that is informative as to quantities and underlying causes. The aim is to present the evidence and suggest its potential implications.

Each chapter begins with a brief discussion that relates the analysis to some of the themes discussed above, and specifically to the policy landscape. This is intended to draw attention to implications or telling examples relating to the relationship between evidence and policy. Some of the work presented exemplifies the issues raised above. Other elements of the research raise further questions for consideration in the final chapter, where we revisit the relationship between evidence and policy in light of the material presented.

The chapters are organised according to the schema presented above, beginning at the bottom and moving towards the top. Chapter 2 considers not only a specific policy, namely the systematic evaluation of infrastructure projects, but focuses on two particular methodological aspects of the evaluation process. In other words, it looks at evidence in favour of two specific alterations to established evaluation policy. Chapters 3 and 4 consider the evidence for introducing two specific policies that are in operation elsewhere but not yet in Ireland: loan-to-value limits on residential mortgages and pay-for-performance in healthcare. The first of these policies relates to a policy area that is developing in response to crisis, while the second is relevant to a long-established policy area currently undergoing major reform. As we will see, this distinction alters the way the available evidence must be weighed. Chapters 5 and 6 present evidence relating to the primary aims of mature policy areas: education policy (improving the quality of second-level education) and industrial policy (boosting innovation in enterprises). The focus in each case is on understanding the role of specific policies within the unique Irish system, with implications for interpreting the lessons from international and domestic evidence.

Chapters 7 and 8 relate to somewhat more dynamic policy areas, namely, labour-activation policy and competition (and associated regulatory) policy. In both cases, there is a clear direction in which policy has moved internationally, with Ireland lagging behind developments elsewhere. This leads to a greater focus on how policy is evolving in the context of the Great Recession and on international evidence from countries that have travelled further in the given policy direction.

Chapters 9 and 10 explore further evidence directly related to the causes and impact of the recession itself. In the first case the focus is on the role played by consumer financial decision-making in the period leading up to the crisis and on the policies needed to ensure that such mistakes are not repeated. Consumers' financial decision-making is an area where knowledge is developing and new policy challenges are being identified, with some initial policy options sketched out by international researchers. Hence, most of the evidence in Chapter 9 relates to understanding the policy challenge in this area, and what this might imply for some of the initial policy responses that have been proposed. Chapter 10 explores the policies adopted by different countries seeking to achieve fiscal consolidation from an unsustainable fiscal position. It seeks to draw lessons for how to complete a successful consolidation in Ireland, exploiting case studies that appear most relevant for Ireland's current predicament.

Lastly, two chapters concern themselves with new statistical analyses that highlight policy challenges. Chapter 11 explores the extent to which private-sector labour costs adjust through market processes in a time of very high unemployment, and asks whether policy interventions can be designed that would help the labour market to clear. Chapter 12 presents an example of where analysis of new data raises potential policy challenges for Ireland, namely, the varying perceptions of public service quality across different policy domains. The marked differences between Ireland and other EU countries might prompt some to consider that policy responses are necessary, while others might judge that policy intervention either should not or could not be considered.

Thus, as the topics move from specific policies, through policy areas, to options and eventually to challenges for which policy response options are more matters of debate than development, while evidence remains highly relevant, the use of evidence changes. In the early chapters the focus is on specific policy evaluation. By the latter three chapters, the evidence no longer relates to the evaluation of specific policies or even to estimates of the likely impact of policy options. Instead, the provision of evidence informs policymakers about outcomes presently beyond their control and aims to increase understanding of the forces that produce them.

The final chapter draws together the findings and links them back to the issues discussed in this opening chapter and to the growing international literature on evidence-based policy. Clear themes and commonalities can be identified, which vary across the policy landscape, and which give insight into the primary relationship of interest: how evidence relates to policy.

REFERENCES

Bartholemew, J. (2002). 'James Lind's Treatise of the Scurvy (1753)'. *Postgraduate Medical Journal*, 78, 695–696.

Best, A. and Holmes, B. (2010). 'Systems thinking, knowledge and action: towards better models and methods'. *Evidence & Policy*, 6, 145–159.

Boden, R. and Epstein, D. (2006). 'Managing the research imagination? Globalisation and research in higher education'. *Globalisation, Societies and Education*, 4, 223–236.

Cartwright, N. and Hardie, J. (2012). *Evidence-Based Policy: A practical guide to doing it better*. Oxford: Oxford University Press.

Charness, G. and Rabin, M. (2002). 'Understanding social preferences with simple tests'. *Quarterly Journal of Economics*, 117, 817–869.

Coalition for Evidence-Based Policy (2012). *Our Mission*. www.coalition4evidence.org

Daly, M. E. (1997). *The Spirit of Earnest Inquiry: The Statistical and Social Inquiry Society of Ireland, 1847–1997*. Dublin: Institute of Public Administration.

European Commission (EC) (2007). *Towards More Knowledge-based Policy in Education and Training*. Brussels: EC.

Freeman, C. (1995). 'The National System of Innovation in Historical Perspective'. *Cambridge Journal of Economics*, 19, 5–24.

Gaffney, M. and Harmon, C. (2007). 'Overview and policy conclusions' in *Evidence-Based Policy: Getting the evidence, using the evidence and evaluating the outcomes*, pp. 6–11. Dublin: National Economic and Social Forum.

House of Commons Science and Technology Committee (2006). *Scientific Advice, Risk and Evidence-Based Policymaking*. London: The Stationery Office.

Levin, B. (2004). 'Making research matter more'. *Education Research Policy Archives*, 12, 56.

Lundvall, B-Å. (ed.) (1992). *National Innovation Systems: Towards a Theory of Innovation and Interactive Learning*. London: Pinter.

Magnuszewski, P., Sodomkova, K., Slob, A., Muro, M., Sendzimir, J., Pahl-Wostl, C. (2010). *Report on Conceptual Framework for Science–Policy Barriers and Bridges*. EC FP7 Project PSI-Connect, www.psiconnect.eu.

Mayer, I., van Daalen, C. and Bots, P. (2004). 'Perspectives on Policy Analyses: A Framework for Understanding and Design'. *International Journal of Technology, Policy and Management*, 4, 169–190.

National Economic and Social Forum (NESF) (2007). *Evidence-Based Policy: Getting the Evidence, Using the Evidence and Evaluating the Outcomes*. Dublin: NESF.

Nelson, R. (ed.) (1993). *National Innovation Systems. A Comparative Analysis*. New York/Oxford: Oxford University Press.

Nutley, S., Morton, S., Jung, T. and Boaz, A. (2010). 'Evidence and Policy in Six European Countries: Diverse Approaches and Common Challenges'. *Evidence and Policy*, 6, 131–144.

Pawson, R. (2006). *Evidence-Based Policymaking: A Realist Perspective*. London: Sage Publications.

Ruane, F. (2012). 'Research Evidence and Policymaking in Ireland'. *Administration*, 60, 119–38.

Sanderson, I. (2009). 'Intelligent Policymaking for a Complex World: Pragmatism, Evidence and Learning'. *Political Studies*, 57, 699–719.

Tombs, S. and Whyte, D. (2003). 'Scrutinizing the Powerful: Crime, Contemporary Political Economy, and Critical Social Research' in Tombs, S. and Whyte, D. (eds.), *Unmasking the Crimes of the Powerful*, pp. 3–48. New York: Lang.

UK Treasury (2011). *The Magenta Book: Guidance for Evaluation*. London: HM Treasury.

CHAPTER 2

Using Evidence to Improve Evaluation Methods for Public Infrastructure

Edgar Morgenroth

Capital investment is an important area of government expenditure. With competing demands for capital investment and limited resources it is not surprising that formal methods for the evaluation of different investments have been developed. One of the most common methods and one that is obligatory for most public capital projects is cost-benefit analysis. This chapter deals with specific aspects that need to be considered when applying cost-benefit analyses. In relation to the policy landscape (Figure 1.1), therefore, this chapter considers specific policies within a mature policy area.

While project evaluation and cost-benefit analysis are well established policy areas, the application of such methodologies requires the identification of appropriate parameters such as discount rates, which change over time thus requiring continual research to ensure the validity of the results from an evaluation. Furthermore, new research provides evidence on some important shortcomings in the application of the methodologies and highlights ways to overcome these shortcomings.

Here the recent international literature is reviewed, as the setting of appropriate discount rates has been considered in other jurisdictions, such as Australia. Furthermore, with regard to the application of cost-benefit analysis and in particular the *ex ante* projection of costs and benefits, systematic studies have been conducted for a number of countries. Because of data limitations similar studies currently cannot be undertaken in Ireland. In order to illustrate the implications of alternative parameters some example calculations are provided.

The evidence surveyed suggests that the discount rates applied in cost-benefit analysis of projects should have been set at a higher level than recommended in the guidelines issued by the Department of Finance. The chapter also highlights the potential use of hyperbolic discounting for costs and benefits that occur in the very far distance, which has become more relevant as climate change impacts are very long term. It also shows that across many developed countries costs and benefits are often systematically miscalculated, with costs being underestimated and benefits being overestimated. The chapter suggests that methods to account for this optimism bias should be considered in Ireland.

There are a number of areas for further research. First, while this chapter has focused on just one parameter used in cost-benefit analysis, others such as the cost of public funds, and the shadow price of labour will also need updating on a regular basis. Estimates for optimism bias are not available for Ireland but would be a valuable insight to develop a practical approach to dealing with optimism bias. While evaluation methods typically measure the direct costs and benefits of a project, the wider costs and benefits of this project are not generally accounted for. This might be important particularly for projects that generate spillovers (positive or negative) but appropriate methods have largely not been developed.

BACKGROUND

An extensive literature has shown that infrastructure yields a positive long-run macroeconomic return (see Lighthart and Martin-Suarez, 2011). The return on such investment depends on the size and quality of the existing infrastructure stock and the level of demand for (e.g., congestion of) it. Thus, if the current infrastructure stock is adequate and no constraints exist then the likely return on further investment at this point is low or even negative, or as Pritchett (1996, p.1.) noted – 'the value of infrastructure is not equal to its cost'.

The fact that a positive return to infrastructure investment is not guaranteed and that different investments have different impacts, together with the fact that the demand for resources for potential projects tends to outstrip the available public resources even during 'normal' times, implies that investment decisions should be based on careful evaluation. The economic crisis in Ireland has radically changed the fiscal environment and consequently, public capital budgets have been cut successively since the National Development Plan (NDP) 2007–2013 was published. The public capital budget now amounts to just 50 per cent of what had been planned in 2007, even when one takes into account that tender prices have fallen by about 25 per cent.[10] Given the smaller total budget and the fact that the cost of public funds has increased it is more important than ever to ensure that spending is prioritised properly in order to derive maximum benefit. In order to prioritise we must evaluate.

There are a number of alternative evaluation methodologies that can be applied. These include macroeconometric models, input output models, multi-criterion decision analysis and cost-benefit analysis (CBA). Cost-benefit analysis is perhaps the most widely used method and a cost benefit analysis is required in

---

10 These calculations are based on the figures contained in the NDP and the public capital programme that accompanied the budgets. The price deflator is that implied by the CSO National Accounts.

Ireland for public projects costing in excess of €50 million (Department of Finance, 2005).[11] CBA relies on the specification of a range of parameters such as the cost of public funds, shadow cost of labour, taxation, and a discount rate. Furthermore, in order to ensure comparability across projects, common baseline assumptions about economic and demographic development need to be used, which are important inputs into estimates of costs and benefits and projects should also be tested against a range of credible counterfactuals.

This chapter considers two issues in the application and usefulness of cost benefit analysis for infrastructure prioritisation namely the impact of risk in the form of inaccurate cost or benefit estimates and the setting of the appropriate discount rate. These two issues are chosen first, because they crucially determine the usefulness of a CBA and second, because there have been interesting developments in the international literature on these issues that have yet to be reflected in the application of CBA in an Irish setting. These issues are quite general and apply to all types of infrastructures (transport projects, hospitals, schools, flood defences, public offices etc.).

EVALUATION METHODOLOGIES

Before turning to the two specific issues that will be considered below it is useful to consider why CBA is perhaps the most widely applied methodology. This is most readily achieved by considering some of the strengths and weaknesses of other evaluation methodologies as well as CBA.

Fully specified macroeconometric models have been used to evaluate the impact of programmes of investment (e.g., Bradley *et al.*, 2003; Roeger, 1996), but in principle they could also be used to evaluate individual projects. They are particularly suited to identify the overall short-run and long-run impacts including the wider impacts such as those on prices. However, they are sensitive to the theoretical underpinnings used, as these can have an important bearing on the impact estimates,[12] and are not well-suited to assess alternative projects within a specific investment area as they lack the required detail.

Computable General Equilibrium (CGE) models are theory based multi-equation models that are parameterised using estimates from the literature and calibrated to actual data. They have been used by a number of researchers for project evaluation, particularly in the context of regional impacts where the data required to estimate fully specified macroeconometric models is not available (e.g., Gillespie *et al.*, 2001 or Törmä, 2008). Their advantage is the general equilibrium nature that captures all effects, their theoretical consistency and the reduced need for data. However, the latter, along with the fact that the parameters

---

11 Since January 2006 projects costing in excess of €30 million are subjected to a cost-benefit analysis.
12 For example in the QUEST model (Roeger, 1996), crowding out mechanisms reduce the overall estimated impact of the Structural Funds.

are taken from the literature or where appropriate parameters are not available these are assumed, risks that the model does not reflect the real structure of the economy. Furthermore, as the structure is imposed, this approach is less well suited to the estimation of long-run impacts that arise from structural change.

Another approach to project evaluation is to use an input-output (I-O) model. I-O models identify the interconnection of input and output of different sectors and/or regions of an economy. They have been used for the evaluation of individual projects (e.g., Juri and Kockelman, 2006) and programmes of investment (e.g., Beutel, 2002). The I-O approach is ideally suited to analyse the short-term impacts, such as the employment impact and the wider distributional impact of a project or a programme of projects. However, I-O models are less well suited to the evaluation of the long-term supply side impacts as it is difficult to incorporate supply-side (or neo-classical) adjustment mechanisms into a static input-output framework.

A less technical evaluation methodology is multi-criterion decision analysis, which has been used in Ireland (see Honohan, 1997; FitzGerald et al., 2003) and which has become more popular in other countries in recent years (see Bradley et al., 2006; Cundric et al., 2008; De Brucker et al., 2011). Multi-criteria analysis (MCDA) describes any structured approach used to determine overall preferences among alternative options, where the options accomplish several objectives. This methodology is used to make a comparative assessment of alternative projects or heterogeneous measures. It involves scoring each project or programme of investment using a common set of criteria, each of which are given a weighting according to the range of objectives, constraints and rationale for investment. MCDA allows decision-makers to take account of a full range of social, environmental, technical, economic, and financial criteria simultaneously. Therefore, it is particularly applicable to cases where a single-criterion approach falls short, especially where monetary values are difficult to estimate. However, it can suffer from subjectivity and requires a degree of knowledge of the performance of projects, which is not usually available for new projects.

Cost-benefit analysis aims at comparing costs and benefits of government policies. It involves calculating a comprehensive set of costs and benefits accounting for the fact that these do not necessarily arise simultaneously, that the public intervention can have a range of distortionary effects and reflecting the fact that market outcomes are not necessarily efficient. As such it is a method that identifies whether a project passes basic investment criteria, namely that a project is expected to yield a positive net return. Perhaps more importantly, it is a methodology that can be used to compare alternative projects and variations of the same project in order to identify that which yields the highest return. CBA is well grounded in welfare economics although the degree to which a particular CBA conforms to welfare economic theory is highly dependent on the thoroughness of the analysis and the assumptions and parameters that are chosen. While making all the costs, benefits and distortions explicit is a great strength of cost-benefit analysis, the requirement to quantify all of these can be very onerous and does involve the choice of specific parameters. As such this methodology is more readily applied to a smaller number of projects rather than a large number of diverse projects (see Morgenroth and FitzGerald, 2006). Furthermore, by relying on the choice of parameters and the quantification of costs and benefits the choice and accuracy of these has an important bearing on the results. Consequently, some researchers have cautioned against blindly following the results of a CBA and have highlighted that it is important to address the shortcomings of CBA (e.g., Hahn and Dudley, 2007 and van Wee, 2012). However, CBA is the cornerstone of project evaluation in many countries (e.g., Australia, UK, USA) and is also used as the key appraisal method in Ireland.

In many countries a difference between planning outcomes and the policy decision-making process can be observed and there is no convergence on best practice in terms of planning methods and institutions (Short and Kopp, 2005). Thus, while it is recognised that infrastructure decision-making is often sub-optimal it is difficult to identify the best system of decision-making. In the absence of clear evidence that one system of decision-making is superior, the focus should be on improving the quality of decisions made within the existing system, which is the focus of this chapter.

PROJECT RISKS – THE ACCURACY OF COST AND BENEFIT ESTIMATES

Projects are subject to a range of risks. For example, time delays can arise during construction resulting in cost escalation (construction risk), the operating costs can be underestimated or the output of the infrastructure can be overestimated (operating risk), the demand for and 'willingness to pay for' an infrastructure can be overestimated (demand risk), there can be significant financial risks if the project needs to be refinanced or if at an early stage the cost of funds changes, consumers may also choose alternatives (e.g., un-tolled roads or a bus rather than rail) and finally projects are also subject to political risk in that political priorities may change due to changed circumstances or a changed government. Nevertheless, projects are typically promoted on an 'everything goes according to plan' basis.

A large number of studies have considered whether costs, demand and land-use impacts of transport infrastructure projects have been mis-estimated and whether they have been systematically biased in order to improve the likelihood that decision-makers will support a particular project. Interestingly, there appear to be no such papers for other forms of infrastructures even though there are numerous examples of other types of infrastructure where costs were underestimated and benefits were not realised.

Flyvbjerg *et al.* (2003) analysed 258 projects from 20 countries covering rail, bridge, tunnel and road projects. They found that 90 per cent of projects were subject to cost overruns. The average cost overrun for rail projects was 45 per cent, bridges and tunnels were subject to an average 34 per cent cost overrun and roads cost on average 20 per cent more than initially estimated. Another large scale study by Bain (2009) found traffic forecasts to be 23 per cent higher than outturn and that this bias is not confined to first-year forecasts, which are difficult to make but also into the medium term.

The degree to which demand for infrastructure is accurately predicted at the planning stage was investigated by Pickrell (1990) with respect to ten rail projects in the USA. He found that for nine projects the actual passenger numbers were 50 per cent lower than expected while for one project the passenger numbers exceeded the predicted level by 50 per cent. Flyvbjerg et al. (2004) analysed 210 projects from 14 countries and found that the passenger numbers for rail projects were overestimated in 90 per cent of projects with the overestimate compared to the actual outturn averaging 51 per cent. For roads the estimates on average understated traffic by 9.5 per cent, but there was a large spread with some overestimates and some underestimates. A more recent study by Parthasarathi and Levinson (2010) considered 391 road projects in Minnesota constructed in the 1960s and compared the traffic forecasts with the traffic counts taken in 1978. They found that on average traffic on roads was underestimated by 19.5 per cent and that the deviations of actual from projected traffic ranged from −60 per cent to +57 per cent. They found that the deviations varied across road types with traffic on major roads being underpredicted at the time of planning while that for smaller roads was overpredicted. They also highlight that the inaccuracies arise out of the failure of the underlying models to incorporate behavioural change and flaws in demographic forecasts.

Given the strong evidence that there is systematic optimism bias, particularly on costs and also on demand for rail, it is important to consider why this bias emerges, which has been the subject of a number of studies and a number of explanatory factors have been identified. Flyvbjerg et al., (2003) consider the impact of the length of the project implementation phase, the size of the project and the type of project ownership on cost escalation. Specifically, they found that an additional year from the decision to build a project and the end of construction adds 4.6 per cent to costs. For bridges and tunnels larger projects are found to have higher cost escalation and that roads projects were found to increase in size over time. Finally, they also found that there was no systematic difference in cost over-runs between traditional public projects and public private partnerships (PPPs).

Mackett and Edwards (1998) argue that the objectives of decision-makers and the legislative and planning framework are important determinants of optimism bias. They highlight that often it is easier to get support from central government for more 'high-tech' discrete projects than more incremental improvements of existing systems. Furthermore, they contend that decision-makers prefer to support what they term 'glamorous' projects instead of simpler less visible projects. Pritchett (2002) constructs a simple political economy model where projects/

programmes are supported by 'advocates' who are more committed to pursuing their project than the general public and where the latter is split into three groups according to their attitudes towards the project. He finds that except in the case where advocates know that the project will have the desired outcome, they will prefer not to evaluate the project, i.e., they will prefer ignorance.

The implications of the findings of this literature are best illustrated by applying them to an example of a rail project with benefit to cost ratio of 2:1. For rail projects the findings are that the benefit (demand) is overestimated by 50 per cent and that costs are underestimated up by 40 per cent at the time of project proposal. Adjusting the benefits and costs accordingly reduces the Benefit to Cost Ratio (BCR) to less than 0.75:1.

In the UK it is considered best practice to make an explicit allowance for optimism bias at the evaluation stage. The UK Department for Transport published a set of guidelines (see Flyvbjerg and COWI, 2004). These guidelines recommend that a fixed percentage be added to the costs for the purposes of a cost benefit analysis. These guidelines make explicit allowance for the fact that the cost over-runs vary considerably. For example, in order to ensure that the final costs of a rail project are on budget with a 50 per cent certainty then the initial cost estimate should be increased by 40 per cent.[13] To ensure the project ends up on budget with an 80 per cent certainty, 57 per cent should be added to the initial cost estimate (and 68 per cent if a 90 per cent chance of staying on budget is necessary).[14] For roads, the recommended uplift is smaller reflecting the lower optimism bias found in research.

DISCOUNT RATE

Given that costs and benefits do not accrue immediately, but rather are spread over time it is necessary to account for the fact that the value today of these future streams is not equal to their value in the future, i.e., a euro to be received in 10 years time is worth less than a euro received today. Converting future values to a present value is accomplished using a discount rate.

Setting the appropriate discount rate has been a topic of countless research papers (e.g., Stiglitz,1994) and long literature reviews, so that a full review of this literature is beyond the scope of this chapter.[15] Instead this section considers the appropriate rate of discount and the valuation of costs and benefits that arise in the distant future.

---

13 Of course setting such rules runs the risk that the initial cost estimates are adjusted downwards accordingly. The degree to which this happens in practice does not appear to have been investigated yet.

14 They also highlight that the *ex-post* bias on IT projects can be particularly large and recommend that the initial costs are increased by between 10 per cent and 200 per cent.

15 Harrison (2010) provides a very comprehensive review of the literature and identifies its implications for setting discount rates in Australia.

It is useful to set out the implication of setting different discount rates, which is best achieved by considering a simple example of €1,000 received at different points in the future discounted by different discount rates, as shown in Table 2.1.[16] The first column shows the valuation today of €1,000 received in the future without discounting. The first row clearly shows that €1,000 received in one years' time would be valued today at less than €1,000, but even with this short-time horizon, the discount rate has a significant impact on the valuation. For the 20 year horizon the valuation of €1,000 using the 4 per cent discount rate is just over twice that using the 8 per cent discount rate which in turn is just over twice that for the 12 per cent discount rate, which shows the implication of different discount rates over a typical time horizon.[17] Once the discount rate is positive, the valuation today of €1,000 received in 100 years time is zero or very close to zero regardless of the discount rate once the traditional model of exponential discounting is applied, where the discount rate remains constant over time. This has important implications since the very long-run benefit of projects is often put forward as a reason to go ahead with projects with modest short- to medium-term benefits. On the basis of Table 2.1 these benefits would be irrelevant.

Table 2.1: Variation in the Value Today of €1,000 Received in the Future Using Alternative Discount Rates

Years	Discount Rate			
	0 per cent	4 per cent	8 per cent	12 per cent
1	€1,000	€962	€926	€893
10	€1,000	€676	€463	€322
20	€1,000	€456	€215	€104
50	€1,000	€141	€21	€3
100	€1,000	€20	€0	€0

Note: These are derived using the conventional exponential discounting.

16 The table applies what is referred to as exponential discounting, which is formally stated as θ=1/(1−δ), where denotes the discount factor by which the value is multiplied in order to convert it into a present value, denotes the discount rate and t denotes the number of years into the future when the cost/benefit occurs.
17 The choice of discount rate can also have a significant impact on certain types of public private partnerships. For example, Vassallo (2010) considers the impact of the discount rate on a flexible-term highway concession known as least present value of revenues (LPVR), where the concession is awarded to the bidder that offers the lowest present value of revenues discounted by the discount rate set by the government. A lower discount rate was found to increase the traffic risk to the concession holder.

Alternative approaches to explain and derive the discount rate have been put forward. First, the discount rate is argued to reflect the rate of time preference of individuals with respect to consumption decisions. This corresponds to the fact that the benefits of public projects are typically enjoyed by consumers, and that the public resources expended could have been used for other consumption. Another approach is to consider the discount rate as a measure of the opportunity cost of funds that could have been invested in alternative projects which would have a return which is forgone. The alternative measures point to different proxies to measure the discount rate.

If the underlying approach is based on the opportunity cost of funds then financial market rates can be used. For example, the most common measure of the riskless rate of return is the long-run government bond rate. For Ireland, the real rate of interest on long-run bonds over the last 35 years has been 3.3 per cent.[18] For Germany, the UK and the US the respective rates have been 3.7 per cent, 3.3 per cent and 3.1 per cent. Of course, most projects are not riskless so that a rate incorporating risk should be used to evaluate projects.

The real after-tax rate of return on private capital in Ireland for the period 2002 to 2009 averages 10 per cent, which is slightly higher than the 8.5 per cent found by Harrison (2010) for Australia over a four decade period.[19] The difference might be explained by either the higher return in Ireland or an upward bias due to the importance of foreign multinational companies in Ireland and their ability to shift profits. An alternative would be to consider a share index. However, as an index implies a degree of diversification the rate of return should be considered an intermediate between the riskless and the risky rate of return.

Using the consumption approach the common estimate of the discount rate is calculated as the sum of the pure rate of time preference and the rate of consumption growth multiplied by the elasticity of marginal utility of consumption.[20] Over the period 1970 to 2010 per capita real consumption growth in Ireland has averaged 4.1 per cent per year.[21] Evans (2005) provides estimates of the elasticity of marginal utility of consumption for Ireland that range from 1 to 1.47. There is much debate about the correct value of the pure rate of time preference, but a range of 1 per cent to 3 per cent is often used. Utilising these estimates yields a social discount rate between 5.1 per cent and 9 per cent using the consumption growth over the full period.

The current official test discount rate in Ireland is 4 per cent (used to discount future costs and benefits), with financial discount rates ranging from 5.82 per cent

---

18 This is the average long-run interest rate taken from the OECD data base OECD Statistics.
19 The real after-tax return was calculated as the ratio of the net operation as published in the CSO *Institutional Sector Accounts* (2010) and the capital stock as published by the CSO *Estimates of the Stock of Fixed Assets* (2011).
20 This is the so called Ramsey equation based on the Ramsey growth model (see Ramsey, 1928).
21 For the period 1970 to 2000, excluding the boom years, real per capita consumption growth averaged 4.7 per cent.

to 6.7 per cent (used to discount project cash flows) depending on the type and length of project (Department of Public Expenditure and Reform, 2011).

The underlying model of discounting used in Table 2.1 is exponential discounting where the rate does not vary across years. As was shown, the consequence of this is that costs or benefits that occur in the distant future (e.g., 100 years) have almost no impact at all on the results of the analysis. For example, the cost of storing nuclear waste that has to be borne for thousands of years into the future is largely removed from the analysis of the costs and benefits of the construction of a nuclear reactor if the exponential approach is used. Likewise, any climate change impacts of a project (e.g., the emission reductions of a public transport project) that accrue in the long run will be virtually eliminated if the exponential discounting approach is used. It is, therefore, not surprising that the parameters and calculation of the discount rate have been subject to substantial debate particularly in the context of valuing climate change (see Anthoff, Tol and Yohe, 2009).

While there has been a particular focus on discounting the distant future more recently due to the interest in the effects of climate change, the issue is not new and substantial experimental and empirical work suggests that individuals apply a declining discount rate which is captured well using a hyperbolic curve.[22] A range of papers in the 1970s and 1980s showed that observed decisions by individuals deviated from what would be expected by conventional theory, with empirical studies finding both extremely large discount rates and even negative rates (Loewenstein and Thaler, 1989). Using experiments Thaler (1981) showed that individuals did not use a constant discount rate but rather that their rates decline for more distant events. Viscusi *et al.* (2008) found strong evidence for hyperbolic (declining) discounting in a study of visitors to water bodies.

Weitzman in a series of papers (e.g., 1998; 2001; 2010) made an important contribution to this literature. He showed that if future discount rates are uncertain then the expected net present value should be used, which implies a decreasing term structure with the discount rate approaching the lowest possible rate. He further argued that since discount rates are not known *ex ante* this uncertainty should be explicitly reflected in any model. A common approach to incorporating such uncertainty into a model is to assume that the outcomes are distributed according to a probability distribution. Weitzmann (1998) assumes that the probability of predicting the discounted value follows a gamma distribution, which results in decreasing discount rates.[23]

To understand the implications of the alternative discounting approaches it is again useful to consider the example of €1,000 received at different times in the

---

22 The most general form of the hyperbolic discount is formally stated as $\theta = 1/(1-\alpha t)^{y/\alpha}$

23 Processes for which the time between events is relevant are often found to follow a gamma distribution. Given that there is a time span between the point at which a valuation is made and the point in time when the outcome is realised, the gamma distribution is a natural choice.

future using the two approaches, which is shown in Figure 2.1. The figure clearly shows the more rapid initial decline in valuations and the less rapid decline in valuation in the more distant future using the hyperbolic (declining) discounting compared to exponential discounting. A €1,000 received (lost) in 100 years is valued just over €200 using the hyperbolic (declining) approach, while it is only worth €20 using the exponential discounting approach.

Figure 2.1: Comparison of the Value Today of €1,000 Received in the Future Using Exponential (4 per cent) and Hyperbolic (Declining) Discounting

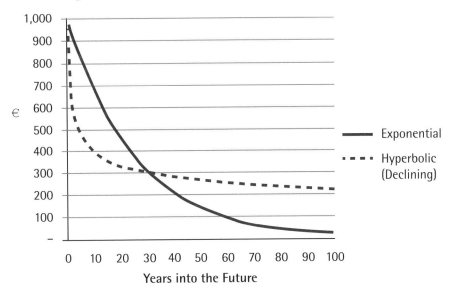

Note: The parameters for the hyperbolic discounting are taken from Angeletos *et al.* (2001) page 51.

While there is significant evidence in favour of some kind of hyperbolic discounting, the debate is ongoing (e.g., Bugess and Zerbe, 2011). Nevertheless, the response in a number of countries has been to use hyperbolic (declining) discounting for costs and benefits that accrue more than 50 years into the future (e.g., HM Treasury, 2011). This approach is appealing since it does not bias the analysis against projects with benefits that arise in the near future by applying exponential discounting to these, while allowing for costs and benefits that arise in the distant future by applying hyperbolic (declining) discounting. A practical approach would be to apply the higher discount factor (lower discount rate) of the two, i.e., the exponential discounting up to the point where the two lines in Figure 2.1 cross and the hyperbolic (declining) thereafter. In Figure 2.1 the two lines cross at 31 years, where the crossing point is determined by the parameterisation and discount rates chosen. For use in actual evaluation these would need to be chosen carefully.

CONCLUSIONS

In order to prioritise investment it is important to evaluate. This chapter has considered just two issues that have a crucial impact on the usefulness of evaluations using a cost-benefit analysis.

The evidence on the expected costs and benefits of projects highlights that projects often do not go according to plan and that these estimates are subject to systematic optimism bias, which while not universal appears to be widespread. In particular it appears to be a significant problem in rail projects.

There is no systematic evidence on optimism bias in Ireland, which of course does not imply that optimism bias is absent. However, the Comptroller and Auditor General has identified some projects as having cost significantly more than had been expected (e.g., refurbishment of Cork Courthouse). Therefore, as a first step to protecting the tax payer, it is important to establish whether projects in Ireland have been subject to optimism bias. This requires thorough *ex post* evaluation of a comprehensive set of all types of infrastructure projects. This analysis should not be restricted to transport infrastructure but should also consider other types of infrastructure. If optimism bias is found, then the UK approach would be a useful first step to protect the tax payer against cost escalation and underperformance of infrastructure.

Of course, a finding that optimism bias has not been an issue does not imply that projects have been good value; it only means that the projections were correct. If a project comes in on budget this does not mean that the costs of the project were minimised, or indeed, that it was the cheapest option to provide the desired outcome. An *ex post* analysis of projects can also be used to compare prices across projects, identify their determinants and allows for an international comparison.

As was highlighted above, projects face a variety of risks. While the implications of risk to the value of a cost-benefit analysis are well known and guidelines usually require these to be priced, in practice risks are often not taken into account (Van Ewijk and Tang, 2003). Therefore, the use of a riskless rate of discount is inappropriate in most cases and thus the discount rates currently used for the assessment of public projects are lower than the estimates of the discount rate provided above, and are almost certainly too low. This implies a lower threshold for projects and biases the results of a cost benefit analysis in favour of projects with substantial medium-term benefits.

The risk free rate should not be used unless a project is indeed risk free, that is all risk has been spread to the market,[24] the risks are not covered by either the

---

24 This could be achieved through the purchase of insurance, which has a cost that should then enter the calculations.

beneficiaries of the project and tax payers or if the costs and benefits have been converted to 'certainty equivalents' (see Harrison, 2010).[25] Instead, sensitivity analysis should be carried out using a range of discount rates that should be centred on a plausible risky rate of return. This reflects the fact that a 'one size fits all' approach is not consistent with the heterogeneity of the projects that are being assessed. For Australia, Harrison (2010) recommends a base rate of 8 per cent and sensitivity analysis over a range of 3 to 10 per cent, where the base is derived from the return to capital. Given the evidence on discount rates presented, a similar approach in Ireland would imply a range with a slightly higher upper value. Where the results are found to be sensitive to the choice of discount rate, further analysis on the appropriate rate should be carried out.

Another important implication from the recent literature is that exponential discounting may be inappropriate, particularly when it comes to valuing costs and benefits that accrue in the very long run. For costs and benefits that accrue in the distant future hyperbolic discounting should be applied. A pragmatic approach is to apply a hybrid between the exponential and the hyperbolic (declining) discounting using the lower rate of the two. This avoids biasing the analysis against projects with benefits in the near future by applying exponential discounting, while it allows for costs and benefits that arise in the distant future by applying the hyperbolic (declining) discounting.

The apparently narrow focus of this chapter should not be taken to imply that only the two issues considered here are important in getting quality cost benefit evaluations, although they are among the most important. A range of other factors also should be reviewed periodically to ensure that the project appraisal guidelines guarantee the best possible analysis. For example, choosing an appropriate comparator is important in choosing the right project. If a project is only compared to a 'do nothing' comparator, then if that project is in any way effective it will dominate the 'do nothing' comparator. Consequently, such a comparison yields no insights for project prioritisation. Therefore, projects should be compared to alternative projects, and variations of the same project should also be considered in order to identify the most effective option.

The implicit assumption in this paper is that some preliminary analysis was used to establish the need for a project, which should be done on the basis of a full assessment of the existing infrastructure and the likely future needs. A fundamental prerequisite for this analysis should be a central asset register, proper condition surveys and asset management plans. These appear to be lacking in some cases in Ireland.[26] Such knowledge should also be used to decide between the building of new infrastructure, maintenance or incremental improvement of

---

25 In many PPP projects the risks of a project are not completely transferred to the market and indeed it can be argued that it is impossible to completely transfer risk to the market, when the projects concern strategic infrastructures.

26 This is common practice in the private sector and in many other countries, e.g., the UK.

existing infrastructure. Likewise, it should not be assumed that investment in new infrastructure is necessarily the most effective solution. In many cases proper maintenance of existing infrastructures would be a more efficient substitute to future investment in new structures. Furthermore, measures other than investment, such as appropriate fiscal incentives, may also lead to the desired outcome. Finally, it is difficult to have confidence in any analysis that is not made public or of which only selected aspects are made public. As such, it is imperative that all evaluations should be published in full in order to allow public scrutiny.

REFERENCES

Angeletos, G-M., Laibson, D., Repetto, A., Tobacman, J. and Weinberg, S. (2001). 'The Hyperbolic Consumption Model: Calibration, Simulation and Empirical Evaluation', *Journal of Economic Perspectives*, 15, 47–68.

Anthoff, D., Tol, R.J. and Yohe, G. (2009). 'Discounting for Climate Change.' *Economics: The Open-Access, Open-Assessment E-Journal*.

Bain, R. (2009). 'Error and Optimism Bias in Toll Road Traffic Forecasts', *Transportation*, 36, 469–482.

Beutel, J. (2002). *The Economic Impact of Objective 1 Interventions for the period 2000–2006*, Final Report to DG-REGIO, May.

Bradley J., Morgenroth, E. and Untiedt, G. (2003). 'Macro-regional evaluation of the Structural Funds using the HERMIN modelling framework', *Italian Journal of Regional Science*, 3, 5–28.

Bradley J., Mitze, T., Morgenroth, E. and Untiedt, G. (2006). *How can we know if EU cohesion policy is successful? Integrating micro and macro approaches to the evaluation of Structural Funds*. Münster: GEFRA.

Burgess, D. and Zerbe, R. (2011). 'Appropriate Discounting for Benefit Cost Analysis', *Journal of Cost Benefit Analysis*, 2, 1–18.

Cundric, A., Kern, T. and Rajkovic, V. (2008). 'A qualitative model for road investment appraisal', *Transport Policy*, 15, 225–231.

De Brucker, K., Macharis, C. and Verbeke, A. (2011). 'Multi-criterion Analysis in Transport Project Evaluation: An Institutional Approach', *European Transport*, 47, 3–34.

Department of Finance (2005). *Guidelines for the Appraisal and Management of Capital Expenditure Proposals in the Public Sector*. http://www.finance.gov.ie/documents/publications/other/capappguide05.pdf

Department of Public Expenditure and Reform (2011). *Project Discount and Inflation Rates*. http://per.gov.ie/project-discount-inflation-rates/

Evans, D. (2005). 'The Elasticity of Marginal Utility of Consumption: Estimates for 20 OECD Countries', *Fiscal Studies*, 26, 197–224.

FitzGerald, J., McCarthy, C., Morgenroth, E. and O'Connell, P.J. (2003). *The Mid-Term Evaluation of the National Development Plan (NDP) and Community*

Support Framework (CSF) for Ireland, 2000–2006. Policy Research Series No. 50, Dublin: Economic and Social Research Institute.

Flyvbjerg, B., in association with COWI (2004). *Procedures for Dealing with Optimism Bias in Transport Planning – Guidance Document.* London: Department of Transport.

Flyvbjerg, B., Holm, M., Skamris, K. and Buhl, S.L. (2003). 'How Common and How Large Are Cost Overruns in Transport Infrastructure Projects?', *Transport Reviews,* 23, 71–88.

Flyvbjerg, B., Holm, M., Skamris, K. and Buhl, S.L. (2004). 'What Causes Cost Overrun in Transport Infrastructure Projects?', *Transport Reviews,* 24, 3–18.

Flyvbjerg, B., Holm, M., Skamris, K. and Buhl, S.L. (2005). 'How (In)accurate Are Demand Forecasts in Public Works Projects? The Case of Transportation', *Journal of the American Planning Association,* 71, 131–46.

Gillespie, G., McGregor,P., Swales, K. and Yin, Y.P. (2001). 'The Displacement and Multiplier Effects of Regional Assistance: A Computable General Equilibrium Analysis', *Regional Studies,* 35, 125–139.

Hahn, R. and Dudley, P. (2007). 'How Well Does the U.S. Government Do Benefit-Cost Analysis?', *Review of Environmental Economics and Policy,* 1, 192–211.

Harrison, M. (2010). *Valuing the Future: The Social Discount Rate in Cost-Benefit Analysis.* Visiting Researcher Paper, Australian Government Productivity Commission.

HM Treasury (2011). *The Green Book: Appraisal and Evaluation in Central Government.* London: TSO.

Honohan, P. (ed.) (1997). *EU Structural Funds in Ireland: A Mid-Term Evaluation of the CSF 1994–1999,* Policy Research Series, No. 31, Dublin: The Economic and Social Research Institute.

Juri N. R. and Kockelman, K. (2006). 'Evaluation of the Trans-Texas Corridor Proposal: Application and Enhancement of the Random-Utility-Based Multiregional Input-Output Model', *Journal of Transport Engineering,* 132, 531–539.

Lightart, J. and Martin Suarez, R. (2011). The Productivity of Public Capital: A Meta-analysis', in Jonkhoff, W. and Manshandenr, W. (eds.), *Infrastructure Productivity Evaluation.* New York: Springer.

Loewenstein, G. and Thaler, R. (1989). 'Anomalies: Intertemporal Choice', *Journal of Economic Perspectives,* 3, 181–193.

Mackett, R.L. and Edwards, M. (1998). 'The Impact of New Urban Public Transport Systems: Will the Expectations Be Met?', *Transportation Research A,* 32, 231–45.

Morgenroth, E. and FitzGerald, J. (2006). *Ex-ante Evaluation of National Investment Priorities 2007–2013,* Policy Research Series Paper No 59. Dublin: Economic and Social Research Institute.

Parthasarathi, P. and Levinson, D. (2010). 'Post-construction evaluation of traffic forecast accuracy,' *Transport Policy*, 17, 428–443.

Pickrell, D.H. (1990). 'Urban Rail Transit Projects: Forecast versus Actual Ridership and Costs', US Department of Transportation.

Pritchett, L. (1996). 'Mind Your P's and Q's: The Value of Infrastructure is not Equal to its Cost', World Bank Working Paper No. 1660.

Pritchett, L. (2002). 'It Pays to be Ignorant: A Simple Political Economy Model of Rigorous Program Evaluation' *Policy Reform*, 5, 251–269.

Ramsey, F. (1928). 'A Mathematical Theory of Saving', *Economic Journal*, 38, 543–559.

Roeger, W. (1996). *Macroeconomic Evaluation of the Effects of Community Structural Funds with QUEST II*. Mimeo, European Commission, DG-ECFIN.

Short, J. and Kopp, A. (2005). 'Transport Infrastructure: Investement and Planning. Policy and Research Aspects', *Transport Policy*, 12, 360–367.

Stiglitz, J. (1994). 'Discount Rates: The Rate of Discount for Cost-Benefit Analysis and the Theory of the Second Best' in Layard, R. and Glaister, S. (eds.), *Cost-Benefit Analysis*, Cambridge: Cambridge University Press.

Thaler, R. (1981). 'Some Empirical Evidence on Dynamic Inconsistency', *Economics Letters*, 8, 201–207.

Törmä, H. (2008). 'Do Small Town Development Projects Matter, and can CGE Help?', *Spatial Economic Analysis*, 3, 247–268.

Van Ewijk, C. and Tang, P. (2003). 'How to Price Risk In Public Investment', *De Economist*, 151, 317–328.

Van Wee, B. (2012). 'How Suitable is CBE for the Ex-Ante Evaluation of Transport Projects: A Discussion from the Perspective of Ethics' *Transport Policy*, 19, 1–7.

Vassallo, J. (2010). 'The Role of the Discount Rate in Tendering Highway Concessions under the LPVR Approach', *Transportation Research Part A*, 44, 806–814.

Viscusi, K., Huber, J. and Bell, J. (2008).'Estimating Discount Rates for Environmental Quality from Utility-based Choice Experiments', *Journal of Risk and Uncertainty*, 37, 199–220.

Weitzman, M. (1998). 'Why the Far-Distant Future Should be Discounted at its Lowest Possible Rate', *Journal of Environmental Economics and Management*, 36, 201–208.

Weitzman, M. (2001). 'Gamma Discounting', *American Economic Review*, 91, 260–271.

Weitzman, M. (2010). 'Risk-adjusted Gamma Discounting', *Journal of Environmental Economics and Management*, 60, 1–13.

CHAPTER 3

Should Loan-to-Value Ratios be Limited? The International Evidence

David Duffy

This chapter examines international evidence on whether there could be a role for Loan-to-Value (LTV) limits as an instrument of macroprudential regulation in Ireland. As the duration and depth of the international housing market downturn has continued, a growing body of international research has sought to examine the factors that contributed to the crisis and to outline possible responses. The potential policy response examined in this chapter emerges from the broader and evolving policy area of macroprudential regulation.

Macroprudential polices have been in existence for some time. However, the scale of the current crisis in terms of house price declines, personal debt levels and weakness of the banking system in the face of the economic downturn means that there is currently an increased focus on this area. Policymakers are looking for solutions and possible mechanisms by which large negative impacts from such a crisis can be avoided in the future. The research examined assesses whether the introduction of loan-to-value limits can help to either avoid rapid and unsustainable house price growth, limit the impact of a housing market downturn on the macroeconomy and the financial system, or both. For policymakers, answers to these questions help determine if there is a role for LTV limits imposed as a policy instrument rather than determined by the market. With respect to the policy landscape (Figure 1.1), this chapter, therefore, looks at evidence in relation to a specific policy designed to meet a clearly identified policy challenge.

To date regulatory imposed LTV limits have not been a feature of the Irish market. Thus, the methodological approach is to review international evidence on the introduction of LTV limits. Consideration is also given to international evidence, where available, that looks at how such limits might interact with other measures aimed at dampening the housing market.

While evidence is not entirely conclusive, there may be a role for LTV limits as one of a set of macroprudential policy instruments. The international evidence finds support for the view that LTV ratios are linked to boom and bust cycles in housing markets, including the level of personal debt and exposure to negative equity. In an Irish context, where homeownership is high, the evidence points to an important consideration for policymakers – the impact that the introduction of LTV limits can have on the rate of homeownership, particularly in younger households. Where LTV limits have been introduced there is evidence that, while they do not prevent booms from occurring, they may contribute to reducing house price volatility and limit the extent of damage to the banking sector at the end of a boom.

Lastly, the suggestion is made that policymakers should monitor the use of and results from the managing of LTV limits by regulators in other economies. In many cases the use of LTV limits is relatively recent and their use in conjunction with other measures makes it difficult to isolate their impact.

BACKGROUND

While the extent of the rise and the depth of the fall may vary, Ireland in common with many other developed economies has experienced a housing market boom and crash. As the duration and depth of the international housing market downturn has continued a growing body of international research has sought to examine the factors that contributed to the crisis and outline possible responses. Three broad policy areas emerge from the literature – monetary policy, fiscal policy and macroprudential regulation.[27] According to the Committee on the Global Financial System (2010), the aim of macroprudential policy is 'to reduce systemic risk, strengthening the financial system against shocks', with systemic risk considered to be the 'risk of disruption to financial services that is caused by an impairment of all or parts of the financial system and has the potential to have serious negative consequences for the real economy'. Macroprudential policy has two main aims: to strengthen the financial system's resilience and to actively limit the build-up of financial risks.

This chapter does not examine the causes of the housing market boom, either internationally or in Ireland. Rather, it is concerned with one specific macroprudential policy response that relates to the housing market. Macroprudential measures are usually designed to target specific objectives, such as household borrowing. Given their narrow focus they are usually considered to be able to tackle an issue more directly and at a lower cost than the broader sweep of monetary or fiscal policy. In the context of the housing market, measures could include higher capital requirements, dynamic provisioning (mandating higher loan loss provisions during upswings), or limits on debt-to-income ratios. The focus of this chapter is on a specific macroprudential measure aimed at borrowing in the housing market, namely, a limit on loan-to-value ratios (LTV). The introduction of such a limit can have both individual borrower and macroeconomic effects. A limit on the maximum LTV ratio might help to curtail the build-up of debt by mortgage borrowers, reducing the risk associated with house price volatility. Lower borrowing means that greater declines in house prices are needed

---

27 Clement (2010) reviews the use of the term macro-prudential, stating that it refers to 'the use of prudential tools with the explicit objective of promoting the stability of the financial system as a whole, not necessarily the individual institutions within it'.

to place borrowers in negative equity. It is argued that limits on the amount that can be borrowed may also contain the extent of a boom by reducing the number of borrowers at a given price (Crowe et al., 2011a, 2011b). For the macroeconomy, LTV limits can have the effect of lowering house price volatility and reducing the impact of a residential property market downturn on the banking sector. In addition, there is some evidence that LTV limits lower house price expectations, which can have a dampening effect on house price growth.

This chapter reviews the international evidence on caps to loan-to-value ratios, with the aim of assessing their potential value as a policy tool. First, it examines the trend in average LTV ratios in Ireland as well as looking at published data on the distribution of LTV ratios. Section 2 also reviews some of the international evidence on the links between LTV ratios and housing markets, while section 3 discusses the international evidence on the role that LTV ratios have played in housing booms. Section 4 outlines the published evidence to date which suggests that while LTV limits can have some impact on the property market, their main result has been to strengthen the resilience of the banking system to economic shocks. Section 5 discusses some of the issues surrounding the implementation of LTV limits. Section 6 concludes.

WHAT HAPPENED TO LOAN-TO-VALUE RATIOS IN IRELAND?

Research at the IMF by Crowe et al. (2011a) found that, across a sample of 21 countries, the average LTV ratio was 71 per cent. However, the Committee on the Global Financial System (2006) show data indicating that while most housing markets have LTV ratios of between 80 and 100 per cent, the average can range from 60 per cent (Australia) to, until recently, 125 per cent (Netherlands).[28] In addition, while there remains variation by individual market, longer mortgage contracts are associated with higher LTV ratios.

It is possible to construct a long-run time series of the average LTV ratio for the period 1974 to 2010 for Ireland. Having remained relatively low for most of the period the average LTV ratio began to increase sharply from 2005, which may, in part at least, be due to the introduction of 100 per cent mortgages. At their peak in 2009 the annual average LTV ratio was 94.2 per cent for new and 85 per cent for second-hand houses.

Figure 3.2 shows average house prices in Ireland. In an Irish context, house prices began to rise rapidly prior to any increase in LTV ratios. This may point to higher LTV ratios becoming a factor late in the boom and allowing the boom to continue for longer than it otherwise would.

---

28 According to the Netherlands Authority for the Financial Markets, new standards mean that the mortgage loan may amount to 112 per cent of the purchase value of the residence. The part of the debt that is in excess of the purchase value has to be redeemed within 7 years, or covered by accumulated assets. Until now, there was no maximum for the amount of the mortgage loan compared with the value of the residence. Press release, April 21, 2010.

Figure 3.1: Average Loan-to-Value Ratio, Ireland

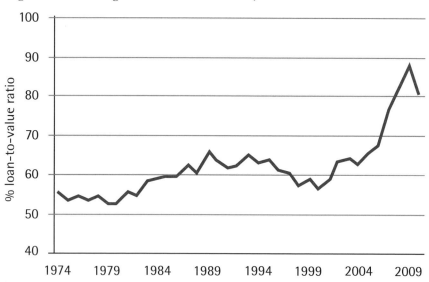

Source: Based on Department of the Environment data for mortgage loans paid, 1970–2006; Data from 2006–2010 from Irish Banking Federation and Local Authorities. Data available at Department of the Environment website (www.environ.ie).

Figure 3.2: Average House Price, Ireland

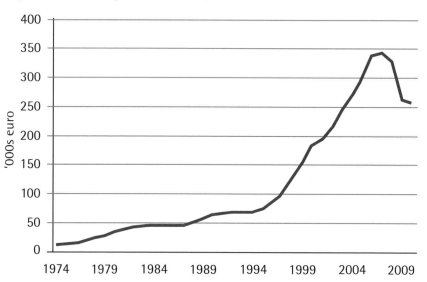

Source: Based on Department of the Environment Housing Statistics.

Figure 3.3a: Percentage of Mortgages with LTV> 90 per cent, First-time Buyers

Source: Based on Department of the Environment Housing Statistics.

Figure 3.3b: Percentage of Mortgages with LTV> 90 per cent, Repeat Buyers

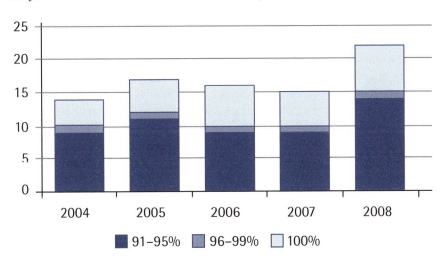

Source: Based on Department of the Environment Housing Statistics.

As pointed out by Committee on the Global Financial System (2006), the national average LTV ratio could be high but it could be that the high LTV ratios are all concentrated in high income or high wealth households who have more scope to respond to shocks and a lower probability of receiving a negative income shock. Household vulnerability is lower in this situation than if the high LTV ratios are concentrated in higher credit risk borrowers, who are likely to have low or variable incomes. Thus, in assessing the role of LTV limits data should ideally be available at the household level to enable a more accurate analysis of the size of the most vulnerable subgroup of the population and the extent of the risks they face.

Average LTV ratios may not be representative of the risks in the market – what may be more indicative of risk is the distribution of ratios. For example, while the average LTV ratio in the US was 76 per cent in the years prior to the crisis, loans with a LTV ratio of 100 per cent were widely available (IMF, 2011). While data on the distribution of LTV ratios for Ireland are limited, the Department of the Environment has published the range of LTV ratios for the period 2004 to 2008. What is most noticeable is the high proportion of first-time buyers (FTB) with a very high LTV ratio. In 2007 and 2008 around one in four first-time buyers had a LTV ratio of 100 per cent (Figure 3.3a). In contrast, in 2008 only 7 per cent of repeat buyers had an LTV of 100 per cent (Figure 3.3b). As pointed out by Doyle (2009) by the end of 2008, 100 per cent mortgages were no longer available as, following house price falls, banks became more restrictive with respect to LTV ratios.

In response to the crisis a number of countries have taken steps to increase mortgage market regulation, including setting LTV limits. For example, amongst others, Sweden has set a maximum LTV ratio of 85 per cent, while Finland has set a limit of 90 per cent (IMF, 2011). The Honohan report (2010) into the Irish banking crisis reveals that the introduction of LTV limits was identified in 2006 as a potential measure to dampen the property boom by the Financial Regulator. Capital requirements were raised for high LTV ratio mortgages in 2006, although this was after much debate and is considered 'belated and relatively modest'. Alternatives, such as banning (or disapproving publicly of) 100 per cent LTV ratio mortgages, were not considered seriously as they were felt to be out of tune with the principles-based approach[29] and with the international regulatory fashion of the time (Honohan, 2010). In addition there were concerns that stronger regulatory action would have had a negative impact on the competitiveness of institutions under the remit of the Financial Regulator and may have made Ireland a less attractive location for international investment. Again these issues are discussed in more detail in Honohan (2010).

In Ireland, while there is currently no direct regulation of credit limits, as part of Central Bank restructuring, broader regulatory powers which would include the ability to prescribe lending limits are anticipated (CBFSAI, 2010). The Central Bank aims to improve the identification and control of credit risk by enhancing

---

29 Principles-based regulation relied very heavily on making sure that appropriate governance structures and systems were in place in banks and building societies (Honohan, 2010).

credit history information about borrowers. The lack of comprehensive credit information can lead to poor lending decisions resulting in overleveraged borrowers. With regard to credit limits, the Central Bank is keeping under review the potential for credit limits to be applied as a macro-prudential measure.

THE ROLE OF LOAN-TO-VALUE RATIOS IN HOUSING BOOMS

Among the factors identified internationally as facilitating the boom in housing markets has been the trend towards a more deregulated mortgage market, increased competition within the mortgage market and high levels of mortgage product innovation.[30] Ellis (2006) argues that these factors, combined with the effect of lower inflation on nominal interest rates and increased credit supply, supported increased demand for housing. Given the relatively inelastic nature of housing supply, higher house prices resulted. Andrews (2010), in an analysis of a panel of OECD countries, finds that financial deregulation and mortgage innovations have been associated with a noticeable increase in the effective demand for housing and, thus, real house prices. Duca, Muellbauer and Murphy (2011) using US data show that LTV ratios rose over the period 2000 to 2005 and find that changes to credit standards played a major role driving real US house prices. Andrews et al. (2011) found that over the past three decades, having accounted for a number of macroeconomic and structural factors, demand pressures arising from financial deregulation may have translated into increases in house prices of some 30 per cent in an average OECD country over the period.

Part of the mortgage market innovation that took place included an increase in LTV ratios internationally. Borio and Shim (2007) and Borio, Furfine and Lowe (2001) suggest that LTV ratios are inclined to be pro-cyclical, as lenders tend to relax LTV ratios in good times in response to competitive pressures and perceptions of declining risk. In an analysis of the US housing market, Ellis (2008a) argues that, in part, the depth of the housing downturn in the US was caused by an easing of lending standards. This included the use of second mortgages, (resulting in higher overall LTV ratios), higher initial LTV ratios on new mortgages, and the availability of 100 per cent mortgages. Furthermore, the introduction of interest only[31] mortgages meant that not only were initial LTV ratios high, but they stayed high on an ongoing basis.

As part of a wider examination of the influence of structural and policy factors on real house prices, Andrews (2010) looks at the role played by the LTV ratio. Based on his analysis of 20 OECD counties he finds that an increase in the LTV ratio is associated with higher real house price volatility, where house price

---

30 For example, see André (2010) or Ellis (2008a).
31 An interest only mortgage means that the borrower does not repay any of the principal but instead just pays the interest due. Typically, for this type of mortgage a borrower would have an interest only period at the commencement of the mortgage, say for 3 years, after which they would then begin to repay both interest and capital.

volatility is measured as the standard deviation of annual real house price growth over 5 year intervals between 1980 and 2005. The empirical results show that half a standard deviation rise in the LTV ratio (equivalent to 5 percentage points) is associated with a 7 per cent increase in real house price volatility, although the impact is lower in countries with a more responsive housing supply and higher transactions costs. In addition, Andrews finds that house price volatility tends to be higher in environments characterised by high rates of leverage (proxied by using maximum LTV ratios). On the basis of his wider analysis, Andrews (2010) concludes prudential banking supervision and polices aimed at containing the build up of borrowing reduce the extent of house price volatility, and that these results support the argument for ongoing prudential reform.

Empirical analysis in IMF (2011) using data from 19 advanced OECD economies covering the period 1980 to 2010 shows a positive, significant, relationship between LTV ratios and the magnitude of house price downturns. The analysis finds countries where LTV ratios are high, on average, have deeper downturns. Crowe et al. (2011b) acknowledge that establishing a causal link running from LTV ratios to house price dynamics is difficult due to lack of time series data, lack of variation in LTV limits over time, or the lack of mandatory LTV limits in many countries. Nonetheless, using data from 21 countries they find that maximum LTV limits are positively related to house price appreciation between 2000 and 2007, estimating that a 10 percentage point increase in the maximum LTV ratio allowed is associated with a 13 per cent increase in nominal house prices. Other research has also shown the influence of LTV ratios on house prices, with positive shocks to income leading to larger house price increases where LTV ratios are higher (Lamont and Stein, 1999; Almedia, Campello and Liu, 2006, Benito, 2006). Thus, there is a wide range of papers using cross-country analysis showing that higher LTV ratios are associated with higher house prices and higher house price volatility.

EVIDENCE ON LIMITS ON LOAN-TO-VALUE RATIOS

As part of the discussion on what caused the boom and possible means of containing future booms, there has been some focus on the potential role to be played by capping LTV ratios. Crowe et al. (2011b) cite examples of the effectiveness of LTV limits. For example, in Korea the introduction of LTV limits in September 2002 saw monthly house price inflation fall from 3.4 per cent to 0.3 per cent and then remain low until April 2003. Subsequent lowering of the LTV limit was followed by reductions in house price inflation.

The Use of LTV Limits in Hong Kong

One housing market with long-run experience of LTV limits is Hong Kong, where maximum LTV limits have been in place since 1991, as well as the adjustment of these limits to intervene in the market. The policy of LTV limits was introduced with two main aims: to strengthen bank resilience to asset price volatility, and to reduce the risk of bank credit becoming a source of cycle amplification. Prior to 1991 the maximum LTV ratio was 90 per cent. Initially, a LTV limit of 70 per cent was adopted voluntarily by the banking sector, until November 1995 when the policy became part of regulatory policy. Since then the LTV limit has remained in place although the limit has varied in the face of property market conditions. For example, in its most recent move, the Hong Kong Monetary Authority reduced the maximum LTV for properties valued at over HK$12 million (approximately 1.2 million euro) to 50 per cent, lowered the maximum LTV ratio for properties valued over HK$8 million (€785,000 approx.) and below HK$12 million from 70 per cent to 60 per cent and capped the maximum loan amount at HK$6 million (€590,000 approximately). For residential properties with a value below HK$8 million the maximum LTV ratio was held at 70% but the maximum loan amount was capped at HK$4.8 million (€470,000 approximately). For all non-owner-occupied residential properties, the limit has also been reduced to 50 per cent regardless of the property value. These measures were introduced amid concerns that the housing and mortgage markets would grow too rapidly, exposing the banking system to higher risks.[32]

Using loan level data for Hong Kong, Wong et al. (2004) find that the LTV ratio is statistically significant, the higher the current LTV ratio the greater is the default probability. In addition they undertake a simulation exercise, allowing the LTV limit to be relaxed from 70 per cent to 90 per cent. This results in a sharp increase in negative equity loans and a default rate twice that which actually occurred. The evidence presented in the analysis suggests that the policy of limiting LTV ratios has a role in reducing negative equity and mortgage defaults.

Using panel data from 13 economies, some of which do not have a LTV policy, Wong et al. (2011) assess the sensitivity of the mortgage delinquency ratio[33] to property prices and find that sensitivity is lower in economies with a LTV policy. A 1 per cent drop in property prices would increase the delinquency ratio for economies with LTV policies by 0.35 basis points, whereas there would be a 1.29 basis point increase for economies without a LTV policy. Thus, the policy is considered to be an effective one with regard to reducing systemic risk. In addition, the limits have played a role guarding the system against the house price crash in 1997. They find that 'if maximum LTV ratios were to have been relaxed from 70 per cent to 90 per cent before 1997, the delinquency ratio right after the 40 per cent decline in property prices in 1997 98 would have been 1.7 per cent compared to the actual level of 0.84 per cent at the end of 1998.' These results are consistent with the earlier Wong et al. (2004) study which used loan level data.

Wong et al. (2011) use data for Hong Kong, Singapore and Korea, three economies with LTV limits, to examine the effectiveness of LTV policy and the tightening of this policy in stabilising the property market. The results in relation to the property market are mixed. However, they find strong empirical evidence

---

32 Hong Kong Monetary Authority Press Release, November 19, 2010.
33 The mortgage delinquency ratio is measured by a ratio of total amount of overdue loans to total outstanding loans.

that tightening LTV caps reduces household leverage, leading the authors to suggest that LTV policy may affect systemic risk via effects on household leverage with the property market playing a minor role.

Although limited to a LTV ratio of 70 per cent, credit is available in the Hong Kong property market under a mortgage insurance programme allowing qualified borrowers to obtain a loan of up to 90 per cent of the house value. However, the lenders exposure remains at 70 per cent as the remaining 20 per cent is insured by the Hong Kong Mortgage Corporation. The mortgage insurance programme does allow qualifying borrowers overcome the hurdle of a substantial downpayment, even if the loan repayments were affordable. Wong et al. (2011) show that usage of mortgage insurance increased between 1999 and 2009, arguing that this indicates that the concerns about LTV limits and liquidity constraints should not be lightly dismissed. As part of their panel data analysis they examine whether mortgage insurance programmes reduce the effectiveness of a LTV policy but find no evidence that such an effect occurs. Mortgage insurance of high LTV loans is also a feature of the Canadian mortgage market (Kiff, 2009).

Gerlach and Peng (2005) find the introduction of LTV limits to have a significant impact on bank lending and property prices in Hong Kong. They find that bank lending adjusts to property prices, with a 10 per cent increase in real property prices leading to a 4 per cent rise in real bank credit prior to 1991 but by only 1.3 per cent after 1991, at least in part due to the introduction of an LTV limit. These results show that the prudential regulation and risk controls limited the exposure of the banking sector to swings in property prices.

Crowe et al. (2011b), based on the Hong Kong experience, suggest that while LTV limits may not prevent a boom, their presence helps to limit damage to the banking system. The positive experience using LTV limits in Hong Kong is pertinent in an Irish context, as Hong Kong is also a small open economy. Furthermore, the pegging of their currency to the US dollar means that monetary policy cannot be used to control asset prices (Gerlach and Peng, 2005).

LTV Limits and Debt-to-Income Limits

LTV limits are one of the macroprudential measures that have been introduced in some economies and considered in the literature as a means of containing the effects of a real estate boom and bust. In some cases they have been introduced in conjunction with other measures, such as debt-to-income limits, for example, China introduced LTV limits in 1997 and followed with debt-to-income limits in 2004 (IMF, 2011). Similarly, debt-to-income limits were introduced in Korea approximately three years after the introduction of LTV limits. There is little empirical evidence available of the use of debt-to-income limits with much of the macroprudential literature focusing on LTV limits. Igan and Kang (2011) examine the introduction of LTV and debt-to-income limits in Korea. Combining a regional data set and survey data they find evidence that transactions levels fall after the introduction of such limits. In a series of regressions, Igan and Kang found that the implementation of a LTV limit had a negative statistically-significant impact on house price growth. Although the coefficients for a debt-to-income limit were also negative they were not statistically-significant. In the three month period following a tightening of regulations, they found an average drop of 16 per cent in transaction activity in response to a tightening of LTV limits and a 21 per cent average drop in response to tightening debt-to-income regulations. In addition, using survey data they are able to model the effect of limits on property buying decisions and perceptions on the direction of house prices. The results show that both LTV and debt-to-income ratio tightening delay property-buying decisions and push down house price expectations.

LTV Limits and Homeownership

The implementation of LTV limits can have an impact on the attainment of homeownership. The imposition of such limits may involve either the exclusion of low-income households from owner occupancy or postponement of the decision to become a homeowner due to the need to meet a higher downpayment constraint. Using data from a survey of US borrowers, Mayer and Engelhardt (1996) find that the size of the downpayment required can act as a constraint to homeownership. Using Canadian data, Engelhardt (1994) shows that for a given house price, as the proportion of the price required as a downpayment rises, by increasing the amount of savings required for a deposit, this acts to discourage homeownership. Andrews and Caldera Sánchez (2011), based on analysis of a panel of 12 OECD countries, show the relaxation of downpayment constraints has increased homeownership rates, particularly among credit-constrained and younger households over recent decades. They show that, overall, a 10 percentage point increase in the LTV ratio raises the aggregate homeownership rate by 3 per cent from the sample median. The effect is much stronger for those households that are financially constrained, with the homeownership rate rising by 12 per cent for households in the second income quartile with a head of household aged between 25–34 years. Caldera Sánchez and Andrews (2011), using household data for 25 OECD countries, find that the relaxation of downpayment constraints on mortgage loans, reducing deposit requirements, has increased residential mobility, with a stronger effect on younger households.[34] Caldera Sánchez and Andrews (2011) also discuss the risks associated with high rates of homeownership or high LTV ratios, as very high borrowing to achieve homeownership may constrain mobility by increasing vulnerability to shocks and to negative equity.[35]

---

34 Households where the head of household is aged 44 years or younger.

35 They cite evidence from Chan (2001) who uses a sample of US loan level data and shows that those with high initial LTV ratios are more likely to be 'locked-in' and unable to move as a result of a house price shock. Ferreira et al. (2010) using American Housing Survey also finds a negative relationship between negative equity and mobility. However, there is some debate about this finding in a paper by Schulhofer-Wohl (2010).

As pointed out by Catte *et al.* (2004), high LTV ratios allow a higher level of debt, which can require longer repayment terms to keep the debt service cost to income ratio affordable. Longer repayment terms reduce the amount of capital repaid in any period. A lower LTV ratio provides the borrower with a buffer to protect against house price falls and so can reduce the incidence and depth of negative equity (Ellis, 2008a; Ellis, 2008b). Ellis (2008b) shows the implications for negative equity of different stylised LTV distributions, with a lower average initial ratio resulting in a lower incidence of negative equity. In an Irish context, Duffy (2010) shows that those with high LTVs are much more likely to experience negative equity.[36]

ISSUES SURROUNDING THE IMPLEMENTATION OF LTV LIMITS

In constructing an LTV ratio for regulatory purposes, the value against which the loan is measured can have a significant impact, particularly on the procyclicality of bank lending. If house prices are rising rapidly, in part due to easing credit standards, then the value component could be considered unreliable and would also artificially lower the LTV ratio. The majority of economies use the market value of the property, although a number use a mortgage lending value. The market value is based on the transaction price for the property, while the mortgage lending value is an 'estimate of the realisable value of the property that is sustainable in the longer term' (Borio *et al.*, 2001). Use of the market value, based on primarily short-term factors, can therefore result in higher procyclicality in the value component. In Hong Kong properties were usually valued by a professional surveyor who took account of factors such as property age and location as well as the latest transaction price for similar properties. The maximum loan was calculated based on the lower of the purchase price or the valuation amount (Gerlach and Peng, 2005).

An important consideration is the timing of the introduction of LTV limits in the house price cycle. In this regard empirical analysis is scarce. At present Irish house prices continue to fall and lending standards have tightened. As already noted, Doyle (2009) finds that by the end of 2008, 100 per cent mortgages were no longer available in Ireland. Based on the small number of countries where LTV limits have been introduced, it appears that the introduction generally occurs at a time of strong house price growth and worries about excessive exposure to property sector loans. In the case of Hong Kong a voluntary LTV limit was first introduced by the banking sector in 1991 during a period of rapid house price growth to 'provide a cushion for banks should the market come back down' (Yue, 2001). The limit was then adopted by the Hong Kong Monetary Authority as a

---

36 An overview of the literature on the effects of negative equity for individual borrowers and the macroeconomy is discussed in Duffy (2010).

prudential measure. Similarly, the Financial Supervisory Service in Korea first introduced LTV limits around 2003 to 'prevent potential distress from an overheated housing market on the financial system' (Lee, 2006).

As pointed out by the Committee on the Global Financial System (2010), the use of macroprudential tools is in its infancy and so the full impact of any measures may not yet be fully understood. For example, the introduction of lower LTV ratios may lead to a redeployment of capital to other sectors. In addition, the transmission mechanism may change over time as financial innovation in response to policy measures may change the risk distribution. In order to be able to operate macro-prudential policies, particularly in a countercyclical manner, policymakers must be able to identify the build up of financial risk and so observable and reliable indicators are needed. In addition, micro data, such as survey data, may provide information about the distribution that aggregate macro data do not provide. In applying a limit to the LTV ratio, policymakers could set the cap at a certain level and leave it there. This would contribute to the aim of enhancing financial system resilience, but may also act as an automatic stabiliser which helps moderate the financial cycle. This latter effect could be enhanced by adjusting the LTV limit around its norm in a countercyclical manner. A Committee on the Global Financial System 2010 workshop[37] on the use of property related measures found that an 80 per cent LTV ratio maximum was generally seen as the norm with tightening of this usually in the order of 10–20 percentage points, some of which was reversed when conditions normalised.

While policy interventions may help to reduce future risks, intervention is not without costs or possibly market distortions. A difficulty implementing macro-prudential measures is that once they are put in place the market works to find ways of overcoming the restriction. Attempts to overcome LTV limits have the potential for serious consequences. Multiple loans can make sorting out debt problems much more difficult in the event of a bust. There is also the risk of pushing borrowers outside the mainstream financial system to non-bank or less regulated borrowing. To avoid this regulatory arbitrage, it is important that LTV limits apply to the entire financial system. In addition such regulatory arbitrage can, over time, reduce the effectiveness of LTV limits (IMF, 2011).

Crowe et al. (2011a; 2011b) cite the example from the US of combining one or more loans to avoid mortgage insurance above an 80 per cent LTV. This could be overcome by banning second loans or by using LTVs ratios applied to aggregate borrowings. Crowe et al. also cite the example of Korea where lower LTV limits for loans with less than three years of maturity lead to a boom in loans with a term of three years and one day. Macroprudential measures can suffer from being a 'blunt' instrument. Studies of homeownership rates indicate that those impacted by LTV limits would be those more in need of credit, for example younger and/or

---

37 Committee on the Global Financial System (2010). 'Macroprudential instruments and frameworks: a stocktaking of issues and experiences', CGFS paper no. 38, Bank for International Settlements, May.

poorer individuals. Some solutions have been adopted to try to overcome, or minimise, the unintended negative consequences from LTV limits. Again Crowe et al. (2011a; 2011b) cite a range of examples – Korea differentiates limits across regions based on house price appreciation, while China and Singapore impose lower limits on second mortgages. However, there is also empirical evidence showing that LTV limits have a role in reducing house price volatility, and experience showing that LTV limits can offer some protection to consumers and the banking system in the event of a bust. Crowe et al. (2011b), in their model based analysis, find that the use of LTV limits has the advantage of a narrow focus on a specific objective, and by addressing a specific issue can perform better than other interventions. However, Crowe et al. (2011a; 2011b) also argue that their narrow focus means that they may be easier to circumvent. When this happens, the result may be more difficult to resolve or renegotiate in the event of a bust, in which case the measures are ultimately counter-productive.

Crowe et al. (2011a; 2011b) undertake a model based evaluation of policy responses, monetary policy, fiscal policy and macroprudential measures, to house price fluctuations and find support for the view that tools with a narrow focus, macroprudential measures, addressing a specific rigidity can perform better, and suggest that LTV limits might be a policy tool that could operate in a counter-cyclical manner. As argued by Crowe et al. (2011a; 2011b), 'Each policy will entail costs and distortions, and its effectiveness will be limited by loopholes and implementation problems. Broad reaching measures (such as change in monetary policy) will be more difficult to circumvent, and hence potentially more effective, but will typically involve greater costs. More targeted measures (such as maximum LTV ratios) may limit costs, but will be challenged by loopholes, jeopardizing efficacy.' Borio and Shim (2007) make the point that prudential policy alone is not sufficient, monetary and fiscal policy may also play a role and take a share of the burden.

CONCLUSIONS

With increasing attention being paid to the causes of the housing market boom and bust, the international evidence suggests that LTV limits on mortgages may have a role to play. Data from Ireland shows that LTV ratios rose in the latter half of the boom, which suggests that they may have contributed to prolonging the boom in Irish house prices. If Ireland were to decide to regulate LTV ratios then this would have a number of possible impacts on the future housing market. The introduction of LTV limits could lower house price volatility. In addition, the evidence indicates that LTV limits do not prevent house price booms but can help to protect the financial system from sharp declines in house prices. Although the literature shows that LTV limits would not prevent future growth in Irish house prices they can serve to dampen growth by lowering purchaser's house price expectations.

LTV limits have generally been introduced during a housing market boom or as a result of the experience gained from an economic shock. Evidence from Korea shows lower transaction levels following the imposition of LTV limits. Other research shows that LTV ratios tend to be procyclical. Furthermore, as pointed out by Doyle (2009), by the end of 2008, 100 per cent LTV ratio mortgages had disappeared from the Irish market. On that basis average LTV ratios in the Irish market are probably already lower than during the boom period. This represents a market response. The introduction of LTV limits in Ireland as a regulation instrument would represent a direct policy intervention, which could prevent LTV ratios increasing during future periods of strong house price growth. If LTV limits are to be introduced then the timing of the introduction and the level at which any limit is set needs careful consideration. At present, the Irish housing market is still experiencing a contraction in prices and low levels of activity. However, as there is a low volume of transactions at present, this may well represent a good opportunity to put a new policy framework in place. Thus, in the future if house prices began to increase rapidly a policy framework would exist. There is also evidence that suggests that the existence of such a policy tool would in itself have a dampening impact on price expectations. The experience of Hong Kong is particularly relevant for Ireland, indicating that LTV limits can be actively adjusted to take account of the property market cycle, suggesting a much more active role for regulation.

Although the use of macro-prudential tools is the focus of a growing body of research it is, as yet, difficult to fully assess their effectiveness as in many cases the use of such tools is in its infancy. In addition, they may be used in conjunction with other monetary or fiscal policy instruments and so their impact may be difficult to assess. Despite this, the empirical evidence to date suggests that the introduction of LTV ratios can have an impact, particularly on the robustness of the banking system in the face of property related shocks.

REFERENCES

Almeida, H., Campello, V. and Liu, C. (2006). 'The Financial Accelerator: Evidence from International Housing Markets,' *Review of Finance*, Oxford University Press for European Finance Association, 10, 321–352, September.

André, C. (2010). 'A Bird's Eye View of OECD Housing Markets', OECD Economics Department Working Papers, No. 746, Paris: OECD Publishing.

Andrews, A. (2010). 'Real House Prices in OECD Countries: The Role of Demand Shocks and Structural and Policy Factors', OECD Economics Department Working Papers, No.831, Paris: OECD Publishing.

Andrews, D. and Caldera Sánchez, A. (2011). 'Drivers of Homeownership in Selected OECD Countries', OECD Economics Department Working Papers, No. 849, Paris: OECD Publishing.

Andrews, D., Caldera Sánchez, A. and Johansson, A. (2011). 'Housing Markets and Structural Policies in OECD Countries', OECD Economics Department Working Papers No. 836, Paris: OECD Publishing.

Benito, A. (2006). 'The Down-payment Constraint and the UK Housing Market: Does the Theory Fit the Facts?', *Journal of Housing Economics*, 15, 1–20.

Borio, C., Furfine, C. and Lowe, P. (2001). 'Procyclicality of the Financial System and Financial Stability Issues and Policy Options', BIS Papers, No 1, March.

Borio, C., and Shim, I. (2007). 'What Can (Macro-)prudential Policy Do to Support Monetary Policy?', Bank for International Settlements Working Papers No. 242, December.

Caldera Sánchez, A. and Andrews, D. (2011). 'To Move or Not to Move: What Drives Residential Mobility Rates in the OECD?', OECD Economics Department Working Papers, No. 846, Paris: OECD Publishing.

Catte, P., Girouard, N., Price, R. and Andre, C. (2004). 'Housing Markets, Wealth and the Business Cycle', OECD Economics Department Working Papers, No. 394. Paris: OECD Publishing.

Central Bank and Financial Services Authority of Ireland (CBFSAI) (2010). 'Banking Supervision: Our New Approach', June 21, Dublin: CBFSAI.

Central Bank of Ireland (2011). 'Banking Supervision: Our Approach 2011 Update', June 30, Dublin: CBFSAI.

Chan, S., (2001), 'Spatial Lock-in: Do Falling House Prices Constrain Residential Mobility?' *Journal of Urban Economics*, 49, 567–586.

Clement, P. (2010). 'The Term "Macroprudential": Origins and Evolution' *BIS Quarterly Review*, March.

Committee on the Global Financial System (2006). 'Housing Finance in the Global Financial Market', CGFS Paper No. 26, Bank for International Settlements, January.

Committee on the Global Financial System (2010). 'Macroprudential Instruments and Frameworks: A Stocktaking of Issues and Experiences', CGFS Paper No. 38, Bank for International Settlements, May.

Crowe, C., Dell'Ariccia, G., Igan, D. and Rabanal, P. (2011a). 'Policies for Macrofinancial Stability: Options to deal with Real Estate Booms: Lessons from Country Experiences' Washington: IMF Staff Discussion Note SDN/11/02, February.

Crowe, C., Dell'Ariccia, G., Igan, D. and Rabanal, P. (2011b). 'How to Deal with Real Estate Booms: Lessons from Country Experiences', Washington: IMF Working Paper WP/11/91, April.

Doyle, N. (2009). 'Housing Finance Developments in Ireland', *Central Bank Quarterly Bulletin 04*, October.

Duca, J.V., Muellbauer, J. and Murphy, A. (2011). 'Shifting Credit Standards and the Boom and Bust in US House Prices', Centre for Economic Policy Research, Discussion Paper No. 8361, April.

Duffy, D. (2010), 'Negative Equity in the Irish Housing Market', *The Economic and Social Review*, Spring 2010, 41.

Ellis, L. (2006).'Housing and Housing Finance: The View from Australia and Beyond', Reserve Bank of Australia Research Discussion Papers RDP 2006–12, Reserve Bank of Australia.

Ellis, L. (2008a). 'The Housing Meltdown: Why Did It Happen in the United States', Bank for International Settlements Working Papers No. 259, September.

Ellis, L. (2008b). 'How Many in Negative Equity? The Role of Mortgage Contract Characteristics', Bank for International Settlements *Quarterly Review*, December.

Engelhardt, G.V. (1994). 'House Prices and the Decision to Save for Down Payment', *Journal of Urban Economics*, 36, 209–237.

Ferreira, F., Gyourko J. and Tracy J. (2010). 'Housing Busts and Household Mobility', *Journal of Urban Economics*, 86, 34–45.

Gerlach, S. and Peng, W. (2005). 'Bank Lending and Property Prices in Hong Kong, *Journal of Banking and Finance*, 29.

Honohan, P. (2010). *The Irish Banking Crisis Regulatory and Financial Stability Policy 2003–2008*, A Report to the Minister for Finance by the Governor of the Central Bank, May.

Igan, D. and Kang, H. (2011). 'Do Loan-to-Value and Debt-to-Income Limits Work? Evidence from Korea', IMF Working Paper, March.

IMF (2011). 'Housing Finance and Financial Stability – Back to Basics', Chapter 3 in *Global Financial Stability Report*, April.

Kiff, J. (2009). 'Canadian Residential Mortgage Markets: Boring but Effective', IMF Working Paper WP/09/130, June. Washington: IMF.

Lamont, O. and Stein, J.C. (1999). 'Leverage and House Price Dynamics in US Cities', *The RAND Journal of Economics*, 30, Autumn.

Lee, Jang Yung (2006). 'Macroprudential Supervision in Korea: Experiences and Case Studies', Macroprudential Supervision Conference (FSC/FSS/IMF), Seoul, November 7–8.

Mayer, C.J. and Engelhardt, G.V. (1996). 'Gifts, Down Payments and Housing Affordability', *Journal of Housing Research*, 7, Fannie Mae Foundation.

Schulhofer-Wohl, S. (2010). 'Negative Equity Does Not Reduce Homeowners' Mobility', Federal Reserve Bank of Minneapolis, Working Paper No. 682.

Wong, J., Fung, L., Fong, T., Sze, A. (2004). ' Residential Mortgage Default Risk and the Loan-to-Value Ratio', Hong Kong Monetary Authority, *Quarterly Bulletin*, December.

Wong, E., Fong, T., Li, K. and Choi, H. (2011). 'Loan-to-Value Ratio as a Macro-prudential Tool – Hong Kong's Experience and Cross Country Evidence', Hong Kong Monetary Authority Working Paper 01/2011, February.

Yue, E. (2001). 'Marrying the Micro- and Macro-prudential Dimensions of Financial Stability – the Hong King Experience', Bank for International Settlements Papers Number 1.

CHAPTER 4

The Potential Role of Pay for Performance in Irish Healthcare: Lessons from the International Evidence

Anne Nolan, Jacqueline O'Reilly, Samantha Smith, Aoife Brick

This chapter considers evidence for policy in the area of payment of providers in healthcare, and in particular, the use of pay-for-performance (P4P) incentives. In terms of the policy landscape (Figure 1.1), the payment of healthcare providers is relevant to a long-established policy area that is undergoing substantial reform at present in Ireland. The specific policy of P4P is one that is an aspect of the remuneration of healthcare providers in many countries. However, while there has been reference to the potential role of P4P in Irish healthcare, it is not yet a feature of the Irish system and its introduction is not an established government policy. The available evidence on P4P is limited at present.

The key research question examined in this chapter is whether there is evidence that P4P can increase the efficiency and quality of healthcare services. If so, then the argument for introducing P4P in the Irish health system would be strengthened. As a labour intensive sector, supply-side measures that influence provider behaviour offer a clear avenue for improving efficiency. P4P incentives, in which payments are tied to performance, are becoming increasingly common in international healthcare systems. An answer to the main research question can help policymakers to assess the contribution of P4P incentives to particular Irish policy challenges (e.g., how to achieve increased efficiency in healthcare, without compromising on quality). The research also highlights the importance of context in assessing the applicability of P4P to the Irish healthcare system.

The methodological approach is to review and critically assess the existing international evidence on P4P in healthcare. The focus is on P4P programmes in the areas of primary care, acute care and integrated care that have been introduced by national public sector organisations such as the UK National Health Service (NHS) and US Medicare system.

The review of the international evidence highlights key implications for Irish policy. First, despite the popularity of P4P in many countries, the available evidence is limited, largely due to technical limitations in evaluating existing initiatives (e.g., lack of a control group). This highlights the importance of facilitating on-going evaluation when designing any new policy option. Second, even where rigorous evaluations of P4P are undertaken, there is no clear answer to the question of whether P4P is effective (in terms of health outcomes, cost control, etc.). Third, context is important in assessing the potential role of P4P in Irish healthcare. In contrast to the settings in which the available evidence on P4P is concentrated, the Irish healthcare system is characterised by a complex system of financial incentives that have well-documented adverse effects on equity and efficiency. In addition, many of the supportive structures that are in place in other countries, such as a unique health identifier, are not yet in place in Ireland. Finally, the review highlights that while a lack of conclusive evidence does not necessarily imply that P4P should not be adopted (or at least piloted) in Ireland, it follows that Irish policymakers can learn from 'second mover advantage' by learning from future P4P experience in other countries.

BACKGROUND

Over the period 2000–2009, public health expenditure more than doubled in real terms (Brick *et al.*, 2010). Since then, a severe and prolonged recession, the banking crisis and the resulting EU-IMF bailout have combined to create an environment in which large real decreases in public expenditure are required. Already, public health expenditure has fallen by €1.3 billion (or over 8 per cent in nominal terms) from its peak in 2009.[38] As the second largest component of public expenditure, healthcare is particularly vulnerable to the effects of the further cuts in expenditure that are required.

In this context of diminishing financial resources, there is increasing emphasis on maximising the value of expenditure by ensuring efficient delivery of high quality healthcare services. While the Public Service Agreement contains a number of commitments to reform work practices, the use of involuntary redundancies is prohibited. With this constraint, ensuring that existing resources are used efficiently, without compromising on quality of care, is crucial. As a labour intensive sector, supply-side measures that influence provider behaviour offer a clear avenue for improving efficiency (Simeons and Giuffrida, 2004). Pay for performance (commonly referred to by the acronym P4P), in which payments are tied to performance, is becoming increasingly common in international healthcare systems.[39] This trend is occurring despite the lack of evidence on its effectiveness and a lack of consensus on how to design and implement such programmes

---

38 http://per.gov.ie/databank/ [last accessed 22 May 2013].
39 In some cases, pay is not strictly for performance, but rather sanctions for underperformance. While it may be more accurate to refer to performance-related pay, we follow the convention in the literature of referring to the concept as P4P.

(Cromwell et al., 2011; Maynard, 2012). Nevertheless, P4P is attracting notable attention in the international literature and there has also been reference to the potential role for P4P in the Irish healthcare sector (Gantly, 2011).[40] In addition, the recent *Programme for Government* contains a number of commitments that relate to how healthcare providers are paid.

This reflects the growing realisation that the structure of financial incentives is crucial for improving efficiency and equity in healthcare. Financial incentives have been shown to influence both provider and patient behaviour (Newhouse and Insurance Experiment Group, 1993; Croxson et al., 2001; Dusheiko et al., 2003) and thus it is important that they are structured appropriately. The recent Expert Group on Resource Allocation and Financing in the Health Sector highlighted the many, and often conflicting, financial incentives in the Irish healthcare system, most of which arise from the complex interaction between the public and private sectors (Ruane, 2010). Private sources account for a relatively small proportion of total health financing in Ireland. However, across the system, publicly- and privately-financed care is often administered by the same staff, using the same facilities. In many cases, different provider payment methods exist for public and private healthcare, generating financial incentives on the part of providers that differ by patient type.[41] The consequences of these often conflicting financial incentives for efficiency and equity have been well documented (Brennan, 2003; Tussing and Wren, 2006; Brick et al., 2010), and re-aligning existing financial incentives to support equitable and efficient healthcare is a first priority (Ruane, 2010).

Thus, in light of the need for measures to enhance value for money in Irish healthcare, and in the context of the current financial incentive structures in the system, this chapter examines international evidence on P4P and determines its potential role as a policy option in Ireland. Overall, the available literature indicates that there is insufficient evidence of significant positive effects of P4P initiatives. This, coupled with an already complex set of financial incentives in Irish healthcare, has implications for the use of P4P in the Irish system.

---

40 It is important to clarify what we mean by P4P (see below). While there are a number of current initiatives in the Irish healthcare system that are experimenting with alternative methods of provider payment (e.g., the Heartwatch programme in primary care, the orthopaedic prospective funding pilot in acute hospitals, etc.), they are not explicitly characterised by defined payments for achievement of efficiency or quality goals.

41 Unless otherwise stated, throughout this chapter, the term 'incentives' refers to financial incentives, which can be generated by the method by which healthcare providers are paid, or by the method by which users/patients pay for care. It is also important to acknowledge that although outside the scope of this chapter, non-financial incentives such as ethical standards, professional norms, altruism, etc. also impact on the behaviour of healthcare providers (Scott, 2011).

PAY FOR PERFORMANCE IN HEALTHCARE

Cromwell et al. (2011, p. 7) define P4P as 'an approach used to provide incentives to physicians and healthcare provider organisations to achieve improved performance'. P4P was originally designed to improve quality of care, but with increasingly scarce resources, it is also used as a mechanism to reduce costs. The development of P4P was in part motivated by concerns about relying solely on providers to ensure sufficient quality in healthcare. In addition, there are failings in the traditional methods of provider payment (Cromwell et al., 2011). P4P mechanisms provide a way to reinforce the desired financial incentives embodied in existing payment mechanisms, or to provide incentives for performance that the traditional reimbursement mechanisms are lacking.

There are four main categories of P4P, namely programmes that pay for reporting of quality-related data, for quality, for efficiency (i.e., reduction or containment of costs), or for value (combined quality and cost measures). Cromwell et al. (2011) provide a useful framework for describing P4P programmes (see Table 1 in Nolan et al., 2011).[42] First, P4P programmes can be voluntary or mandatory. Voluntary programmes are likely to be easier and cheaper to implement but may be subject to selection effects whereby providers who expect to do well are more likely to participate. Programmes that involve penalties for poor performance may need to be mandatory. Second, in any P4P programme, there are three core elements concerning whom to pay, how to measure performance, and how and how much to pay. For each element, there are a number of options, indicating that P4P programmes can be structured in many different ways, and as yet the optimal combination of options has not been identified.

Payments can be directed at individuals, groups of providers, or larger organisations such as hospitals. Where payments are directed at small groups of providers, the payment incentives affect only a small proportion of the patient's overall care, which could exacerbate fragmentation in the system. Measuring performance requires decisions on the domains of performance (e.g., clinical outcomes or processes), and appropriate indicators. Paying for performance can draw on existing resources (i.e., redistribution), on savings generated by high performance, or on new money. Adding new money could be justified if improving and reporting performance requires new investment and higher costs, but the cost effectiveness of the programme needs to be assessed in this case. Decisions are also needed on the benchmarks for assessing performance (e.g., targets, relative performance). The incentives facing providers can be 'positive' (e.g., bonuses, extra per-patient pay), or 'negative' in terms of withholding payments or penalties. Finally, it is important to recognise that P4P programmes can also incorporate non-financial incentives (e.g., publicising provider performance, providing technical assistance).

The Evidence section presents available evidence on selected P4P programmes in healthcare. For ease of presentation, we discuss programmes undertaken in

---

42 See also Eijkenaar (2012); Emmert et al. (2012); Wilson (2013).

primary, hospital and integrated care settings separately. The emphasis is on large-scale P4P schemes introduced by national public sector organisations.

EVIDENCE

Primary Care

Traditional methods of provider payment in primary care include fee-for-service (FFS), capitation and salary. Gosden et al. (2006) provide an overview of the theoretical and empirical literature on the various methods, highlighting the lack of consensus on the 'ideal' method of payment, and the trade-offs involved in choosing any one method.[43] In light of these trade-offs, many countries are experimenting with blended methods which include a capitation or salary component, FFS payments for the provision of defined services (e.g., out-of-hours, house calls, etc.), and P4P elements for the achievement of specific objectives (e.g., quality, chronic disease management, etc.).

We examine the main features of three selected case studies of the largest international P4P programmes in primary care, the UK Quality and Outcomes Framework (QOF), the Australian Practice Incentives Program (PIP) and the US Physician Group Practice (PGP) Demonstration (see Table A1 in Nolan et al., 2011 for full details). The characteristics of the three schemes differ considerably, principally in terms of the number and type of indicators used to measure performance. Despite the popularity of P4P in primary care, there is little rigorous evidence on the effects of P4P on quality of care and other outcomes (Christianson et al., 2008; Scott et al., 2011). In terms of quality of care for chronic disease, Campbell et al. (2007) found that while there were significant improvements in quality of care for asthma and diabetes after the introduction of QOF, later research suggests that the rates of improvement have slowed (Campbell et al., 2009). Campbell et al. (2007) also observed no significant differences for chronic heart disease before and after the introduction of QOF. Serumaga et al. (2011) similarly found that the QOF hypertension targets had no significant impact on blood pressure measures, intensity of treatment or on hypertension-related clinical outcomes such as stroke. Scott et al. (2009) found that GPs working in practices that participated in the PIP were more than 20 per cent more likely to order a diabetes test than a comparable GP in a non-participating practice.

A number of studies have questioned whether improvements attributed to P4P incentives were simply the continuation of pre-P4P trends (NHS Information Centre, 2007; Calvert et al., 2009; Centers for Medicare and Medicaid Services, 2009; Iglehart, 2011). One key area of concern with any form of financial

---

43 For example, while FFS payments promote productivity and access, they also provide a disincentive to engage in preventive care and score poorly in terms of cost containment. Capitation payments discourage productivity, but (with appropriate risk adjustment) promote access and preventive care and can be effective in controlling costs (Brick et al., 2010).

incentive is the potential for unintended consequences[44] whereby the incentives encourage behaviours that are not aligned with the underlying objectives. One such consequence is gaming, whereby providers engage in undesirable behaviour (e.g., selecting patients who are healthier in order to make targeted levels of performance easier to achieve). While Gravelle et al. (2010) found that lower rates of achievement in the first year of the QOF in Scotland were associated with higher exception reporting in the following year, Doran et al. (2006) could not determine whether the positive association between performance and exception reporting was due to gaming.[45] Doran et al. (2008) noted that, in general, exception reporting rates were low and suggested that exception reporting is being used appropriately to exclude patients on clinical grounds.

Selection of activities is also a concern; Doran et al. (2011) found that improvements on indicators associated with the QOF seem to have been achieved at the expense of small detrimental effects on areas of care that were not incentivised. In Australia, concerns have been raised that the structure of the PIP allows providers to select those areas in which they have the greatest potential for reward (e.g., electronic reporting), with much lower uptake of the incentives that require much more effort on the part of the practices (Cashin and Chi, 2011).

The potentially negative impact of P4P on the motivation of GPs, and the relationship between GPs and patients has also been highlighted. Gillam et al. (2011) report that the focus on targets and record-keeping may discourage GPs from taking a broader population health perspective (see also Roland, 2004; Smith and York, 2004; McDonald and Roland, 2009). Indirect effects of the QOF on practice organisation in terms of the diversification of nurse roles has been viewed as a positive development (Gillam and Siriwardena, 2011). The role of the QOF in reducing health inequalities is also subject to conflicting evidence (Millett et al., 2008; Dixon et al., 2011; Gillam and Siriwardena, 2011; Alshamsan et al., 2012).

The QOF is the only P4P programme that we examine that has been subject to any evaluation of its cost effectiveness (see Cashin and Chi, 2011 and Centers for Medicare and Medicaid Services, 2009 for discussion of the PIP and PGP). In the UK, there is some tentative evidence in favour of the cost effectiveness of certain QOF indicators (Fleetcroft and Cookson, 2006; Mason et al., 2008; Walker et al., 2010; Dusheiko et al., 2011). However, the administrative costs associated with the QOF were not considered, nor the overall opportunity costs (Gillam et al., 2012). The administrative burden of P4P has also been discussed in Australia and

---

44 Unintended consequences are not necessarily unanticipated; Smith et al. (2004) discuss the potential consequences (such as gaming) that might arise from the way in which the QOF was structured.

45 Exception reporting refers to the practice whereby GP practices can exempt patients from inclusion in the QOF for a number of reasons (e.g., non-toleration or allergic reaction to prescribed medication). The overall exception rate was 5.4 per cent in 2009/10 (Audit Commission, 2011).

the US (Mathematica Policy Research, 2009; Australian National Audit Office, 2010).

Hospital Care

In the hospital sector, P4P programmes are a relatively recent innovation, implemented to fine-tune existing payment mechanisms so that funders' financial incentives are aligned with those of providers (Mehrotra et al., 2009; Cromwell et al., 2011). Here we review the literature on two case studies from the US (the first country to apply P4P to hospitals) (see Table A2 in Nolan et al., 2011 for full details).

The Premier Hospital Quality Incentive Demonstration (PHQID) combines quality reporting with a conventional P4P programme. Evidence on its effectiveness is mixed. Comparing four participating hospitals with a control group of six non-participants over the relatively short period 2002–2004, Grossbart (2006) found quality of care improved by a greater extent in the former group for all three conditions under consideration.[46] Studying the same three conditions in a larger sample over 2003–2005, using more robust analytical techniques, Lindenauer et al. (2007) concluded that PHQID hospitals achieved greater improvements in quality of care compared to those undertaking public reporting only. However, Werner et al. (2011) found that initial performance improvements among 260 PHQID hospitals relative to non-participants were not sustained over the five-year study period between 2004 and 2008. Ryan et al. (2012) found that the PHQID did not succeed in encouraging greater quality improvement among previously low-performing hospitals. The results from these studies were based on process measures; the estimated empirical effects of PHQID participation on health outcomes are even less encouraging. Glickman et al. (2007) found no statistically significant difference in AMI mortality between PHQID hospitals and those participating in a voluntary quality improvement initiative – a finding subsequently supported by Ryan (2009), not only for AMI but also for three other conditions. Jha et al. (2012) found no evidence that participation in the PHQID led to a statistically significant decline in 30-day mortality. Limited evidence is currently available on other impacts of the PHQID: Ryan (2009) found that it had no statistically significant effect on patient costs for four conditions, Kruse et al. (2012) similarly found no statistically significant effects on hospital or Medicare costs for AMI, while Ryan (2010) concluded that there was weak evidence of patient selection.[47]

The second case study – non-payment for poor performance – is the antithesis of the PHQID and other schemes that pay for quality. While it is too soon to evaluate its impact properly, the initiative has generated much discussion on its

---

46 Acute myocardial infarction (AMI), heart failure and pneumonia.
47 To date, only one known cost-effectiveness analysis of a hospital-based P4P initiative has been published. Although the study did not include a control group, the initiative was found to be cost effective (Galvin, 2006; Nahra et al., 2006; Conrad, 2010).

potential to produce cost savings and unintended consequences (Hoff and Soerensen, 2010). Estimates of the potential cost savings from not paying for preventable complications range from 0.001 per cent of hospital payments (McNair et al., 2009) to 9 per cent of total inpatient cost (Fuller et al., 2009) depending, to a large extent, on the number and type of conditions deemed preventable. McNair et al. (2009) recommended that the initiative could be strengthened by incorporating additional conditions or expanding it to include readmissions (as proposed by Averill et al., 2009). The potential for unintended consequences pertains to the extent to which the preventable complications are entirely within the control of the hospital. If they are not, unintended consequences and opportunity costs might arise if hospitals' efforts focus on minimising the incidence of such events to the detriment of other aspects of quality of care (Wald and Kramer, 2007; Pronovost et al., 2008). For example, Inouye et al. (2009) argued that patient falls during hospitalisation are unlikely to be completely within the control of hospitals and, consequently, could encourage the use of physical restraints to reduce patient mobility, possibly adversely affecting patient outcomes.[48] A further potential disadvantage of the initiative is that hospitals may be incentivised to select healthier patients and to avoid higher-risk cases (Gemmill, 2006; Rosenthal, 2007). Consequently, any cost savings could be offset by higher expenses due to increased screening and changed coding practice (Pronovost et al., 2008; Wachter et al., 2008; McNutt et al., 2010).

These and other hospital sector P4P programmes are becoming increasingly popular internationally, despite the available empirical evidence on their effectiveness being, at best, limited and inconclusive. Public reporting schemes for hospitals operate in Germany and England, for instance, although there are national differences in the content of the quality reports and the role of financial incentives. As with the PHQID, the Commissioning for Quality and Innovation (CQUIN) payment framework, introduced in England in 2009, provides financial rewards to hospitals for quality improvements; although unlike the PHQID, it operates within existing financial resources. The concept of not reimbursing hospitals for emergency readmissions that occur within 30 days of the initial episode is expected to result in estimated cost savings of £490million in England, and a similar scheme is in operation in Germany (NHS Confederation, 2011; Or and Häkkinen, 2011) (see Table A2 in Nolan et al. (2011) for further details on these schemes).

Integrated Care

While the above sections focused on P4P within primary care and the hospital sector, the application of financial incentives to reward performance across sectors of the healthcare system is even less developed. Although not a P4P initiative per

---

48 Wald et al. (2007) and Saint et al. (2009) have discussed analogous implications for catheter-associated urinary tract infection, another complication covered by the initiative.

se, bundled or episode-based payments offer one potential mechanism to incentivise quality improvements within an integrated system (Davis, 2007). By paying a fixed price to all healthcare providers involved in an episode of care, bundled payments should encourage increased efficiency, improved quality of care, and reduced risk of cost shifting between sectors and there is some empirical evidence to support this (Cromwell *et al.*, 1997; Hackbarth *et al.*, 2008; Miller, 2009; RAND, 2010; Sutherland, 2011).

Further benefits may arise where P4P elements are incorporated explicitly into bundled payments. For example, under Geisinger Health System's ProvenCare in the US, an incentive to reduce complications and readmissions was built into the calculation of the fixed payment rate for coronary artery bypass surgery (Mechanic and Altman, 2009).[49] In its first year, ProvenCare achieved reductions in readmissions (10 per cent), hospital charges (5 per cent) and length of stay (16 per cent) (Casale *et al.*, 2007; Mechanic and Altman, 2009). Extrapolating from available evidence, Hussey *et al.* (2009) estimated that 5.4 per cent of health expenditure in the US could be saved over the period 2010–2019 if bundled payments were applied to all chronic diseases and all payers. However, it is not clear whether the success of such initiatives – which operate within an integrated delivery network and a system of electronic health records – could be replicated at a national level given the fragmented nature of most healthcare systems (Goldfield *et al.*, 2008; Paulus *et al.*, 2008; Hussey *et al.*, 2009; Miller, 2009).

Implementing bundled payments is not without challenges. Miller (2009) has argued that the transition to bundled payments may be easier for surgical, rather than medical, conditions where hospitals and surgeons are paid on the same basis (i.e., case-based payments). Conflict between providers is another potential problem, although this could be negated to some extent if an independent 'financial integrator' was responsible for allocating funds to providers (de Brantes *et al.*, 2009). There are concerns that bundled payments may reduce necessary (especially preventive) care, but increase unnecessary episodes, and encourage unbundling of services to increase income (Robinson, 2001; Crosson *et al.*, 2009; Miller, 2009).

Summary of the Evidence on P4P

The preceding sections highlight the wide variation in the structures of P4P programmes and the often inconclusive evidence on their effectiveness. Generating policy recommendations is difficult due to the limited number of rigorous evaluations of P4P. Recent systematic reviews of P4P (Giuffrida *et al.*, 2009; Mehrotra *et al.*, 2009; de Bruin *et al.*, 2011; Scott *et al.*, 2011; Emmert *et al.*, 2012; Gillam *et al.*, 2012; Eijkenaar *et al.*, 2013) highlight the absence of studies

---

49 Other examples of bundled payments include the Prometheus Model (de Brantes *et al.*, 2009) and the Acute Care Episode Demonstration (Centers for Medicare and Medicaid Services, 2010; Greenwald, 2011).

of sufficient quality on P4P effectiveness.[50] Limited and often poor quality evidence stems partly from technical challenges in evaluating P4P schemes. Attributing performance improvements to P4P is difficult in the absence of pre-P4P baseline data. One of the main criticisms of the UK QOF was that the absence of baseline data and the ease with which practices were able to hit targets raised questions about the extent to which the QOF produced better quality care, improved recording of care (McDonald et al., 2009), or merely rewarded what had already been achieved (NHS Information Centre, 2007; Calvert et al., 2009). P4P initiatives are often accompanied by other interventions (e.g., IT investment), making it difficult to isolate the effect of the scheme itself. In addition, the evaluation may fail to identify changes in outcomes if the study period is too short or may be subject to confounding if the study period is too long. Participation in such schemes is often voluntary meaning that selection effects are a concern (Lindenauer et al., 2007; Scott et al., 2011). Finally, there is the problem of generalisability; the context in which such schemes operate can be influential in explaining the results (McDonald et al., 2009).

Notwithstanding these technical difficulties in evaluating P4P initiatives, the available evidence does not provide a clear answer to the question of whether P4P should be implemented. However, the research literature does suggest a number of limitations with existing P4P initiatives (e.g., Cromwell et al., 2011). Obtaining valid, reliable and important performance indicators in healthcare is difficult and leads to P4P programmes that are focused on areas that can be measured easily, but are not necessarily highly correlated with health outcomes (Bhattacharyya et al., 2009). The performance measurement approach can also be too prescriptive, discouraging innovation and elements of personal and holistic care not easily measured or rewarded financially (Buetow, 2008). It can also 'crowd out' intrinsic motivation by interfering with provider autonomy and professional judgement (Cromwell et al., 2011; Janus, 2011). The scope for unintended consequences is a concern. P4P may encourage patient selection, misrepresentation of performance data, or decisions to practice in areas with 'compliant' patient populations. This may reinforce/increase disparities between providers and areas (Buetow, 2008) although appropriate risk adjustment of payments can help (Cromwell et al., 2011).

The lack of evidence on cost effectiveness is of particular concern in the context of limited resources. P4P programmes may impose large costs on funders (especially where new money is required) and on providers in the form of administrative costs. The business case for P4P may be particularly hard to make when the costs are immediate, but any financial gains are likely to accrue mostly in the future.

While most evaluations have reported only limited impact of P4P, it must be remembered that the size of the financial incentives is often quite small relative to

---

50 Emmert et al. (2012) focused solely on cost effectiveness of P4P, while de Bruin et al. (2011) focused on P4P in chronic disease management.

overall remuneration (Cromwell *et al.*, 2011). However, one review suggests that incentives of about 5 per cent of total physician earnings are enough to induce behavioural change from physicians (Young *et al.*, 2005).[51] It is also important to recognise the role of non-financial incentives, as well as the incentives facing patients, in enhancing or diluting the effects of financial incentives.

POLICY IMPLICATIONS AND LESSONS

General Lessons

Given the mixed experience and limitations with existing P4P programmes, a number of recommendations have been made for their future development. A central message is to proceed with caution, to learn from available experience and to undertake rigorous evaluation of pilot programmes (Propper and Wilson, 2003; Davis, 2007).

Cromwell *et al.* (2011) identify a set of requirements for what they term 'second generation' P4P initiatives. A central theme is the importance of integrated healthcare and the need for P4P programmes to support integration. This includes directing payments towards large provider organisations rather than individual physicians (to encourage team-based care)[52] and making providers more accountable for reducing fragmentation in healthcare (e.g., requiring one provider organisation to take responsibility for the complete care of a patient (Iglehart, 2011)).

Other recommendations for second generation P4P programmes include the adoption of bundled payment methods; increases in the size of both financial risks and rewards; more ambitious quality improvement goals; use of electronic health record systems; and involving patients as well as providers in the programmes (e.g., lower co-payments). In contrast to the QOF approach in the UK, the recommendation is to ensure that the performance payments in second generation P4P programmes are self-financing, particularly pertinent during an economic recession. Crucially, the recommendations also emphasise the need to acknowledge the limitations of P4P. Evidence-based guidelines are, and will continue to be, unavailable for many medical situations meaning that there will be limits on the size and scope of P4P programmes. P4P may be necessary, but not sufficient, for improving quality; other policy, IT, healthcare delivery and organisational factors must also be aligned towards the same goals (Cromwell *et al.*, 2011).

---

51 The recent Affordable Care Act in the US requires that 1 per cent of annual Medicare hospital payments be dispersed as P4P (Epstein, 2012).

52 However, a recent systematic review of P4P initiatives noted that P4P is more effective when payments are directed at individuals or small groups of providers (Eijkenaar *et al.*, 2013).

Lessons for Ireland

Although there is an obvious need for greater efficiency and quality in the Irish healthcare system (Ruane, 2010), there are reasons why P4P initiatives are not recommended at this stage. First, many of the supportive factors are not in place, including integrated IT systems, adequate data reporting, and a unique health identifier. Progress on these factors is required regardless of the introduction of P4P in the Irish system.

Second, applying P4P initiatives to existing provider payment mechanisms would add new complications to an already complex system. In primary care, GPs are currently paid on the basis of capitation (plus allowances and fees for special items of service) for public (i.e., medical/GP Visit card) patients, but on a FFS basis for private patients.[53] Any P4P initiative by the Government for GP care would apply only for the 40 per cent of the population covered by a medical/GP Visit card. In fact, the mechanism for paying GPs to care for medical card/GP Visit card holders already incorporates a mix of capitation and FFS (for special items of service). As such, it could be interpreted as a P4P initiative, except that the additional FFS payments are not directed at specific areas of performance, or subject to monitoring and adjustment in line with policy priorities.[54]

Financial incentives in the hospital sector are complex due to the treatment of private patients in public hospitals. Consultants in public acute hospitals are paid a salary for public patients and, where relevant, FFS for private patients. Under existing arrangements, public hospitals can levy maintenance charges on private patients who occupy a private-designated bed, in addition to the statutory inpatient bed charge. There is evidence that private patients in acute public hospitals are publicly subsidised and for many treatments, private health insurers have an incentive for private patients to be treated in public, rather than private, hospitals. In this context, acute hospital care comes under criticism for crowding out public patients (Wren, 2003; Ruane, 2010). Introducing a P4P initiative in this context without first addressing the underlying perverse incentives that potentially favour the treatment of private patients in public hospitals would be unlikely to succeed in influencing patient care and outcomes.[55]

Finally, to follow the recommendations for second generation P4P programmes, the core theme of healthcare integration needs to be addressed before considering P4P initiatives (Ruane, 2010). Within a dynamic policy area already undergoing reform, the sequencing of policies needs to be carefully considered, irrespective of

---

53 See Brick *et al.* (2010) for a full description of public healthcare entitlements in Ireland.
54 The list of 18 special items of service (e.g., influenza vaccination) reimbursed by the Primary Care Reimbursement Service to GPs in respect of medical card holders has not changed in at least 10 years (Nolan *et al.*, 2011).
55 Legislation will be introduced during 2013 to provide for charging of private inpatients in public hospitals, where they are not in a designated private bed (HSE, 2013).

the international evidence regarding the effectiveness of a specific type of policy. On the demand side, the requirement for the majority of the population to pay the full cost of primary care at point of use may interfere with patients' decisions on seeking care at the most appropriate time and level in the system. On the supply side, there is as yet limited capacity to oversee and monitor performance and delivery of integrated care. Introducing P4P without first dealing with these factors is unlikely to succeed in promoting integration.

Notwithstanding the complex structure of financial incentives in the Irish healthcare system, the above examples illustrate that the potential for using existing payment mechanisms to encourage enhanced quality and value for money has yet to be fully explored. The commitments in the *Programme for Government* in relation to provider payment afford an important opportunity in this regard. For example, the pilot initiative of prospective funding for selected elective orthopaedic procedures in a subset of public hospitals has already resulted in increased activity, shorter hospital stays and higher rates of day of surgery admission (Donovan, 2011).[56] There is also potential for further benefits if the prospective tariff is explicitly set to incentivise a shift away from inpatient treatment. In England, there was a statistically significant increase in the proportion of day case activity as a result of such an initiative (Farrar et al., 2009). As highlighted by the shortage of rigorous studies of P4P schemes, appropriate *ex post* evaluation of any new initiatives will be crucial to assess their performance in achieving the stated health policy objectives.

CONCLUSIONS

The current recession dictates that large decreases in public expenditure are required. Already, public health expenditure has fallen substantially since its peak in 2009. As the second largest component of public expenditure, healthcare is particularly vulnerable to the effects of the further cuts in expenditure that are required. In this context of diminishing financial resources, there is increasing emphasis on maximising the value of expenditure by improving efficient delivery of high quality healthcare services.

As a labour intensive sector, initiatives that focus on provider behaviour offer a clear avenue for improving efficiency. Pay-for-performance, in which payments are tied to performance, is becoming increasingly common in international healthcare systems, and the *Programme for Government* contains a number of commitments that relate to provider payments. This reflects the growing realisation that the structure of financial incentives is crucial for improving efficiency and equity in healthcare. However, the Irish health system is characterised by a complex set of financial incentives. In light of the need for measures to enhance

---

56 These results relate only to those procedures under study. In evaluating the full impact of the pilot project, it is important to also consider any spillover effects on other areas of hospital activity.

value for money in Irish healthcare, and in the context of the current financial incentive structures in the system, this chapter examined international evidence on P4P and assessed its potential role as a policy option in Ireland.

Overall, the available literature indicates that there is insufficient evidence to conclude that introducing P4P improves efficiency and quality in healthcare. Given the emphasis on evidence-based policy, it is perhaps surprising that so many countries are now considering, or have already introduced, P4P programmes. Of course, a lack of conclusive empirical evidence does not necessarily imply that P4P should not be adopted (or at least piloted), particularly given the weaknesses of the existing P4P evaluations. It follows that Ireland can benefit from 'second mover' advantage if the time then comes to learn from future P4P experience in other countries. Experience elsewhere highlights the importance of programme design and on-going data collection in facilitating appropriate *ex post* evaluation of any new initiatives. In conclusion, as discussed above, there are legitimate arguments as to why Ireland should not consider introducing P4P mechanisms at least until the many complexities in provider reimbursement, public/private interaction, and patient access to the system are resolved.

REFERENCES

Alshamsan, R., Lee, J.T., Majeed, A., Netuveli, G. and Millett, C. (2012). 'Effect of a UK pay-for-performance program on ethnic disparities in diabetes outcomes: interrupted time series analysis'. *Annals of Family Medicine*, 10, 228–34.

Audit Commission (2011). *Paying GPs to Improve Quality – Auditing Payments under the Quality and Outcomes Framework*. Health Briefing – February 2011. London: Audit Commission.

Australian National Audit Office (2010). 'Practice Incentives Program': Department of Health and Ageing Medicare Australia. *Audit Report No.5 2010–11*. Available at: http://www.anao.gov.au/~/media/Uploads/Documents/2010%2011_audit_report_no5.pdf [last accessed 20 May 2013].

Averill, R. F., McCullough, E. C., Hughes, J. S., Goldfield, N. I., Vertrees, J. C. and Fuller, R. L. (2009). 'Redesigning the Medicare Inpatient PPS to Reduce Payments to Hospitals with High Readmission Rates'. *Healthcare Financing Review*, 30, 1–15.

Bhattacharyya, T., Freiberg, A., Mehta, P., Katz, J. and Ferris, T. (2009). 'Measuring the report card: the validity of pay-for-performance metrics in orthopedic surgery'. *Health Affairs*, 28, 526–32.

Brennan, N. (2003). *Commission on Financial Management and Control Systems in the Health Service*. Dublin: Stationery Office.

Brick, A., Nolan, A., O'Reilly, J. and Smith, S. (2010). 'Resource Allocation, Financing and Sustainability in Healthcare'. *Evidence for the Expert Group on Resource Allocation and Financing in the Health Sector*. Dublin: Department of Health and Children and Economic and Social Research Institute.

Buetow, S. (2008). 'Pay-for-performance in New Zealand primary healthcare'. *Journal of Health Organisation and Management*, 22, 36–47.

Calvert, M., Shankar, A., McManus, R., Lester, H. and Freemantle, N. (2009). 'Effect of the Quality and Outcomes Framework on Diabetes Care in the United Kingdom: Retrospective Cohort Study'. *British Medical Journal*, 338, b1870.

Campbell, S., Reeves, D., Kontopantelis, E., Middleton, E., Sibbald, B. and Roland, M. (2007). 'Quality of Primary Care in England with the Introduction of Pay for Performance'. *New England Journal of Medicine*, 357, 181–190.

Campbell, S., Reeves, D., Kontopantelis, E., Sibbald, B. and Roland, M. (2009). 'Effects of Pay for Performance on the Quality of Primary Care in England'. *New England Journal of Medicine*, 361, 368–377.

Casale, A. S., Paulus, R. A., Selna, M. J., Doll, M. C., Bothe, A. E., Jr, McKinley, K. E., Berry, S. A., Davis, D. E., Gilfillan, R. J., Hamory, B. H. and Steele, G. D., Jr. (2007). 'ProvenCareSM: A Provider-Driven Pay-for-Performance Program for Acute Episodic Cardiac Surgical Care'. *Annals of Surgery*, 246, 613–623.

Cashin, C. and Chi, Y. (2011). Australia: The Practice Incentives Program (PIP). Washington DC: The World Bank. Available at: http://www.rbfhealth.org/rbfhealth/system/files/Case%20study%20Australia%20Practice%20Incentive%20Program.pdf [last accessed 20 May 2013].

Centers for Medicare and Medicaid Services (2009). 'Physician Group Practice Demonstration Evaluation Report'. *Report to Congress*. Available at: www.cms.gov/DemoProjectsEvalRpts/downloads/PGP_RTC_Sept.pdf [last accessed 20 May 2013].

Centers for Medicare and Medicaid Services (2010). 'Medicare Acute Care Episode Demonstration for Orthopedic and Cardiovascular Surgery'. Available at: www.cms.gov/DemoProjectsEvalRpts/downloads/ACE_web_page.pdf [last accessed 20 May 2013].

Christianson, J., Leatherman, S. and Sutherland, K. (2008). 'Lessons from Evaluations of Purchaser Pay-for-Performance Programs: A Review of the Evidence'. *Medical Care Research and Review*, 65(Supplement), 5S-35S.

Conrad, D. (2010). 'Incentives for healthcare performance improvement' in Smith, P. C., Mossialos, E., Papanicolas, I. and Leatherman, S. (eds.), *Performance Measurement for Health System Improvement*. New York: Cambridge University Press.

Cromwell, J., Dayhoff, D. A. and Thoumaian, A. H. (1997). 'Cost savings and physician responses to global bundled payments for Medicare heart bypass surgery'. *Healthcare Financing Review*, 19, 41–57.

Cromwell, J., Trisolini, M., Pope, G., Mitchell, J. and Greenwald, L. (eds.) (2011). *Pay for Performance in Healthcare: Methods and Approaches*, New York: RTI Press.

Crosson, F. J., Guterman, S., Taylor, N., Young, R. and Tollen, L. (2009). 'How Can Medicare Lead Delivery System Reform?', *The Commonwealth Fund: Issue Brief*.

Croxson, B., Propper, C. and Perkins, A. (2001). 'Do Doctors Respond to Financial Incentives? UK Family Doctors and the Fundholding Scheme'. *Journal of Public Economics*, 79, 375–398.

Davis, K. (2007). 'Paying for Care Episodes and Care Coordination'. *New England Journal of Medicine*, 356, 1166–1168.

de Brantes, F., Rosenthal, M. B. and Painter, M. (2009). 'Building a Bridge from Fragmentation to Accountability – The Prometheus Payment Model'. *New England Journal of Medicine*, 361, 1033–1036.

de Bruin, S. R., Baan, C. A. and Struijs, J. N. (2011). 'Pay-for-performance in disease management: a systematic review of the literature'. *BMC Health Services Research*, 11:272.

Dixon, A., Khachatryan, A., Wallace, A., Peckham, S., Boyce, T. and Gillam, S. (2011). *The Quality and Outcomes Framework (QOF): does it reduce inequalities?* London: The King's Fund.

Donovan, B. (2011). 'Casemix Funding in Ireland: From Retrospective to Prospective? Progress since 2010'. *Presentation to 2011 Patient Classification Systems International (PSCI) Conference*.

Doran, T., Fullwood, C., Gravelle, H., Reeves, D., Kontopantelis, E., Hiroeh, U. and Roland, M. (2006). 'Pay-for-Performance Programs in Family Practices in the United Kingdom'. *New England Journal of Medicine*, 355, 375–384.

Doran, T., Kontopantelis, E., Valderas, J., Campbell, S., Roland, M. and Reeves, D. (2011). 'Effect of financial incentives on incentivised and non-incentivised clinical activities: longitudinal analysis of data from the UK Quality and Outcomes Framework'. *British Medical Journal*, 342, 1–12.

Dusheiko, M., Gravelle, H., Jacobs, R. and Smith, P. (2003). 'The Effect of Budgets on Doctor Behaviour: Evidence from a Natural Experiment'. *Journal of Health Economics*, 25, 449–478.

Dusheiko, M., Gravelle, H., Martin, S., Rice, N. and Smith, P. C. (2011). 'Does better disease management in primary care reduce hospital costs? Evidence from English primary care'. *Journal of Health Economics*, 30, 919–932.

Eijkenaar, F. (2012). 'Pay for performance in healthcare: an international overview of initiatives'. *Medical Care Research and Review*, 69, 251–76.

Eijkenaar, F., Emmert, M., Scheppach, M. and Schoffski, O. (2013). 'Effects of pay for performance in healthcare: A systematic review of systematic reviews'. *Health Policy*, 110, 115–30.

Emmert, M., Eijkenaar, F., Kemter, H., Esslinger, A. S. and Schoffski, O. (2012). 'Economic evaluation of pay-for-performance in healthcare: a systematic review'. *European Journal of Health Economics*, 13, 755–67.

Epstein, A. M. (2012). 'Will pay for performance improve quality of care? The answer is in the details'. *New England Journal of Medicine*, 367, 1852–3.

Farrar, S., Yi, D., Sutton, M., Chalkley, M., Sussex, J. and Scott, A. (2009). 'Has Payment by Results Affected the Way that English Hospitals Provide Care? Difference-in-Differences Analysis'. *British Medical Journal*, 339(aug27_2), b3047–.

Fleetcroft, R. and Cookson, R. (2006). 'Do the incentive payments in the new NHS contract for primary care reflect likely population health gains?' *Journal of Health Services Research & Policy*, 11, 27–31.

Fuller, R., McCullough, E., Bao, M. and Averill, R. (2009). 'Estimating the costs of potentially preventable hospital acquired complications'. *Healthcare Financing Review*, 30, 17–32.

Galvin, R. S. (2006). 'Evaluating the Performance of Pay for Performance'. *Medical Care Research and Review*, 63(1 suppl), 126S-130S.

Gantly, D. (2011). 'P4P schemes are on the horizon for GPs'. *Irish Medical Times*. Dublin: *Irish Medical Times*. Available at: http://www.imt.ie/news/latest-news/2011/05/p4p-schemes-are-on-the-horizon-for-gps.html [last accessed 20 May 2013].

Gemmill, M. (2006). 'Pay-for-Performance in the US: What lessons for Europe?' *Eurohealth*, 13, 21–23.

Gillam, S. and Siriwardena, N. (eds.) (2011). *The Quality and Outcomes Framework*, Oxford: Radcliffe Publishing.

Gillam, S. J., Siriwardena, A. N. and Steel, N. (2012). 'Pay-for-performance in the United Kingdom: impact of the quality and outcomes framework: a systematic review'. *Annals of Family Medicine*, 10(5), 461–8.

Giuffrida, A., Gosden, T., Forland, F., Kristiansen, I., Sergison, M., Leese, B., Pedersen, L. and Sutton, M. (2009). 'Target payments in primary care: effects on professional practice and healthcare outcomes'. *The Cochrane Collaboration*, 2009, 1–11.

Glickman, S. W., Ou, F.-S., DeLong, E. R., Roe, M. T., Lytle, B. L., Mulgund, J., Rumsfeld, J. S., Gibler, W. B., Ohman, E. M., Schulman, K. A. and Peterson, E. D. (2007). 'Pay for Performance, Quality of Care, and Outcomes in Acute Myocardial Infarction'. *Journal of the American Medical Association*, 297, 2373–2380.

Goldfield, N., Averill, R., Fuller, R. and Vertrees, J. (2008). 'A Response to the Prometheus Proposal –Well Intended but Impossible to Implement'. *American Journal of Medical Quality*, 23, 85–89.

Gosden, T., Forland, F., Kristiansen, I., Sutton, M., Leese, B., Giuffrida, A., Sergison, M. and Pedersen, I. (2006). 'Capitation, Salary, Fee-For-Service and Mixed Systems of Payment: Effects on the Behaviour of Primary Care Physicians'. *Cochrane Database of Systematic Reviews*, 31–25.

Gravelle, H., Sutton, M. and Ma, A. (2010). 'Doctor Behaviour Under a Pay for Performance Contract: Treating, Cheating and Case Finding?' *The Economic Journal*, 120(February), 129–156.

Greenwald, L. M. (2011). 'Who gets the payment under pay for performance?' in

Cromwell, J., Trisolini, M. G., Pope, G. C., Mitchell, J. B. and Greenwald, L. M. (eds.), *Pay for Performance in Healthcare: Methods and Approaches*. North Carolina: RTI Press.

Grossbart, S. R. (2006). 'What's the Return? Assessing the Effect of "Pay-for-Performance" Initiatives on the Quality of Care Delivery'. *Medical Care Research and Review*, 63(1_suppl), 29S-48.

Hackbarth, G., Reischauer, R. and Mutti, A. (2008). 'Collective accountability for medical care – Toward bundled Medicare payments'. *New England Journal of Medicine*, 359, 3–5.

Hoff, T. J. and Soerensen, C. (2010). 'No Payment for Preventable Complications: Reviewing the Early Literature for Content, Guidance, and Impressions'. *Quality Management in Healthcare*, 20, 62–75.

HSE (2013). 'National Service Plan 2013'. Dublin: HSE. Available at: http://www.hse.ie/eng/services/Publications/corporate/NSP2013.pdf [last accessed 12 February 2013].

Hussey, P., Sorbero, M., Mehrotra, A., Liu, H. and Damberg, C. (2009). 'Episode-Based Performance Measurement and Payment: Making it a Reality'. *Health Affairs*, 28, 1406–1417.

Iglehart, J. (2011). 'Assessing an ACO Prototype - Medicare's Physician Group Practice Demonstration'. *New England Journal of Medicine*, 364, 198–200.

Inouye, S. K., Brown, C. J. and Tinetti, M. E. (2009). 'Medicare Nonpayment, Hospital Falls, and Unintended Consequences'. *New England Journal of Medicine*, 360, 2390–2393.

Janus, K. (2011). 'Pay-for-Performance does not always "pay"'. *Eurohealth*, 17, 31–34.

Jha, A. K., Joynt, K. E., Orav, E. J. and Epstein, A. M. (2012). 'The long-term effect of premier pay for performance on patient outcomes'. *New England Journal of Medicine*, 366, 1606–15.

Kruse, G. B., Polsky, D., Stuart, E. A. and Werner, R. M. (2012). 'The impact of hospital pay-for-performance on hospital and Medicare costs'. *Health Services Research*, 47, 2118–36.

Lindenauer, P. K., Remus, D., Roman, S., Rothberg, M. B., Benjamin, E. M., Ma, A. and Bratzler, D. W. (2007). 'Public Reporting and Pay for Performance in Hospital Quality Improvement'. *New England Journal of Medicine*, 356, 486–496.

Mason, A., Walker, S., Claxton, K., Cookson, R., Fenwick, E. and Sculpher, M. (2008). 'The GMS Quality and Outcomes Framework: Are the Quality and Outcomes (QOF) Indicators a Cost-Effective Use of NHS Resources?': Available at: http://www.york.ac.uk/media/che/documents/papers/jointexecutivesummaryUEA-York-%20270308final.pdf [last accessed 20 May 2013].

Mathematica Policy Research (2009). 'Using Payment Incentives to Improve Care for the Chronically Ill in Medicare: First Year Implementation of the Medicare Care Management Performance Demonstration (MCMP)'.

Washington: Mathematica Policy Research. Available at: https://www.cms.gov/Reports/Downloads/Felt-Lisk_2009.pdf [last accessed 20 May 2013].

Maynard, A. (2012). 'The Powers and Pitfalls of Payment for Performance'. *Health Economics*, 21, 3–12.

McNair, P., Luft, H. and Bindman, A. (2009). 'Medicare's Policy Not To Pay For Treating Hospital-Acquired Conditions: The Impact'. *Health Affairs*, 28, 1485–1493.

McNutt, R., Johnson, T. J., Odwazny, R., Remmich, Z., Skarupski, K., Meurer, S., Hohmann, S. and Harting, B. (2010). 'Change in MS-DRG Assignment and Hospital Reimbursement as a Result of Centers for Medicare & Medicaid Changes in Payment for Hospital-Acquired Conditions: Is It Coding or Quality?' *Quality Management in Healthcare*, 19, 17–24.

Mechanic, R. and Altman, S. (2009). 'Payment Reform Options: Episode Payment is a Good Place to Start'. *Health Affairs*, 28, W262–W271.

Mehrotra, A., Damberg, C. L., Sorbero, M. E. and Teleki, S. S. (2009). 'Pay for Performance in the Hospital Setting: What is the State of the Evidence?' *American Journal of Medical Quality*, 24, 19–28.

Miller, H. (2009). 'From Volume To Value: Better Ways To Pay For Healthcare'. *Health Affairs*, 28, 1418–1428.

Millett, C., Gray, J., Bottle, A. and Majeed, A. (2008). 'Ethnic Disparities in Blood Pressure Management in Patients With Hypertension After the Introduction of Pay for Performance'. *Annals of Family Medicine*, 6, 490–496.

Nahra, T. A., Reiter, K. L., Hirth, R. A., Shermer, J. E. and Wheeler, J. R. C. (2006). 'Cost-Effectiveness of Hospital Pay-for-Performance Incentives'. *Medical Care Research and Review*, 63(1 suppl), 49S-72S.

Newhouse, J. P. and Insurance Experiment Group (1993). *Free for all? Lessons from the RAND Health Insurance Experiment*. RAND.

NHS Confederation (2011). 'The impact for non-payment for acute readmissions'. Available at: http://www.chks.co.uk/userfiles/files/The%20impact%20of%20non-payment%20for%20acute%20readmissions%20FINAL%20FOR%20WEB.pdf [last accessed 20 May 2013].

NHS Information Centre (2007). 'Time Series Analysis for selected clinical indicators from the Quality and Outcomes Framework 2001–2006'. London: NHS Information Centre. Available at: https://catalogue.ic.nhs.uk/publications/primary-care/qof/time-seri-anal-shed-clin-ind-qof-01–06/time-seri-anal-shed-clin-ind-qof-01–06-rep.pdf [last accessed 20 May 2013].

Nolan, A., O'Reilly, J., Smith, S. and Brick, A. (2011). *The Potential Role of Pay-for-Performance in Irish Healthcare*. ESRI Renewal Series Paper No. 4. Dublin: Economic and Social Research Institute.

Or, Z. and Häkkinen, U. (2011). 'DRGs and quality: For better or worse?' in Busse, R., Geissler, A., Quentin, W. and Wiley, M. (eds.), *Diagnosis Related Groups in Europe. Moving Towards Transparency, Efficiency and Quality in Hospitals*. Maidenhead: Open University Press.

Paulus, R., Davis, K. and Steele, G. (2008). 'Continuous Innovation in Healthcare: Implications of the Geisinger Experience'. *Health Affairs*, 27, 1235–1245.

Pronovost, P. J., Goeschel, C. A. and Wachter, R. M. (2008). 'The Wisdom and Justice of not Paying for "Preventable Complications"'. *Journal of the American Medical Association*, 299, 2197–9.

Propper, C. and Wilson, D. (2003). 'The Use and Usefulness of Performance Measures in the Public Sector'. *Oxford Review of Economic Policy*, 19, 250–267.

RAND (2010). 'Analysis of Bundled Payment'. Available at: http://www.rand.org/pubs/technical_reports/TR562z20/analysis-of-bundled-payment.html [last accessed 20 May 2013].

Robinson, J. C. (2001). 'Theory and Practice in the Design of Physician Payment Incentives'. *The Milbank Quarterly*, 79, 149–177.

Roland, M. (2004). 'Linking Physicians' Pay to the Quality of Care – A Major Experiment in the United Kingdom'. *New England Journal of Medicine*, 351, 1448–1454.

Rosenthal, M. B. (2007). 'Nonpayment for Performance? Medicare's New Reimbursement Rule'. *New England Journal of Medicine*, 357, 1573–5.

Ruane, F. (2010). *Report of the Expert Group on Resource Allocation and Financing in the Health Sector*. Dublin: Department of Health and Children.

Ryan, A. M. (2009). 'Effects of the Premier Hospital Quality Incentive Demonstration on Medicare Patient Mortality and Cost'. *Health Services Research*, 44, 821–842.

Ryan, A. M. (2010). 'Has pay-for-performance decreased access for minority patients?' *Health Services Research*, 45, 6–23.

Ryan, A. M., Blustein, J. and Casalino, L. P. (2012). 'Medicare's flagship test of pay-for-performance did not spur more rapid quality improvement among low-performing hospitals'. *Health Affairs*, 31, 797–805.

Saint, S., Meddings, J. A., Calfee, D., Kowalski, C. P. and Krein, S. L. (2009). 'Catheter-Associated Urinary Tract Infection and the Medicare Rule Changes'. *Annals of Internal Medicine*, 150, 877–884.

Scott, A., Schurer, S., Jensen, P. and Sivey, P. (2009). 'The Effects of an Incentive Program on Quality of Care in Diabetes Management'. *Health Economics*, 18, 1091–1108.

Scott, A., Sivey, P., Ait Ouakrim, D., Willenberg, L., Naccarella, L., Furler, J. and Young, D. (2011). 'The effect of financial incentives on the quality of healthcare provided by primary care physicians' (Review). *Cochrane Database of Systematic Reviews*, 1–59.

Serumaga, B., Ross-Degnan, D., Avery, A., Elliott, R., Majumdar, S., Zhang, F. and Soumerai, S. (2011). 'Effect of pay for performance on the management and outcomes of hypertension in the United Kingdom: interrupted time series study'. *British Medical Journal*, 342(d108), 1–7.

Simeons, S. and Giuffrida, A. (2004). 'The Impact of Physician Payment Methods

on Raising the Efficiency of the Healthcare System: An International Comparison'. *Applied Health Economics and Health Policy*, 3, 39–46.
Smith, P. and York, N. (2004). 'Quality Incentives: The Case of UK General Practitioners'. *Health Affairs*, 23, 112–118.
Sutherland, J. M. (2011). 'Hospital payment mechanisms: An overview and options for Canada'. *CHSRF Series on Cost Drivers and Health System Efficiency: Paper 4*. Available at: http://www.chsrf.ca/Libraries/Hospital_Funding_docs/CHSRF-Sutherland-HospitalFundingENG.sflb.ashx [last accessed 20 May 2013].
Tussing, D. and Wren, M.A. (2006). *How Ireland Cares: The Case for Health Reform*. Dublin: New Island.
Wachter, R. M., Foster, N. E. and Dudley, R. A. (2008). 'Medicare's Decision to Withhold Payment for Hospital Errors: The Devil is in the Details'. *Joint Commission Journal on Quality and Patient Safety*, 34, 116–123.
Wald, H. L. and Kramer, A. M. (2007). 'Nonpayment for Harms Resulting from Medical Care: Catheter-Associated Urinary Tract Infections'. *Journal of the American Medical Association*, 298, 2782–4.
Walker, S., Mason, A., Claxton, K., Cookson, R., Fenwick, E., Fleetcroft, R. and Sculpher, M. (2010). 'Value for money and the Quality and Outcomes Framework in primary care in the UK NHS'. *British Journal of General Practice*, May, e213–e220.
Werner, R. M., Kolstad, J. T., Stuart, E. A. and Polsky, D. (2011). 'The Effect of Pay-for-Performance in Hospitals: Lessons for Quality Improvement'. *Health Affairs*, 30(4), 690–698.
Wilson, K. J. (2013). 'Pay-for-Performance in Healthcare: What Can We Learn From International Experience?' *Quality Management in Healthcare*, 22, 2.
Wren, M.A. (2003). *Unhealthy State: Anatomy of a Sick Society*. Dublin: New Island.
Young, G. J., White, B., Burgess, J. F., Jr., Berlowitz, D., Meterko, M., Guldin, M. R. and Bokhour, B. G. (2005). 'Conceptual issues in the design and implementation of pay-for-quality programs'. *American Journal of Medical Quality*, 20, 144–50.

CHAPTER 5

Learning from the Evidence: Using Educational Research to Inform Policy

Emer Smyth, Selina McCoy

This chapter draws on Irish and international research to look at the way in which evidence can inform the future direction of second-level education. Education is a distinctive policy area in that the schooling system reflects the long-term interaction of complex social, economic, cultural and political factors. With respect to the policy landscape (Figure 1.1), although education can be regarded as an established policy area, the reform of junior cycle means that the system is currently in the process of significant change.

Another distinctive feature of the education arena is that research and policy questions are often inextricably linked, oriented as they are towards the factors enhancing young people's educational development, broadly defined. Although the Irish educational system is relatively highly centralised, schools have a certain degree of control over dimensions, such as ability grouping and subject choice, which significantly shape student learning experiences. Thus, in an important sense, national policy is mediated and reshaped at the school level.

The chapter identifies a number of key areas in which research evidence can contribute to enhanced policy and practice at the national and school levels. Evidence is drawn from a wide range of studies conducted in different national contexts and using varied methodologies. The analysis of the Irish context relies mainly on large-scale quantitative and mixed methods research conducted at the Economic and Social Research Institute (in which the authors were involved) and at the Educational Research Centre, Drumcondra. The argument presented is that rather than engage in 'policy borrowing', seeking to emulate practices from very different social and cultural contexts, international evidence can provide the basis for 'policy learning', marrying insights regarding potential levers for change with an in-depth knowledge of the specificities of the Irish context.

The chapter highlights clear policy implications, centring on three features which can make an appreciable difference to student outcomes. First, rigid ability grouping (streaming) is associated with underperformance among those assigned to lower stream classes, without any corresponding gains for those in higher stream classes. Second, the quality of teacher-student relations is found to be predictive of a range of student outcomes, including retention and achievement. Third, students are more positive about classes that involve active learning rather than passive listening. Thus, a move away from rigid ability grouping coupled with high expectations for all students, promoting a positive school climate, and providing active and engaging teaching and learning in the classroom will enhance young people's educational outcomes.

The reform of junior cycle is likely to move the educational system closer to realising these goals, but effective implementation will be contingent on support for principals and teachers in developing the skills required to implement these practices. Systematic evaluation of the new junior cycle programme will, therefore, be crucial in assessing how implementation occurs across a range of school and classroom settings.

BACKGROUND

Education matters because it is intrinsically valuable, allowing young people to develop intellectually, socially and personally. Education plays a central role in developing human capital and this is crucial to our long-term economic prosperity and, in particular, to our recovery over the coming decade. It matters too because it is a strong predictor of adult life chances, influencing access to, and quality of, employment, income levels and even health (Smyth and McCoy, 2009). How best to invest in education to enhance individual and social benefits has, therefore, been the subject of a good deal of debate in Ireland and internationally. International research has shown that the benefits of certain educational interventions considerably exceed their costs, revealing the longer term pay-off of increased (targeted) educational investment (Levin, 2009). The recent situation in Ireland has been one of reductions in some elements of educational provision. In the context of constrained expenditure on education, it is all the more important that policy development be informed by sound evidence. This chapter draws on Irish and international research to look at the way in which evidence can inform the future direction of second-level education.

Comparing educational achievement across countries

There has been considerable debate internationally about how to assess and improve the quality of education. Cross-national surveys (such as the PISA studies of 15 year olds conducted by the OECD) have been used by countries to compare themselves against international benchmarks and are 'increasingly used as the ultimate reference on the 'quality of education" (Mortimore, 2009). Such data have been used not only as a source of information on different educational systems but as a basis for policy prescription (Porter and Webb, 2008; Alexander, 2010). Ranking countries in this way has had a good deal of popular appeal, receiving considerable coverage in the media and prompting policymakers in a number of countries to embark on educational reform in the wake of 'PISA panic'. However, there are considerable difficulties in using cross-national surveys as a basis for policy development. First, there is a difficulty in achieving true comparability across countries because of fundamental differences in language and culture, and in the types of skills and competencies developed in different schooling systems (Bradshaw et al., 2009; Goldstein, 2004; Mortimore, 2009). Second, questions have been raised as to whether and how such data can be used to bring about the improvement of national educational systems. Commentators make an important distinction between approaches which are based on 'policy borrowing' and those based on 'policy learning' (Lingard, 2010; Raffe, 2011). A policy borrowing approach looks for a unique, transferable example of 'best practice' and seeks to 'transplant' elements of that system into another country. However, this approach fails to take account of the complex ways in which education systems are embedded in broader historical, cultural, social and economic circumstances. In contrast, a 'policy learning' approach uses international evidence not for a 'quick-fix' solution but to inform thinking about policy development in the specific national context, looking at how 'good' rather than 'best' practice varies by context, time and place (Raffe, 2011).

If we are to learn from international experience in this way, what kind of evidence is likely to provide useful insights for policy development? Looking across existing literature, the kind of research evidence which is likely to facilitate policy learning is found to have certain features, which include:

- A range of outcomes should be considered. The vast majority of research studies focus on academic achievement (often defined as performance on standardised tests) but less is known about the factors shaping student engagement and motivation, early school leaving, take-up of particular subjects, and later participation in lifelong learning. Children and young people themselves emphasise the affective (emotional) as much as the cognitive (learning) domain in discussing their school experiences (Alexander, 2008).
- Findings should be placed within their overall context (Seidel and Shavelson, 2007), taking account of the extent to which particular findings reflect the specific educational system and/or broader structures of socio-economic inequality.
- The processes and outcomes for different groups of children and young people should be considered – what works for whom? Many studies focus on 'average' effects but the impact of certain factors may vary by gender, social class, ethnicity and prior achievement.
- Evidence should ideally draw on a mix of sources, including students' own perspectives. An increasing body of work shows the value of taking account of the student voice in school improvement (Rudduck and McIntyre, 2007). Further, a review of a large number of research studies conducted by Seidel and Shavelson (2007) indicates that student reports of teaching methods are more strongly predictive of academic outcomes than teacher reports.

In the following sections, these criteria are used as a guideline in discussing what conclusions can be drawn from existing research on the quality of second-level education.

Challenges for Second-Level Education in Ireland

The discussion so far has looked at international debates about educational quality and standards. How does Ireland fare from this perspective? Using international benchmarks, expenditure on second-level education relative to per capita GDP in 2009 was above the OECD average (albeit after a sustained period in which expenditure had been below this average); rates of upper secondary attainment among young adults were above the average for EU21 countries; and the ratio of students to teachers at junior cycle was around the European average (though this may have changed since 2009). In 2009, performance among 15-year olds in PISA was below average for mathematical literacy, average for reading literacy, and above average for science literacy and digital literacy (Cosgrove *et al.*, 2010, 2011; Shiel *et al.*, 2010). The low, and relatively declining, levels of Irish performance in reading and mathematics literacy attracted a good deal of attention and prompted a new policy emphasis on promoting literacy and numeracy in primary and post-primary education (DES, 2011). However, such benchmarks give a very partial view of the 'quality' of Irish education and taken in isolation give no indication as to what the appropriate policy response might be. In some ways, the reaction to the PISA results has deflected attention away from long-standing evidence which provides more detailed insights into the challenges facing the Irish second-level system; this evidence includes the following:

- There is persistent variation and inequality in educational outcomes: young people from working-class backgrounds have lower scores on literacy and numeracy tests, achieve lower exam grades at both Junior and Leaving Certificate levels, and are more likely to drop out of school before reaching the Leaving Certificate (Cosgrove *et al.*, 2010; Smyth, 1999; Smyth *et al.*, 2007; Byrne and Smyth, 2010). This inequality has significant societal and individual costs (Smyth and McCoy, 2009).
- A significant number of young people make the transition to second-level education with literacy levels that make it difficult for them to engage fully with the curriculum (Smyth *et al.*, 2004).
- There has been persistent evidence of lack of engagement in mathematics, with significant failure rates in mathematics exams, low levels of take-up of higher level mathematics at senior cycle level, and a focus on drill and repetition rather than deeper understanding in mathematics classes (Lyons *et al.*, 2003; Smyth and Hannan, 2002; SEC, 2011), issues which have prompted the introduction of the new Project Maths curriculum.
- There is a mismatch between the more teacher-centred methods used in

second-level schools and the more active methods which young people find engaging (Smyth *et al.*, 2007, 2011).
- The pace of instruction in many second-level classrooms does not match student needs (Smyth *et al.*, 2004), with less use of differentiation (that is, tailoring teaching approaches to meet the range of abilities in the class) than desirable in some settings (DES, 2007, 2008).
- The exam-focused nature of the system has had the effect of narrowing the range of learning experiences to which young people are exposed and has focused both students and teachers on 'covering the course' or 'teaching to the test' rather than achieving deeper understanding (Smyth *et al.*, 2007, 2011).

Such evidence provides a firm basis for highlighting (some of) the issues to be addressed to improve the quality of second-level education.

WHAT REALLY WORKS?

The previous section outlined how research evidence can potentially contribute to policy formulation. In the current economic climate, increased investment in education is unlikely in the near term and the emphasis is likely to lie, as in other areas, on getting the best value from the resources available. Fortunately, there is now a large body of research which shows how policy and practice at the school level can make a substantive impact on student outcomes by identifying 'drivers' or 'levers' of improvement. Many of these changes would require relatively modest levels of expenditure. The remainder of this section outlines some of the ways in which evidence might inform policy development in these domains.

School Effects

There is a large body of robust research which shows that 'schools matter', that is, what happens within the school can make a difference to how students fare, even taking account of student characteristics on entry to the school (for an overview, see Teddlie and Reynolds, 2000). A number of studies, mainly in Britain and the US, have pointed to the characteristics of 'effective' primary and second-level schools, including high (but realistic) teacher expectations, staff commitment and involvement, student involvement, an orderly environment, and parental involvement (Brookover *et al.*, 1979; Mortimore *et al.*, 1988; Rutter *et al.*, 1979; Teddlie and Stringfield, 1993).

While some research has focused on the effect of school processes on 'average' student outcomes, a growing body of research indicates that the impact of schools may vary across different groups of students. Thus, some schools in England have been found to be more effective for lower ability students while others enhance the achievement levels of higher ability students (Thomas *et al.*, 1997; Dearden *et al.*, 2011). Schools may also be differentially effective for different social class, ethnic or gender groups (Smith and Tomlinson, 1989; Sammons *et al.*, 1997).

In Ireland, research has indicated significant differences between schools in a range of student outcomes, including achievement, attendance, early school leaving, subject take-up and personal-social development, controlling for differences in student intake (Hannan *et al.*, 1996; Smyth, 1999; Smyth *et al.*, 2011). Junior and Leaving Certificate achievement are found to be higher in schools with a more positive disciplinary climate, less negative teacher-student interaction, a more flexible approach to subject choice, greater student involvement and higher teacher expectations, all else being equal (Smyth, 1999). School practice is found to be more important for students with initially lower levels of academic ability (Smyth, 1999). Student attendance is higher where young people experience positive relations with their teachers and those teachers have high expectations, and where staff are more involved in school decision-making (Smyth, 1999). Negative interaction with teachers and peers is also associated with early school leaving (Byrne and Smyth, 2010). In keeping with international research, schools in Ireland matter less for personal development than for academic outcomes (Teddlie and Reynolds, 2000; Opendakker and Van Damme, 2000). Even so, certain aspects of the school process, especially relations with teachers and peers, are found to have a significant effect on student self-image and stress levels (Smyth, 1999).

While international and Irish studies point to a range of factors associated with student outcomes, two aspects of school organisation and process are worth highlighting here: ability grouping and school climate (measured in terms of the quality of teacher-student relationships).

Ability Grouping

Types of ability grouping can generally be classified as streaming, setting or mixed ability. **Streaming** involves using performance on a test (or another metric) to allocate students to different classes on the basis of (assessed) ability. In this system, students are placed in a lower stream class for all subjects, including Physical Education and Metalwork as well as English and Mathematics. **Setting** is a more flexible form of ability grouping, whereby students are allocated to 'higher' or 'lower' sets depending on their ability in a particular subject. Thus, a student may be in the lower set for Mathematics but in the higher set for English. **Mixed ability** grouping may occur by design (if a school wishes to have a genuine mix of students in each class) or as a result of random allocation to class groups.

International studies have found that streaming results in very different educational and social experiences for students attending the same school. Students allocated to lower streams experience very different learning processes, with lower academic demands and less emphasis on the kinds of discussion-based approaches which facilitate achievement (Applebee *et al.*, 2003; Oakes, 1990, 2005). As a result of being labelled in this way, many students develop very negative views of their own abilities (Hansell and Karweit, 1983), resulting in some instances in the development of an anti-school culture (Lacey, 1970; Hargreaves, 1967). Streaming is also found to reinforce prior differences in terms of social class and ethnicity since working-class and ethnic minority students are more likely to be allocated to lower stream classes (Oakes, 1990, 2005; Gamoran and Mare, 1989; Gamoran et al., 1995).

In the Irish context, the use of streaming has declined since the 1980s but is now more highly concentrated in schools serving disadvantaged populations (Smyth et al., 2004). A large nationally representative study of Junior Certificate students showed significant underperformance among those allocated to lower stream classes with no grade advantage accruing to those in higher stream classes (Smyth, 1999). Later longitudinal research replicated this finding and indicated the way in which underperformance among lower stream students reflects the interaction of low teacher expectations, slower pace of instruction and negative labelling (Smyth et al., 2007). Streaming is found to account for part of the social class gap in academic achievement; in other words, working-class young people achieve lower exam grades, at least in part, because they are more likely to attend schools where streaming is used and more likely to be allocated to lower stream classes in these schools (Smyth et al., 2007).

Although the use of mixed ability base classes in Irish second-level schools has increased over time, the majority of schools allocate students to 'set' groups for at least some subjects, generally Mathematics, Irish and English (and sometimes a foreign language) (Smyth et al., 2007, 2011). Research indicates a complex interaction between school policy regarding allocation to ability groups, teacher and student expectations in shaping the proportion of students who take higher level subjects (Smyth et al., 2007, 2011). Thus, setting is employed differently in different contexts – in some schools, all students are encouraged to take higher level while in others, access to the 'higher' set is strictly rationed on the basis of prior performance.

This research provides strong evidence for moving away from rigid ability grouping in order to enhance achievement and reduce educational inequality. In the reformed junior cycle (discussed in greater detail below), the majority of subjects will be studied at a common level, thus removing some of the impetus for ability grouping. This is likely to enhance the potential achievement of young people. However, separate higher and ordinary levels will remain for Irish, English and Mathematics, the subjects in which setting is most commonly used currently. The way in which allocation to higher and ordinary level is handled at the school and class level will therefore remain central to ensuring improved take-up of higher level.

Research has indicated that the majority of base classes in Irish second-level schools are now mixed ability in composition (Smyth et al., 2004). As noted, this does not necessarily translate into mixed ability teaching since setting is commonly used for some subjects. Again the issue of how mixed ability is implemented emerges as central. In mixed ability groupings, a significant proportion of second-level students report that the pace of instruction in class is too fast or too slow for them, indicating the need for teaching methods that cater for the diversity of students in the classroom (Smyth *et al.*, 2007, 2011). Inspection reports also point to the need for a greater use of differentiation in teaching methods within second-level classes (DES, 2007, 2008). The use of differentiation is all the more important in the context of increased diversity in the student population, reflecting the proportion of newcomer (immigrant) students and the mainstreaming of young people with special educational needs (McCoy and Banks, 2012).

The Social Climate of the School

Two syntheses of international research (Martin and Dowson, 2009; Jennings and Greenberg, 2009) highlight the importance of relationships in student engagement, with supportive teacher-student relationships found to have positive effects on student academic and social-emotional outcomes (see also Crosnoe *et al.*, 2004; Opdendakker *et al.*, 2012). 'Connective instruction' (also termed 'relational pedagogy'), where students feel supported and cared for by their teacher, is associated with enhanced motivation and achievement (Martin and Dowson, 2009). In Ireland, the cross-sectional PISA study indicates that reading literacy scores are higher in schools with better teacher-student relations (OECD, 2010), though it is difficult to interpret this relationship as causal. Longitudinal research provides a more robust way of isolating the impact of teacher-student interaction on young people as they move through the school system. In the Irish context, such research indicates that the quality of student-teacher relations has a significant effect on a range of student outcomes, including academic performance, early school leaving, academic self-image (that is, how students view their own capacity to cope with schoolwork) and planned post-school pathways. Students who experience negative interaction with their teachers (that is, those who are frequently 'given out to' or reprimanded) achieve lower exam grades, are more likely to drop out of school and are less likely to intend to go on to higher education, all else being equal (McCoy *et al.*, 2010; Smyth *et al.*, 2011). More negative disciplinary climates are found in schools serving disadvantaged populations (McCoy *et al.*, 2012; Gilleece *et al.*, 2009; Smyth *et al.*, 2007) and in larger classes (Gilleece *et al.*, 2009).

National and international research has provided a clear message that teacher-student relations matter a great deal for student outcomes. However, less is known about how to bring about a more positive social climate in the school. Existing studies find that more punitive measures, such as suspension from school, serve to further alienate students, culminating in disengagement or early school leaving (Blomberg, 2004; Fenning and Bohanon, 2006; Skiba and Peterson, 2000). In contrast, emphasising positive behaviour and providing engaging learning opportunities have been found to reduce the incidence of misbehaviour in schools (Bradshaw *et al.*, 2009; Osher *et al.*, 2010). Research in Ireland shows that some young people, particularly working-class boys, become caught up in a cycle of being 'given out to' by teachers and 'acting up' in response, with lower levels of achievement and higher drop-out rates among this group of students (Smyth et al., 2004, 2011; Byrne and Smyth, 2010). How student behaviour is handled therefore appears central to reducing educational inequality and enhancing retention and achievement.

Teacher Effects

A large number of research studies have indicated that student outcomes, especially academic achievement, vary according to their teacher (Day et al., 2007). At primary level, it is generally easy to isolate the effects of teachers and schools since children usually have one main class teacher. In second-level schools, it is more difficult to disentangle the effect of individual teachers as students are taught by many different teachers. Many studies have pointed to considerable variation in academic achievement levels across different subjects within second-level schools (Goldstein et al. 1993; Luyten, 1994; Thomas et al., 1997). Others, however, have pointed to school effects as being substantial, in some cases being on a par or larger than teacher effects (Opendakker and Van Damme, 2000). It is likely that the relative importance of teacher, classroom and school effects is cross-nationally variable, reflecting differences in school structure, the use of ability grouping and the degree of teacher autonomy (see Teddlie and Reynolds, 2000). It can be concluded therefore that both schools and teachers matter in shaping student outcomes within second-level education.

Teacher Characteristics

Whether teachers matter has rarely been disputed but how teachers matter has been the subject of much debate (Palardy and Rumberger, 2008). Studies can be classified as those which assess the impact of teacher characteristics and/or those which look at instructional practices. Findings on the effect of teacher qualifications are inconsistent. Where studies have found some effects, they have generally been limited to a subset of outcomes (Nye et al., 2004; Palardy and Rumberger, 2008). It should be noted, however, that in Western countries there is unlikely to be very significant differences in the level of teacher qualifications. There is a lack of evidence on the impact of different types (rather than levels) of teacher qualifications. However, a review of research by Wayne and Youngs (2003) indicates that students make more progress in Mathematics when taught by teachers who had more Mathematics training in their degree. A German study (Baumert et al., 2010) points to the need to distinguish between the teacher's content knowledge ('knowing the subject') and their pedagogical content knowledge ('knowing how to teach the subject'), finding the latter to be a strong influence on student achievement in Mathematics. There has been no Irish research to date on the effect of teacher qualifications on second-level student outcomes.

As with teacher qualifications, findings on the impact of teacher experience (number of years teaching) tend to be non-significant (Day et al., 2007; Palardy and Rumberger, 2008) or limited to a subset of outcomes (Nye *et al.*, 2004). In a study of Chicago public schools, Aaronson *et al.* (2007) concluded that tenure and qualifications explain, at most, 1 per cent of the variance. Other factors such as being positive about professional practice and support, and feelings of self-efficacy, are found to be associated with teacher effectiveness (Day *et al.*, 2007). The vast majority of research on teacher effects has focused on differences in the way in which they teach, an issue we discuss in the following subsection.

Teaching Methods

Recent years have seen considerable debate internationally about the kinds of teaching methods which enhance student engagement and learning (Muijs and Reynolds, 2011). The fault-lines have been crudely characterised as the conflict between 'teacher-centred' and 'student-centred' methods. Much of the debate has been quite polarised, asserting the superiority of one method over the other. However, other researchers have argued that teachers often use a broad repertoire of methods and it is important therefore to identify elements of good practice (which are not necessarily mutually exclusive) (James and Pollard, 2010). On this basis, there is some consensus that certain kinds of approaches enhance student outcomes; all of these elements emphasise the active engagement and interaction of the learner, although this may occur in different contexts (including whole-class teaching). These include the following elements:

- Goal Setting: The teacher setting clear goals for the lesson at the outset is found to enhance achievement (Mortimore *et al.*, 1988; Creemers and Kyriakides, 2008).
- Classroom Focus: A less disruptive and more focused classroom fosters more time on task, thus enhancing student progress (Brookover *et al.*, 1979; Scheerens and Bosker, 1997; Teddlie and Stringfield, 1993).
- Challenging Material: An emphasis on providing challenging material to students, using higher order (open) rather than procedural (or factual) questioning and discussion, is associated with enhanced achievement (Nystrand and Gamoran, 1991; Camburn and Han, 2008; Yair, 2000; Mortimore *et al.*, 1988; Rosenshine *et al.*, 1996).
- Active Engagement: The active engagement of students in practical investigation is found to enhance conceptual understanding of, and achievement in, science (Minner *et al.*, 2010).
- Group-Work: Cooperative learning and peer tutoring through small group-work enhance achievement (Kamps *et al.*, 2008; Topping, 2005; Scheerens and Bosker, 1997; Veenman *et al.*, 2005; Webb and Mastergeorge, 2003; Galton *et al.*, 2009).
- Formative Assessment: The use of assessment for learning (formative assessment) enhances learning (James and Pollard, 2010).

- Expectations: Teacher expectations have a strong impact, with, for example, lower reading achievement gains where teachers hold negative expectations (e.g., view children as incapable of learning) (Palardy and Rumberger, 2008; Brookover *et al.*, 1979; Teddlie and Stringfield, 1993).

There appears to be a consensus favouring active teaching and learning methods among young people in very different national settings, with studies of student perspectives indicating their desire for greater discussion and interaction in class (for example, EPPI, 2005; Gorard and See, 2011; Osler, 2010; Lumby, 2011). In keeping with the discussion of the importance of teacher-student relationships above, the quality of the interaction with teachers is seen as key to student learning. Students appear to respond to teachers who they feel trust them, give them more responsibility, care about them, are patient with them, encourage them to do their best and treat them with respect (see, for example, Hallinan, 2008).

There is a lack of systematic evidence on the use of different teaching methods at post-primary level in Ireland and the extent to which the methods used vary across year groups, subject areas and different groups of students. However, insights can be gleaned from the Teaching and Learning International Survey (TALIS) report, where the pattern in Ireland can be placed in international context (Gilleece *et al.*, 2009). As in other countries, Irish teachers (at junior cycle level) have more positive attitudes to constructivist (student-centred) methods than to direct transmission (where teachers do most of the talking). However, compared with those in other countries, teachers in Ireland are more likely to use a highly structured (and teacher-centred) approach and much less likely to use student-centred activities. Variation is also evident by subject area, with Mathematics being taught in a more structured way than other subjects. More student-centred practices are used with higher ability students and are less prevalent in larger classes (Gilleece *et al.*, 2009). Student reports of classroom practices further indicate the continuing reliance on teacher-centred approaches in second-level classrooms, with exam years in particular characterised by teachers doing most of the talking, less use of group work, less active student involvement and an emphasis on practising previous examination papers (Smyth *et al.*, 2011) Inspection reports have also highlighted the dominance of teacher talk and an over-emphasis on learning through memorisation in some subjects (DES, 2007, 2008).

In conclusion, there is considerable debate about the most effective teaching methods but some consensus that more active engagement of the learner enhances outcomes, especially the development of deeper understanding. There is a paucity of research on teaching practices in Irish second-level education, but existing evidence suggests that approaches tend to be teacher-centred.

Curriculum and Assessment

The discussion so far has focused on school processes independently of the issue of what is taught (curriculum) and how we know what students have learned (assessment). Indeed, Teddlie and Reynolds (2000) have acknowledged that research on school effects has tended to take the existing curriculum as given. In Ireland, potential reform of junior and senior cycle education has been on the agenda for some time. Research clearly indicates that the current Junior and Leaving Certificate models tend to narrow the range of student learning experiences and to focus both teachers and students on 'covering the course' (Smyth et al., 2007, 2011). The Post-Primary Longitudinal Study points to a number of elements which should be considered in any curriculum reform: ensuring continuity between primary education, junior and senior cycle in the standards expected of students; moving away from the very detailed content of many subjects, which currently appears to contribute to a pace of instruction not always conducive to student learning and to a more teacher-centred approach rather than the kinds of active teaching methods which students find most engaging; the need to embed key skills, such as critical thinking, learning to learn and ICT skills, in the curriculum in order to equip young people for the future; a consideration of the possibility of making work experience available to all students, regardless of the programme they take; the crucial role of school climate, especially positive teacher-student relations, in student engagement; and the need to move to a broader range of assessment modes, which reflect the full range of skills and knowledge developed within schooling. Such a shift in approach is likely to enhance student engagement and provide young people with richer educational experiences as a preparation for adult and work life.

The junior cycle reform to be implemented from 2014 onwards represents a sea-change in the nature of Irish second-level education. It involves a shift away from an exam-dominated mode of assessment, less detailed curriculum specifications, fewer subjects to be assessed than currently, a focus on embedding key skills in teaching and learning, and a concern with more innovative approaches to teaching and learning (NCCA, 2011). There are a number of challenges for successful curriculum implementation. First, the number of subjects to be assessed will be reduced. While schools are free to offer a larger number of subjects, recent experience points to a close link between what is assessed and what is taught. Depending on how schools organise subject choice, there is a risk of differential student access to a broad range of subject areas, an issue which has important implications for later options at senior cycle and in post-school education. Second, to date the Transition Year programme has been the only outlet for teachers to engage in course design so the new junior cycle will require a new set of skills for many teachers, with initial and continuing teacher education playing a crucial role in developing these skills. Finally, the junior cycle document envisages a more interactive learning environment with young people playing a more active role in their own learning. Currently, second-level education in Ireland can be characterised as quite hierarchical in nature (Lynch and Lodge, 2002). The more active engagement of young people will, therefore, require greater student involvement in the operation of the school. Even more crucially, effective curriculum implementation will require a significant broadening of the repertoire of teaching and assessment methods used in the classroom, which necessitates a strong emphasis on continuous professional development for teachers.

The consequences for the quality of Irish education will also depend on the extent to which innovations at junior cycle are followed through into senior cycle education (and beyond). Without senior cycle reform, young people will move from a richer and engaging learning experience to a narrower one focused on the terminal exam. There is also a danger that even though assessment approaches will become more varied at junior cycle, the high-stakes nature of the Leaving Certificate will (continue to) have a 'back-wash' effect on earlier stages.

CONCLUSIONS AND IMPLICATIONS FOR POLICY

Investment in education is perhaps unique in having the potential to impact on generations to come. In the context of scarce resources, it is all the more important that policy decisions should be guided by the existing evidence base. We can potentially learn a lot from what other educational systems have 'got right' and from the measures that have not succeeded. However, it is vital that, in drawing on such evidence, we do not fall into the trap of advocating 'policy borrowing'. The nature and structure of national educational systems reflect a multiplicity of historical, social, cultural and economic factors, making it impossible to 'transplant' certain measures from one country to the other. We can, however, usefully engage in 'policy learning', by reflecting on existing international research and policy development through the specific lens of the Irish educational system and its societal context. Irish research can provide a further basis for assessing 'what works' in terms of school organisation and process.

This chapter has presented evidence on aspects of schooling which can enhance student outcomes, not only academic achievement but engagement, retention and social-personal development. The three factors on which the chapter focuses (ability grouping, school climate, and teaching methods) are ones which operate largely at the school and classroom level. Even in a centralised educational system, schools 'do' policy in an important sense (Ball et al., 2012), shaping the context for teaching and learning. Some changes can therefore be enhanced by national policy, mainly through initial and continuous professional development for teachers, rather than driven by it. However, the specific school context is also shaped by wider structures relating to curriculum and assessment. Evidence presented in the chapter has pointed to the way in which the current exam structures in Ireland tend to narrow student learning experiences to preparing for the test. Thus, broader curricular reform at the national level has the potential to profoundly reshape teaching and learning at the school level.

There is robust research which shows that rigid forms of ability grouping (streaming) have a significant and large negative impact on student achievement for those allocated to lower stream classes without any corresponding gains for those allocated to higher stream classes. Moving away from streaming will, therefore, enhance average student achievement and play a part in reducing the social inequality in educational outcomes resulting from the disaffection found among working-class boys in lower stream classes. There are challenges, however, in catering to the heterogeneous needs of students within a class, with a significant proportion of second-level students currently reporting difficulties with the pace of instruction. Investment in continuous professional development for teachers to support effective differentiation is, therefore, likely to significantly enhance student achievement.

There is robust evidence too that the nature of the school climate, that is, day-to-day interactions between teachers and students, significantly influences a range of student outcomes, including early school leaving, academic achievement, academic self-image, stress levels, and intended post-school pathways. Furthermore, students see care and respect on the part of teachers as key to effective teaching and learning in the classroom. The school disciplinary policy is an important lever for school climate; Irish research (in keeping with evidence from other countries) indicates that punitive measures can actually fuel a cycle of misbehaviour and disengagement while international research points to the value of positive behaviour policies in bringing about a climate of respect. It is vital that the creation of a positive climate be seen as a central component of school development planning. Again, investment in continuous professional development for principals and teachers is likely to facilitate change; initial teacher education should also emphasise school and classroom climate as many new teachers may not realise the impact they actually have on their students.

The junior cycle reform being introduced from 2014 will represent a very significant shift in educational policy and practice. It promises, inter alia, an emphasis on the kinds of active teaching and learning methods which second-level students find engaging and much more flexibility at the school level to engage in course design. The success of the reform will ultimately depend on the extent to which principals and teachers are supported in acquiring the skills to develop their practice in this way. Its impact on the skills and competencies young people acquire will also depend on the degree to which similar changes are brought about within senior cycle education.

REFERENCES

Aaronson, D., Barrow, L., Sander, W. (2007). 'Teachers and Student Achievement in the Chicago Public High Schools', *Journal of Labor Economics*, 25, 95–135.

Alexander, R.J. (2008). *Education for All, the Quality Imperative and the Problem of Pedagogy*. London: Institute of Education.

Alexander, R.J. (2010). '"World class schools" – noble aspiration or globalised hokum?', *Compare*, 40, 801–817.

Applebee, A.N., Langer, J.A., Nystrand, M. and Gamoran, A. (2003). 'Discussion-Based Approaches to Developing Understanding: Classroom Instruction and Student Performance in Middle and High School English', *American Educational Research Journal*, 40, 685–730.

Ball, S.J., Maguire, M. and Braun, A. (2012). *How Schools do Policy: Policy Enactments in Secondary Schools*. London: Routledge.

Baumert, J., Kunter, M., Blum, W. *et al.*, (2010). 'Teachers' Mathematical Knowledge, Cognitive Activation in the Classroom, and Student Progress', *American Educational Research Journal*, 47, 133–180.

Blomberg, N. (2004). *Effective Discipline for Misbehavior: In School vs. Out of School Suspension*. Philadelphia: Villanova University.

Bradshaw, C. P., Mitchell, M.M. and Leaf, P.J. (2009). 'Examining the Effects of School-wide Positive Behavioral Interventions and Supports on Student Outcomes: Results from a Randomized Controlled Effectiveness Trial in Elementary Schools', *Journal of Positive Behavior Interventions*. Available at http://pbi.sagepub.com/cgi/content/abstract/1098300709334798v1.

Brookover, W., Beady, C., Flood, P., Schweitzer, J. Wisenbaker, J. (1979). *School Social Systems and Student Achievement: Schools Can Make a Difference*. New York: Praeger.

Byrne, D. and Smyth, E. (2010). *No Way Back? The Dynamics of Early School Leaving*, Dublin: Liffey Press/ESRI.

Camburn, E. and Han, S.W. (2008). *What Do We Know About Instruction From Large-Scale National Surveys?* Wisconsin: WCER Working Paper No. 2008–1.

Cosgrove, J., Perkins, R., Moran, G., Shiel, G. (2011). *Digital Reading Literacy in the OECD Programme for International Student Assessment (PISA 2009): Summary of Results for Ireland*. Dublin: Educational Research Centre.

Cosgrove, J., Shiel, G., Archer, P. and Perkins, R. (2010). *Comparisons of Performance in Ireland PISA 2000 to PISA 2009: A Preliminary Report to the Department of Education and Skills*. Dublin: Educational Research Centre.

Creemers, B.P.M. and Kyriakides, L. (2008). *The Dynamics of Educational Effectiveness*. London: Routledge.

Crosnoe, R., Johnson, M. and Elder, G. (2004). 'Intergenerational Bonding in School: The Behavioral and Contextual Correlates of Student-Teacher Relationships', *Sociology of Education*, 77, 60–81.

Day, C., Sammons, P., Stobart, G., Kington, A. and Gu, Q. (2007). *Teachers Matter: Connecting Work, Lives and Effectiveness*. Milton Keynes: Open University Press.

Dearden, L., Micklewright, J., Vignoles, A. (2011). 'The Effectiveness of English Secondary Schools for Pupils of Different Ability Levels', *Fiscal Studies*, 32, 225–244.

Department of Education and Skills (2007). *Looking at English: Teaching and Learning English in Post-primary Schools*. Dublin: Department of Education and Skills.

Department of Education and Skills (2008). *Looking at Science: Teaching and Learning in Post-primary Schools*. Dublin: Department of Education and Skills.

Department of Education and Skills (2011). *Literacy and Numeracy for Learning and Life*. Dublin: Department of Education and Skills.

EPPI (2005). *A Systematic Review of What Pupils, Aged 11–16, Believe Impacts on Their Motivation to Learn in the Classroom*. London: EPPI Centre, University of London.

Fenning, P.A. and Bohanon, H. (2006). 'Schoolwide discipline policies: An analysis of discipline codes of conduct' in C.M. Evertson and C.S. Weinstein (eds.), *Handbook of Classroom Management: Research, Practice, and Contemporary Issues* (pp. 1021–1040). Mahwah, NJ: Erlbaum.

Galton, M., Hargreaves, L. and Pell, T. (2009). 'Group Work and Whole-class Teaching with 11- to 14-year-olds Compared', *Cambridge Journal of Education*, 39, pp. 119–140.

Gamoran, A. and Mare, R.D. (1989). 'Secondary School Tracking and Educational Inequality: Compensation, Reinforcement, or Neutrality?', *American Journal of Sociology*, 94, 1146–1183.

Gamoran, A., Nystrand, M., Berends, M., LePore, P.C. (1995). 'An Organizational Analysis of the Effects of Ability Grouping', *American Educational Research Journal*, 32, 687–715.

Gilleece, L., Shiel, G., Perkins, R. and Proctor, M. (2009). *Teaching and Learning International Survey (2008) National Report for Ireland*. Dublin: Educational Research Centre.

Goldstein, H. (2004). 'International Comparisons of Student Attainment: Some Issues Arising from the PISA Study', *Assessment in Education: Principles, Policy & Practice*, 11, 319–330.

Goldstein, H., Rasbash, J., Yang, M., Woodhouse, G., Pan, H., Nuttall, D. and Thomas, S. (1993). 'A Multilevel Analysis of School Examination Results', *Oxford Review of Education*, 19, 425–433.

Gorard, S. and See, B.H. (2011). 'How Can We Enhance Enjoyment of Secondary School? The Student View', *British Educational Research Journal*, 37, 671–690.

Hallinan, M.T. (2008). 'Teacher Influences on Students' Attachment to School', *Sociology of Education*, 81, 271–283.

Hannan, D.F., Smyth, E., McCullagh, J., O'Leary, R. and McMahon, D. (1996). *Coeducation and Gender Equality. Exam Performance, Stress and Personal Development*. Dublin: Oak Tree Press/ESRI.

Hansell, S. and Karweit, N. (1983). 'Curricular Placement, Friendship Networks and Status Attainment' in J.L. Epstein and N. Karweit (eds.), *Friends in School, Patterns of Selection and Influence*. New York: Academic Press.

Hargreaves, D.H. (1967). *Social Relations in a Secondary School*. London: Routledge.

James, M. and Pollard, A. (2010). 'Learning and Teaching in Primary Schools: Insights from TLRP' in R. Alexander (ed.), *The Cambridge Primary Review Research Surveys*. London: Routledge.

Jennings, P. and Greenberg, M. (2009). 'The Prosocial Classroom: Teacher Social and Emotional Competence in Relation to Student and Classroom Outcomes', *Review of Educational Research*, 79, 491–525.

Kamps, D.M., Greenwood, C. Arreaga-Mayer, C., et al. (2008). *The Efficacy of Class-Wide Peer Tutoring in Middle Schools*. Virginia: West Virginia University Press.

Lacey, C. (1970) *Hightown Grammar*. Manchester: Manchester University Press.

Levin, H.M. (2009). 'The Economic Payoff to Investing in Educational Justice', *Educational Researcher*, 38, 5–20.

Lingard, B. (2010). 'Policy Borrowing, Policy Learning: Testing Times in Australian Schooling', *Critical Studies in Education*, 51, 129–147.

Lumby, J. (2011). 'Enjoyment and Learning', *British Educational Research Journal*, 37, 247–264.

Luyten, H. (1994). 'Stability of School Effects in Dutch Secondary Education', *International Journal of Educational Research*, 21, 197–216.

Lynch, K. and Lodge, A. (2002). *Equality and Power in Schools*. London: Routledge/Falmer.

Lyons, M., Lynch, K., Close, S., Sheerin, E. and Boland, P. (2003). *Inside Classrooms: The Teaching and Learning of Mathematics in Social Context*, Dublin: Institute of Public Administration.

McCoy, S. and Banks, J. (2012) 'Simply Academic? Why Children with Special Educational Needs Don't Like School', *European Journal of Special Needs Education*, 27, 1: 81–97.

McCoy, S., Byrne, D., O'Connell, P.J., Kelly, E. and Doherty, C. (2010) *Hidden Disadvantage? A Study on the Low Participation in Higher Education by the Non-Manual Group*. Dublin: Higher Education Authority.

McCoy, S. Smyth, E. and Banks, J. (2012) *The Primary Classroom: Insights from Growing Up in Ireland Study*. Dublin: ESRI/NCCA.

Martin, A.J. and Dowson, M. (2009). 'Interpersonal Relationships, Motivation, Engagement, and Achievement: Yields for Theory, Current Issues, and Educational Practice', *Review of Educational Research*, 79, 327–365.

Minner, D.D., Levy, A.J. and Century, J. (2010). 'Inquiry-based Science Instruction – What is it and Does it Matter? Results from a Research Synthesis Years 1984 to 2002', *Journal of Research in Science Teaching*, 47, 474–496.

Mortimore, P. (2009). *Alternative Models for Analysing and Representing Countries' Performance in PISA*. Brussels: Education International Research Institute.

Mortimore, P., Sammons, P., Stoll, L., Lewis, D. and Ecob, R. (1988). *School Matters: The Junior Years*. London: Open Books.

Muijs, D. and Reynolds, D. (2011). *Effective Teaching: Evidence and Practice*. London: Sage Publications.

National Council for Curriculum and Assessment (2011). *Towards a Framework for Junior Cycle*. Dublin: NCCA.

Nye, B., Konstantopoulos, S. and Hedges, L.V. (2004). 'How Large are Teacher Effects?', *Educational Evaluation and Policy Analysis*, 26, 237–257.

Nystrand, M. and Gamoran, A. (1991). 'Instructional Discourse Student Engagement, and Literature Achievement', *Research in the Teaching of English,*. 25, 261–290.
Oakes, J. (1990). *Multiplying Inequalities: The Effects of Race, Social Class, and Tracking on Opportunities to Learn Mathematics and Science*. Santa Monica: Rand.
Oakes, J. (2005). *Keeping Track: How Schools Structure Inequality, Second Edition*. New Haven: Yale University Press.
OECD (2010). *PISA 2009 Results: What Students Know and Can Do*. Paris: OECD.
Opdenakker, M.C., Maulana, R. and den Brok, P. (2012). 'Teacher–student Interpersonal Relationships and Academic Motivation Within One School Year: Developmental Changes and Linkage', *School Effectiveness and School Improvement*, 23, 95–119.
Opdenakker, M.C. and Van Damme, J. (2000). 'Effects of Schools, Teaching Staff and Classes on Achievement and Well-Being in Secondary Education: Similarities and Differences Between School Outcomes', *School Effectiveness and School Improvement*, 11, 165–196.
Osher, D., Bear, G.G., Sprague J.R. and Doyle W. (2010). 'How Can We Improve School Discipline?', *Educational Researcher*, 39, 48–58.
Osler, A. (2010). *Students' Perspectives on Schooling*. Milton Keynes: Open University Press.
Palardy, G.J., and Rumberger, R.W. (2008). 'Teacher Effectiveness in First Grade: The Importance of Background Qualifications, Attitudes, and Instructional Practices for Student Learning', *Educational Evaluation and Policy Analysis*, 30, 111–140.
Porter, T. and Webb, M. (2008). 'The Role of the OECD in the Orchestration of Global Knowledge Networks' in R. Mahon and S. McBride (eds.), *The OECD and Transnational Governance*. Vancouver: University of British Columbia Press.
Raffe, D. (2011). *Policy Borrowing or Policy Learning? How (Not) to Improve Education Systems*. Edinburgh: CES Briefing.
Rosenshine, B., Meister, C. and Chapman, S. (1996). Teaching Students to Generate Questions: A Review of the Intervention Studies. *Review of Educational Research*, 66, 181–221.
Rudduck, J. and McIntyre, D. (2007). *Improving Learning Through Consulting Pupils*. London: Routledge.
Rutter, M., Maughan, B., Mortimore P. and Ouston, J. (1979). *Fifteen Thousand Hours: Secondary Schools and Their Effects on Children*. London: Open Books.
Sammons, P., Thomas, S. and Mortimore, P. (1997). *Forging Links: Effective Schools and Effective Departments*. London: Paul Chapman.
Scheerens, J. and Bosker, R.J. (1997). *The Foundations of Educational Effectiveness*. Oxford: Pergamon Press.
Seidel, T. and Shavelson, R.J. (2007). 'Teaching Effectiveness Research in the Past Decade: The Role of Theory and Research Design in Disentangling Meta-Analysis Results', *Review of Educational Research*, 77, 454–499.

SEC (2011). State Examinations Statistics (www.examinations.ie).

Shiel, G., Moran, G., Cosgrove, J. and Perkins, R. (2010). *A Summary of the Performance of Students in Ireland on the PISA 2009 Test of Mathematical Literacy and a Comparison with Performance in 2003*. Dublin: Educational Research Centre.

Skiba, R. and Peterson, R. (2000). 'The Dark Side of Zero Tolerance: Can Punishment Lead to Safe Schools?', *Phi Delta Kappan*, 80, 372–382.

Smith, D.J. and Tomlinson, S. (1989). *The School Effect: A Study of Multi-Racial Comprehensives*. London: Policy Studies Institute.

Smyth, E. (1999). *Do Schools Differ?* Dublin: Oak Tree Press/ESRI.

Smyth, E., Banks, J. and Calvert, E. (2011). *From Leaving Certificate to Leaving School*. Dublin: Liffey Press/ESRI.

Smyth, E., Dunne, A., Darmody, M. and McCoy, S. (2007). *Gearing Up for the Exam? The Experiences of Junior Certificate Students*. Dublin: Liffey Press/Economic and Social Research Institute.

Smyth, E. and Hannan, C. (2002). *Who Chooses Science?* Dublin: Oak Tree Press/Economic and Social Research Institute.

Smyth, E. and McCoy, S. (2009). *Investing in Education: Combating Educational Disadvantage*, Dublin: Economic and Social Research Institute/Barnardos.

Smyth, E., McCoy, S. and Darmody, M. (2004). *Moving Up: The Experiences of First Year Students in Post-primary Education*. Dublin: Liffey Press/Economic and Social Research Institute.

Teddlie, C. and Reynolds, D. (2000). *The International Handbook of School Effectiveness Research*. London: Falmer.

Teddlie, C. and Stringfield, S. (1993). *Schools Make a Difference: Lessons Learned from a 10–year Study of School Effects*. New York: Teachers College Press.

Thomas, S., Sammons, P. Mortimore, P. and Smees, R. (1997). 'Differential Secondary School Effectiveness: Comparing the Performance of Different Pupil Groups', *British Educational Research Journal*, 23, 451–469.

Topping, K.J. (2005). 'Trends in Peer Learning', *Educational Psychologist*, 25 (6), 631–645.

Veenman, S., Denessen, E., van den Akker, A. and van der Rijt, J. (2005). 'Effects of a Cooperative Learning Program on the Elaborations of Students During Help Seeking and Help Giving', *American Educational Research Journal*, 42, 115–151.

Wayne, A.J. and Youngs, P. (2003). 'Teacher Characteristics and Student Achievement Gains: A Review', *Review of Educational Research*, 73, 89–122.

Webb, M. and Mastergeorge, A.M. (2003). 'The Development of Students' Helping Behaviour and Learning in Peer-Directed Small Groups', *Cognition and Instruction*, 21, 361–428.

Yair, G. (2000). 'Educational battlefields in America: the tug of war over students' engagement with instruction', *Sociology of Education*, 73, 247–269.

CHAPTER 6

Boosting Innovation and Productivity in Enterprises: What Matters? What Works?

Frances Ruane, Iulia Siedschlag

The focus of this chapter is on the insights from research on innovation and productivity for policy design in relation to Ireland's enterprise sector. In terms of the policy landscape (Figure 1.1), enterprise policy is part of a mature policy system which has its origins in the 1950s and which is evolving continuously to encapsulate appropriate responses to the more rapid pace of technological change and globalisation in the past two decades. The chapter discusses evidence that is relevant to innovation in the indigenous enterprise sector. While over the past thirty years Irish economic growth has been dominated by the contribution to exports by multinationals in the manufacturing and internationally traded services sectors, the competitiveness of the indigenous sector is essential for sustainable employment growth and economic recovery. The key to competitiveness lies in enhancing the innovative capacity of Irish-owned companies and thereby increasing their productivity so that they can grow their global market exports.

In this chapter, we explore what we can learn from the international evidence about what drives investment in innovation, innovation outputs and how that translates into productivity growth. This involves careful conceptualisation of the innovative process and an analysis centred on the enterprise itself, since this is where innovation takes place. We take into account Ireland's being a small open economy and this is reflected in the emphasis on enterprise internationalisation and innovation.

While there are many case studies of innovation, our approach is to look at evidence from the international empirical research literature based on large-scale enterprise innovation surveys carried out by countries in the European Union. We select those studies that we see as being a priori relevant to Ireland. These studies allow us to examine what makes enterprises more likely to invest in innovation and to innovate and, if they innovate, what makes them likely to translate this successful innovation into increased productivity (which is associated with more jobs and more tax revenues). We concentrate on studies that are based on the econometric model developed by Crépon, Duguet and Mairesse (1998), which provides a structured approach to analysing the innovation process. We also estimate this model using data for the Irish indigenous sector, since that is the focus of our analysis.

We set out what this evidence shows and what it suggests for policy intervention to enable and foster innovation. The findings point to considerable complexity and to very significant enterprise heterogeneity. This indicates that a policy-mix approach that allows interventions to be fine tuned is needed. We find that key elements of such a policy mix are in place in Irish innovation policy.

We complete our analysis by noting the challenges that current policy should address and by noting the potential for policy insights from future research based on analyses using longer longitudinal data sets for EU countries and for Ireland, and the potential for data linking which would allow yet further analysis of the innovation-exporting relationship.

BACKGROUND

In the context of intensified global competition over the past two decades, there has been a growing emphasis on innovation in all developed countries.[57] For OECD economies, innovation at enterprise level is widely acknowledged as the key driver of sustainable long-term economic growth (OECD, 2006; OECD, 2009a) through new product/service creation, process development and organisational change. Innovation results from enterprises' own innovation efforts and also from their collaborations with other entities on the supply chain (suppliers and consumers) and with knowledge institutions (higher education and research). Furthermore, innovation is not limited by national boundaries or systems, as today's knowledge networks are both global and local.

The importance of having framework conditions in place that are conducive to innovation within countries and within regions (e.g., European Union) is recognised in the policy environment and is strongly supported by empirical evidence (see Box, 2009).[58] The key framework conditions include: a stable macroeconomic policy environment; international openness to flows of goods, services, capital and knowledge (embodied in both technologies and people); appropriate levels of competition and regulation; a developed and well functioning

---

57 The increased emphasis on innovation in the EU dates back to the Lisbon Strategy in 2000, as the lag between innovation rates in the EU compared with the US and Japan were noted. This emphasis was reinforced at the European Council meeting in Spring 2006 when investment in knowledge and innovation was identified as one of the four priority areas in the revised strategy.

58 The importance of framework conditions is also emphasised in Porter (1990), who looks at innovation from an enterprise-strategy perspective, drawing on case studies to explore innovation processes. Our approach complements Porter's.

financial system; a coherent intellectual property system; flexible labour markets; a well-performing education system and a high-performing infrastructure.

Policies that improve the framework conditions in a particular economy will also support innovation, and consequently other policy efforts to increase innovation will be undermined by ignoring the impact of these framework conditions. While Ireland has committed to improving the framework conditions facing the enterprise sector, it has still some considerable distance to travel (OECD, 2009b; OECD, 2011). Furthermore, the current international crisis is particularly damaging because of the global uncertainty it has generated, and the consequential problems for financing enterprise innovation caused by the difficulties in financial institutions in Ireland.

Market and systemic failures in the innovation process can result in the levels of investment in innovation within enterprises and industries being less than socially optimal (OECD, 2006). The key market failures identified in the literature are well known. Positive externalities, due to knowledge spillovers, mean that the private returns to an enterprise investing in innovation are less than the total returns to society from that investment. These knowledge externalities, which reflect the public good aspect of knowledge generation, also underpin government funding of basic research in most countries. Information asymmetry regarding the risks associated with investments in innovation makes it difficult for enterprises to raise funds for innovations that have a high research component, and hence market processes generate less investment in innovation than is optimal. This problem is exacerbated in the case of small and medium-size enterprises (SMEs) which cannot attract the funds needed to support their investments and hence cannot achieve the economies of scale needed for growth.

In addition, there are several systemic failures that can undermine the development of an innovation eco-system and thereby reduce the level of innovation below its optimal level and/or undermine its potential efficiency. These arise from several sources: successful innovation often requires the cooperation of market and non-market institutions (e.g., enterprises and universities) which have incompatible incentives; knowledge flows can be restricted by suboptimal networking and personnel mobility; enterprises may not have the capability to absorb knowledge that could enhance their capacity to innovate and remain competitive; SMEs may not have the resources to allow them to benefit from international developments in science, technology and innovation, etc.

Throughout the OECD economies, these market and systemic failures are seen as providing the rationale for governments to develop policies designed to support innovation and higher productivity levels within enterprises. However, government intervention is not automatically justified by such failures as the costs of the intervention, both direct and indirect, may be high relative to the benefits. This is more likely to be the case where interventions are complex and administratively burdensome, giving rise to the risk of replacing market or systemic failures with government failures (OECD, 2006). So whether such policies in any particular country will be effective, i.e., generate net benefits relative to their costs, depends on their being appropriately targeted to address the specific failures that are present. To succeed, these policies must recognise how enterprise characteristics and performance vary between and within industries and understand the determinants of innovation and productivity at enterprise level.

Ireland only began to focus on innovation in the early 1990s (Mjøset, 1992) and from the late 1990s onwards there has been significant support given to the development of the country's scientific, technological and innovative capacity (ICSTI, 1999; Forfás, 2004). Direct support has been given for building research and innovation capacity within the enterprise sector, and the funding challenges faced by SMEs have led to considerable investment by the State in venture capital funds. Furthermore, a series of tax changes have enhanced the attractiveness of Ireland as a base for enterprise-led R&D and innovation.

The competition for internationally mobile innovation intensive projects has also influenced the government's emphasis on building research excellence in the last decade, where earlier and more limited support had simply focused on the relevance of research in universities to enterprise interests. Consequently, there has been a significant up-scaling of the research capacity and science and technology infrastructure in Ireland's universities, colleges and other public research organisations.

Notwithstanding the pressure on public expenditure, the 2007–2011 government signalled its intention to continue to support research as part of its economic strategy (Department of An Taoiseach, 2008) and this emphasis is evident in the *Programme for Government* of the 2011–2016 government. This support is set to continue both at enterprise level and in the public research system, with the focus increasingly on investment in those areas that are most likely to yield measurable returns in the medium term (Forfás, 2011).

The tight fiscal constraints and the urgency of achieving successful outcomes require that government policies aimed at enhancing enterprise innovation and raising productivity need to be very effective. This means understanding the relationship at enterprise level between productivity and innovative sales and between investment in innovation and innovation performance. Specifically, we draw on the new international literature based on enterprise level data to explore:

- Does innovation contribute to higher productivity?
- Which types of enterprises invest in innovation?
- Which enterprises have higher innovation expenditure per employee?
- Which types of enterprises are more likely to translate innovation inputs into innovation outputs (innovate successfully)?

We then look at what these findings imply for policy in relation to indigenous enterprises, whether the current policy mix is appropriate, and how it might develop to be more effective. While crucially important, the evaluation of the impacts of R&D and innovation policies is beyond the objectives of this chapter.

The next section of the chapter sets out the conceptual framework underpinning the analysis, while the following section summarises the data sets used. We then discuss the findings of the international literature in relation to the four questions before exploring these questions specifically in the context of the indigenous sector. Finally, we present some brief conclusions.

ANALYTICAL FRAMEWORK

To answer the questions this chapter addresses, we propose a conceptual framework to contextualise the large existing empirical evidence on the complex relationships between innovation inputs, innovation outcomes and productivity. This framework derives from four literature strands which are relevant to the four questions this chapter addresses.

Size, market power and innovation

The importance of technological change and innovation for sustainable long-term economic growth was first highlighted by Schumpeter (1942). He introduced the concept of 'creative destruction' to describe innovative entry and argued that large enterprises operating in concentrated markets are more likely to innovate. Following on from Schumpeter's contribution, the literature on *industrial organisation* has focused on the relationships between enterprise size, market structure and innovation (measured by R&D expenditures) and neglected other determinants of technological change and innovation such as knowledge spillovers and innovation capability (Cohen, 2010).

A positive relationship between enterprise size and innovation is underlined by factors such as: i) economies of scale in R&D; ii) economies of scope in R&D; iii) diversification of risks; and iv) availability and stability of external and internal funds.[59] However, as enterprises grow, there may be efficiency losses associated with performing R&D, in particular from losing managerial control and diminished ability of innovators to appropriate the benefits from their innovative efforts (Cohen and Levin, 1989). Schumpeter (1942) also highlighted the role of market power in enabling and fostering innovation. Thus, while the rents from *ex ante* market power provide enterprises with internal financial resources for innovative activities, anticipated *ex post* market power incentivises enterprises to invest in R&D.

Empirical evidence on the relationship between market concentration and innovation is mixed with most recent studies suggesting that this relationship is non-linear and bi-directional as market structure itself is influenced by innovation (Cohen and Levin, 1989; Geroski and Pomroy, 1990; Sutton, 1996, 1998), a

---

59 For a detailed discussion of these underlying factors see Cohen and Levin (1989), Symeonidis (1996), and Ahn (2002).

factor often ignored in earlier studies. More recent studies have considered additional enterprise and industry characteristics as additional variables to explain innovation activity.[60]

R&D investment, knowledge spillovers and productivity growth

The *endogeneous growth* literature (Grossman and Helpman 1990; Romer, 1990; Aghion and Howitt, 1992; Griliches, 1996) has established that technological change is endogenous and that private R&D investment and knowledge spillovers affect productivity growth. The point of departure of the theories of endogenous growth are two related characteristics of knowledge: i) knowledge is non-rival (the marginal costs for an additional technology user are negligible); ii) knowledge is partially non-excludable due to imperfect intellectual property protection which implies that the return to investments in knowledge/innovation is partly private and partly public (social).

Existing empirical evidence at enterprise and industry levels suggests that social rates of return to R&D/innovation investment are higher than the private rates of return (Griliches, 1992). Jones and Williams (1998) relate the theoretical models of new growth theory to empirical results in the productivity literature and show that these results can be taken as lower bounds for the social rate of return to R&D.

A key policy message of this literature is that the presence of knowledge spillovers and other market failures in the innovation process provides the rationale for government intervention to incentivise investment in innovation.

Innovation systems

The main contribution of the literature on *national innovation systems* (Freeman, 1987; Lundvall, 1992; Nelson, 1993) is towards understanding innovation at the national macro level as being the result of interactions between enterprises and institutions at the micro levels which are governed by both market forces and non-market institutions.[61] The efficiency of the national innovation system depends on the performance of individual actors and the institutions that govern their interactions. The main policy message of this literature is the central role the government can play as a co-ordinating agent to correct systemic failures. One policy limitation of this national innovation system concept is its failure to take account of the growing internationalisation of R&D and innovation and consequently of the need to consider the international context in which innovation takes place.

---

60 For recent review of this literature see Cohen (2010).
61 A recent survey of the national innovation systems literature is provided by Soete *et al.* (2010).

International trade with heterogeneous firms

The most recent international trade theory, known as the *new-new trade theory* (Melitz, 2003; Helpman *et al.*, 2004) has established that enterprises with international linkages are more productive than enterprises serving only the domestic markets. Existing empirical evidence indicates that enterprises with international linkages (exporters, importers and multinational firms) differ systematically from enterprises that serve only the national market.[62] Specifically, they are larger, generate higher value added, employ more capital per worker, have higher skilled workers and have higher productivity.

While this literature has assumed that enterprise productivity is exogenous, more recent theoretical contributions allow for the possibility of enterprises increasing their productivity through innovation activities (Yeaple, 2005; Bustos, 2011). A positive correlation between exporting and innovation activity has been found in several studies (Wagner, 1996; Roper and Love, 2002). In addition, a number of recent empirical studies have found that exporters are more likely to introduce product innovation (Liu and Buck, 2007; Salomon and Shaver, 2005; Bratti and Felice, 2012). Furthermore, additional recent empirical evidence suggests that foreign-owned enterprises and exporters are more likely to innovate (Criscuolo *et al.*, 2010; Siedschlag *et al.*, 2010).

In summary, this analytical framework allows us to think of innovation as a complex and non-linear process which is the result of many interactions between enterprises and institutions including government. Innovation takes place in the context of increased internationalisation of economic activities including a growing internationalisation of R&D, innovation and production activities. Furthermore, this analytical framework highlights the rationale for government intervention to foster innovation and productivity in enterprises. However, the cost of government intervention also needs to be taken into account when policy choices about allocation of scarce public financial resources are made.

MEASUREMENT AND DATA

Until the beginning of the 1990s, innovation was measured and analysed using two measures, namely, R&D expenditures and patents. However, it became apparent in the late 1980s that both R&D expenditures and patents have major shortcomings as measures of innovation. R&D expenditure measures just one input, albeit a major one, into innovation. Patents cover only a subset of invention successes and the extent of patent use varies widely across industries. In addition, most patents describe inventions that are of little value (Hall, 2011). In effect, both measures are more suited to measuring technological innovation and innovation in manufacturing.

---

62 Recent micro-econometric evidence has been surveyed by Helpman (2006), Greenway and Kneller (2007) and Wagner (2007).

With the growing share of services in the economic activity of developed economies, innovation in services and, more broadly, non-technological innovation are recognised as being increasingly important. Innovation in services is less directly dependent on R&D expenditures and, given the intangible nature of services, less likely to be patented. To capture these new economic developments and to overcome the shortcomings of the traditional measures of innovation, qualitative and quantitative data on innovation at enterprise level have been collected through innovation surveys. In Europe, these innovation surveys are known as the Community Innovation Surveys (CIS).[63]

The concept of innovation has been developed over the past two decades and different types of innovation are set out formally in the Oslo Manual (OECD, 2005, p. 46). The Manual defines innovation as:

the implementation of a new or significantly improved product (good or service), or process, a new marketing method, or a new organisational method in business practices, workplace organisation or external relations.

This definition distinguishes four types of innovation: product innovation, process innovation, organisational innovation, and marketing innovation. Using this conceptual framework, an innovative enterprise is defined as an enterprise that had successfully introduced one of these types of innovations in the period under consideration. Alternatively, using an input-based definition, an innovative enterprise is defined as one that engages in investment in R&D/innovation.

The Oslo Manual has also broadened the definition of innovation expenditures beyond R&D expenditure to include expenditure on training, purchasing of equipment, designs and licences.

EMPIRICAL EVIDENCE ON INNOVATION AND PRODUCTIVITY IN ENTERPRISES

A growing empirical literature has explored the links between innovation inputs (R&D/ innovation expenditure), innovation outcomes and output/productivity. This strand of research is based on an econometric framework developed by Crépon, Duguet and Mairesse (1998), hereafter referred to as the CDM model, and most studies use data from the Community Innovation Survey (CIS).

The CDM model estimates three sets of relationships. The first set consists of two equations relating to the innovation investment phase, viz., the propensity of enterprises to invest in innovation and the innovation expenditure intensity conditional on innovation investment. The second set relates the various types of innovation outcomes to innovation expenditure intensity (innovation

---

63 Between 1990 and 2005, the CIS were conducted every 4 years. Since 2007, CIS are conducted every 2 years and enterprises are asked questions in relation to their innovation activities over the previous 3–year period.

expenditure per employee) and other enterprise and industry characteristics. The third set links output/productivity to innovation outcomes and other enterprise characteristics.

There are two econometric issues associated with estimating the CDM model. First, selection bias might arise due to the fact that a number of questions in surveys are only asked of innovative enterprises and this set of enterprises might be non-random. Second, innovation inputs, innovation output and productivity might be simultaneously determined. These econometric issues are corrected for using appropriate estimation techniques.[64] The multivariate econometric analyses reviewed here allow one to distinguish the influence of each relevant factor on the key outcome variables over and above the influence of other factors (covariates). Hence this type of evidence is more robust than analyses based on univariate correlations. The CDM econometric model and a summary of empirical evidence from selected country studies are discussed in Ruane and Siedschlag (2011). The selected studies estimate variants of the CDM model and use CIS data from developed European countries. The countries covered in this summary include large ones (France, Germany, United Kingdom, Spain, Italy) and small countries (Sweden, Finland, Norway, Switzerland, Denmark, the Netherlands, Belgium, Austria, Luxembourg) as well as Ireland.[65]

While the selected studies address the same issues, they differ in several respects such as: the types of innovation that are considered, the explanatory variables used, and the econometric methods used to account for selectivity and simultaneity. Given the fact that the Community Innovation Surveys do not observe the same firms over time, most of the reviewed studies use cross-sectional data which implies that the estimates can be interpreted as correlations and not necessarily as causal relationships. In contrast, Polder *et al.* (2010) and Siedschlag *et al.* (2010) linked two or three CIS waves to analyse the connections between innovation and productivity at enterprise level over time. The added value of these two studies is that they account for the heterogeneity of unobserved firm characteristics and dynamic responses of innovation and productivity outcomes to lagged explanatory variables. These additional empirical controls lead to more robust evidence. Because of data availability, most studies focus on the intensity of *product innovation*, i.e., innovative sales share; innovative sales per employee; and patents per employee. However, some recent studies have considered additional types of innovation – process, organisational and marketing innovation.

---

64 For details on these estimation techniques, see Siedschlag *et al.* (2010) and Ruane and Siedschlag (2011).

65 The CDM model has also been estimated for developing countries, such as Chile (Benavente 2006), Argentina, Brazil, Mexico (Raffo *et al.*, 2008; Chudnovsky *et al.*, 2006) and China (Jefferson *et al.*, 2006). Because these countries have different underlying structural characteristics in comparison to developed countries, we do not review them here. The evidence suggests that enterprises in developing countries tend to have weaker interactions with their national innovation systems.

Specifically, these latter studies look at innovation output in terms of the probability that the enterprises introduce product, process, or organisational innovations.

Given that productivity gains are often related to efficiency improvements due to process and organisational innovations, we report the results of both of these where available. The analyses in most cases cover manufacturing enterprises only but we also report the small number of studies that cover services (for example Polder *et al.*, 2010 for the Netherlands; Siedschlag *et al.*, 2010 for Ireland; Mairesse and Robin, 2009 for France; Lööf and Heshmati, 2006, for Sweden).

We consider the empirical findings in relation to each question in turn.

What is the innovation productivity link?

The existing empirical evidence indicates that enterprises with product innovation do have higher productivity levels (measured as sales per employee, value added per employee). There is also evidence, albeit more limited, of a positive link between process innovation and productivity levels. Some further studies, (for example, Polder *et al.*, 2010, for the Netherlands; Siedschlag *et al.*, 2010 for Ireland) uncover a positive link between organisational innovation and productivity that is stronger than that for product and process innovation.[66] The estimated productivity elasticity with respect to the product innovation intensity (innovative sales share) in manufacturing ranges from 0.07 (France) to 0.26 (Norway), while the corresponding elasticity for services is 0.09 (Sweden). The corresponding estimates for Ireland (0.09/0.10) imply that on average, a doubling of the share of sales due to new products is associated with a labour productivity that is higher by 9 per cent in manufacturing and by 10 per cent in services. The productivity elasticity with respect to the probability of introducing new product innovation in manufacturing ranges from 0.05 (France) to 0.69 (Italy) while the corresponding elasticity for services is lower (0.17 for France). In Ireland, the productivity elasticities imply that being a product innovator is associated with labour productivity being 26 per cent higher in manufacturing and 61 per cent higher in services. Taken together, the evidence supports a strong emphasis on innovation as a key driver of productivity at enterprise level.

Which enterprises are more likely to invest in R&D/innovation?

The most robust result across the reviewed empirical evidence is that larger enterprises have a greater propensity to invest in R&D/innovation. Over and above size, enterprises operating in international markets (exporters) are more likely to invest in innovation. Other factors positively associated with the propensity of enterprises to invest in innovation include higher innovation

---

66 The role of organisational innovation has been less analysed due to unavailable data in earlier CIS and innovation surveys.

capability,[67] previous successful innovation, formal and strategic protection of intellectual property, larger market shares, more diversified activities, receiving public funding, and belonging to a business network.

The empirical evidence for Ireland (Siedschlag *et al.*, 2010) indicates that the propensity of enterprises to invest in innovation is positively linked to size, the internationalisation of enterprises (foreign ownership and exporting) and a higher innovation capability. The Irish results are in line with the international evidence. While other studies have not specifically modelled the role of foreign ownership, given the large share of foreign affiliates in the business R&D in Ireland (70 per cent in 2005, European Commission, 2008), this variable was included for Ireland to avoid biased estimates.

Which enterprises have higher innovation expenditure per employee?

While larger enterprises are more likely to invest in innovation, existing empirical evidence suggests that the innovation expenditure intensity (R&D/innovation expenditure per employee) either decreases with or is independent of enterprise size. Other factors found to be positively linked to the R&D/innovation effort intensity include larger market shares, more diversified activities, international competition (from exporting), engagement in co-operation for innovation activities, receiving public funding for innovation, formal and strategic protection of intellectual property, continuity of R&D investment, previous successful innovation, and higher innovation capability.

The evidence from Ireland indicates that, for a given probability of investing in innovation, smaller enterprises have higher innovation expenditures per employee. A similar result is found in other small countries such as Finland, Sweden and the Netherlands. Not surprisingly, innovation expenditure per employee is found to be positively correlated with foreign-ownership and higher innovation capability.

Which enterprises are more likely to innovate successfully?

Successful innovation implies that innovation inputs are translated into innovation outputs such as product, process or organisational innovation. In relation to enterprise size, the empirical evidence is mixed. While several studies find that larger enterprises are more likely to have successful innovations, particularly product innovation, other studies find that size is not significantly linked to innovation outcomes. Furthermore, while some studies find that higher R&D/innovation expenditure intensity appears positively linked to successful innovation, especially product innovation, other studies find that R&D/innovation

---

67 Innovation capability is measured as the productivity gap between enterprise productivity and the productivity of global leaders (top 10 per cent most productive enterprises) in the same industry.

expenditure does not translate into innovation output directly. This result is particularly sensitive to model specification and to the econometric methods used. Interactions with national innovation systems, as captured by co-operation in innovation activities with other agents, in particular suppliers and customers and research institutions (universities and R&D institutes), appear in most cases to contribute to successful innovation. Other factors with a positive influence on successful innovation include formal and/or strategic protection of intellectual property, greater ICT investment and greater ICT use (particularly in services).

The evidence for Ireland indicates that enterprises with international linkages are more likely to have product, process and organisational innovation as well as a higher intensity of product innovation (innovative sales share). While larger enterprises are more likely to be innovators, the innovative sales associated with product innovation are not significantly linked to enterprise size. With the exception of organisational innovation, enterprise level R&D/innovation expenditure intensity is not significantly linked to positive innovation outcomes when account is take of foreign linkages, enterprise size and interactions with the national innovation system.[68] A similar result is found for process and organisational innovation in the Netherlands (Polder *et al.*, 2010) and for product innovation intensity in Austria, Switzerland, Luxembourg (OECD, 2009c). This finding suggests that the relationship between R&D/innovation expenditure intensity and innovation outcomes is a complex one and that particular care is needed when drawing policy implications from the existing evidence. One possibility for this finding is that the relationship between innovation expenditure intensity and innovation outcome is a lagged one and hence, cannot be captured due to data limitations. Another possible explanation might be that service enterprises represent a larger number in the analysed sample in comparison to manufacturing enterprises and that innovation in services is less dependent on R&D/innovation expenditure. Further, the growing internationalisation of R&D and innovation might substitute for enterprises' own innovation efforts/inputs. Existing empirical evidence suggests that co-operation in innovation activities within the national innovation system has become increasingly important for enterprise innovation in Ireland (see Siedschlag *et al.*, 2010).

In summary, the international empirical evidence as well as evidence from Ireland suggests three key policy relevant findings:

- Innovation is positively linked to productivity, and this link appears to be robust to different data sets, model specifications, and econometric methods;
- The impact of innovation on productivity varies by innovation type and enterprise scale;

---

[68] OECD (2009c) and Doran and O'Leary (2011) using cross-section data, different CDM model specifications and different econometric methods find that product innovation intensity was higher in enterprises with higher R&D intensity.

- The relationships between innovation inputs, innovation outcomes and productivity are complex, non-linear and unlikely to be contemporaneous.

KEY POLICY MESSAGES FOR INDIGENOUS INNOVATION

While the international evidence reviewed above informs our understanding of how innovation is linked to productivity, its purpose is not to evaluate the relevant R&D and innovation policies. Nonetheless, it is possible to explore the key policy messages associated with these findings and we do this now for indigenous enterprises. We recognise that these enterprises account for the smaller share of investment in innovation[69] but we suggest Ireland urgently needs to raise the productivity of indigenous enterprises if it is to achieve sustainable economic renewal and employment growth. To put this policy objective into perspective, a few statistics calculated on the basis of the data provided by the Central Statistics Office (2012) are helpful. In 2010 Irish-owned enterprises accounted for 98 per cent of the total number of enterprises and 78 per cent of the total number of persons engaged in Ireland. However, they represented only 44 per cent of the total gross value added produced by all enterprises. Labour productivity (gross value added per person engaged) in Irish-owned enterprises was €39,328 compared to €171,387 in foreign-owned enterprises and €68,781 for all enterprises. In order to contextualise the international results discussed, we have estimated the CDM model for the indigenous sector only.[70] In this section, we review the four questions discussed above for the indigenous sector and draw out the policy messages in the context of the programmes currently being operated by Enterprise Ireland.[71]

What is the link between innovation and productivity at enterprise level?

The striking results for Irish-owned enterprises are (a) the strong link between organisational innovation and productivity; (b) that product innovation is only associated with higher productivity when combined with organisational innovation;[72] and (c) that the effect of process innovation is stronger when

---

69 In 2011 indigenous enterprises accounted for 29 per cent of business expenditure on R&D in Ireland. http://cso.ie/shorturl.aspx/143.
70 These results are reported in Ruane and Siedschlag (2011). The results of a similar analysis for foreign-owned enterprises are available on request.
71 The data used in the econometric analysis come from the CIS; all information related to current policies come from Enterprise Ireland.
72 It appears that product innovation intensity, measured as the share of sales from new or improved products, is negatively associated with enterprise productivity. The CIS data do not allow us to distinguish price and quantity effects of product innovation and so we could not explain what determines this relationship.

combined with organisational innovation.[73] Taken together, these results suggest that, among Irish indigenous enterprises, over the analysed period 2004–2008, higher productivity has been generated more by improvements in the efficiency of production than by the introduction of new and improved products.

The overall results in the previous section validate the government's commitment to supporting innovation at enterprise level. This commitment is reflected in the suite of programmes operated by Enterprise Ireland and the introduction of more generous tax credits for R&D expenditures in the past decade. However, this validation does not necessarily imply that the particular programmes being operated are the most cost effective means of supporting the link between investment in innovation and productivity. The international results in relation to enterprise-level heterogeneity support the adoption of a 'policy mix' approach to innovation in order to take account of scale, capability, exporting and cooperation with external bodies. Such an approach, as has been adopted by Enterprise Ireland, means that individual enterprises are likely to receive funding under several different programmes. This has implications for how data on enterprises are maintained, how project proposals are appraised, how agency effectiveness is measured and how programmes are evaluated.[74] While, as noted in the Background section, the evaluation of the impacts of such R&D and innovation policies is beyond the scope of this chapter, we highlight in the Conclusions section the need for developing appropriate evaluation methodologies to take account of the complexity of the innovation process and the mixture of interventions in place.

Which enterprises are more likely to invest in R&D/innovation?

One of the most striking results from the international evidence and linked back to Schumpeter (1942) is the strong impact of enterprise scale on the decision to invest in innovation. Put simply, smaller enterprises are less likely to invest in innovation than large enterprises. This result, confirmed by the evidence for the Irish indigenous sector, is unsurprising given that innovation activities, especially in relation to product innovation, are associated with risk and with financial requirements that are likely to be more challenging for smaller enterprises. The importance of scale suggests that policies that promote enterprise growth or reduce impediments to enterprise growth will enhance the probability of enterprises engaging in innovation. Indigenous enterprises that are exporters are also more likely to invest in R&D/innovation.[75]

---

73 This result contrasts strongly with the finding for foreign-owned enterprises, where product innovation is associated with higher productivity while the process innovation has no significant impact on productivity.

74 Martin (2009) notes the complications in relation to programme evaluation.

75 The empirical evidence is not sufficient to determine unambiguously the direction of causation between innovation and exporting but it does suggest that policies that promote exporting are likely to support innovation behaviour.

Enterprise Ireland operates a two-pronged approach to increasing the numbers of enterprises engaging in R&D and innovation (RDI) i) by providing support to encourage existing enterprises to begin to invest in RDI and ii) by supporting entrepreneurs who are seeking to establish High Potential Start-Ups (HPSUs), which are defined as new enterprises focused on export markets that engage in significant RDI investments *ab initio*.[76] Over 70 HPSUs have been established in each year since 2005, and these now provide a sufficiently large pool to evaluate the effectiveness of this programme.[77]

Which enterprises have higher innovation expenditure per employee?

While scale affects the decision of Irish-owned enterprises to invest in innovation, it does not impact proportionately on innovation expenditure per employee. In fact, smaller enterprises are more likely to spend relatively more on innovation per employee than larger enterprises. The key determinant of innovation expenditure per employee in Irish indigenous enterprises is the enterprise's innovation capability. This suggests that any support given to promote increased innovation needs to take account of the enterprise's capacity to innovate and that a starting point for encouraging enterprises to innovate is the assurance that they have the skill capacity to reap the benefits of such innovation investments.

Again Enterprise Ireland takes a twin-track approach when encouraging enterprises to expand their investment in RDI by i) providing individual enterprises with R&D grants to co-finance the R&D cost, and ii) by investing in private sector seed and venture capital funds that operate primarily in innovation-intensive industries. The question that now arises is to whether these investments are being converted into successful innovations.

Which enterprises are more likely to innovate successfully?

Once again, the international evidence that enterprise scale matters is found for Irish indigenous enterprises. Larger enterprises are more likely to have successful process innovation, organisational innovation and process and organisational innovation combined. However, smaller enterprises have higher product innovation intensities (innovative sales share). In the case of Irish-owned enterprises only, innovation expenditure per employee is found to impact significantly only in the case of organisational innovation. By contrast, the impact of exporting on successful innovation is highly significant – Irish exporters are more likely to have successful innovation outcomes than non-exporters when they invest in process innovation, organisational innovation, and in a combination of product and organisational innovation. What is important for policymakers to note is that we

---

76 Details on the various policy supports to RDI enterprises can be found on www.enterprise-Ireland.com and are summarised in Ruane and Siedschlag (2011).

77 Forfás is currently completing an evaluation of this programme.

do not find this result when investment is solely in product innovation, or even in product combined with process innovation. A further result of note is that there is no evidence that exporters' shares of new products in total sales are higher than non-exporters' shares.

These results raise questions for whether current policy is succeeding in growing indigenous exporting enterprises that are capable of creating new products for export markets. The fact that enterprise characteristics, such as size and exporting behaviour, impact strongly on innovative success points to the importance of formulating policy at enterprise as well as at sectoral level. This enterprise-centred approach is deeply ingrained in Enterprise Ireland operations as it has been a defining feature of the Irish industrial policy since the 1950s. Ireland benefits from the integration of all aspects of enterprise development within one agency as it facilitates an integrated approach to enterprise supports and the application of sophisticated project-appraisal methods.

The importance of scale points to the benefits of growing Irish indigenous enterprises. In addition to the programmes above, Enteprise Ireland operates a Business Development Programme aimed at 'scaling up' existing enterprises with the potential to become significant middle-sized entities. Since a targeted approach is adopted, involving the selection of a small number of enterprises annually, the mechanisms for enterprise selection are crucial.

The operational framework in Enterprise Ireland integrates exporting and innovation – in effect virtually all Enterprise Ireland companies are exporters or soon to be exporters.[78] Agency personnel identify several factors as being crucial to successful exporting: sales and marketing capabilities, innovation and R&D activity, continuous competitiveness through lean improvements, and on-going leadership and management development. On average, the agency has funded training for 200 managers a year to support the building of capability and funding for such capability building has increased from €4.3 million to €14.7 million over the period.

The evidence for Irish-owned enterprises also indicates that many forms of co-operation for innovation activities[79] appear to contribute significantly to successful innovation by Irish-owned enterprises. The exceptional case is co-operation with competitors which is found to be negatively associated with innovative success. This finding could be interpreted as indicating that some Irish-owned enterprises with a weak innovation performance turn to co-operation with competitors as a strategy for survival or growth. The strong influence of co-operation on innovative success reflects the impact of the innovation eco-system, as discussed above. In other words, while enterprises' innovative activities and their innovative successes are influenced by their own characteristics, they are also influenced by their

---

78 This is one of the positive results of the integration of agencies in the 1990s.
79 Particularly co-operation with suppliers of equipment, materials, components or software; with consultants, commercial labs or private R&D institutes; and with universities or other higher education institutions.

interactions with outside agents in the system. Consequently, policy that supports co-operation between target enterprises and other agents will have differential effects depending on the type of agent involved and the type of innovation being supported.

The major support from Enterprise Ireland for co-operation with the Higher Education Institute (HEI) sector comes primarily in the form of the Competence Centre Initiative established to assist enterprises in accessing the expertise of researchers in the Institutes of Technology, and the research networks programme, which supports groups of enterprises in linking to HEIs via a shared research programme. In addition, Enterprise Ireland supports commercialisation activities (technology transfer offices and commercialisation funds). The rationale for such programmes is supported by the evidence of the positive link between innovation success and cooperation with HEIs. However, it is a separate research question whether the specific supports in place are the most cost effective and whether the metrics required to monitor these are adequate.

Overall, there is a positive alignment between Ireland's strategic approach to providing direct support for innovation in indigenous enterprises and what emerges from the international literature and from the analysis of innovation in the Irish indigenous sector. Three key issues for policy merit further consideration:

- The likelihood of innovation success depends crucially on the capacity of enterprises to internalise knowledge spillovers. Are indigenous enterprises growing that capability?
- While the current policy mix approach makes sense in terms of addressing heterogeneity, it may be timely to review whether or not existing schemes could be rationalised to provide more focus and reduce the Exchequer costs associated with supporting innovation?[80]
- Do the measures and methodologies currently in place evaluate objectively the effectiveness of policy measures (including returns to innovation investment)?

CONCLUSIONS

As noted in the introduction, the international evidence points to the fact that successful innovation is more likely to occur when enabling framework conditions are in place. The international literature shows that productivity is positively affected by innovation, which in turn depends on a range of factors which vary by enterprise both across and within sectors. Research in this area is still at a relatively early stage and most analysis is still based on cross-sectional data. Analyses based on longitudinal data are required to ensure that the findings are fully robust.

---

80 The counter argument in relation to having a large number of schemes is that they can handle the heterogeneity better, i.e., deal with companies at different stages of development.

The messages coming from the international and national research literature point to the complexity of the innovative process and to the potential for policy to support innovation. This complexity means that a mix of policies is likely to be more successful than a single policy approach. However, the mixture of policies must be carefully designed and assessed and all new programmes should be piloted. It may be timely to review how policies in relation to both foreign and indigenous enterprises might be further integrated to promote synergies. Furthermore, with a complex mix of policies, the selection of metrics used to measure performance must be made carefully, and appropriate methods used to evaluate success/failure and indicate where improvements can be made.

Crucially, and not an area where international evidence is yet helpful, evaluation of policy success should seek to take greater account of the time period over which success/failure should be evaluated, i.e., how many years does it take to realise the benefits of investment in innovation within the enterprise or in cooperation with a HEI, as measured in terms of productivity, output growth, enterprise survival rates, export sales and employment? Multi-period panel analysis is required to explore the causal factors underpinning the relationship between innovation expenditure, innovation performance and productivity. For Ireland, it would be important that future waves of the Community Innovation Survey provide the basis for a strong longitudinal element which will allow policy to be informed by such analysis. This will ensure that realistic expectations can be formed about what can be expected from expenditure on innovation, and programmes refined to be as efficient and effective as possible.

In relation to systemic failures, Irish policies continue to promote co-operative agreements, both among enterprises in Ireland, between enterprises in Ireland and HEIs, and between enterprises and HEIs in Ireland and suitable partners outside Ireland. Strategies have been put in place to enhance knowledge flows, by supporting researcher mobility and developing career opportunities, etc. However, much remains to be done in this area as noted by Martin (2009).

Many Irish innovation policy documents identify the market and systemic failures in the innovation process in Ireland that underpin the actions introduced to address them. Knowledge spillovers are seen as justifying the very significant investment in research and development in the past decade, and the current focus of that investment on areas relevant to Ireland's growth potential (Forfás, 2011). The potential for knowledge spillovers also underpins the decision to invest in fostering HEI–enterprise linkages through the Centres for Science, Engineering and Technology and the Competence/ Technology Centres. However, the international evidence (see Ruane and Siedschlag, 2011) suggests that knowledge spillovers are not automatic but are conditioned and enhanced by enterprises' absorptive capacity including past R&D/innovation investments and human capital.

The evidence also suggests that domestic expenditure on R&D and innovation improves the capacity to absorb foreign country technology. Taken together, Irish innovation policy has strong evidential support from the international literature.

However, while a policy mix is appropriate, the number of Enterprise Ireland schemes is large and they merit review with a view to possible rationalisation. Given this number of schemes, it is not easy or indeed meaningful to measure the effectiveness of any one scheme. Evaluation of the success/failure of these schemes is only possible using carefully chosen metrics and econometric methodologies, estimated on the integrated Enterprise Ireland data base. Such an analysis would assist in measuring impact and in refining the schemes in place.

In essence, the key policy messages that emerge from our review of the international literature are:

- Government needs to keep focus on the framework conditions that enable innovation. This includes actions that generally support enterprise growth, that strengthen the national innovation system, and that promote international links with the international innovation system.
- Policy to promote innovation at enterprise level needs to take account of differences across enterprises and especially in their capacity to absorb new knowledge. In the current context with limited budgets, all programmes should be evaluated for effectiveness, using metrics and methods that take account of complexity of the innovation process and the mixture of policies in place.

REFERENCES

Aghion, P. and Howitt, P. (1992). 'A Model of Growth through Creative Destruction', *Econometrica*, 60, 323–351.

Ahn, S. (2002). 'Competition, Innovation and Productivity Growth: A Review of Theory and Evidence', *OECD Economics Department Working Papers* No. 317, OECD Publishing. http://dx.doi.org/10.1787/182144868160.

Benavente, H. J. M. (2006). 'The Role of Research and Innovation in Promoting Productivity in Chile', *Economics of Innovation and New Technology*', 15, 301–315.

Box, S. (2009). 'OECD Work on Innovation – A Stocktaking of Existing Work', *OECD Science, Technology and Industry Working Papers*, 2009/2, OECD Publishing. http://dx.doi.org/10.1787/227048273721.

Bratti, M. and Felice, G. (2012). 'Are Exporters More Likely to Introduce Product Innovations?' *The World Economy*, 35, 1559–1598.

Bustos, P. (2011). 'Trade Liberalization, Exports, and Technology Upgrading: Evidence on the Impact of MERCOSUR on Argentinian Firms,' *American Economic Review*, 101, 304–40.

Chudnovsky, D., Lopez, A. and Pupato, G. (2006). 'Innovation and Productivity in Developing Countries: A Study of Argentine Manufacturing Firms' Behaviour (1992–2001), *Research Policy*, 35, 266–288.

Cohen, W. M. (2010). 'Fifty Years of Empirical Studies of Innovative Activity and Performance' in B. H. Hall, and N. Rosenberg (eds.), *Handbook of the Economics of Innovation*, 1, 129–213, Oxford: Elsevier.

Cohen, W.M. and Levin, R. (1989). 'Empirical Studies of Innovation and Market Structure' in R. Schumalensee and R. D. Willig (eds.), *Handbook of Industrial Organization*, 2, Amsterdam: North Holand.

Crépon, B., Duguet, E. and Mairesse, J. (1998). 'Research, Innovation, and Productivity: An Econometric Analysis at the Firm Level', *Economics of Innovation and New Technology*, 7, 115–156.

Criscuolo, C., Haskel, J., Slaughter, M. J. (2010) 'Global Engagement and the Innovation Activities of Firms', *International Journal of Industrial Organization*, 28, 191–202.

Central Statistics Office (2012). *Business in Ireland 2010*, Dublin: The Stationery Office.

Department of An Taoiseach (2008). *Building Ireland's Smart Economy: A Framework for Sustainable Economic Renewal*, Dublin: Stationery Office.

Doran, J. and O'Leary, E. (2011). 'External Interaction, Innovation and Productivity: An Application of the Innovation Value Chain to Ireland', *Spatial Economic Analysis*, 6, 199–222.

European Commission (2008). *A More Research-Intensive and Integrated European Research Area, Science, Technology and Competitiveness Key Figures Report 2008/2009*, Luxembourg: Office for Official Publications of the European Communities.

Forfás (2004). *Building Ireland's Knowledge Economy – The Irish Action Plan for Increasing Research and Development to 2010*, Dublin: Forfás.

Forfás (2011). *Report of the Steering Group of the Research Prioritisation Exercise*, Dublin: Forfás.

Freeman, C. (1987). *Technology Policy and Economic Performance: Lessons from Japan*, London: Pinter.

Geroski, P.A. and Pomroy, R. (1990). 'Innovation and the Evolution of Market Structure', *Journal of Industrial Economics*, 38, 299–314.

Greenaway, D. and Kneller, R. (2007). 'Firm Heterogeneity, Exporting and Foreign Direct Investment: A Survey', *Economic Journal*, 117, F134–F161.

Griliches, Z. (1992). 'The Search for R&D Spillovers', *Scandinavian Journal of Economics*, 94, Supplement, S29–S47.

Griliches, Z. (1996). 'The Discovery of the Residual: A Historical Note', *Journal of Economic Literature* 34, 1324–1330.

Grossman, G.M. and Helpman, E. (1990). 'Trade, Innovation and Growth', *American Economic Review*, 80, 86–91.

Hall, B. H. (2011). 'Innovation and Productivity', *Nordic Economic Policy Review*, 167–203.

Helpman, E. (2006). 'Trade, FDI and the Organisation of Firms', *Journal of Economic Literature*, XLIV, 589–630.

Helpman, E., Melitz, M. and Yeaple, S. (2004). 'Export versus FDI with Heterogeneous Firms', *American Economic Review*, 94, 300–316.

ICSTI (1999). *Technology Foresight Ireland: An ICSTI Overview*, Dublin: Forfás.

Jefferson, G.H., Bai, H., Guan X. and Yu, X. (2006). 'R&D Performance in Chinese Industry', *Economics of Innovation and New Technology*, 15, 345–366.

Jones, C. I. and Williams, J. C. (1998). 'Measuring the Social Return to R&D', *The Quarterly Journal of Economics*, 113, 1119–1135.

Liu, X. and Buck, T. (2007). 'Innovation Performance and Channels for International Technology Spillovers: Evidence from Chinese High-Tech Industries', *Research Policy*, 36, 355–366.

Lööf, H. and Heshmati, A. (2006). 'On the Relationship between Innovation and Performance: A Sensitivity Analysis', *Economics of Innovation and New Technology*, 15, 317–344.

Lundvall, B.A. (ed.) (1992). *National Systems of Innovation: Towards a Theory of Innovation and Interactive Learning*, London: Pinter.

Mairesse, J. and Robin, S. (2009). *Innovation and Productivity: a Firm-Level Analysis for French Manufacturing and Services Using CIS3 and CIS4 Data (1998–2000 and 2002–2004)*, mimeo, Paris, CREST-ENSAE.

Martin, T. (2009). *Erawatch Country Report 2009: Analysis of Policy Mixes to Foster R&D Investment and to Contribute to ERA, Ireland*, Luxembourg: Office for Official Publications of the European Communities.

Melitz, M.J. (2003). 'The Impact of Trade on Intra-Industry Reallocations and Aggregate Industry Productivity', *Econometrica*, 71, 1695–1725.

Mjøset, L. (1992). *The Irish Economy in a Comparative Institutional Perspective*, Report No. 93, Dublin: National Economic and Social Council.

Nelson, R. (1993). *National Innovation Systems: A Comparative Analysis*, New York: Oxford University Press.

OECD (2005). Oslo Manual: 'Guidelines for Collecting and Interpreting Innovation Data', Third Edition, Paris: OECD.

OECD (2006). *Economic Policy Reforms: Going for Growth, 2006*, Paris: OECD.

OECD (2009a). *OECD Economic Surveys: European Union, 2009*, Paris: OECD.

OECD (2009b). *OECD Economic Surveys: Ireland, 2009*, Paris: OECD.

OECD (2009c). *Innovation in Firms. A Microeconomic Perspective*, Paris: OECD.

OECD (2011). *OECD Economic Surveys: Ireland, 2011*, Paris: OECD.

Polder, M., Van Leeuwen, G., Mohnen, P. and Raymond, W. (2010). 'Product, Process and Organisational Innovation: Drivers, Complementarity and Productivity Effects', CIRANO Working Papers 2010s-28, CIRANO, Montréal, Canada.

Porter, M.E. (1990). 'The Competitive Advantage of Nations', New York: Free Press, 1990.

Raffo, J., l'Huillery, S. and Miotti, L. (2008). 'Northern and Southern Innovativity: A Comparison across European and Latin American Countries', *European Journal of Development Research*, 20, 219–239.

Romer, P. (1990). 'Endogenous Technological Change', *Journal of Political Economy*, 98, S71–102.

Roper, S. and Love, J. (2002). 'Innovation and Export Performance: Evidence from UK and German Manufacturing Plants.' *Research Policy*, 31, 1087–1102.

Ruane, F. and Siedschlag, I. (2011). 'Boosting Innovation and Productivity in Enterprises: What Works?', ESRI Renewal Series Paper 3, Dublin: Economic and Social Research Institute.

Salomon, R. and Shaver, M. (2005). 'Learning by Exporting: New Insights from Examining Firm Innovation', *Journal of Economics & Management Strategy*, 14, 431–460.

Schumpeter, J. A. (1942). *Capitalism, Socialism and Democracy*, New York: Harper and Row.

Siedschlag, I., Zhang, X. and Cahill, B. (2010). 'The Effects of the Internationalisation of Firms on Innovation and Productivity', ESRI Working Paper No. 363, Dublin, Ireland: Economic and Social Research Institute.

Soete, L., Verspagen, B., Ter Weel, B. (2010). 'Systems of Innovation' in B. H. Hall and N. Rosenberg (eds.), *Handbook of the Economics of Innovation*, 2, 1156–1180, Oxford: Elsevier.

Sutton, J. (1996). 'Technology and Market Structure', *European Economic Review*, 40, 511–530.

Sutton, J. (1998). *Technology and Market Structure: Theory and History*, Cambridge, Mass., The MIT Press, USA.

Symeonidis, G. (1996). 'Innovation, Firm Size, and Market Structure: Schumpeterian Hypotheses and some New Themes', *OECD Economic Studies*, 27, 1996/II, 35–70.

Yeaple, S. R. (2005). 'A Simple Model of Firm Heterogeneity, International Trade, and Wages', *Journal of International Economics*, 65, 1–20.

Wagner, J. (1996). 'Export Performance, Human Capital, and Product Innovation in Germany: A Micro View', *Jahrbuch fur Wirtschaftswissenschaften*, 47, 40–45.

Wagner, J. (2007). 'Exports and Productivity: A Survey of the Evidence from Firm-level Data', *The World Economy*, 30, 60–82.

CHAPTER 7

Do Active Labour Market Policies Activate?

Elish Kelly, Seamus McGuinness, Philip J. O'Connell

Ireland is again facing a crisis of mass unemployment. Active labour market policies (ALMPs) – consisting of a range of assistance, training and employment programmes to support the unemployed back to work – have been identified as being an essential part of the policy response to the current unemployment problem.' This chapter examines a wide range of national and international evidence on the effectiveness of ALMPs. In relation to the policy landscape (Figure 1.1), it identifies and examines a body of research for a specific policy area that is currently being reformed to deal with the unemployment crisis the country now faces. Evidence relating to some specific policies within the area is also considered.

The chapter addresses the following questions: i) what can ALMPs do for the unemployed?, ii) are some types of programmes more effective than others?, and iii) what can we expect ALMPs to achieve in a recession? It is hoped that the answers to these questions will assist in the design and implementation of an effective labour market activation policy. The aim is a system that assists those unemployed to find a job or places them on a specific pathway that will eventually reintegrate them into the labour market.

Our approach is to review both the international and national literature on the effectiveness of various ALMPs, along with international documentation on how Public Employment Services (PESs) activate the unemployed and how the main active labour market programmes are utilised. Given that countries differ with respect to economic and institutional settings, active labour market programme characteristics, outcomes measured in evaluations and time-periods covered, the chapter draws heavily on two recent studies that used a meta-analytical framework to overcome these cross-country comparison problems and identify what countries can learn from each other regarding active labour market programme effectiveness.

Research on the effectiveness of active labour market programmes is not conclusive. Nevertheless, there are some findings that are sufficiently consistent to serve as a guide to policy in this area. The implied causal effects are not straightforward, however, but depend on certain other factors being in place. For example, job search assistance tends to be effective, fast and relatively inexpensive, but the results suggest it is more successful when combined with regular monitoring of job search activities and sanctions for non-compliance. Training also tends to increase employment prospects, provided it is strongly linked to skill demands in the labour market. Public sector job creation programmes, such as the Community Employment Scheme, do not work as an activation policy, and this is mainly because such programmes lack market linkages.

Finally, it is recommended that the various programmes implemented are regularly monitored and evaluated, in order to ensure that they are effective in assisting the unemployed to re-integrate into the labour market. Otherwise, both unemployed individuals and society will incur unnecessary costs from an ineffective activation system.

BACKGROUND

The collapse in economic activity since 2007 has had severe knock-on effects in the labour market. In particular, the unemployment rate has increased from 4.4 per cent in 2006 to 14.7 per cent in 2012 (Central Statistics Office, 2012 and 2013a), while the employment rate has fallen from 68.8 per cent to 59.3 per cent (Central Statistics Office, 2013b). Thus, as in the 1980s Ireland again faces a crisis of mass unemployment. Active labour market policies (ALMPs), consisting of a range of assistance, training and employment programmes to support the unemployed to reintegrate back into the labour market, have been held out as an essential part of the policy response to the unemployment problem (see, for example, OECD, 2007).

This chapter examines the national and international evidence on the effectiveness of ALMPs and asks: i) what do ALMPs do for the unemployed?, ii) are some programmes more effective than others?, and iii) what can we expect ALMPs to achieve in a recession?

We begin by providing some background to ALMPs. This is followed by an outline of the key instruments used by Public Employment Services (PESs) to activate the unemployed, and also the main active labour market programmes utilised. Evidence on the effectiveness of various ALMPs is then presented. Finally, drawing on two meta-analysis studies, we highlight the ALMPs that have been found to be the most effective in reintegrating the unemployed back into employment.

ACTIVE LABOUR MARKET POLICIES AND ACTIVATION STRATEGIES

In most European countries there has been some shift in emphasis and resource allocation from passive to active measures. Passive measures provide income support to unemployed people. In Ireland this mainly includes insurance-based Jobseekers Benefit and assistance-based Jobseekers Allowance. Active measures, such as the range of job placement, assistance and employment services, training programmes, employment subsidies and direct employment provision, are intended to assist the unemployed back to work. Increased emphasis on activation was initially advocated by the OECD in its 1994 *Jobs Strategy*,[81] adopted by the European Commission in its *European Employment Strategy* in 1997, and reiterated by the OECD in its revised *Jobs Strategy* in 2006.[82] In practice, there has been limited adoption of the activation agenda and just a few countries have substantially increased their spending on active measures relative to passive measures. Higher levels of unemployment have been put forward as a reason for the limited transfer of public resources into active measures in many countries, since spending on passive income support will automatically increase during periods of high unemployment. However, even during periods of low unemployment in the last decade, public spending on passive measures was greater than on active measures in most countries (see Kelly, McGuinness and O'Connell (2011) for more details).

The issue of replacement rates,[83] the standard indicator of the generosity of an unemployment benefit system, came to the fore in the 1994 OECD *Jobs Strategy*. The evidence at the time suggested that replacement rates were sufficiently large to act as a disincentive to work for many welfare recipients, thus leading to the creation of unemployment traps (Martin, 2000). In light of this, the adoption of the *OECD Jobs Strategy* led a number of countries to examine whether active labour market policies could be used more effectively to both curb the unemployment trap and reduce high levels of unemployment. This examination in turn either led to the introduction of, or increased emphasis on, 'activation' strategies in many countries, which had the objective of encouraging jobseekers to be more active in their efforts to find work and/or to improve their employability (OECD, 2007). Activation strategies apply the principle of 'mutual obligation', which means that benefit recipients are expected to engage in job search and/or education, training or employment programmes in exchange for receiving benefit payments and efficient employment services. In applying this principle, PESs aim to monitor benefit recipients' compliance with eligibility conditions and to implement, where necessary, temporary sanctions or benefit exclusions (OECD, 2007), thus linking activation measures with the replacement rate.

The increased role of activation/mutual obligation strategies has been one of the main labour market policy reforms in the OECD in the last decade.[84] If such

---

81 OCED (1994a). *The OECD Jobs Study: Facts, Analysis, Strategies*. Paris: OECD. The publication of the OECD Jobs Strategy was supported by two volumes of research: OECD (1994b). *The OECD Jobs Study: Evidence and Explanations*, Volumes I and II. Paris: OECD.
82 OECD (2006a). Boosting Jobs and Income: Policy Lessons from Reassessing the OECD Jobs Strategy. Paris: OECD.
83 The replacement rate is the proportion of expected income from work which is replaced by unemployment and related welfare benefits (Martin, 2000).
84 See Eichhorst and Konle-Seidl (2008) for a good overview of the evolution and development of activation strategies across various OECD countries.

strategies are designed appropriately then they can result in jobseekers having a better chance of finding employment, along with reducing the disincentive effect of high and long-lasting unemployment benefits. Research by the OECD (2003, 2007) indicates that better labour market outcomes, particularly in terms of reducing benefit dependence, have been achieved in those countries that have implemented an effective activation/mutual obligations scheme.

INSTRUMENTS USED TO ACTIVATE THE UNEMPLOYED

The primary objective of activation strategies is to encourage jobseekers to be more active in their efforts to find work and/or increase their employability. The key components of such a strategy are as follows (OECD, 2007):[85]

  i. Registration for placement and assessment of work availability as preconditions for benefit payment;
 ii. Regular and intense interventions in the unemployment spell by the PES;
iii. Explicit regulations regarding job search requirements;
 iv. Direct referrals to vacant jobs;
  v. Referrals to ALMPs, with compulsory participation for some jobseekers.

In most countries, registration with the placement service and assessment of work availability are preconditions for benefit payment. However, there are a few countries, where registration for benefit precedes that for placement. The rationale for such a system is not clear, with the time lag to registration leading to a number of potential matches of jobseekers to suitable jobs being missed when benefit is already being paid (OECD, 2007), thus implying an inefficient use of public resources. Interventions in the unemployment spell refer to compulsory scheduled contacts between the jobseeker and the PES. These may include: i) the initial registration interview, ii) detailed registration interview,[86] iii) regular intensive interviews to report and monitor job search activities and work availability, iv) referrals to vacant jobs, v) feedback on job applications, vi) discussion of individual action plans and vii) referrals to ALMPs. An individual action plan

---

85 Voluntary interviews and collective information sessions are also used by some countries to activate the unemployed.

86 Full registration interviews are conducted in those countries that only collect basic information at the initial placement interview. This interview is needed to obtain more detailed information on the benefit claimant (e.g., education qualifications, work history, etc.) so that the person can be referred to an appropriate vacant job or to an active labour market programme. Such interviews are also used to explain the full range of services provided by the PES, the rights and duties of the benefit claimant, application of a profiling instrument (if in existence) and to establish an individual action plan. In some countries, these latter tasks are carried out at the initial registration interview.

is an agreement signed by both the jobseeker and the PES officer: typically such a plan describes the jobseeker's situation, outlines the actions to be undertaken by the jobseeker, and the duties of the employment service in facilitating the jobseeker to find a job and/or to increase their employability.

A number of countries now have explicit regulations relating to job search requirements and stipulate that jobseekers regularly report and document their job search actions. The frequency of reporting and number of job search activities to be undertaken varies by country and jobseeker type. A direct referral to a vacant job is when the PES offers a specific vacancy to a jobseeker. This activation measure can occur at the initial interview[87] and/or at subsequent intensive interviews. The main benefit of a direct job referral is that it can speed up the matching process and, thus, reduce benefit payment along with the risk of prolonged unemployment.

Referrals to ALMPs are also an important feature of an activation strategy. The types of ALMPs that are employed by PESs, which are discussed in more detail later in the chapter, vary substantially across countries, and countries are continuously modifying their programmes, or introducing new ones, with the result that there is rarely a stable set of ALMPs to evaluate (Martin, 2000).

The revised OECD *Jobs Strategy* recommended that effective ALMPs should be compulsory after a certain period of unemployment (OECD, 2007). Research indicates that participation in such programmes can speed up the re-employment process. It has also been found that referral to ALMPs with the threat of benefit sanctions for non-participation can lead to increases in the number of individuals going from benefit to work around the formal deadline for programme entry. This 'motivation' or 'threat' effect, whereby individuals cease claiming benefits and re-enter the labour market in order to avoid the obligation of programme participation, can have a positive impact on re-employment rates (see Black et al., 2003; Rosholm and Svarer, 2004; Geerdsen, 2006; Geerdsen and Holm, 2007; and Graversen and van Ours, 2006). Most countries do not require jobseekers to continue with their job search obligations when participating in an ALMP. However, the OECD (2007) recommends that some time should be set aside for individuals participating in publicly subsidised employment schemes to continue their job search, as take up of market-sector jobs is viewed as being of greater benefit to the jobseeker.

In implementing activation strategies, the PES can impose temporary sanctions or benefit exclusions on jobseekers that do not comply with job-search requirements and activation measures. Several studies have found that the imposition of a sanction has a positive effect on re-employment rates (OECD, 2007).

In most countries, activation policies are implemented by the country's PES. However, some countries[88] contract private providers to implement their policies,

---

87 If work availability is evaluated at the initial placement interview as a pre-condition for benefit entitlement then the PES can intervene immediately with job offers.

88 For example, Australia, Germany, Netherlands and United Kingdom.

either in full or in conjunction with the PES. The evaluation results on the effectiveness of such out-sourcing mechanisms are mixed, largely due to the implementation of such mechanisms as opposed to the quality of the services offered by private providers in general.[89]

Poorly controlled access to non-employment income-maintenance schemes, such as disability, lone-parent and early retirement, can undermine the impact of activation measures for unemployment benefit recipients, as some of the long-term unemployed enter benefit schemes that facilitate economic inactivity. This suggests the need for non-employment benefit gate-keeping (Tergeist and Grubb, 2006).

ACTIVE LABOUR MARKET PROGRAMMES

The main ALMPs to assist jobseekers to reintegrate into the labour market are:[90]

  i. Job search assistance, monitoring and sanctions
  ii. Training programmes;
  iii. Public-sector job creation programmes;
  iv. Private-sector incentive schemes (e.g., wage subsidies and/or start-up grants).[91]

Job Search Assistance (JSA) includes a variety of measures that aim to increase the effectiveness of job search. Examples of such measures include: counselling; job search courses; vocational guidance; establishment of individual action plans; and direct referrals to vacant jobs. Job Search Assistance is often combined with monitoring and the imposition of sanctions when jobseekers do not comply with the job search activities that are required for receipt of unemployment benefits. Job Search Assistance tends to be the least costly ALMP (Martin, 2000; Kluve, 2006). Furthermore, compared to other ALMPs, JSA rates well in evaluation studies. However, the evidence suggests that JSA needs to be combined with increased monitoring of jobseekers.

The key objective of training programmes is to enhance jobseekers' human capital and, thus, their employment prospects. Training programmes vary according to jobseeker type. For example, some jobseekers require basic job search training or other general skills, while others undertake more intensive and specific

---

89 See Tergeist and Grubb (2006) for further information on the use of quasi-market mechanisms in the provision of employment services.
90 Programmes are often targeted at specific groups, e.g., young workers (25 years of age and younger), disabled, lone-parents, immigrants, etc. See Aakvik et al.,(2005) and Kirby and Riley (2004) for disability and lone-parent programme evaluations, while some of the literature that has evaluated youth programmes is discussed below.
91 A strict classification of an ALMP into one of these four categories is not always feasible as some countries have schemes that contain elements of two or more of these programmes.

training to either enhance their employability or to secure better quality jobs. Training tends to account for the largest share of spending on active measures (Martin, 2000). However, evaluations of the performance of public training programmes, which are discussed in more detail below, are mixed. According to Martin (2000), the design of public training programmes is critical to their effectiveness. Specifically, such programmes need to be tightly targeted at participants, relatively small in scale and to establish strong links with local employers through the inclusion of an on-the-job component in the programme.

Job search assistance and training mainly seek to influence the supply side of the labour market, while direct job creation in the public sector and incentives to create jobs in the private sector seek to influence the demand side. Public-sector job creation programmes focus on the creation of public jobs that produce public goods and services. The main objective of this type of programme is to keep the unemployed jobseeker in contact with the labour market and, thus, to prevent the erosion of their human capital while unemployed. However, such jobs are often not close to the regular labour market (Kluve, 2006).

The aim of private sector incentive programmes is to create incentives that alter employer and/or worker behaviour. For example, wage subsidies in the private sector are intended to encourage employers to either create new jobs or to maintain existing positions. Such subsidies, which can be given directly to the employer or employee, tend to be for a fixed period of time and are often targeted at more disadvantaged individuals. Start-up incentives, which are provided to unemployed individuals that want to establish their own business, are another type of private sector incentive programme.

EVIDENCE ON THE EFFECTIVENESS OF ACTIVE LABOUR MARKET PROGRAMMES

There is a substantial body of research seeking to evaluate the effectiveness of ALMPs. This work, which goes back to the mid-1970s, aims to assess the impact of programme participation on an individual's employment, unemployment and/or earnings after he/she has left the programme relative to a benchmark group of similar individuals that did not participate (Martin, 2000). The research presented in this chapter is, for the most part, evaluations of ALMPs that were implemented in various European countries in the 1990s and 2000s, and which focus on employment and/or unemployment outcomes. An overview of the studies is presented in Table A1 in the Appendix, while a more complete discussion of the literature can be found in Kelly, McGuinness and O'Connell (2011).

Job Search Assistance, Monitoring and Sanctions

A number of studies have found that JSA measures (e.g., interviews, counselling, etc.), combined with monitoring of job search behaviour and the threat and/or imposition of sanctions for non-compliance, can be effective in increasing the transition from unemployment to work. Some studies have shown that JSA measures on their own can have positive employment effects (e.g., Crépon, Dejemeppe and Gurgand, 2005). Other researchers (e.g., Cockx and Dejemeppe, 2007) have found that the threat of monitoring job search activities in isolation from JSA measures can improve unemployed workers probability of employment, and increasingly so as benefit claimants approach the time at which monitoring takes place. However, there is some concern that the threat of increased monitoring may result in workers accepting lower quality jobs, although it is argued by some (e.g., Cockx and Dejemeppe, 2007) that this outcome can be countered by appropriate scheduling of JSA interviews and the provision of effective counselling.

Positive results have also been found for the imposition of sanctions for non-compliance with job search requirements (see, for example, van den Berg et al., 2004; and Abbring, van den Berg and van Ours, 2005), while others (e.g., Lalive et al., 2005) have found that both sanction warning and enforcement have a positive effect on the exit rate from unemployment. A number of other evaluations have found that JSA measures coupled with increased monitoring of job search behaviour and sanctions have been successful in getting unemployed individuals back to work (see, for example, Müller and Steiner, 2008; Svarer, 2007; Dolton and O'Neill, 1996; and Sianesi, 2008).

While there is some debate in the literature over the optimal combination of assistance, monitoring and the threat and/or enforcement of sanctions, it would appear that, by and large, a combination of all components is needed to produce benefits for both unemployed workers and society at large (Martin, 2000; OECD, 2005 and 2006b; and Kluve, 2006).

Job Search Assistance in Ireland

Evaluations of job search assistance and monitoring in Ireland have been quite limited, and have mainly centred on the National Employment Action Plan (NEAP), which is currently being replaced by a new model called *Intreo*.[92] When the NEAP was evaluated, the process required that those who had been unemployed for a period of three months had to be referred by the Department of Social Protection (DSP) to FÁS, formerly Ireland's national employment and training authority,[93] for interview, which in turn could initiate further assistance with job search, guidance, counselling, referral to employment or, in some cases, training or other ALMPs. Early evaluations of the NEAP were positive but hampered by the absence of adequate data to support rigorous econometric

---

92 *Intreo* is a component of the Government's labour market activation strategy: more information on Intreo can be found at www.welfare.ie

93 FÁS is currently being disbanded. In January 2012, the organisation's employment services and employment programmes were transferred to the DSP, and its training function is to be taken over by the Department of Education and Skills.

analysis (O'Connell, 2002a; Indecon, 2005). The most recent evaluation of the NEAP, as it operated between 2006 and 2008 (McGuinness, O'Connell, Kelly and Walsh, 2011; and McGuinness, O'Connell and Kelly, 2013), found that there were problems of access to NEAP programmes with the result that not all those who should have participated in an activation measure did so. A substantial group of jobseekers, about 25 per cent, who were eligible for assistance under the NEAP were not identified and referred. Another group, over 25 per cent, were not eligible for NEAP referral because they had received some form of assistance in a previous unemployment spell. This practice of excluding those who went through the NEAP process during a previous period of unemployment would appear to run counter to the underlying rationale of activation policies: to assist those most likely to encounter difficulties in finding work. The evaluation also showed that those who participated in the NEAP activation interview were less likely to become employed. Specifically, comparing the outcomes of those who were referred for a FÁS interview under the NEAP, including both those who attended and those who did not attend the interview, with a control group of those who were not referred, it was found that the NEAP was associated with a *negative* impact, with the chances of entering employment being about 17 per cent lower for those who went through the interview process. This suggests that the interview element of the NEAP was an ineffective route to employment. It is too early to assess the effectiveness of the new system that is replacing the NEAP, *Intreo*, as the new model is currently being rolled out and will not be available in every DSP office until 2014.

Training Programmes

The findings from the empirical literature on the effectiveness of training programmes are mixed. Some studies have found positive effects of participation in training programmes on employment (e.g., Cockx, 2003; and Richardson and van den Berg, 2006) found that vocational training had a positive impact on exits to work, while others (e.g., Rosholm and Skipper, 2009) have found that classroom training programmes increased participants' unemployment rates in the period immediately after the training ended – a result attributed to a 'lock-in effect'. The lock-in effect, which is when job search declines during (or immediately after) participation in a training course, may be one of the main reasons for the poor performance of some training programmes that have been evaluated over a short time horizon. Some studies have found that training had positive employment effects in the medium and long term in Germany (e.g., Fitzenberger, Osikominu and Paul, 2010; Lechner, Miquel and Wunsch, 2011; Lechner, Miquel and Wunsch, 2007; Lechner and Wunsch, 2009; and Fitzenberger, Osikominu and Völter, 2006). However, earlier evaluations of the same training programmes (e.g., Lechner, 2000; and Hujer and Wellner, 2000) found no significant effects.

Results from evaluations of the impact of the duration of training have also been mixed (e.g., Crépon *et al.*, 2011; Fitzenberger *et al.*,2010; Kluve, Schneider,

Uhlendorff and Zhao, 2007; Biewen, Fitzenberger, Osikominu and Waller, 2007; and Hujer, Thomsen and Zeiss, 2006), as have the findings from studies that have evaluated the differential impact of different types of training programmes (e.g., Biewen et al., 2007; Lechner et al., 2011; Lechner et al., 2007; Fitzenberger and Völter, 2007; Fitzenberger, Osikominu and Völter, 2006; and Arellano, 2010).

The results from studies comparing the effectiveness of training programmes against other types of ALMPs, such as wage subsidies, JSA, public sector subsidised jobs, etc., are also mixed (e.g., Kluve, Lehmann and Schmidt, 1999; Van Ours, 2001; Fitzenberger, Orlyanskaya, Osikominu and Waller, 2008; Neubäumer, 2010; Jespersen, Munch and Skipper, 2008; Sianesi, 2008; Carling and Richardson, 2004; Lalive, van Ours and Zweimüller, 2008; and Gerfin and Lechner, 2002).

Training in Ireland

Compared to many other OECD countries, there is a shortage of rigorous evidence on the impact of training in Ireland. O'Connell (2002b) and O'Connell and McGinnity (1997) argued that in relation to both supply- and demand- side measures, programmes with strong linkages to the labour market are more likely to enhance the employment prospects of their participants. In relation to training programmes delivered during the 1990s, they found that training in specific skills was more likely to increase participants' subsequent probability of employment. This is consistent with findings for Sweden (e.g., Sianesi, 2008; and Carling and Richardson, 2004). Conniffe, Gash and O'Connell (2000) focused on young unemployed individuals and found that general training had no significant effect on this group's probability of gaining employment. McGuinness, O'Connell and Kelly (2011) found that, on average, training did increase the probability of exiting unemployment in the 2006–2008 periods. Their analysis also showed that the type of training matters: job-search training and high-level specific skills training are most likely to increase the probability of their participants exiting from unemployment. There was no consistent evidence to suggest that low-level skills training significantly increase employment prospects. In general shorter duration training programmes were found to be more effective, with the exception of high-level skills training where there appears to be a pay-off to more extended training durations.

Public Sector Job Creation Programmes

Direct employment schemes in the public sector are generally targeted at disadvantaged individuals and provide subsidised work usually in the social economy. Where such programmes are well organised, they can generate socially useful goods and services. However, the evidence from the evaluation literature indicates that direct job creation in the public sector has not, for the most part, been successful in assisting unemployed individuals to secure permanent jobs in the ordinary labour market (e.g., Kluve, Lehmann and Schmidt, 1999; Sianesi,

2008; Carling and Richardson, 2004; Gerfin and Lechner, 2002; Lalive *et al.*, 2008; Jespersen *et al.*, 2008). Overall, the evidence suggests that direct job creation in the public sector has not been successful in improving the labour market prospects of unemployed workers (Martin, 2000; Kluve and Schmidt, 2002; and OECD, 2005).

Direct Employment Schemes in Ireland

The evidence for Ireland on direct employment schemes is consistent with the pessimistic international findings. Most of the research has focused on Community Employment (CE), the largest such direct employment scheme and, indeed, the single largest active labour market programme implemented in Ireland over the last decade and a half. Evaluations comparing CE participants with control groups of non-participants found that participation in CE was not associated with increased post-programme employment chances (O'Connell and McGinnity, 1997; and O'Connell, 2002b). While CE has not been the subject of a rigorous evaluation in recent years, an analysis of the factors associated with long-term unemployment in the 2006–2008 period found that previous participation in a CE scheme was associated with an increased risk of long-term unemployment, even when a range of personal characteristics and labour market experience was taken into account (O'Connell, McGuinness, Kelly and Walsh, 2009).

Private Sector Incentive Schemes

Private-sector incentive schemes consist of both wage subsidies to private sector employers and start-up grants for self employment. While a few studies have obtained negative or insignificant employment effects for private subsidised employment programmes (e.g., Kluve *et al.*, 1999; and van Ours, 2001), positive results from such schemes have been found in most countries (e.g., Jespersen *et al.*, 2008; Rosholm and Svarer, 2004; Lalive *et al.*, 2008; Gerfin and Lechner, 2002; Sianesi, 2008; Carling and Richardson, 2004; Jaenichen and Stephan, 2009; and Boockmann *et al.*, 2007). However, most studies do not account for the potential deadweight and displacement effects associated with such schemes,[94] which are issues that need to be borne in mind when assessing the findings from wage subsidy evaluation studies.

---

94 The net effect of any policy intervention targeting employment levels will be total employment growth less deadweight and displacement. Deadweight refers to any change in the key outcome variable, for example, employment growth in the context of a wage subsidy that would have occurred even if the wage subsidy was absent. Displacement refers to the extent to which the employment growth in subsidised firms occurs at the expense of lower growth in non-subsidised firms.

Private Sector Incentives in Ireland

Research on the effectiveness of incentives to support employment in the private sector in Ireland is limited and quite dated. Breen and Halpin (1989) found that subsidies to support self-employment targeted at the long-term unemployed in the 1980s had positive effects on their subsequent employment chances. O'Connell (2002b) and O'Connell and McGinnity (1997) showed that wage subsidies to support employment experience in private sector firms were more likely to enhance post-programme employment prospects, compared with a comparison group of non-participants and controlling for other relevant personal characteristics and labour market experience. A number of internship programmes have recently been initiated in Ireland. One such programme that has been recently evaluated is *JobBridge*: the objective of this programme is to provide those seeking employment with an opportunity to gain work experience, maintain close links with the labour market and develop their skills through their internship, thereby improving their chances of finding employment in the future. The evaluation concluded that *JobBridge* was an effective labour market intervention as it displayed an overall progression rate of 61 per cent into employment. However, the study of *JobBridge*, while making some comparisons with the exit rates of non-participants, did not explicitly estimate the programme value added controlling for differences in the age, education, labour market experience levels, etc., of programme participants versus non-participants. Thus, the study failed to explicitly account for i) observable differences in participants versus non-participants; ii) sample selection bias, whereby more able applicants were more likely to obtain places, iii) unobservable differences and iv) dynamic lock-in effects. Given the absence of the previous components from the *JobBridge* evaluation, all of which are deemed to be essential elements of effective labour market activation, it is not possible to accurately assess the value added of the *JobBridge* programme from the published report.

Youth Measures

Many young people have short spells of unemployment during their transition from school-to-work. However, some get trapped in unemployment and risk becoming long-term unemployed (OECD, 2009a).[95] The severity of the most recent global recession has increased the danger of this outcome among young adults, particularly disadvantaged youth that left school early without basic education (Scarpetta, Sonnet and Manfredi, 2010). In general, young people are somewhat more vulnerable to unemployment during an economic downturn due to their concentration in temporary jobs and cyclically-sensitive industries (OECD, 2009b).[96] Thus, a key priority of current governments is the introduction of measures to minimise the impact of the recession on young people and, in

---

95 http://www.oecd.org/dataoecd/54/62/43765276.pdf
96 http://www.oecd.org/dataoecd/54/50/43766254.pdf

particular, policies to prevent them from falling into long-term unemployment. However, the objective of youth measures is often not only to enhance young unemployed individuals' employment prospects but to encourage re-entry to education.

There has been a particular research focus on the impact of ALMPs among young people, possibly due to their greater exposure to unemployment and to the risk of long-term unemployment during recessions. However, as is the case in respect of adult programmes, results from studies that have evaluated the effectiveness of youth ALMPs are mixed (e.g., Hardoy, 2005; Brodaty, Crépon and Fougère, 2002; Fougère, Kramarz and Magnac, 2000; Hämäläinen and Ollikainen, 2004; Jensen, Rosholm and Svarer, 2003; Larsson, 2003; Dorsett, 2006; Blundell, Costa Dias, Meghir and van Reenen, 2004; van Reenen, 2003; and Lissenburgh, 2004). Nevertheless, the results are, by and large, supportive of wage subsidies, although, the potential deadweight and displacement effects associated with wage subsidies are not accounted for in the evaluations of youth programme evaluations. Mandatory participation and/or the imposition of sanctions for non-compliance seem to be common in countries where youth measures have proven to be successful (e.g., Denmark and the United Kingdom).

WHAT WORKS?

It is difficult to identify what one country can learn from other countries' experiences with ALMPs, particularly in terms of identifying what programmes have been found to work. This is due to variations in economic and institutional settings across countries, along with specific programme characteristics (e.g., type, scale,[97] target group, etc.), methodological issues in conducting the evaluations[98] (e.g., data used, methodology employed, outcome measured, use of selection controls, etc.) and the time period over which programmes are assessed.[99] In their recent surveys of the evaluation literature, both Kluve (2006) and Card, Kluve

---

97 Many programmes that have been evaluated tend to be small scale or trial programmes; thus, while such programmes might produce positive outcomes, the positive results might not hold if the programme was extended in terms of participant numbers or geographic coverage (Martin, 2000).

98 See Heckman *et al.* (1999), Blundell and Costa Dias (2000) and Kluve and Schmidt (2002) for a discussion of the methodological issues that arise in evaluating active labour market programmes (see also Heckman, Ichimura and Todd, 1998). Imbens and Wooldridge (2008) provide a survey of the most recent methodological advances in evaluating active labour market programmes (see also Cahuc and Le Barbanchon, 2010).

99 The majority of evaluations focus on short-term outcomes (e.g., one to two years after the person has participated in a programme); consequently, a programme that is found to be effective in the short run might not necessarily have long-term benefits, and vice-versa.

and Weber (2010) use a meta-analytical framework[100] to overcome these cross-country comparison problems and draw conclusions on what countries can learn from each other on ALMP effectiveness.

The two meta-analysis studies, each of which is based on more than 100 evaluations, took account of: (i) programme type, (ii) methodology, (iii) institutional context, (iv) the economic background in the country at the time the particular programme was in operation, (v) the country the programme relates to and (vi) the decade in which the programme was run, to identify the effectiveness of various ALMPs.[101] In particular, the two studies assessed the effectiveness of: (i) JSA and sanctions, (ii) training programmes, (iii) public sector job creation programmes and (iv) private sector incentive schemes, in terms of whether each programme had a positive, negative or insignificant treatment effect on post-programme employment rates.

In terms of the results, overall both Kluve (2006) and Card *et al.* (2010) found that once the *type* of ALMP is taken account of, e.g., JSA, training, etc., there is little systematic relationship between programme effectiveness and the other contextual factors. Kluve (2006) showed that relative to training programmes, JSA combined with sanctions, and private sector incentive schemes, had higher probabilities of positive treatment effects, while the opposite was the case for direct employment schemes in the public sector. Card *et al.* (2010) found similar results. However, Card *et al.* (2010) assessed both the short-term and long-term effectiveness of ALMPs and found that JSA had more favourable short-term impacts, whereas training programmes produced better outcomes in the medium term. Public sector job creation programmes, on the other hand, had negative outcomes in both the short and medium runs. Card *et al.* (2010) also concluded that ALMPs do not have differential effects on males and females.

The main policy implication that follows from Kluve (2006) and Card *et al.* (2010) is that programme type is what matters most for ALMP effectiveness. Training generally leads to a modest improvement in employment chances, while JSA and private sector employment incentives tend to show more favourable outcomes. However, public job creation schemes have generally been found to be less effective. Other contextual factors tend to be less important.

CONCLUSION

International research on the impact of active labour market programmes is far from conclusive and faces several difficult methodological challenges, although it

---

100 A meta-analysis is a statistical procedure that combines the results from different studies that address the same scientific question (e.g., ALMP effectiveness) in order to obtain a quantitative estimate of the overall effect of a particular intervention (e.g., ALMP participation) on a defined outcome (e.g., re-entry to the labour market).
101 Card *et al.* (2010) also took account of the heterogeneity of programme participants (e.g., gender, age, disadvantaged, etc.) in their meta-analysis.

does suggest a number of tentative conclusions that can serve to guide policy. Rigorous Irish research is limited to a small number of studies and much of it relates to earlier historical periods characterised by different macro-economic conditions to those prevailing today. Nevertheless, both international and domestic research indicate that the type of active labour market programme is important – some programmes work better than others – and help to identify the types of programmes that are more likely to enhance the employment prospects of unemployed participants. The principal conclusions are as follows:

- Job Search Assistance, including counselling, job-placement, monitoring and the development of action plans, as well as training in job search techniques, tends to be effective, fast, and relatively inexpensive. Effective job search and monitoring should be the corner-stone of all services to unemployed people and serve as the gateway to employment and training opportunities, irrespective of prevailing labour market conditions. Activation is essential to maintain connection with the labour market, even during a recession. Such activation tends to be more effective when combined with regular monitoring of job search activity and sanctions for non-compliance.
- Training tends to increase employment prospects, but it is important that training be strongly linked to skill demands in the labour market. Even in a slack labour market, training remains important to enable job seekers to compete for the limited opportunities that do exist and to maintain and develop human capital to enable them to participate in any upturn in the economy and labour market. To ensure that training reflects labour demand, it is crucial that the skill requirements of employers are effectively communicated to training providers on an ongoing basis, for example, through the development of sectoral skills councils. Such councils, which should include employers, training providers and government, could inform both the overall composition and content of skills training.
- Market links are also vital in supply side measures. This is why incentives to increase demand among private sector employers, or at least to real jobs in the public sector, can increase employment probabilities of participants. In effect, such incentivised work experience is equivalent to training: both types of active labour market programme increase participants' human capital. Lack of market linkages is also why public sector job creation in the social economy does not enhance the employment prospects of participants, in Ireland as elsewhere, notwithstanding the useful social output of many such schemes.
- While the evidence on the impact of youth measures is mixed, there are encouraging results in respect of wage subsidies. In general ALMPS for young people tend to be more effective when implemented in a context of compulsory engagement with the PES.

A number of important institutional reforms have been initiated in the very recent period in Ireland and are currently being implemented. These include: i) the introduction of *Intreo*, which is a new service from the DSP that provides unemployed individuals with a single point of contact for all employment and income support: this new service, which is replacing the NEAP, is currently being rolled out across the country and is expected to be available in all DSP offices by end 2014; ii) the development of a case management system with stronger emphasis on activation; iii) the introduction of sanctions for non-compliance with job-search and engagement with employment and training opportunities; iv) the development of a profiling system to allow targeting of scarce resources on those who need and can benefit from activation; and v) the abolition of FÁS, its replacement with the new further education and training authority, SOLAS,[102] and the assumption of responsibility for all labour market training and education by the Department of Education and Skills. These are important reforms and represent a welcome shift to a more active labour market policy response to unemployment. The integration of income support with activation is welcome and is in line with best practice in many other European countries. However, it is as yet unclear how the provision of training is to be organised between DSP, SOLAS and the education and training providers. The core principle governing that relationship between activation and training provision should be that the transition needs to be seamless, based on the needs of both unemployed individuals and current and future employers.

An active labour market policy regime is based on effective programmes. Ireland invests substantial resources in ALMPs. In the context of mass unemployment and the fiscal crisis of the State, it is essential that this investment achieves the best value for money: we need to identify and allocate spending to those ALMPs that do most to enhance the employment prospects of those who participate in them.

While this review of the evidence provides some clarity on the kinds of ALMPs that work in more than one context, the scale of the Irish crisis is daunting and aspects of it are unusual or even unique. There is a substantial structural component to the Irish unemployment problem arising from the collapse of the construction sector. A very large number of unemployed individuals possess skills that are no longer in demand and are unlikely to be so for the foreseeable future. This leaves policymakers with a two-fold challenge. First, it is necessary to identify the areas for which former construction workers can be retrained. There has been little debate on this point. Research is needed that identifies expanding areas of the economy, particularly those to which the skills of former construction workers can be readily transferred. Second, given the budget constraint, which rules out the provision of training for all, careful and informed consideration needs to be given as to how to allocate limited public resources in a manner that balances effectiveness and equity.

---

102 Seirbhísí Oideachais Leanunaigh agus Scileanna.

APPENDIX

Table A1 is available to download at http://www.esri.ie/pubs/EC001App.pdf.

REFERENCES

Aakvik, A., Heckman, J.J. and Vytlacil, E.J. (2005). 'Estimating Treatment Effects for Discrete Outcomes when Responses to Treatment Vary: An Application to Norwegian Vocational Rehabilitation Programs', *Journal of Econometrics*, 125, 15–51.

Abbring, J.H., van den Berg, G.J. and van Ours, J.C. (2005). 'The Effect of Unemployment Insurance Sanctions on the Transition Rate from Unemployment to Employment', *The Economic Journal*, 115, 602–630.

Arellano, F.A. (2010). 'Do Training Programmes Get the Unemployed Back to Work? A Look at the Spanish Experience', *Revista de Economía Aplicada*, 18, 39–65.

Biewen, M., Fitzenberger, B., Osikominu, A. and Waller, M. (2007).'Which Program for Whom? Evidence on the Comparative Effectiveness of Public Sponsored Training Programs in Germany', IZA Discussion Paper 2885.

Black, D.A., Smith, J.A., Berger, M.C. and Noel, B.J. (2003). 'Is the Threat of Reemployment Services More Effective than the Services Themselves? Experimental Evidence from the UI System', *The American Economic Review*, 93, 1313–1327.

Blundell, R. and Costa Dias, M. (2000). 'Evaluation Methods for Non-Experimental Data', *Fiscal Studies*, 21, 427–468.

Blundell, R., Costa Dias, M., Meghir, C. and van Rennen, J. (2004). 'Evaluating the Employment Impact of a Mandatory Job Search Program', *Journal of the European Economic Association*, 2: 569–606.

Boockmann, B., Zwick, T., Ammermüller, A. and Maier, M. (2007). 'Do Hiring Subsidies Reduce Unemployment Among the Elderly? Evidence from Two Natural Experiments', ZEW Discussion Paper No. 07-001.

Breen, R. and Halpin, B. (1989). *Subsidising Jobs: An Evaluation of the Employment Incentive Scheme*. ESRI General Research Series Number 144. Dublin: Economic and Social Research Institute.

Brodaty, T., Crépon, B. and Fougére, D. (2002). 'Do Long-term Unemployed Workers Benefit from Active Labor Market Programs? Evidence from France, 1986–1998', *mimeo*.

Cahuc, P. and Le Barbanchon, T. (2010).'Labor Market Policy Evaluation in Equilibrium: Some Lessons of the Job Search and Matching Model', *Labour Economics*, 17, 196–205.

Card, D., Kluve, J. and Weber, A. (2010). 'Active Labour Market Policy Evaluations: A Meta-Analysis'. *The Economic Journal*, 120, F452–F477.

Carling, K. and Richardson, K. (2004). 'The Relative Efficiency of Labour Market Programs: Swedish Experience from the 1990s', *Labour Economics*, 11 (3): 335–354.

Central Statistics Office (2012). *Live Register: December 2011*. Cork: Central Statistics Office.

Central Statistics Office (2013a). *Live Register: February 2013*. Cork: Central Statistics Office

Central Statistics Office (2013b). *Quarterly National Household Survey: Quarter 4 2012*. Cork: Central Statistics Office.

Cockx, B. (2003). 'Vocational Training of Unemployed Workers in Belgium', IZA Discussion Paper 682.

Cockx, B. and Dejemeppe, M. (2007). 'Is the Notification of Monitoring a Threat to the Unemployed? A Regression Discontinuity Approach', IZA Discussion Paper 2854.

Conniffe, D., Gash, V. and O'Connell, P.J. (2000). 'Evaluating State Programmes: 'Natural Experiments' and Propensity Scores', *The Economic and Social Review*, 31 (4): 283–308.

Crépon B., Dejemeppe, M. and Gurgand, M. (2005). 'Counseling the Unemployed: Does It Lower Unemployment Duration and Recurrence?', IZA Discussion Paper 1796.

Crépon, B., Ferracci, M. and Fougère, D. (2011). 'Training the Unemployed in France: How Does It Affect Unemployment Duration and Recurrence?', *Annales d'Economie et de Statistique* (forthcoming).

Dolton, P. and O'Neill, D. (1996). 'Unemployment Duration and the Restart Effect: Some Experimental Evidence', *The Economic Journal*, 106, 387–400.

Dorsett, R. (2006). 'The New Deal for Young People: Effect on the Labour Market Status of Young Men', *Labour Economics*, 13, 405–422.

Eichhorst, W. and Konle-Seidl, R. (2008). 'Contingent Convergence: A Comparative Analysis of Activation Policies', IZA Discussion Paper No. 3905.

Fitzenberger, B., Osikominu, A. and Paul, M. (2010). 'The Heterogeneous Effects of Training Incidence and Duration on Labour Market Transitions', IZA Discussion Paper No. 5269.

Fitzenberger, B., Orlyanskaya, O., Osikominu, A. and Waller, M. (2008). 'Déjà Vu? Short-Term Training in Germany 1980–1992 and 2000–2003', IZA Discussion Paper No. 3540.

Fitzenberger, B. and Völter, R. (2007). 'Long-Run Effects of Training Programs for the Unemployed in East Germany', *Labour Economics*, 14, 730–755.

Fitzenberger, B., Osikominu, A. and Völter, R. (2006). 'Get Training or Wait? Long-Run Employment Effects of Training Programs for the Unemployed in West Germany', IZA Discussion Paper No. 2121.

Fougère, D., Kramarz, F. and Magnac, T. (2000). 'Youth Employment Policies in France', *European Economic Review*, 44, 928–942.

Geerdsen, L.P. (2006). 'Is there a Threat Effect of Labour Market Programmes? A Study of ALMP in the Danish UI System', *The Economic Journal*, 116, 738–750.

Geerdsen, L.P. and Holm, A. (2007). 'Duration of UI Periods and the Perceived

Threat Effect from Labour Market Programmes', *Labour Economics*, 14, 639–652.

Gerfin, M. and Lechner, M. (2002). 'A Microeconometric Evaluation of the Active Labour Market Policy in Switzerland', *The Economic Journal*, 112, 854–893.

Graversen, B.K. and van Ours, J.C. (2006). 'How to Help Unemployed to Find Jobs Quickly: Experimental Evidence from a Mandatory Activation Program', IZA Discussion Paper No. 2504.

Hämäläinen, K. and Ollikainen, V. (2004). 'Differential Effects of Active Labour Market Programmes in the Early Stages of Young People's Unemployment', VATT Research Report 115.

Hardoy, I. (2005). 'Impact of Multiple Labour Market Programmes on Multiple Outcomes: The Case of Norwegian Youth Programmes', *Labour*, 19, 425–467.

Heckman, J.J., Ichimura, H. and Todd, P. (1998). 'Matching As An Econometric Evaluation Estimator', *Review of Economic Studies*, 65, 261–294.

Heckman, J.J., Lalonde, R.J. and Smith, J.A. (1999). 'The Economics and Econometrics of Active Labor Market Programs' in O. Ashenfelter and D. Card (eds.), *Handbook of Labor Economics*, Volume 3 (Part 1). North-Holland: Elsevier.

Hujer, R. and Wellner, M. (2000). 'The Effects of Public Sector Sponsored Training on Individual Employment Performance in East Germany', IZA Discussion Paper No. 141.

Hujer, R., Thomsen, S.L. and Zeiss, C. (2006). 'The Effects of Vocational Training Programmes on the duration of Unemployment in East Germany', *Allgemeines Statistisches Archiv*, 90, 299–321.

Imbens, G.W. and Wooldridge, J.M. (2008). 'Recent Developments in the Econometrics of Program Evaluation', IZA Discussion Paper 3640.

Indecon International Economic Consultants (2013). 'Indecon's Evaluation of JobBridge.' www.indecon.ie

Indecon International Economic Consultants (2005). 'Review of National Employment Action Plan Preventative Strategy: Draft Final Report', Dublin: Department of Enterprise, Trade and Employment. (http://www.entemp.ie/publications/labour/2005/neapstrategy.pdf).

Jaenichen, U. and Stephan, G. (2009). 'The Effectiveness of Targeted Wage Subsidies for Hard-to-Place Workers', *Applied Economics*, 43, 1209–1225.

Jensen, P., Rosholm, M. and Svarer, M. (2003). 'The Response of Youth Unemployment to Benefits, Incentives, and Sanctions', *European Journal of Political Economy*, 19, 301–316.

Jespersen, S.T., Munch, J.R. and Skipper, L. (2008). 'Costs and Benefits of Danish Active Labour Market Programmes', *Labour Economics*, 15, 859–884.

Kelly, E., McGuinness, S. and O'Connell, P.J. (2011). 'What Can Active Labour Market Policies Do?', ESRI Economic Renewal Series 001, Dublin: Economic and Social Research Institute.

Kirby, S. and Riley, R. (2004). 'Compulsory Work-Focused Interviews for Inactive Benefit Claimants: An Evaluation of the British ONE Pilot', *Labour Economics*, 11, 415–429.

Kluve, J. (2006). 'The Effectiveness of European Active Labour Market Policy', IZA Discussion Paper No. 2018.

Kluve, J. and Schmidt, C.M. (2002). 'Can Training and Employment Subsidies Combat European Unemployment?', *Economic Policy*, 17, 409–448.

Kluve, J., Lehmann, H. and Schmidt, C.M. (1999). 'Active Labor Market Policies in Poland: Human Capital Enhancement, Stigmatization, or Benefit Churning?', *Journal of Comparative Economics*, 27, 61–89.

Kluve, J., Schneider, H., Uhlendorff, A. and Zhao, Z. (2007). 'Evaluating Continuous Training Programs Using the Generalised Propensity Score', IZA Discussion Paper No. 3255.

Lalive, R., van Ours, J.C. and Zweimüller, J. (2005). 'The Effect of Benefit Sanctions on the Duration of Unemployment', *Journal of the European Economic Association*, 3, 1386–1417.

Lalive, R., van Ours, J.C. and Zweimüller, J. (2008). 'The Impact of Active Labour Market Programmes on the Duration of Unemployment in Switzerland', *The Economic Journal*, 118, 235–257.

Larsson, L. (2003). 'Evaluation of Swedish Youth Labor Market Programs', *The Journal of Human Resources*, 38, 891–927.

Lechner, M. (2000). 'An Evaluation of Public-Sector-Sponsored Continuous Vocational Training Programs in East Germany', *Journal of Human Resources*, 35, 347–375.

Lechner, M. and Wunsch, C. (2009). 'Are Training Programs More Effective When Unemployment is High?', *Journal of Labour Economics*, 27, 653–692.

Lechner, M., Miquel, R. and Wunsch, C. (2007). 'The Curse and Blessing of Training the Unemployed in a Changing Economy: The Case of East Germany after Unification', *German Economic Review*, 8, 468–509.

Lechner, M., Miquel, R. and Wunsch, C. (2011). 'Long-Run Effects of Public Sector Sponsored Training in West Germany', *Journal of the European Economic Association*, 9, 742–784.

Lissenburgh, S. (2004). 'New Deal Option Effects on Employment Entry and Unemployment Exit', *International Journal of Manpower*, 25, 411–430.

Martin, J. (2000) 'What Works Among Active Labour Market Policies: Evidence from OECD Countries' Experiences', *OECD Economic Studies*, No. 30, 2000–1.

McGuinness, S., O'Connell, P.J. and Kelly, E. (2011). 'One Dummy Won't Get it: The Impact of Training Programme Type and Duration on the Employment Chances of the Unemployed in Ireland', ESRI Working Paper 410.

McGuinness, S., O'Connell, P. J. and Kelly, E. (2013). 'Carrots, No Stick, No Driver: The Employment Impact of Job Search Assistance in a Regime with Minimal Monitoring and Sanctions.' UCD Geary Working Paper 2013/08.

McGuinness, S., O'Connell, P.J., Kelly, E. and Walsh, J.R. (2011). *Activation in Ireland: An Evaluation of the National Employment Action Plan*. ESRI Research Series No. 20. Dublin: Economic and Social Research Institute.

Müller, K. and Steiner, V. (2008). 'Imposed Benefit Sanctions and the Unemployment-to-Employment Transition: The German Experience', IZA Discussion Paper No. 3483.

Neubäumer, R. (2010). 'Can Training Programs or Rather Wage Subsidies Bring the Unemployed Back to Work? A Theoretical and Empirical Investigation for Germany', IZA Discussion Paper 4864.

OECD (1994a). *The OECD Jobs Study: Facts, Analysis, Strategies*. Paris: OECD.

OECD (1994b). *The OECD Jobs Study: Evidence and Explanations, Volumes I and II*. Paris: OECD.

OECD (2003). *OECD Employment Outlook*, Chapter 4. Paris: OECD.

OECD (2005). *OECD Employment Outlook*, Chapter 4. Paris: OECD.

OECD (2006a). *Boosting Jobs and Income: Policy Lessons from Reassessing the OECD Jobs Strategy*. Paris: OECD.

OECD (2006b). *OECD Employment Outlook*, Chapter 3. Paris: OECD.

OECD (2007). *OECD Employment Outlook*, Chapter 5. Paris: OECD.

OECD (2009a). *OECD Employment Outlook*, Chapter 1. Paris: OECD.

OECD (2009b). *OECD Employment Outlook*, Chapter 1. Background Document 'Addressing the Labour Market Challenges of the Economic Downturn: A Summary of Country Responses to the OECD-EC Questionnaire'. Paris: OECD.

O'Connell, P.J. (2002a). 'Employability: Trends in Employment and Unemployment; The Impact of Activation Measures; Unemployment Transitions', *Impact Evaluation of the European Employment Strategy in Ireland*. Dublin: Department of Enterprise, Trade and Employment. (http://www.entemp.ie/publications/labour/2004/eesimpactevaluation.pdf).

O'Connell, P.J. (2002b). 'Are They Working? Market Orientation and the Effectiveness of Active Labour-Market Programmes in Ireland', *European Sociological Review*, 18 (1): 65–83.

O'Connell, P.J. and McGinnity, F. (1997). *Working Schemes? Active Labour Market Policy in Ireland*. England: Ashgate.

O'Connell, P.J., McGuinness, S., Kelly, E. and Walsh, J.R. (2009). *National Profiling of the Unemployed in Ireland*. ESRI Research Series No. 10. Dublin: Economic and Social Research Institute.

Richardson, K. and van den Berg, G.J. (2006). 'Swedish Labor Market Training and the Duration of Unemployment', IZA Discussion Paper No. 2314.

Rosholm, M. and Skipper, L. (2009). 'Is Labour Market Training a Curse for the Unemployed? Evidence from a Social Experiment', *Journal of Applied Econometrics*, 24(2): 338–365.

Rosholm, M. and Svarer, M. (2004). 'Estimating the Threat Effect of Active Labour Market Programmes', IZA Discussion Paper No. 1300.

Scarpetta, S., Sonnett, A. and Manfredi, T. (2010). 'Rising Youth Unemployment During the Crisis: How to Prevent Negative Long-term Consequences on a Generation?' *OECD Social, Employment and Migration Working Papers*, No. 106. Paris: OECD Publishing.

Sianesi, B. (2008). 'Differential Effects of Active Labour Market Programs for the Unemployed', *Labour Economics*, 15, 370–399.

Svarer, M. (2007). 'The Effect of Sanctions on the Job Finding Rate: Evidence from Denmark', Economics Working Paper 2007–10, School of Economics and Management, University of Aarhus.

Tergeist, P. and D. Grubb (2006). 'Activation Strategies and the Performance of Employment Services in Germany, the Netherlands and the United Kingdom', OECD Social, Employment and Migration Working Papers No. 42.

van den Berg, G.J., van der Klaauw, B. and van Ours, J.C. (2004). 'Punitive Sanctions and the Transition Rate from Welfare to Work', *Journal of Labour Economics*, 22, 211–241.

van Ours, J.C. (2001). 'Do Active Labour Market Policies Help Unemployed Workers to Find and Keep Regular Jobs?', *ZEW Economic Studies*, 13, 125–152.

van Reenen, J. (2003). 'Active Labour Market Policies and the British New Deal for the Young Unemployed in Context', NBER Working Paper No. 95.

CHAPTER 8

Providing Economic Security Through Competition and Regulatory Policy: What Is the Evidence?

Paul K. Gorecki[103]

This chapter considers the role of competition and regulatory policy in providing economic security. It presents the findings from a substantial body of evidence on the impact of these policies. In terms of the policy landscape (Figure 1.1), competition and regulatory policy is mature, but evolving. Much of the current policy agenda is driven by European Union (EU) legislation and, to a lesser extent, the EU-International Monetary Fund Programme of Financial Support for Ireland.

This chapter addresses these issues by drawing on different kinds of evidence and best practice guidelines developed by international organisations such as the European Commission and Organisation for Economic Co-operation and Development (OECD). While much of the evidence draws on relatively recent events, reference is also made to the experience of the Great Depression, the last time an economic contraction as severe and as global as the current one was experienced.

The key research question is: what is the impact of relaxing or softening the consumer welfare focus of competition and regulatory policy towards favouring the interests of incumbent firms and their labour forces? For policymakers the answer to this question will assist in deciding whether or not, as a general rule, to grant a request from a firm and its employees for the weakening of competition and regulatory policy as a way of providing some relief from economic disruption.

Overall, the evidence surveyed here suggests that providing economic security through relaxing competition (e.g., under-enforcement, carve-outs or exemptions) and regulatory (e.g., restricting entry, changing regulatory objectives to favour the incumbent regulated firm(s)) policy is costly. It creates insiders who benefit from increased security and outsiders who are not in receipt of such protection. The outsiders experience increased prices, poorer service quality, higher unemployment

---

[103] The chapter revises and updates Gorecki (2012b).

and lower wages. However, even for the insiders there is evidence the benefits are short lived. Thus, the implication for policymakers is that competition and regulatory policy should stick firmly to promoting consumer welfare.

Irrespective of the duration of the benefits, providing increased security through relaxing competition and regulatory policy leads to longer term damage to the flexibility and success of the economy, which affects everybody. This raises the issue of what ought to be the process for awarding greater economic security through competition and regulatory policy. Competition and regulatory policy contain provisions that permit otherwise restrictive agreements and regulations to be allowed, but only when the benefits exceed the costs. The implication for policymakers is that these procedures and tests, which are set out in legislation as well as European Commission and OECD guidance, should be strictly followed.

Future research should concentrate on quantifying, evaluating and drawing attention to unnecessarily restrictive or lax competition and regulatory policy. However, researchers also have an important role as gatekeepers, monitoring and commenting on the quality of analysis used to justify the restrictive competition or regulatory policy in the first place, whether it is a regulatory impact analysis or a commissioned research report.

BACKGROUND

The Irish economy's prospects for growth and jobs are not good.[104] People are concerned – quite naturally – about their present and future job prospects both for themselves and their children. Enterprises also face considerable uncertainty as to future demand and access to capital. In these circumstances enterprises, employees and others, either individually or through representative bodies, seek intervention from the State to help them deal with such economic uncertainty and insecurity.

Ireland has few policy instruments or levers it can use at present to improve economic performance, which is the key to creating growth and jobs and so alleviating concerns over economic security. Monetary policy is not an option since Ireland entered the euro in 1999. Equally, on fiscal policy the State has very limited room for manoeuvre, with continuing fiscal and budgetary adjustments. Thus, the State will have to respond sparingly to demands for tax breaks, subsidies or other financial assistance to reduce economic insecurity. This is not to deny, of course, that a more sensible, efficient and fair tax system is likely to boost economic growth, by minimising collection costs and reducing distortions, and thus contribute towards alleviating concerns over economic security.

Competition and regulatory policy are, however, off-budget *al*ternatives by which the State can address the demand for economic security.[105] Concerns over

---

104 See, for example, Duffy and Timoney (2013).

105 Regulatory agencies are typically funded in Ireland through a levy on the regulated entities. However, the State funds the body charged with administering and enforcing competition policy, the Competition Authority, out of tax revenue.

excessive or destructive competition, for example, can be addressed by regulatory controls on entry or by exempting from competition law a trade association's efforts to organise the market to ensure 'fair' incomes.[106] Nevertheless, the EU and the EU-IMF Programme of Financial Support for Ireland place certain constraints on the State in respect of competition and regulatory policy.[107]

There are two quite different and opposing approaches as to how competition and regulatory policy can be used to promote economic security. First, and this is the traditional view of competition and regulatory policy, by making markets work well for consumers (including treating businesses as consumers of goods and services) so that markets operate effectively and efficiently. This approach sees arrangements that restrict competition, particularly cartels, prohibited, with offenders caught and appropriately punished. Regulation promotes cost-reflective pricing and investment decisions in vital sectors of the economy such as electricity, gas and telecommunications, through the provision of a transparent, predictable and stable regulatory framework. The success of these policies by stimulating competition and efficiency in the non-traded sector will, it is argued, feed through to lower input prices, better service quality and more choice for the traded sector, thus enhancing competitiveness. The result will be to stimulate growth in output, jobs and income. In short, better and improved economic security.

Second, and this is the entirely opposite approach, it could be argued that in troubled times competition and regulatory policy should be relaxed and administered with flexibility and sensitivity to provide economic security to particular groups that are, or appear to be, especially adversely affected by the recession and austerity. In effect, the first (traditional) approach above should be abandoned or substantially loosened in its application. This alternative approach sees that shelter from market forces can help protect jobs and income and thus provide stability and an opportunity for enterprises and individuals to adjust. Such relaxation would, of course, be temporary; once the economy recovers from the recession then the competition and regulatory regime could return to normal.

The issue thus becomes which way should policy go with respect to competition and regulation.

- Should competition and regulatory policy be relaxed to address concerns over economic security in troubled times?
- What does the international as well as Irish evidence suggest is the economic effect of such relaxation?

---

106 On the choice of policy instruments, see, for example, Trebilcock *et al.* (1982).

107 The EU, for example, insists on the independence of regulatory bodies in energy and telecommunication (Gorecki, 2011a), the European Commission has jurisdiction on competition policy where the alleged breach affects trade between Member States (Whish, 2009), while the European Union (EU)–International Monetary Fund (IMF) Programme of Financial Support for Ireland has measures that promote competition and structural reform, as detailed below.

- Does relaxation of competition and regulatory policy provide economic security? If so, at what price?
- Are there any conditions under which groups or sectors should be sheltered from market forces to provide greater economic security?

This chapter addresses these issues by drawing on different kinds of evidence including surveys, case studies, meta-analysis and best practice guidelines developed by international organisations such as the European Commission (EC) and Organisation for Economic Co-operation and Development (OECD). While much of the evidence draws on relatively recent events and experience, reference is also made to the experience of the Great Depression because it is the last time an economic contraction as severe and as global as the current one was experienced. This evidence is used primarily to examine the impact of relaxing competition and regulatory policy, not only in terms of whether economic security is provided, but also at what cost. In contrast, the best practice guidelines are employed in addressing questions related to the possible conditions under which economic security should be provided through competition and regulatory policy.

The chapter is divided into four sections, including the introduction. In the next section we look at the international and Irish evidence on the impact of relaxing competition and regulatory policy. Attention turns in the penultimate section to an examination of competition and regulatory tests that are (or could be) used by the State. The final section completes the chapter by drawing conclusions in respect of the questions set out above.

RELAXING COMPETITION AND REGULATORY POLICY: THE EVIDENCE

Several sources can be used to cast light on the impact of easing competition and regulatory policy. One set of studies looks at the effect of the relaxation of competition and regulatory policies in troubled times, such as Ireland currently experiences. Other research quantifies the impact of breaches of competition policy or the effects of restrictive or lax regulation in more normal times. Implicit in these studies is the view that vigorous enforcement of competition and regulatory policy is the default position and that relaxing competition and regulatory policy is very much the exception.[108]

---

108 A number of studies discuss the positive relationship between competition and growth, several of which are cited below.

Reduced Enforcement of Competition Law

A number of policy responses are consistent with under-enforcement of competition law in troubled times.[109] For example, the resources allocated to the competition agency could be reduced disproportionately compared to overall reductions in public expenditure. Thus, the agency would not be in a position to conduct as many investigations and prosecutions. Competition law could be amended to make it less effective.[110] Thus, any investigations that were conducted would have a much lower probability of success. Alternatively, the competition agency could be subject to administrative changes which do not have any apparent strategic direction, e.g., reorganised or merged with another agency with little thought or planning.[111] Enforcement activity would be severely hampered by any of these measures and consequently, the probability of being caught breaking competition law would be reduced.

There is a considerable volume of studies on the impact of breaches of competition law. Attention here will be concentrated on cartels, which are commonly considered to be the most pernicious breach of competition law.[112] There is evidence that competition enforcement does impact on the extent of cartel activity. For example, a survey of UK businesses by London Economics (2011, Table 1, p.7), for the UK Office of Fair Trading, found that each cartel investigation deterred 28 cartels.[113] Connor and Bolotova (2006, pp. 1133–1134), in a literature survey and meta-analysis of several hundred cartels across a large number of jurisdictions in the EU, North America and Asia found that the stronger the competition regime, the lower the cartel overcharge.

Nevertheless, it could still be argued that cartels are inherently unstable and provide only temporary protection from the crisis occasioned by the recession.

---

109 The record of the policy response in this respect in Ireland since the onset of the recession in 2008 to competition policy is set out in Gorecki (2012a). Of the three policy responses identified in the paragraph in the text, only one was arguably pursued in Ireland – the October 2008 proposal to merge the Competition Authority and the National Consumer Agency. There is virtually no documentation publicly available to consider the case for this policy proposal, but nearly five years on no legislative proposals have been published, although some are expected later in 2013.
110 For example, breaches of competition law could be redefined to be much narrower, the evidentiary standard required to prove a breach could be raised, and the investigative powers of the competition agency could be reduced.
111 Thus senior managers are likely to become more concerned with turf wars and reorganisation issues than enforcing competition law.
112 'Cartels are the most serious form of anti-competitive behaviour. So stopping cartels remains the Authority's top enforcement priority.' (Competition Authority, 2011b, p. 5). The European Commission (2011, p. 5) takes an equally dim view of cartels.
113 The UK (for individuals only), like Ireland (for individuals and firms), imposes criminal sanctions for hard core cartel offences. In contrast, in most of the rest of the EU cartel offences are civil rather than criminal.

Using this line of thought, investigating and prosecuting cartels is likely to be of limited effectiveness. Furthermore, it could be argued that since cartel arrangements are likely to occur under conditions of fewness, tacit collusion (which is very difficult to detect and prosecute) can be substituted for a cartel. However, the evidence is inconsistent with these views. For example, Connor and Bolotova (2006, pp. 1133–1134) found that cartels raised prices well above the competitive level – on average, 29 per cent, with a median of 19 per cent.[114] They also find that cartels last, on average, for 8.6 years (*ibid*, p. 1128).[115] Research reported by Veljanovski (2011, Table 2, p. 879), in a study of EU cartel decisions from late 2006 to 2010, recorded an average duration of 8.9 years.[116] In terms of the number of cartel members, Hay and Kelly (1974, p. 20) in a study of US cartels between 1963 and 1972, found that the average number of cartel members was 7.25, but this excluded four cases where there were 50 or more cartel members. In terms of concentration, the leading four firms accounted for between 75 and 100 per cent of the market for around 40 per cent of the cartels for which data was available (*ibid*, Table 2, p. 22). Case studies of individual cartels, such as bromine, ocean shipping and stamp auctions, find cartels can actually raise prices to the monopoly level.[117]

While under-enforcement of competition policy is likely to lead to increased cartel activity through which enterprises are able to ameliorate the impact of the recession through securing higher prices in a less competitive environment, it is also likely to have a number of adverse impacts which have wider economic effects.

- Under-enforcement as a policy condones cartel activity, which is a criminal offence in Ireland. This might lead to increased criminal activity if norms of

---

114 However, there were variations depending on, for example, location, geographic scope and time period.
115 The minimum was 1 month, the maximum, 98 years.
116 These estimates of cartel duration may be too low, if subsequent to investigation/prosecution former cartel members are able to collude tacitly. The limited evidence is somewhat mixed on this issue. Kovacic *et al.* (2005), examine post cartel prices for various vitamins and find: vitamins markets with two conspirators were able to tacitly collude post the cartel, but not in vitamins markets where there were three or more conspirators. It should also be remembered that EU and Irish competition law contains provisions against concerted arrangements which are a looser form of agreement than a formal cartel. For further discussion see Whish (2009, pp. 104–113), that quotes a European Court of Justice judgment that defines such a concerted practice as 'a form of coordination between undertakings which, without having reached the stage where an agreement properly so-called has been concluded, knowingly substitutes practical cooperation between them for the risks of competition' (*ibid*, p. 105).
117 See Asker (2010), for details of the stamp auction case study, and Levenstein and Suslow (2006, pp. 79–82).

behaviour of individuals are influenced by such a permissive attitude by the State towards white collar crime.[118]
- No attempt is made to distinguish instances where there may be merit in providing economic security from instances where there is no merit. Enterprises self select where and when to form cartels.
- Cartels are long lasting. Hence if the cartel is formed – encouraged by under-enforcement – it will not necessarily cease once the economy returns to better (more normal) times.[119]
- Cartels lead to higher prices. The prices affected may involve goods or services particularly important for poorer consumers or that are used as inputs into exports, resulting in potential damage to national competitiveness.

These drawbacks reaffirm the traditional case for active competition policy in terms of promoting growth, productivity, innovation, and consumer choice.

Exemptions from Competition Law: Carve-outs

While under-enforcement of competition law can provide some respite for enterprises from the competitive pressures of the marketplace by lowering the probability that cartels will be detected and prosecuted, it nevertheless remains the case that such actions are illegal. When economic circumstances return to normal so will enforcement. Hence enterprises, often with the support of their employees, may request that the State provides a specific legislative exemption or carve out from competition law.

There are historical precedents for exemptions and carve-outs in the US in the 1930s and in Japan in the 1980s.[120, 121] In the US the New Deal cartelisation

---

118 Keizer et al. (2008) show how norms of behaviour of others affects the propensity to break the law.

119 On this issue Levenstein and Suslow (2006, p. 67) comment that, 'successful cartels do not break apart in response to demand fluctuations; they develop organizational machinery of some sort that allows them to weather cyclical fluctuations.' The authors also note that often cartels have a 'rocky start' before being able to manage 'periods of sustained collusion for longer periods' (*ibid*, p. 74). Under-enforcement is likely to facilitate the switch from the rocky start to sustained collusion.

120 The Antitrust Division of the US Department of Justice, based on experience of the 1930s, is 'dedicated to vigorous enforcement of the antitrust laws during these challenging times' (Shapiro, 2009, p. 11). Another difference with the 1930s is that the widespread protectionism that occurred then has not taken place in the current recession. One of the reasons for this is the growth of global supply chains (Datt et al., 2011). The widespread protectionism facilitated the price increases, particularly in the traded sector.

121 For a discussion of Japan in the 1980s, see Porter and Sakakibara (2004); Porter *et al.* (2000); and, Hayashi and Prescott (2002). The findings are similar to those for the US in the 1930s.

policies 'suspended antitrust law and permitted collusion in some sectors provided that industry raised wages above market-clearing levels and accepted collective bargaining with independent unions' (Cole and Ohanian, 2004, p. 781). Industry-wide codes of fair competition were agreed that raised wages and set minimum prices, the latter of which incorporated 'explicit payments to capital' (*ibid*, p. 785). These arrangements covered a large number of industries. The evidence suggests that as a result of these New Deal policies 'in at least manufacturing and some energy and mining industries' (Cole and Ohanian, 2004, p. 793) wages and prices were raised significantly.

The New Deal had other much less beneficial effects. Output and employment were restricted in the cartelised sectors, limiting employment opportunities. Wages in the other sectors of the economy were depressed below their steady state level, even though there was normal productivity growth (*ibid.*, p. 812). Wholesale prices were raised substantially compared with what they otherwise would have been – 24 per cent in 1935 and 14 per cent in 1939 (*ibid.*, Table 5, p. 791). Unemployment was higher than it otherwise would be. In other words, the insiders – those subject to the protection of the codes of fair competition – benefited from the exemption from antitrust laws and associated policies while those outside lost. However, the ramifications extended beyond these redistributive effects to have wider macroeconomic implications. Both Cole and Ohanian (2004) and Romer (1999) argue that these New Deal policies held back the subsequent recovery by preventing adjustment in the 1930s.

Regulation: Changing the Rules of the Game in Favour of the Incumbent

To a considerable extent enterprises in regulated markets, such as fixed line telecommunications networks, energy networks, water supply and airports where there is a clear regulatory rationale, are protected from austerity and economic adversity. They are typically assured of a guaranteed rate of return and protected from competition since they are either a natural monopoly or, at worst, part of a tight oligopoly. That does not mean, however, that these industries are immune from the impact of the recession, since demand for all these areas is likely to be less than it otherwise would be. In the case of airports, for example, demand is likely to be quite income elastic. Furthermore, regulated enterprises might have become highly leveraged and experience debt servicing problems. Incurring such risks may in part reflect a view, given the importance of the regulated enterprise's activity to the wider economy, that the regulator and/or the State would step in to provide assistance if loss of service is threatened due to financial problems.

Governments can alter the regulatory structure in a number of ways to assist regulated enterprises and their labour forces, which are suffering either directly or indirectly because of the recession. First, the objectives of the regulation can be revised to give greater weight to the interests of producers, broadly defined to include the regulated enterprise, its owners and employees. This is most likely to occur where the regulator is given a statutory duty to promote the industry as well as to promote efficient investment and pricing, the more traditional objectives of sector regulators. Until recently, for example, banking legislation in Ireland had the twin objectives of promoting both financial stability and the financial services industry,[122] while the objectives of the Commission for Aviation Regulation were amended in 2004 to be more favourable to the airport authority.[123] Second, the regulatory regime could be changed to give the relevant Minister more control over individual decisions of the regulator. In such a scenario the regulated enterprises and their employees could make direct representations to the Minister so as to influence the regulator's decisions. There can be little doubt that, in the short term at least, such moves provide greater economic security to the regulated network industries. However, there are a number of significant drawbacks for such policies.

- It is not obvious that regulated enterprises and their workforces merit special regulatory treatment. These industries, as noted above, are frequently guaranteed certain rates of return.[124]
- If there is a concern that a regulated enterprise is in financial difficulty that might result in interruption of a vital service, such as electricity or telephone/data transmission, then the solution is not for a regulatory regime that protects the regulated enterprise from the consequences of its own decisions, but rather the introduction of a resolution mechanism that allows the regulator to intervene and take over the enterprise.[125]
- Giving dual objectives to a regulator may hamper effective regulation. What is the correct trade-off between promoting/protecting the regulated industry and promoting more and greater efficiency and consumer welfare? In the UK, for example, '… over [BSE] infected beef, [where] a government department responsible for both consumer protection and industry sponsorship voiced misleadingly reassuring statements until the problem because too serious to ignore. The crisis was a particularly forceful example of the dangers of linking sponsorship with regulation. The results were damaging to both the interests of the industry and the interests of the public.' (Kay, 2009, p. 35).
- Compromising the independence of regulators can increase uncertainty and result in higher prices for consumers of the regulated service. Investments in infrastructure industries are often long lived, with asset lives measured in decades rather than years. Increased uncertainty translates into higher financing costs.[126] Since many of the infrastructure regulated sectors are non-

---

122 Honohan (2010).
123 Gorecki (2011a, pp. 195–196).
124 In some instances, such as electricity, there is some evidence that rents are being earned (Diffney et al. (2009)).
125 Review Group on State Assets and Liabilities (2011, pp. 11–12).
126 Gorecki (2011a, pp. 181–188).

traded inputs into the traded sector, Ireland's competitiveness will be adversely affected by higher prices. This will lead to job destruction and less rather than more economic security.

Restrictive Sector-Specific Entry and Price Regulation

In a period of austerity, with concerns over easy and excessive entry, destructive competition, falling standards, bankruptcies and low returns, one tempting response of the government to ensure economic security is to introduce direct or sector specific regulation (direct regulation). Such regulation typically shields incumbents from competition from outsiders/potential entrants by limiting new entry, while restricting competition between incumbents through, for example, specifying prices and other commercial conditions. Such regulation was, at one time, widespread in sectors such as buses, taxis, trucking, and airlines. In Canada and the US, much of this regulation was introduced during the Great Depression and only abolished in the 1970s and 1980s when the impact of such regulation was evaluated and found to be damaging to growth and productivity.[127] More recently the OECD (2001) evaluated such price and entry regulation in Ireland. Many of the same themes and empirical findings that emerged from the evaluation of direct regulation in North America were echoed in the findings for Ireland. In view of this, much of the discussion in this section draws upon Irish examples.

In terms of providing economic security, the international and Irish evidence is consistent with direct regulation limiting supply and increasing prices. While new greenfield entry is typically restricted under such regulation, entry is still possible through purchasing the right to engage in the regulated activity from an incumbent. This might, for example, be a licence in the case of a taxi or a public house. The price that is paid for the right to engage in the regulated activity is a measure of its 'economic rents', i.e., the difference between the return to employing capital in the regulated compared to a competitive sector, adjusted for any differences in risk.[128]

The extent of these economic rents can be illustrated in Ireland. For example, in 2000 the capital value in Ireland of a taxi licence traded in the secondary market was €101,000, a public house licence €140,000, while prior to road freight deregulation in 1986, a road freight licence traded at €40,000.[129] Restrictive entry regulations in the pharmacy market between 1996 and 2002 resulted in a 40 per cent increase in the value of a pharmacy. The impact of airline regulation was to

---

127 Breyer (1982) and Kahn (1988) on US direct regulation; Economic Council of Canada (1979, 1981) on Canada.
128 Qualitative regulation can, to some extent, substitute for quantitative restrictions. A good example of this is taxi regulation in Ireland. For a discussion see Gorecki (2013).
129 The discussion in this paragraph is based on Gorecki (2009b, Table 2, p. 38; and Table 4, p. 42; 2011b; 2013). The airline price increases refer to the US and Ireland. In the case of Ireland, the estimate of 33 per cent is based on the real decline in the Dublin-London price, 1985–1995.

raise prices by between 18–33 per cent. There is also some evidence that the value of licences increases over time. In the case of a Dublin taxi licence, it increased, measured in constant 1980 €, by a factor of close to 10 between 1980 and 2000, immediately prior to liberalisation of entry controls.

Although direct regulation may be introduced in response to a short-term crisis, the evidence suggests it nevertheless often lasts for decades. In Ireland, for example, the duration of such regulation is: airlines, 54 years (1932–1986); cement, 67 years (1933–2000); public houses 111 years and still extant (1902 to present);[130] taxis 22 years (1978–2000) and three years (2010 and still extant); and, buses 81 years and still extant (1932 to present).[131] An exception is pharmacy restrictions on the location of new pharmacies which lasted only 6 years, from 1996 to 2002, because a High Court judgment caused the entry controls to be dropped by government.[132]

It could, of course, be argued that the transfer of income from consumers of these services through higher prices to the providers of the services is not a cost to society as a whole in terms of forgone output or inefficiency, but rather only a redistribution of income. Furthermore, some of these groups are, it could be claimed, in some sense deserving and so there is an element of social justice involved. However, these arguments do not stand up because direct regulation involves distortions and questionable allocations of resources.

- Resources are consumed in making representations for the creating of direct regulation and for its retention. The evidence suggests that in many cases the alleged oversupply or destructive competition did not justify direct regulation.[133] Such rent seeking behaviour consumes resources that arguably have little social worth or output (Krueger, 1974; Posner, 1975; Tullock, 1967).
- The rents may be dissipated by those subject to direct regulation because of the lack of competition, leading to X-inefficiency and lack of innovation.
- Entry and exit is an important channel of productivity growth.[134] Entrants are often the source of new ideas and innovations that challenge the status quo. Incumbents may be reluctant to invest in new technology that might render

---

130 There was some relaxation in 2000. For details see OECD (2001, p. 204).

131 It should be noted that the discussion is centred on direct regulation that limits or places restriction on entry rather than regulation per se. In the case of taxis, for example, there are good reasons, based on market failure, for setting a maximum price and specifying certain quality standards, but not placing quantitative limits on the number of taxis. For further discussion see Fingleton et al. (1998).

132 Similarly quantitative limits on the number of taxis were found illegal in a 2000 High Court judgment (OECD, 2001, p. 207), but this did not prevent the reintroduction of quantitative limits for taxis in 2010 (Gorecki, 2013).

133 On pharmacy regulation in Ireland see Gorecki (2011b), on taxis in Canada see Economic Council of Canada (1981, p. 25), in Ireland see Fingleton et al. (1998) and Gorecki (2013), on trucking see Kahn (1988, Vol. II, pp. 178–185).

134 Baldwin and Gorecki (1991) and Scarpetta et al. (2002).

existing investment obsolete. By restricting entry through regulation, productivity growth is slowed.
- Consumers experience not just higher prices because of direct regulation on entry, but also enjoy less choice and possibly lower service quality. Waiting times for taxis increase (Goodbody, 2009, Table 6.3, p. 49), some geographic areas may be underserved by pubs (Competition Authority, 1998, pp. 36–50) or pharmacies (Competition Authority, 2001, pp. 12–13) due to entry restrictions.
- Persons and resources that are prepared to enter a sector and are denied access in a period of austerity when jobs are scarce. Unemployment may consequently be higher.
- While the initial enterprises in a market are subject to direct regulation gain, if they subsequently sell their taxi or pub or pharmacy licence, then the new owner will only earn a normal rate of return, unless there are unanticipated price increases. On the other hand, if entry conditions are relaxed the new owner will suffer a capital loss. Tullock (1975) refers to this as the transitional gains trap.
- The impact of the restrictive regulation extends beyond the regulated sector to the economy as a whole. Barone and Cingano (2011), drawing on evidence for OECD countries, find that the less the incidence of such regulation in the service sector (particularly professional services and energy regulation), the better the economic performance of the downstream manufacturing sector in terms of value added, productivity and export growth.

Competition and Regulatory Policy Intervention to Promote Greater Economic Security: Some Conclusions

The evidence suggests that providing economic security through relaxing competition and regulatory policy is costly. It creates two groups in society: insiders who benefit from increased security and outsiders who are not in receipt of such protection. While the insiders receive protection from market forces, the outsiders bear the cost in terms of increased prices, poorer service quality, higher unemployment and lower wages. In part this asymmetry is likely to be a reflection of the fact that the insiders (those that benefit from the relaxation of competition and regulatory law) are concentrated and well organised while the outsiders (those that bear the cost) are disparate and unlikely to be well organised. However, even for the insiders there is evidence that in many cases the benefits are short lived and accrue mostly to the initial group members subject to the greater economic security.[135]

---

[135] This is consistent with the finding that direct regulation lasts for long periods of time while at the same time there is an active secondary market for licences to enter the regulated activity. Equally in the case of cartels that last, on average for close to a decade, a cartel member may be traded either as a private firm or alternatively its shares may be traded.

Irrespective of whether or not the benefits are short lived, providing increased security through relaxing competition and regulatory policy leads to longer term damage to the flexibility and success of the economy, which affects both the insiders and the outsiders.[136] This raises the issue of what ought to be the process for awarding greater economic security through competition and regulatory policy. Is there a framework that should be employed that might command greater and/or more deserved support?

STANDARDS AND TESTS FOR COMPETITION AND REGULATORY POLICY INTERVENTION

A corollary to the potential substantial adverse economic consequences of relaxing competition and regulatory policy is that such relaxation should be invoked only after careful consideration of the rationale as well as weighing the costs and the benefits. There are standards and tests contained within competition and regulatory policy and law that set out instances in which it is appropriate for otherwise anticompetitive agreements to be permitted and/or restrictive regulation to be introduced.

Competition Policy: Section 4 (5) of the Competition Act 2002

Competition law contains provisions to permit what would otherwise be viewed as anticompetitive arrangements.[137] All agreements are subject to competition law, whether they are anticompetitive or not. However, where an arrangement is judged likely to breach competition law there are clear rules for when, despite this arrangement, it can be allowed. Broadly speaking the benefits of the arrangement should outweigh the costs.

---

136 It is no doubt for such reasons that the EU-IMF Programme for Financial Support for Ireland contains structural reforms that promote competition policy, liberalise the regulation of the legal profession and other measures designed to promote competitive markets. For details see EU and IMF Programme reports and updates see: http://www.finance.gov.ie/viewdoc.asp?DocID=6856. Accessed 14 May 2013.

137 In this discussion we concentrate on anticompetitive agreements. However, it should be noted that an abuse of a dominant position might be permitted if the same four conditions set out in the text in reference to agreements are met. (For a discussion see European Commission (2009)). An otherwise anticompetitive merger would be permitted if either: (i) the efficiencies flowing from the merger more than offset the anticompetitive price enhancing effects of the merger; or (ii) the acquired firm is a failing firm. In troubled times both of these defences might be expected to be advanced by the merging parties. However, they are rarely successful due to the stringent requirements that need to be satisfied. These are set out in the merger guidelines of the Competition Authority (2002). See also the Competition Authority's 2008 Kerry Breeo merger determination for its treatment of efficiencies and the 2011 Musgrave/Superquinn merger determination on the failing firm defence. These determinations may be found at: www.tca.ie. Accessed 14 May 2013.

Agreements that would otherwise be anticompetitive are allowed under competition law – at both the Irish (Section 4(5) of the Competition Act, 2002) and EU (Article 101(3) of the Treaty on the Functioning of the European Union) level – if four conditions are satisfied. An agreement must:

- contribute to improving the production or distribution of goods or to promoting technical or economic progress,
- while allowing consumers a fair share of the resulting benefit.

But at the same time the agreement must not,

a. impose on the undertakings concerned restrictions which are not indispensable to the attainment of these objectives; and,
b. afford such undertakings the possibility of eliminating competition in respect of a substantial part of the products in question.

The criteria balance the positive impact of the anticompetitive agreement against the possible price raising impact of the agreement, while at the same time ensuring that the distributional consequences are addressed. The test is a longstanding provision of both EU and Irish competition law, with extensive European Commission (2004) guidance.

In the context of markets and sectors facing difficulties adjusting to adverse economic circumstances, the EU has allowed a limited number of otherwise anti-competitive agreements aimed at restructuring in synthetic fibres, petrochemicals and bricks.[138] In Ireland, a recent attempt to secure an agreement to rationalise over-capacity in beef processing failed.[139] In some cases representative bodies in Ireland have been successful in securing a commitment of a carve out from competition law, despite unsuccessfully arguing to the Competition Authority that the benefits of the agreement exceeded the costs and thus met the conditions set out in Section 4(5).[140, 141] Such policy responses by the State undermine the

---

138 For a discussion of these cases and the treatment of restructuring agreements by the EU, see Whish (2009, pp. 600–601). These cases date mostly from the 1980s and 1990s. An examination of the European Commission's Annual Reports on Competition Policy for 2008 to 2010 shows that restructuring is very much tied in with State Aid, rather than exemptions based on Article 101 (3). Indeed, no examples of the latter were mentioned.
139 Competition Authority (2011a, pp. 22–23).
140 For example, in the case of an anti-competitive agreement concerning voice-over actors and advertising agencies, an attempt was made to argue to the Competition Authority that the agreement met the conditions set out in Section 4(5) of the Competition Act, 2002. The Authority disagreed that the required standard had been met, but the representative body for voice over actors continued to press the Government to agree to a carve out from competition law. This has not, as yet, been enacted. For details see Gorecki (2009a, pp. 222–223).
141 See over.

effectiveness of competition policy and encourage enterprises and employees experiencing difficulty in troubled times to appeal directly to elected representatives to secure an exemption.[142]

Screening New Regulations: Regulatory Impact Analysis

The well-known market failure framework sets out grounds under which governments can intervene to provide economic security to participants in individual markets. There is no need to rehearse that literature here.[143] One of the grounds that is particularly relevant in troubled times is destructive competition, although it is a rationale that while often invoked (e.g., pharmacies, passenger transport, etc.) does not usually stand up to critical scrutiny.[144] Ideally, a carefully designed set of guidelines should set out when regulation is appropriate, based on the market failure framework, together with an institutional mechanism that ensures adherence with the guidelines. Such best practice guidance is developed by bodies such as the OECD (1997) by carefully studying and surveying the record of its member countries. The key requirements are rigorous objective analysis, transparency and strong support from Ministers, backed by a dedicated unit, in order to ensure consistency and compliance with the programme.

In 2005, Ireland introduced such an instrument, Regulatory Impact Analysis (RIA), under which new regulations are, in principle, thoroughly evaluated on an *ex ante* basis.[145] The OECD (2001, pp. 108–109), in advising the State, was able to draw upon its best practice guidelines in formulating its recommendations for improving regulation. In accordance with best practice the Better Regulation

---

141 Although not a carve out in the above sense, the move to impose a Code of Practice for Grocery Goods Undertakings, is likely to shield food processors and primary producers from the full rigours of competition, despite a lack of evidence to support the Code. (Gorecki, 2009c).

142 Under the terms of the EU-IMF Programme for Financial Support for Ireland, which runs until the end of 2013, it is unlikely any such exemptions will be granted. The July 2011 update of the programme states, '[R]equests for exemptions to the competition law framework will not be accepted unless they are consistent with the goals of the EU/IMF supported programme for Ireland and the needs of the economy' (EU and IMF, 2011, p. 29).

143 See, for example, Breyer (1982) and Kahn (1988). Markets fail for a variety of reasons: the presence of firms with market power, such as monopolies; externalities such as pollution and climate change; and, imperfect information leading to financial and health and safety regulation.

144 See discussion above.

145 The methodology is set out in 2005 and 2009 publications issued by the Department of the Taoiseach. Details of these and other Better Regulation Unit publications and regulatory reform agenda may be found at: http://www.taoiseach.gov.ie/eng/Publications/Publications_Archive/Publications_2011/Better_Regulation_Archive.html. Accessed 20 May 2013.

Unit (BRU), which was part of the Department of the Taoiseach, was given responsibility for RIA and the broader better regulation agenda.

The evidence suggests that the implementation and application of the RIA has not lived up to expectations. Goggin and Lauder (2008, p. 6), in a review of the first two to three years sponsored by BRU, reported the perception of external stakeholders that progress was 'disappointing.'[146] The OECD (2010) revisited the better regulation agenda in Ireland in 2010. Although some progress was noted (*ibid*, p. 21), concerns were expressed with respect to the role of BRU (*op. cit*, p.17) as well as criticisms in the application of RIAs (*op. cit*, p.22). The OECD (2010, pp. 28–34) set out a series of key specific recommendations designed to improve not only RIAs but the regulatory agenda more generally. In coming to these judgments the OECD was comparing Ireland to the best practice guidelines it had developed based on the record of what works well in other advanced industrialised countries.

At the present time the future of the RIA and the better regulation agenda is unclear. The BRU itself was abolished in 2011, with the staff assigned to other duties. In February 2012 the government, although recognising the importance of robust and consistent RIAs, acknowledged that 'there is now a lacuna at the centre of Government as this responsibility has yet to be reassigned.'[147] New 'structures to improve coordination and synchronisation'[148] were to be introduced by the end of 2012. However, by May 2013 no such structures have either been announced or created.[149]

In sum, the process of putting in place a rigorous and effective system for evaluating new regulations has been ongoing for in excess of 10 years and remains incomplete. New structures and strengthened procedures are needed. As a result of the weaknesses and shortcomings in the current regime there can be no guarantee that new laws and regulations are being subjected to the prior scrutiny

---

146 Goggin and Lauder (2008, p. 7) also comment, that in 'interviews, representatives of the business sector expressed strong criticism of the lack of visibility of RIAs; they felt that either they were not done, or, if done, many were not published, which meant opportunities for critiques of RIA by business or academics had not developed. Where RIAs had been done, there was a lack of credible consultation; and risk assumptions and estimates of costs and benefits had not been consulted on, and timescales in some cases unrealistic. The timing of RIAs was frequently criticised; they were seen as an "add-on" which happened at the end of the regulatory process, rather than a fundamental part of it. The quality of published RIAs was considered poor...'

147 DJEI (2012, p. 37).

148 *Ibid*, p. 38.

149 The Department of Public Expenditure and Reform has lead responsibility. One element of the new structure is the recently announced Government Economic and Evaluation Service part of the mandate of which includes RIAs. However, the service appears to be more of a support function, rather than an overarching oversight, monitoring and compliance mechanism for government. See Department of Public Expenditure and Reform (2012).

and analysis that they should be, with the result that the adverse consequences outlined in Section 2 are not being avoided.

What Standards and Tests for Intervention?

Internationally there are well thought out and established tests for allowing otherwise anticompetitive agreements to be exempt from competition law and for approving regulatory proposals that might restrict competition. In both cases the test is one of whether the benefits exceed the costs, although the details – as noted above – vary as between competition law and regulatory practice. The approach adopted in Ireland in both cases is based on international best practice. However, in the case of *ex ante* review of regulation through RIAs a number of changes are still necessary in order to comply with international best practice. It is not clear if and when these will be introduced. The very existence of these mechanisms no doubt prevents some anti-competitive agreements and restrictive regulatory proposals, where the benefits are less than the costs.[150]

CONCLUSIONS

The purpose of this chapter has been to address the issue of what role competition and regulatory policy should play in troubled economic times. Should these policies be: (i) relaxed to address concerns over economic security occasioned by the prolonged recession resulting in a series of austerity budgets; or (ii) enforced irrespective of the economic and budgetary conditions in which Ireland finds itself? In a small open economy such as Ireland's, it is important that markets are competitive and regulation that raises costs and inhibits the flow of resources between sectors is avoided. Competition drives productivity growth which increases living standards and promotes competitiveness. Is this rationale still valid in abnormal economic times such as the present recession?

To address the issue of whether or not competition and regulatory policy should be relaxed to address concerns over economic security in troubled times the following questions were posed:

- What does the international as well as Irish evidence suggest is the economic effect of such relaxation?
- Does relaxation of competition and regulatory policy provide economic security? If so, at what price?

---

150 In this context it should be noted that the Competition Authority has a role not only in relation to anti-competitive agreements, but also, under the Competition Act 2002, in advising government on the effects on competition of regulatory proposals. An examination of the Competition Authority (2012) demonstrates the breadth of regulatory proposals that the Authority has commented upon.

- Are there any conditions under which groups or sectors should be sheltered from market forces to provide greater economic security?

Competition policy can be relaxed through under-enforcement and permitting carve-outs or exemptions from competition law. Regulatory policy can be relaxed through changing the mandate of existing regulators to weigh more heavily the welfare of the regulated entity as compared to consumers. It can also allow more direct regulation under which entry into a particular market is restricted. These mechanisms, by providing protection from competition, can deliver a measure of stability and security for incumbent enterprises and their employees. Yet evidence from a wide variety of sources, time periods and jurisdictions suggests that the economic impact of such policies adversely impacts on growth, productivity and competitiveness.

At the level of an individual market, relaxing competition and regulatory policy leads to higher prices and less competitive pressure on enterprises to innovate and grow. The evidence suggests that the impact of relaxing competition and regulatory policy often lasts decades; making reversing these policies once the recession is ended challenging. At a wider economy level, there is less flexibility as resources cannot easily flow between different activities. The export or traded sector is damaged by having to pay higher input prices for goods and services produced in the non-traded sector, thus harming their competitiveness on international markets. The evidence suggests that relaxing competition and regulatory policy in a recession is likely to hold back the subsequent economic recovery.

Nevertheless, despite these adverse economic effects, if relaxing competition and regulatory policy results in increased economic security then this may provide offsetting benefits. Such relaxation involves a redistribution of income from consumers, including businesses (who pay higher prices) to the favoured group. However, such benefits are likely to be transitory, with the result that there will be continued pressure to raise prices. Furthermore, in many cases it is not clear that there is a valid rationale for the relaxation of competition and regulatory policy in terms of favouring a particular group.

Competition and regulatory policy do contain provisions that permit otherwise restrictive agreements and regulations to be allowed, but only when the benefits exceed the costs. These well established precedents are contained in Irish competition law, but the regulatory process in Ireland has, as yet, to fully reflect international best practice in judging *ex ante* regulation. It is not clear when this is likely to happen. The OECD (2010) report sets out the steps that need to be taken in this regard. By adhering to such a framework there is a clear and consistent basis on which decisions to provide economic security can be based; the alternative is *ad hocery* and temporary expedients, which encourage unproductive lobbying. Much better that effort should be concentrated within a framework that promotes sound analysis and careful evaluation of costs and benefits.

REFERENCES

Asker, J. (2010). 'A Study of the Internal Organisation of a Bidding Cartel'. *American Economic Review*, 100, June, 724–762.

Baldwin, J. and Gorecki, P. (1991). 'Entry, Exit, and Productivity Growth' in Geroski, P. and Schwalbach, J. (eds.), *Entry and Market Contestability. An International Comparison*. Oxford: Blackwell, 244–256.

Barone, G. and Cingano, F. (2011). 'Service Regulation and Growth: Evidence from OECD Countries'. *Economic Journal*, 121, September, 931–957.

Breyer, S. (1982). *Regulation and Its Reform*. Cambridge, Mass: Harvard University Press.

Cole, H. and Ohanian, L. (2004). 'New Deal Policies and the Persistence of the Great Depression: A General Equilibrium Analysis', *Journal of Political Economy*, 112, August, 779–816.

Competition Authority (1998). *Interim Study on the Liquor Licensing Laws and Other Barriers to Entry and their Impact on Competition in the Retail Drinks Market*. Dublin: Competition Authority.

Competition Authority (2001). *Submission of the Competition Authority to the Pharmacy Review Group*, Dublin: Competition Authority.

Competition Authority (2002). *Notice in Respect of Guidelines for Merger Analysis*. Decision No. N/02/004. Dublin: Competition Authority.

Competition Authority (2011a). *Annual Report 2010*. Dublin: Competition Authority.

Competition Authority (2011b). *Competition Authority Strategy Statement 2012–2014 (pending amalgamation)*. Dublin: Competition Authority.

Competition Authority (2012). *Annual Report 2011*. Dublin: Competition Authority.

Connor, J. and Bolotova, Y. (2006). 'Cartel overcharges: Survey and meta-analysis.' *International Journal of Industrial Organization*, 24, 1109–1137.

Datt, M., Hoekman, B. and Malouche, M. (2011). 'Taking Stock of Trade Protectionism Since 2008.' *Economic Premise*. Number 72, December.

Department of Jobs, Enterprise and Innovation (DJEI) (2012). *Action Plan for Jobs*. Dublin: DJEI.

Department of Public Expenditure and Reform (2012). 'Minister Howlin announces establishment of new Government Economic and Evaluation Service.' Press Release. 6 March.

Diffney, S., FitzGerald, J., Lyons, S. and Malaguzzi, V. (2009). 'Investment in Electricity Infrastructure in a Small Isolated Market: the Case of Ireland'. *Oxford Review of Economic Policy*, 25, 469–487.

Duffy, D. and Timoney, K. (2013). 'Spring 2013', *Quarterly Economic Commentary*. Dublin: Economic and Social Research Institute.

Economic Council of Canada (1979). *Responsible Regulation*. Ottawa: Supply and Services Canada.

Economic Council of Canada (1981). *Reforming Regulation*. Ottawa: Supply and Services Canada.

European Commission (2004). 'Communication from the Commission. Notice. Guidelines on the Application of Article 81(3) of the Treaty.' *Official Journal*, 27 April, pp. C101/97–C101/118.

European Commission (2009). 'Communication from the Commission – Guidance on the Commission's enforcement priorities in applying Article 82 of the EC Treaty to abusive exclusionary conduct by dominant undertakings.' *Official Journal*, 24 February, pp. C45/7–C45/20.

European Commission (2011). *Report on Competition Policy 2010*. COM(2011) 328 Final. Brussels: the Commission.

EU and IMF (2011). *Programme of Financial Support for Ireland*. 28 July. Dublin: Department of Finance.

Fingleton, J., Evans, J., and Hogan, O. (1998). *The Dublin Taxi Market: Re-Regulate or Stay Queuing?* Studies in Public Policy: 3. Dublin: The Policy Institute, Trinity College.

Goggin, I. and Lauder, G. (2008). *Review of the Operation of Regulatory Impact Analysis*. Dublin: Department of the Taoiseach.

Goodbody Economic Consultants (Goodbody) (2009). *Economic Review of the Small Public Service Vehicle Industry*. Dublin: the Taxi Regulator/Commission for Taxi Regulation.

Gorecki, P. (2009a). 'Future Challenges for Competition Policy in Ireland: A Personal View,' in D. Evans and Jenny, F. (eds) *Trustbusters: Competition Policy Authorities Speak Out*. Boston MA: Competition Policy International, 207–232.

Gorecki, P. (2009b). 'The Recession, Budgets, Competition, and Regulation: Should the State Provide Bespoke Protection?' in Callan, T. (ed.), *Budget Perspectives 2010*. Dublin: Economic and Social Research Institute, 19–53.

Gorecki, P. (2009c). 'A Code of Conduct for Grocery Goods Undertakings and an Ombudsman: How to Do a Lot of Harm by Trying to Do a Little Good'. *The Economic and Social Review*, 40, Winter, 461–488.

Gorecki, P. (2011a). 'Economic Regulation: Recentralisation of Power or Improved Quality of Regulation?' *The Economic and Social Review*, 42, Summer, 177 211.

Gorecki, P. (2011b). 'Do you Believe in Magic? Improving the Quality of Pharmacy Services Through Restricting Entry and Aspirational Contracts, the Irish Experience.' *The European Journal of Health Economics*, 12, December, 521–531.

Gorecki, P. (2012a). 'Competition Policy in Ireland's Recession.' *The Economic and Social Review*, 43, Winter, 597–629.

Gorecki, P. (2012b). *Troubled Times: What Role for Competition and Regulatory Policy?* Renewal Series Paper 10. Dublin: ESRI.

Gorecki, P. (2013). 'The Small Public Service Vehicle Market in Ireland: Regulation and the Recession.' *The Economic and Social Review*. 44, Summer.

Hay, G. and Kelly, D. (1974). 'An Empirical Survey of Price Fixing Conspiracies.' *Journal of Law and Economics*, 17, April, 13–38.

Hayashi, F. and Prescott, E. (2002). 'The 1990s in Japan: A Lost Decade'. *Review of Economic Dynamics*, 5, 206–235.

Honohan, P. (2010). *The Irish Banking Crisis. Regulatory and Financial Stability Policy, 2003–2008*. Dublin: Department of Finance.

Kahn, A. (1988). *The Economics of Regulation. Principles and Institutions*. Cambridge, Mass: MIT Press.

Kay, J. (2009). *Narrow Banking. The Reform of Banking Regulation*. London: Centre for the Study of Financial Innovation.

Keizer, K., Lindenberg, S. and Steg, L. (2008). 'The Spreading of Disorder', *Science*. 322, December, 1681–1685.

Kovacic, W., Marshall, R. Marx, L. and Raiff, M. (2005). 'Lessons for Competition Policy from the Vitamins Cartel', Working Paper Series. Washington DC: George Washington University.

Krueger, A.O. (1974). 'The Political Economy of the Rent-Seeking Society', *American Economic Review*, 64, June, 291–303.

Levenstein, M. and Suslow, V. (2006). 'What Determines Cartel Success?' *Journal of Economic Literature*, 44, March, 43–95.

London Economics (2011). *The Impact of Competition Interventions on Compliance and Deterrence*. Final Report. OFT1391. London: Office of Fair Trading.

Organisation of Economic Co-operation and Development (OECD) (1997). *Regulatory Impact Analysis: Best Practices in OECD Countries*. Paris: OECD.

Organisation of Economic Co-operation and Development (OECD) (2001). *Regulatory Reform in Ireland*. Paris: OECD.

Organisation of Economic Co-operation and Development (OECD) (2010). *Better Regulation in Europe: Ireland*. Paris: OECD.

Porter, M. and Sakakibara, M. (2004). 'Competition in Japan.' *Journal of Economic Perspectives*. 18, Winter, 27–50.

Porter, M., Takeuchi, H. and Sakakibara, M. (2000). *Can Japan Compete?* Basingstoke: Macmillian Press.

Posner, R.A. (1975). 'The Social Costs of Monopoly and Regulation', *Journal of Political Economy*, 83, August, 807–828.

Review Group on State Assets and Liabilities (2011). *Report*. Dublin: Stationery Office.

Romer, C. (1999). 'Why Did Prices Rise in the 1930s?' *Journal of Economic History*, 59, March, 167–199.

Scarpetta, S., Hemmings, P., Tressel, T. and Woo, J. (2002). 'The Role of Policy and Institutions for Productivity and Firm Dynamics: Evidence from Micro and Industry Data', OECD Economics Department Working Papers, No. 329. Paris: OECD.

Shapiro, C. (2009). 'Competition Policy in Distressed Industries.' Remarks prepared for the ABA Antitrust Symposium: Competition as Public Policy, 13

May. This can be accessed at: http://www.justice.gov/atr/public/speeches/245857.pdf.

Trebilcock, M., Prichard, R., Hartle, D. and Dewees, D. (1982). *The Choice of Governing Instrument*. Ottawa: Supply & Services Canada.

Tullock, G. (1967). 'The Welfare Costs of Tariffs, Monopolies, and Theft', *Western Economic Journal*, 5, June, 224–232.

Tullock, G. (1975). 'The Transitional Gains Trap', *Bell Journal of Economics*, 6, Autumn, 671–678.

Veljanovski, C. (2011). 'Deterrence, Recidivism and European Cartel Fines', *Journal of Competition Law & Economics*, 7, December, 871–915.

Whish, R. (2009). *Competition Law*. 6th Edition. Oxford: Oxford University Press.

CHAPTER 9

Protecting Consumers of Financial Services

Pete Lunn

This chapter considers evidence for policy in the area of the regulation of consumer financial services products. In terms of the policy landscape (Figure 1.1), it highlights and analyses a substantial volume of evidence associated with a specific set of policy challenges. Some potential options for policy are then considered, about which less evidence has thus far accumulated. The policy area is relatively new and dynamic, because of both the rapid development of retail financial markets and the global financial crisis, which has exposed serious shortcomings in financial regulation.

The two key research questions addressed are: To what extent are consumers' choices of financial services products subject to systematic phenomena that violate the orthodox model of competitive markets? And, if so, does improved financial education offer a potential policy solution? For policymakers, answers to these questions help to assess the possible effects of disadvantageous consumer decision-making in financial services and the potential of one particular type of policy solution. A further question is whether there are other policy options backed by evidence.

The methodological approach is to review domestic and, in particular, international literature on the two research questions. An assumption underlying this method is that the way consumers choose between financial services products is not subject to strong cultural (or other) effects that might introduce important variation across countries.

Some of the policy implications of the findings are clear. There is a substantial volume of good scientific evidence suggesting that consumers' financial reasoning is subject to systematic and disadvantageous phenomena. Furthermore, at least with respect to financial education programmes undertaken to date, the evidence suggests that they have at best a marginal impact and that, therefore, they are unlikely to address the scale of the problem. More ambiguous is evidence surrounding two other possible policy options: so-called 'nudges' and the safety testing and licensing of financial products.

Lastly, the suggestion is made that policymakers need to take an ongoing empirical approach to this highly dynamic policy area. This involves monitoring closely the effectiveness of pro-consumer interventions in other countries and piloting proposed interventions or pre-testing them for effectiveness.

BACKGROUND

From the perspective of behavioural economics and economic psychology, the global financial crisis has been a watershed. Prior to the crisis, financial regulation in Western capitalist societies largely assumed that economic agents behaved like the infinitely capable yet naively selfish calculating machines modelled in orthodox microeconomics textbooks. This assumption endured despite a mounting body of scientific evidence suggesting otherwise. The present chapter looks at the implications of this evidence for consumer protection in financial services markets. The two primary research questions addressed are whether the financial decision-making of consumers is systematically disadvantageous, and whether policy might be able to improve it. Empirical evidence is presented and assessed from laboratory studies, field experiments and econometric analyses of survey and market data. This evidence is primarily (though not exclusively) international. The aim is to derive lessons for Irish policy, although almost all the findings are relevant elsewhere.

The issue is urgent not only because of the recent crisis. Financial decision-making at the individual level increasingly determines important outcomes. Pension provision has moved towards the defined contribution model. Homeownership based on credit is now the norm, as is borrowing via credit cards and one-off loans for larger purchases. Consumers now routinely purchase multiple forms of insurance. Savers have become investors, extending their ambitions beyond deposit accounts to riskier investments in shares, bonds and property. More generally, increased income and wealth together with an expanded array of financial products mean that the fortunes of citizens probably depend more than ever before on making good financial decisions.

CONSUMERS AND IRELAND'S CRISIS

Disadvantageous Decision-making

At one level, it is obvious that in the years prior to 2008 many consumers in Ireland made decisions that, knowing what they know now, they would not have made. A large proportion of people who bought houses during what turned out to be a gigantic housing and credit bubble ended up in negative equity, in many cases running to over €100,000. Well over 100,000 mortgages were either restructured or went into arrears. Credit card debt rose by 77 per cent in less than five years. This and other forms of consumer credit and household loans (unrelated to house purchase) followed a pattern of dramatic growth followed by slow unwinding of the debt. In short, consumers in Ireland spent like never before. Figure 9.1 shows the progress of the savings ratio from 1970 up to the present time, which twice fell to historic lows of less than 4 per cent during the pre-crisis period.

Figure 9.1: The Savings Ratio, 1970–2011

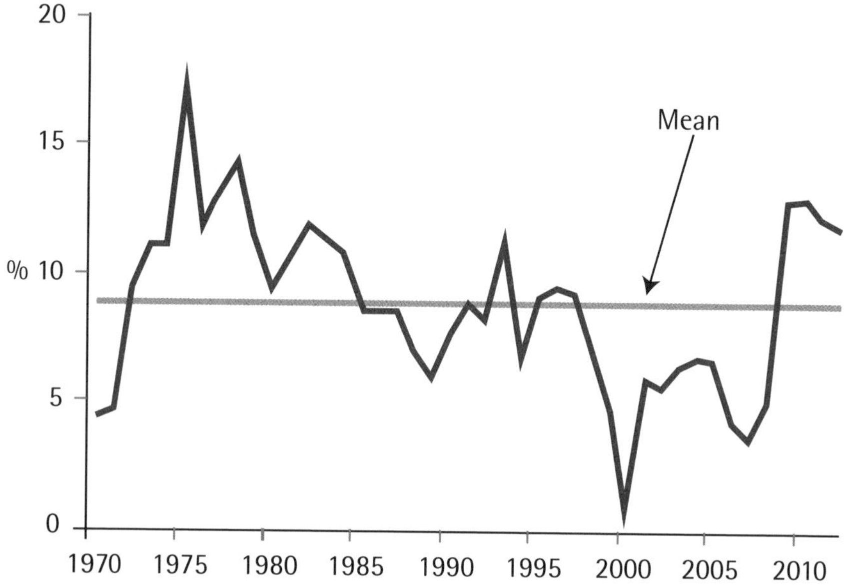

Source: Estimations from the Economic and Social Research Institute Databank.

Assuming that Irish consumers had not suddenly and fundamentally altered their appetite for risk, their behaviour could have made sense only had they formed a reasonable expectation that their likely financial future departed radically from that faced by previous generations and, indeed, the historic fortunes of consumers in other developed nations. Was this a reasonable expectation or a widespread delusion?

Any reasoned expectation ought to be based on an assessment of future income, inflation and interest rates. By coincidence, Ireland's first nationally representative financial capability survey was conducted in late 2007 and early 2008. The data reveal that, given the risks they were taking, a strikingly high proportion of consumers were unaware of basic details of their own finances. According to O'Donnell and Keeney (2009), the 'vast majority' of homeowners with an outstanding mortgage at that time could not say what interest rate applied to it – one-third could not even guess. Similarly, 50 per cent of credit card holders did not know what interest rate applied to their card, while the range of interest rates supplied by those who did claim to know implied that many were mistaken. The survey found that 45 per cent of card holders admitted not paying their balance in full every month, although international evidence suggests that such self-reported figures understate reality and may need to be increased by around half again (Willis, 2008). Data also exist on consumer perceptions of inflation prior to the crisis. Using the EU Consumer Survey (2002–2007), Duffy and Lunn (2009) record that when asked what the percentage increase in prices was over the past 12 months, 34 per cent of consumers could not give any figure while less than 15 per cent could provide a value within two percentage points of the true rate.

Thus, the financial decisions of Irish households during the boom, which for many families were about to have a dramatic impact upon their wealth, were not well informed. The majority of consumers did not know what rate they were borrowing at nor the rate of inflation. Furthermore, though it is harder to examine quantitatively, it seems likely that of the Irish consumers who did save (or were otherwise wealthy) many had poorly diversified investments. Despite holding wealth in property already, a significant number invested in other properties, including a sizeable proportion of those who remortgaged (O'Donnell and Keeney, 2009). Moreover, non-property investment portfolios had an excessive reliance on domestic shares erroneously perceived to be low risk investments, especially bank shares.

Overall, the evidence suggests that poor financial reasoning among consumers prior to Ireland's economic crisis was widespread. Because household decisions were not based on accurate information, it appears that many took on far too much risk unwittingly. Better financial decision-making by consumers might have at least reduced the scale of the bubble. What occurred therefore underlines the potential for gains from policies that improve consumer decision-making.

The Post-Crisis Policy Context

Following the crisis, policy on financial regulation has unsurprisingly begun to reform. The Central Bank Reform Act of 2010 abolished the Irish Financial Services Regulatory Authority, set up a unitary Central Bank, and transferred responsibility for consumer information and education to the National Consumer Agency. This reorganisation was rapidly followed by two rounds of consultation on an updated Consumer Protection Code, which covers Irish regulated providers and came into force in January 2012. The measures are additional to relevant EU directives and largely strengthen or add to provisions contained in the original 2006 Code. Contraventions include failing to live up to 12 principles of business conduct in financial services, which entail being fair to consumers, acting in consumers' best interests, dealing with consumers honestly, and not placing consumers under undue pressure. These principles and many more specific regulations aim to make providers take increased responsibility for their influence on decisions made by their customers.

A number of the Code's rules accord with behavioural evidence. One example is the provision in the original 2006 Code that bans pre-approved credit and automatic increases in credit limits on credit cards, which was partly motivated by evidence on time inconsistent decision-making and behavioural convergence (see Table 9.1). Another example is the requirement for informative and balanced advertising, which mandates warning texts (including equivalence of font sizes) and the ban on unsolicited contact with consumers. These measures should be seen in the context of a large volume of behavioural research on the persuasive power of marketing and selling techniques, including in financial services: Bertrand *et al.* (2010) show surprisingly large impacts of marketing material on consumers' willingness to take out loans, where the attributes promoted were unrelated to any product benefits; de Meza, Irlenbusch and Reyniers (2007) demonstrate the direct persuasive influence of individual salespeople in the insurance market; and the Office of Fair Trading (2004) found that many consumers made inappropriate choices when approached by doorstep sellers. In some markets, such tight regulation of marketing and selling might be thought excessive, but greater precautions may be sensible in financial services. Consumers in these markets make once-off decisions of consequence with limited opportunities for learning through feedback. Indeed, feedback on products such as pensions may only confirm that a key mistake was made decades after the fact, when it is too late to correct it. This arguably justifies a less permissive approach.

Other provisions in the Code require providers to obtain reliable information on consumer circumstances, to ensure the suitability of products for the specific consumer, and to undertake rigorous assessment of the ability to repay loans. Credit products cannot be provided where consumers refuse to supply the necessary personal information. Providers must assess ability to repay a flexible rate mortgage in the event of a 2 per cent (minimum) rise in the interest rate. Meanwhile, the Code strongly mandates the nature and timing of information provided to consumers, such as 'suitability statements' and written consumer warnings, requiring clear and simplified descriptions of products.

Many of these measures aim to prevent excessive indebtedness or risk-taking. To that end, they are consistent with evidence regarding some identifiable problems. Trying to improve consumer decision-making by forcing providers to act in consumers' interests aligns with evidence that consumers have a surprising, perhaps even naive, level of trust in advice from financial service companies and financial advisors, whose incentives may not match their own (see European Commission, 2010). Mandating simplified disclosure is consistent with evidence that the complexity of information can disrupt decision-making (see Table 9.1). Yet evidence supporting the specific policy solutions adopted, as opposed to the nature of the problems, is less apparent. For instance, the effectiveness of mandated disclosures will depend on whether the specific measures adopted do, in fact, improve consumer decisions.

Perhaps most importantly, the ultimate impact of the Code is likely to depend on the extent of enforcement. Honohan (2010) points out that, in the lead up to Ireland's banking crisis, the Financial Regulator had available both information and sanctions that could have been used to tackle the build-up of risk within the financial sector, yet did not take the necessary action. No measures are likely to be effective if they are not enforced.

In addition to the consumer protection regime, there may be potential for policy to improve consumer decision-making through financial education and better provision of helpful consumer information. The National Steering Group on Financial Capability (2009) published a vision for improving financial capability, which includes a 'financial competency framework'. The National Consumer Agency runs financial education courses and provides extensive web-based information about financial products. This route to better decision-making is appealing for policymakers: national strategies to develop financial education and improve financial literacy have been adopted in many countries (OECD, 2011).

Given this policy context, an analysis of international evidence may be helpful in a number of ways. Most obviously, the rapidly increasing volume of research can directly assist our understanding of how modern retail financial services markets work, with respect to the extent of disadvantageous consumer decision-making and the responses of providers. International evidence also relates to specific aspects of Irish policy, such as mandatory disclosure and financial education programmes. Meanwhile, some innovative proposals aimed at improving consumers' financial decision-making are being considered or implemented elsewhere and may be relevant to Irish policy.

COMPETITION, INFORMATION AND BEHAVIOURAL BIASES

Recent events have indicated that orthodox models of competitive markets were inadequate for understanding financial services. The models assumed that competition between firms would incentivise them to offer high quality and low prices, provided consumers had access to the necessary information to choose products to match their preferences. Good consumer decision-making was assumed to follow from complete (or near complete) information. Reality turned out to be quite different.

One immediately striking pattern of consumer behaviour in financial services is the low level of switching between products. Figure 9.2 presents data from Ireland, gathered in 2011 for the National Consumer Agency. With the exception of insurance, rates of switching in financial services are lower than for all other types of product surveyed, with no more than 2 per cent of consumers changing providers for current accounts, saving/investment products, credit cards, mortgages or other loans over a 12–month period. These low rates of switching in Ireland are not dissimilar to those recorded in other countries; low switching is a characteristic of retail financial services.

This pattern of consumer behaviour would make sense if competition meant that little was to be gained from comparison shopping. However, international studies record substantial dispersion in the prices consumers pay across a range of financial services products under different types of regulatory regime, where differences in the nature of the product do not seem sufficient to explain variation.

Examples include Hassink and van Leuvensteijn (2007) for similar products in the Dutch mortgage market; Woodward (2008) for American mortgages; and Martín-Oliver, Salas-Fumás and Saurina (2007) for deposit and loan products at Spanish banks.

Figure 9.2: Proportion of Consumers in Ireland who Switched Provider in the Previous 12 Months

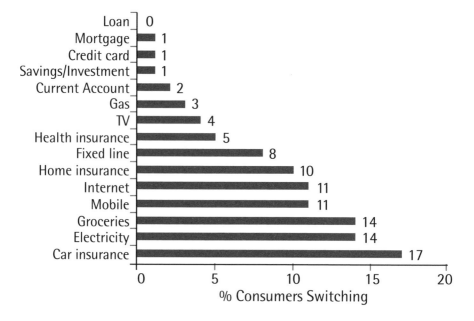

Source: National Consumer Survey, 2011.

Understanding of why consumers fail to switch to more advantageous deals in retail financial services is improving. The market that has received most attention is the US market for mutual funds. By 2010, according to the *Investment Company Institute*, 44 per cent of US households had money invested in a mutual fund.[151] Since the products are disproportionately bought by wealthier households, these consumers can be expected to have above average financial capability. Yet fees associated with these funds can differ by more than ten-fold, despite evidence showing that more expensive funds do not outperform less expensive ones (e.g., Carhart, 1997). Even more striking is that such price dispersion arises for index funds that track stock market indices and hence have virtually no variation in

---

151 These are the most popular form of consumer financial investment in the US. Consumers can invest relatively small sums in a diversified portfolio of shares, bonds and other securities, by pooling their resources with those of other consumers into a larger fund managed by the provider.

returns across providers (Hortaçsu and Syverson, 2004). Choi, Laibson and Madrian, (2010) estimate that American consumers effectively leave in excess of €200 million dollars on the table by not selecting deals with lower fees. Experimental evidence (Choi et al., 2010) and evidence from field data (e.g., Barber, Odean and Zheng, 2005) suggest that this is not the result of inertia or failing to search for the best deal. Rather, consumers are more influenced by information that has little or no impact on the quality of the deal, such as advertising and claims of past performance, than by fees paid to the provider, which more substantially affect their return. The findings, therefore, strengthen the case for tight regulation of advertising in financial services.

The upshot is that price dispersion survives not because consumers are insufficiently active, but because they fail to take good enough decisions to incentivise providers to offer better value. The extent to which this pattern applies to other financial services is not known, but it is ominous that it occurs in a market where consumers are of above average financial capability, product quality is fairly uniform, and it is more straightforward to calculate the full price than it is in, say, the mortgage or credit card market. If consumers struggle to make the easier financial decisions, the implications for more difficult ones are worrying. Some simple evidence is particularly troubling: in a large survey conducted in eight EU countries, 40 per cent of investors in stocks and shares wrongly believed that their initial investment was protected (European Commission, 2010).

Behavioural Biases in Retail Financial Services

The example of work on US mutual funds shows that while trying to explain market-level phenomena, researchers have discovered consumers who fail to act in their own best interests. Much relevant work on consumer decision-making, however, has attacked the issue from the opposite direction. Empirical studies in behavioural economics and economic psychology have documented a long list of systematic influences on economic decision-making, commonly referred to as 'behavioural biases'.[152] Most of these behaviours were initially documented in laboratory experiments, before researchers hypothesised and tested for their presence among consumers and traders in the field, including in financial services. They are also particularly likely to emerge when individuals must make decisions in the face of risk and uncertainty.

Table 9.1 presents a list of established biases, a brief description of each phenomenon, and a selection of empirical studies that have found evidence for

---

152 Due to its prevalence, this terminology has become unavoidable, but it is arguably unfortunate given the negative connotations of "bias". Although in financial markets these phenomena may result in disadvantageous reasoning, it is not clear that they do so more generally. In some contexts the influence may be negative, but in others it may not.

the effect among consumers in experimental or, mostly, field settings. The list is non-exhaustive, as is the evidence cited. All but a few papers referenced are peer reviewed studies published in leading international economics and finance journals. Space does not permit a more thorough review of the extensive research surrounding each phenomenon. Comprehensive overviews exist of evidence for behavioural biases in the laboratory (Kahneman, 2011) and in the field (DellaVigna, 2009), and of the influence of behavioural biases in financial reasoning (de Meza, Irlenbusch and Reyniers, 2008), financial markets (Barberis and Thaler, 2003) and retail financial services (European Commission, 2010). There are overlaps between some biases listed. For instance, framing effects can be caused by contextual changes in the salience of certain information, whether income is sourced from different mental accounts, and so on. It is also possible that some phenomena have common causes, e.g., one reason why people are drawn to default options is because defaults signal the choices usually made by others, so the power of defaults may partly reflect behavioural convergence.

Table 9.1: Behavioural Biases in Judgement and Decision-making of Potential Relevance to Consumers of Financial Services

Bias (Closely related phenomena)	Description	Evidence for the bias among consumers (* = decision involved financial services product)
Choice overload	Being less inclined to make decisions when having to choose among large numbers of options	Iyengar & Lepper (2000); Iyengar, Huberman & Jiang (2004)*; Agnew & Szykman (2005)*; Bertrand et al. (2010)*
Behavioural convergence (Bandwagon effects, Herding, Information cascades)	Being drawn towards or copying similar decisions made by others	Duflo & Saez (2003)*; Hong, Kubik & Stein (2004)*; Huang & Chen (2006); Brown et al. (2008a)*
Time inconsistency (Present bias, Hyperbolic discounting)	Systematic changing of preferences over time, such that more immediate rewards become disproportionately more attractive	Ausubel (1999)*; DellaVigna & Malmendier (2004); Huffman and Barenstein (2004)
Reference dependence (Loss aversion, Endowment effect)	Giving greater weight to losses than to equivalent gains, relative to the present position or to expectations, including greater willingness to take risks when facing losses	Thaler et al. (1997)*; Odean (1998)*; Genesove & Mayer (2001); Thaler & Benartzi (2004)*

Table 9.1: Behavioural Biases in Judgement and Decision-making of Potential Relevance to Consumers of Financial Services (continued)

Bias (Closely related phenomena)	Description	Evidence for the bias among consumers (* = decision involved financial services product)
Status quo bias (Preference for defaults)	Preferring to maintain the present situation or sticking with the default option	Samuelson & Zeckhauser (1988)*; Hartman, Doane & Woo (1991); Madrian & Shea (2001)*; Agnew & Szykman (2005)*
Overconfidence bias (Overoptimism, Miscalibration)	Predicting outcomes too positively and overestimating the accuracy of predictions	Barber & Odean (2001)*; Barber & Odean (2002a)*; Grubb (2009)
Extrapolation bias (Overinference)	When predicting future outcomes based on the past, placing more weight on the most recent events	Muellbauer and Murphy (1997); Benartzi (2001)*; Piazzesi and Schneider (2009)*
Framing effects	Taking a different decision when the same problem is presented in a different way	Thaler & Benartzi (2004)*; Brown *et al.* (2008b)*; European Commission (2010)*
Salience (Inattention)	Placing excessive emphasis on information that is more salient (prominent), or ignoring important information that is less salient	Barber & Odean (2002b)*; Barber, Odean & Zheng, (2005)*; Lacko and Pappalardo (2007)*
Ambiguity aversion	Being more willing to take equivalent risks that the individual feels able to quantify, or feels relatively competent in to assess.	Huberman (2001)*; Grinblatt & Keloharju (2001)*; Benartzi (2001)*; European Commission (2010)*
Mental accounting (Narrow framing)	Taking different decisions according to the history or source of the specific money at stake, i.e. treating wealth in a non-fungible manner	Hastopoulos, Krugman & Poterba (1989)*; Kooreman (2000); Gross & Souleles (2002)*

While the focus of the present chapter is consumers, it is worth noting that professionals and experts are also prone to the biases listed in Table 9.1. While there is a correlation between the quality of decision-making and educational attainment, the estimated correlations tend to be modest and behavioural biases are widespread at all levels of education (De Bruin, Parker and Fischhoff, 2007; Stanovich and West, 2000).

The Impact of Biases at Market Level

Although a comprehensive assessment of the likely impact of all biases listed in Table 9.1 is beyond the scope of the present analysis, it is possible to identify themes that offer possible lessons for consumer protection policy.

First, consumer decision-making is not only influenced by information and prices, but also by timing, form and context, i.e., how and when monies are paid and information is presented. For example, Barber *et al.* (2005) show that the purchase choices of consumers who invest in mutual funds are more sensitive to early fees paid up front than to ongoing fees paid as a percentage of the investment. Another example is a framing effect revealed by Brown *et al.* (2008b). A sample of consumers stated their preferences for securing retirement income from a lump sum, choosing between a life annuity and other options (savings account, consol bond, period annuity). The offers described the same life annuity product with two different forms of language: in one condition it was described as an investment, where a lump sum invested would deliver earnings as a return; in another it was outlined in terms of consumption, as a purchase of a stream of payments for ongoing spending. Although the monetary transaction was identical, pair-wise preferences for the life annuity over the other products approximately doubled from 21–48 per cent in the investment condition, to over 70 per cent in the consumption condition.

A more celebrated example surrounds pension provision. Simply by changing the default position from one where workers have to opt in to a company pension scheme to one where they have to opt out can more than double participation (Madrian and Shea, 2001). Similarly, when Thaler and Benartzi (2004) designed and tested their 'Save More Tomorrow' (SMT) scheme, which offers workers the possibility to commit in advance to participate in a scheme and to increase contributions at the time of future pay increases, they increased average employee savings at one firm from 3.5 per cent of salary to 13.6 per cent in under four years. These are large impacts relative to policy goals for increasing provision.

Thus, a key lesson for policymakers is that contextual differences that tap into at least some of the biases listed in Table 9.1, which seem irrelevant from the perspective of orthodox models of consumer choice, can have very large effects on consumer behaviour.

The second theme to consider is how providers are likely to respond to consumer biases. To take a simple example, consumers who do not comprehend the non-linear acceleration inherent in compound interest are likely to undersave. Providers of savings products have every incentive to try to overcome this problem, and so may help to correct it, by informing consumers and encouraging them to save. By the same token, however, such consumers are likely to overborrow. In this case, providers of credit products stand to make additional revenue from consumers' ignorance and, therefore, have no incentive to tackle it. Lusardi and Tufano (2009) find that the clear majority of a representative national US sample of consumers do not understand compound interest. They estimate that one-third of the fees that this group hand over to credit card companies are attributable to this failing.

A particular concern here relates to time inconsistency (see Frederick, Loewenstein and O'Donoghue, 2002, for review). Many consumers find it hard to resist offers of immediate benefits for which they will pay later, even in circumstances where affordability is a concern. McCarthy (2011) has shown that, controlling for a large range of background characteristics, including socio-economic status and measures of financial literacy, consumers in Ireland and the UK who score poorly on measures of self-control are significantly more likely to experience financial distress. Firms can potentially exploit self-control problems by frontloading benefits and collecting payments later. Ausubel (1999) found that many credit card users who opted for a lower initial 'teaser' rate ended up paying more for credit than had they taken an alternative standard offer. De Meza et al. (2008) note that many shoppers who arrange credit do not intend to do so when setting out and that consumers feel pressurised to take up credit. They conclude, given these circumstances, that an offer of credit without upfront cost amounts to a 'psychological trap'.

Offers of free credit or teaser rates may also prey on overconfidence and extrapolation biases, where consumers overestimate their ability to control spending and extrapolate income increases. It is possible that these products are suitable for some consumers, who for instance may face credit constraints yet want a period of outlay after purchasing a new home. However, analysis of mortgage choice in the UK (Miles, 2004) suggests that this is unlikely to explain why so many mortgage holders opt for initially discounted rates. The more likely explanation is that initial discounts appeal to consumers who combine a straightforward comparison of initial repayments with overly optimistic extrapolations about the future of personal income and house prices. A study that examined the contribution of discounts to current mortgage repayment difficulties in Ireland could be valuable.

More generally, for most of the phenomena in Table 9.1, there are possibilities for the enlightened provider to exploit the biased consumer. Status quo bias may make it more profitable for well-established banks to risk losing a few customers by lowering interest rates on the savings accounts of existing customers than to compete for customers by offering higher rates. Ambiguity aversion might mean that it is easier to sell investment products for a basket of shares in household name companies than for a diversified mix of shares, bonds and property that is more appropriate to most consumers' need to balance risk and return. Each of these hypotheses (and others that could be generated based on Table 9.1) would require specific empirical research to uphold. Yet the general lesson is clear: there are circumstances where profit-maximising providers face incentives not to correct but to exploit consumers' systematically disadvantageous reasoning.

A final theme to consider is whether the market might itself find solutions to these problems. If it is in the interest of at least some providers to compete by educating consumers or marketing products so as to overcome disadvantageous biases, then the market may compete away the problem. However, the studies cited in Table 9.1 show that biases exist in many financial services markets and, therefore, have not yet been competed away, including in markets such as US mutual funds where consumers tend to be more financially literate and experienced. In the 1990s, the entry of new firms into that market was associated with increases in prices (Hortaçsu and Syverson, 2004), perhaps because it increased the complexity of offerings and made it even harder for consumers to compare offerings. Furthermore, theoretical work has established several results showing that biases and associated consumer detriment may be sustained in a competitive market equilibrium where consumers observe prices only approximately (Gabaix, Laibson, and Li, 2005; Carlin, 2009), or fail to take account of a portion of the price that is not initially apparent (Gabaix and Laibson, 2006). In principle, this logic could also apply to consumers failing to appreciate the risks they undertake, such that competition for their business may exploit biases and contribute to consumers unwittingly taking on excessive risk. All three of the official inquiries into Ireland's banking crisis conclude that intensified competition in Irish banking contributed to increased risk-taking in the Irish property market (Honohan, 2010; Regling and Watson, 2010; Nyberg, 2011).

The research on behavioural biases in financial services hence provides three important themes. First, because of behavioural biases, contextual factors that are irrelevant according to orthodox models of consumer behaviour can nevertheless have large effects on consumers' decisions. Second, providers may face incentives to exploit disadvantageous reasoning. Third, there are circumstances where competition is unlikely to drive out products or marketing techniques that do indeed exploit these biases. In a market where consumers struggle to comprehend products, competition may make disadvantageous decision-making worse.

POSSIBLE POLICIES FOR BETTER DECISION-MAKING

The above review of evidence suggests that consumer protection policies based on orthodox microeconomic models are unlikely to be effective in financial services. If not proof, there is at least a persuasive accumulation of evidence that disadvantageous financial reasoning is widespread. Thus, while the ongoing strengthening of consumer protection measures in many countries may owe more to the financial crisis than to papers in scientific journals, there is much evidence to support policies premised on the need to intervene in consumers' decision-making.

But which policies? This section considers a range of possibilities in light of the evidence on consumer decision-making already outlined, and evidence specific to the type of intervention.

Financial Education

Many countries now have strategies to improve financial literacy or financial capability (OECD, 2011), including Ireland. This section offers a brief overview of evidence relating to the potential impact of more and better financial education on market outcomes. More complete literature reviews dedicated solely to this issue are de Meza *et al.* (2008), Atkinson (2008), Willis (2008), Mandell (2009), Lusardi (2010) and Yoong (2011). These six reviews have two notable similarities and one difference, which are instructive for what one might infer for policy. The similarities are, first, a finding of generally low financial literacy by the standards required for sound financial decision-making and, second, relatively disappointing results for interventions designed to improve it. The difference relates to the level of optimism regarding whether it is possible to improve interventions and hence raise financial capability sufficiently to alter market outcomes, or whether public money would be better spent on other ways to protect consumers.

Regarding the general level of financial literacy, the abovementioned reviews are pretty clear. A substantial proportion of consumers cannot correctly answer relatively straightforward questions requiring comparison of interest rates and inflation. Analysing Ireland's financial capability survey, O'Donnell and Keeney (2009) reach a similar conclusion: 'the substantial proportion who performed weakly in all areas gives cause for concern' (p. 3). Without a rudimentary grasp of concepts such as inflation and interest, sound financial decision-making is not possible, even before considering susceptibility to potentially disadvantageous biases.

Turning to financial education interventions, the majority of research has been undertaken in the US, where programmes have been running for some time and it is possible to compare outcomes across states with different policies. Some initially optimistic and widely cited findings by Bernheim, Garrett and Maki (2000) showed that Americans living in states with mandated financial education at high school saved and accumulated wealth more rapidly. Yet few of the many studies conducted since have recorded such positive effects. Tennyson and Nguyen (2001) found little evidence for differences in financial literacy between states with and without a mandate. Mandell (2009) shows that five consecutive waves of the 'Jump$tart' survey, a 31–item multiple-choice financial literacy questionnaire administered to young adults, record no benefit of having received financial education. One possibility is that financial education may influence behaviour without improving financial literacy, perhaps by increasing trust or familiarity with financial transactions. Still, other empirical studies that have looked at behavioural measures have found impacts to be non-existent, small or short-lived (e.g., Clarke *et al.*, 2006; Mandell and Klein, 2009).

The latter authors went as far as to conclude that: 'Until more evidence can be presented to demonstrate that high school courses in personal financial management positively influence subsequent financial behavior, further allocation of scarce educational resources toward mandatory classes of this type should be reconsidered.' (Mandell and Klein, 2009, p. 23) Yet this pessimistic conclusion is not shared by other authors, notably Lusardi (2010), who argues for greater policy effort to increase financial capability.

Discouragingly from a policy perspective, however, the literature cited addresses whether education of consumers can be sufficiently effective to allow a large proportion to acquire knowledge of basic financial concepts. To this difficult long-term aim must be added the challenge presented by behavioural biases, which continue to affect decision-making even once individuals have a grasp of financial concepts, including among experts (de Meza et al., 2008; Lunn, 2013). The implication is that meaningful improvements in financial decision-making through financial education must be considered policies that will act, at best, over a period of decades. Are there potentially quicker policy fixes?

One possibility is that different types of financial education may be more effective, such as face-to-face counselling. An experiment in Illinois found that referring high-risk mortgage applicants to a third-party review by a state-certified counsellor reduced the likelihood that they opted for the risky mortgage (Agarwal et al., 2009). Furthermore, once mortgage providers knew that an external review would occur there was a marked reduction in the riskiness of offers. The financial advice in this case had heavy state involvement, making this an effective but probably expensive policy. Counselling sessions lasted one to two hours and focused not on advice regarding optimal choice but on educating applicants about common pitfalls. Furthermore, the positive findings were gathered in a context where borrowers were routinely taking on very high-risk loans.

The findings of Agarwal et al., contrast with those relating to financial advice generally, which suggests that financial advice does little for consumer decision-making. In some contexts obtaining financial advice is correlated with less advantageous decisions (e.g., Hackethal, Inderst and Meyer, 2011). Disclosures of potential conflicts of interest are often ignored or, when responded to, taken into account excessively (Lacko and Pappalardo, 2007; European Commission, 2010). The offer of free unbiased advice to retail investors has a minimal effect, because the advice is taken up by those who least need it and is largely ignored (Bhattacharya et al., 2012).

The experiment of Agarwal et al. raises the possibility that interventions that highlight common mistakes might be more effective than efforts to educate consumers about financial matters. A few researchers (e.g., Kahneman and Riepe, 1998; Larrick, 2004) have begun to examine methods of 'de-biasing': interventions in decision-making intended to counter specific disadvantageous behaviours. Kahneman and Riepe developed a ten-point checklist for investment advisors to help them teach clients to avoid pitfalls illuminated by behavioural economics. To some extent, the warnings mandated by Ireland's Consumer Protection Code attempt to alert consumers to some known pitfalls, although the salience of these warnings is mediated by the attitude providers take towards them. However, it may be possible to exploit the de-biasing approach and to pilot schemes that target prevention of common mistakes.

Soft Paternalism – 'Nudges'

Thaler and Sunstein's (2008) book *Nudge* has had a profound impact on policymakers in the US and UK, not least with the appointment of Cass Sunstein in 2009 to head the Office of Information and Regulatory Affairs at the White House. Its central thesis is that behavioural science can be employed to design policies that make beneficial decisions more likely, without imposing bans or limits on choice. In the jargon, this is called 'soft paternalism', with policymakers setting the 'choice architecture' to 'nudge' people towards better choices.

In financial services, some mandatory disclosures fit this description. The requirement in Ireland's Consumer Protection Code that providers give consumers a 'Statement of Suitability' outlining why the offered product is suitable is arguably an example of a 'nudge'; the hope is that it makes both parties consider the deal more carefully. Mandated disclosure has been used at different times by regulators, mostly to simplify or standardise the information available to consumers, in pursuit of greater transparency with respect to price, quality and the risks associated with products. Unfortunately, evidence for its effectiveness is not very positive, at least with respect to consumers' ability to choose better deals. For instance, concerns about the complexity of the UK mortgage market led to the introduction in 2004 of the MCOB (Mortgage Conduct of Business) regulation, which provided consumers with prescribed information intended to assist comparison of mortgage offerings. Evidence suggests that MCOB increased business costs and prices, with no discernible decrease in price dispersion (Monteiro and Zaidi, 2007). Similar attempts to mandate simplified and standardised information have been undertaken with respect to investment products through the EU's Key Investor Information Document and the US Securities and Exchange Commission's 'Summary Prospectus' for mutual funds. Beshears *et al.* (2010) conducted an experiment with a sample of white collar staff at Harvard University – a group with relatively high financial literacy. Subjects chose between real mutual funds based on available literature and were rewarded by the performance of the fund over a subsequent period, standing to earn roughly $100 each depending on the success of their choices. Beshears *et al.*, found that choices paid too much heed to irrelevant aspects of the funds and insufficient attention to fees, leading to suboptimal decisions. The Summary Prospectus made no difference. In a similar experiment Choi, Laibson and Madrian (2009) designed and tested three forms of information provision, including a cheat sheet and an FAQ sheet designed to be as clear and straightforward as the experimenters could make it. They managed a measurable if modest improvement in decision-making, but the majority of subjects still made costly mistakes. Lastly, similarly modest improvements in investment decisions following simplification of information were recorded in experiments conducted by the European Commission (2010), but these involved a choice between only two products with a small volume of information compared to any real market decision.

Combining these results with the evidence relating to the provision of advice suggests limitations to what can be achieved through simplification and information provision. Thus, while state-funded financial information and advice schemes, such as those operated by the National Consumer Agency in Ireland, will probably have positive effects for some consumers who engage successfully with them, the overall market impact is likely to be small.

It is possible that more personalised and specific feedback might be more effective. Barr, Mullainathan and Shafir (2008) propose a range of such measures. Lenders would have to reveal to borrowers their estimated probability of default. Investment products would have to include total fees paid with worked examples of possible returns. Credit card companies would have to detail on the main page of bills how long it would take to pay off the debt at the minimum monthly rate and the total interest that would be paid, with worked examples of how much late payment would cost. (A version of these ideas was taken up in America's 2009 Credit CARD Act, though it is too early to evaluate the impact.) Another possibility would be to require providers of savings accounts to send a clear annual statement showing growth in real (not just nominal) terms. Another possibility suggested by Thaler and Sunstein (2008) is to mandate providers to produce key personalised information, such as their credit card usage pattern over the previous year, in a machine-readable standardised form that can be inputted to price comparison software. The potential for consumer learning through such explicit and personalised feedback is based on psychological studies of effective learning generally and ought, in theory, to be measurable through experimental studies and pilots.

A final potential 'nudge' style policy is also more interventionist. Barr, Mullainathan and Shafir (2008) argue that regulators should mandate default products. Mortgage and other credit providers would be compelled to provide a standard 'plain vanilla' product, the terms and conditions of which, with the exception of the interest rate, would be dictated by regulation. Default products could include prudent limits on borrowings relative to income. Room would remain for innovation, but the idea is that the consumer's choice would always be whether or not to opt out of a default product that the state had deemed to be safe. Behavioural evidence on defaults suggests that this might establish good norms and thus limit how far products could depart from those norms yet remain popular. Proposals for plain vanilla products were originally in the Obama administration's plans for financial regulatory reform, but failed to get past the US Congress.

In summary, behavioural evidence has spawned some creative ideas for how financial regulation might plausibly improve decision-making without becoming what some would see as excessively prohibitive. Pilot schemes and experiments are needed before many of these policy proposals can be judged.

Safety Tests for Financial Products

If there is 'soft paternalism', there must presumably also be 'hard paternalism'. Though the authors would doubtless not describe it as such, the case for harder paternalism following the financial crisis is probably most forcefully put by two leading US lawyers in *Making Credit Safer* (Bar-Gill and Warren, 2008). The argument centres on a rhetorical question: why is safety regulation applied to all manner of physical products, from toasters to toys yet policing the safety of credit products is left largely to consumer choice? In essence, Bar-Gill and Warren argue that consumers can no more be expected to understand the potential dangers of complex financial products designed to make the lender maximum profit than the potential dangers of unsafe electrical appliances. Their conclusion is, straight-forwardly, that there should be parity of treatment between financial products and physical products, such that financial products are also safety-checked by a powerful regulator before being let loose on the market.

How does this proposal relate to the evidence presented in preceding sections? Bar-Gill and Warren's interpretation of the empirical evidence can be summarised by the following statements: (1) financial products can cause great harm, including to third parties; (2) consumers are not able to assess the price, quality and risk associated with financial products; (3) providers have little incentive to provide safe financial products, but instead to offer products that exploit consumers, hide important features and hence expose them to unperceived risks; and (4) the combination of competition and consumer education and learning is unable to overcome these problems. Given all of these conclusions and the fact that unperceived risks associated with physical products are disallowed through safety regulation, Bar-Gill and Warren draw their ultimate conclusion that financial products should also be rigorously safety tested before being marketed.

Based on the evidence cited, two statements might be inferred with respect to Bar-Gill and Warren's analysis. First, the conclusions they draw are more definite than is implied by the empirics, perhaps especially with respect to outstanding avenues of consumer learning and potential de-biasing. Second, it is nevertheless the case that statement (1) is evident and, given current evidence, each of the remaining three statements holds on the balance of probabilities. There are strong reasons to be sceptical about the possibilities for combining improved consumer education and learning with smarter regulation to fix the problem. Consequently, Bar-Gill and Warren's more radical approach to consumer protection should be taken seriously.

CONCLUSIONS

There is now overwhelming evidence that orthodox microeconomic models fail to describe markets for retail financial services accurately, because they assume that consumers will make optimal decisions in their own interest. The proportion of consumers lacking the basic financial knowledge necessary to do this is substantial. Furthermore, even those who have higher financial capability appear to be subject to a range of behavioural biases in judgement and decision-making, which are also likely to lead to some disadvantageous decisions. Moreover, there is evidence to suggest that competition is unlikely to drive out the problem. Consumer detriment caused by paying over the odds for financial services may be considerable, while damage due to consumers taking on too much risk has been painfully apparent in recent years, both in Ireland and globally. Improving financial decision-making therefore constitutes an important policy challenge.

There is less conclusive evidence that relates to the potential of different policy options to tackle the challenge, but nevertheless some implications can be drawn. Better financial education and information for consumers is probably of marginal benefit, unless new and creative ideas emerge to improve its effectiveness. There is scant evidence that financial education programmes produce meaningful shifts in consumer behaviour and even consumers of above average financial literacy do not seem to make appreciably better financial decisions after receiving simplified descriptions of available products. Nevertheless, further attempts to improve policy in this area, perhaps concentrating on the broader notion of financial 'capability' rather than 'literacy', could potentially produce better methods with larger impacts, most likely over the longer term. Consumer education and information targeted at known pitfalls in financial reasoning may prove more effective, as may face-to-face counselling, though widespread use of the latter is expensive. Laboratory and field experiments to test these alternative approaches could be devised and executed.

Restrictions on marketing and selling practices contained in Ireland's 2012 Consumer Protection Code effectively ban provider behaviour that has been shown empirically to disrupt consumers' decision-making. Restrictions on prearranged credit also have empirical support. However, the evidence that in some cases simplified product information has had little influence on consumer choices suggests that the many mandatory information disclosures may have limited impact. Much of the remainder of the Code's effectiveness will depend on how it is enforced, particularly with respect to whether providers can genuinely be expected to act in the best interests of consumers, notwithstanding regulations stipulating that they must. The evidence reviewed here suggests that providers frequently face incentives to capitalise on consumer biases and to hide portions of the full price. Thus, provider behaviour is only likely to change if enforcement of the Code is strong enough to outweigh these market incentives.

Evidence, therefore, supports much tougher financial regulation than was the pre-crisis norm, such that providers have genuine incentives to help consumers to take better decisions, with respect to both the price they pay and the suitability of products. Thorough inspections of practice, mystery shopping and monitoring of advertising can be combined with effective punishment, which might include publicising violations given the limited threat of fines. Investment of the resources necessary to police the Consumer Protection Code in this manner might well repay. That said, tough regulation requires resolve and the return on the investment is hard to observe. It may prove unpopular among providers and those who find it harder to get credit; meanwhile the biggest successes, which consist of the avoidance of very negative outcomes, may go unseen.

A number of 'behaviourally informed' approaches to regulation have been suggested in recent times. These include proposals for more explicit mandated feedback (e.g., information tailored to specific consumers, estimates of the full price paid over the product lifetime), for mandated machine readable product information and for state regulated plain vanilla products. There is little evidence regarding the effectiveness of such policies, so it will be important to scrutinise the outcome if and when they are adopted elsewhere. In particular, the US Consumer Financial Protection Bureau has begun to conduct some relevant experiments and pilots. This highlights an important development in international research in this area, which is the increased use of empirical approaches to policy development. Ireland could also benefit from adopting this strategy to road test regulations.

Lastly, a perfectly reasonable if not definitive interpretation of the available evidence is that consumer detriment in retail financial services requires much stronger product regulation, involving the testing and licensing of financial products. Should post-crisis regulatory reform fail to generate evidence of consumer benefit, this case may become too compelling to ignore. It ought not to take the dawning of another crisis to persuade us to take much stronger action.

REFERENCES

Agarwal, S., Amromin, G., Ben-David, I., Chomsisengphet, S. and Evanoff, D.D. (2009). 'Do Financial Counseling Mandates Improve Mortgage Choice and Performance? Evidence from a Legislative Experiment'. Federal Reserve Bank of Chicago, Working Paper 2009-07.

Agnew, J.R. and Szykman, L.R. (2005). 'Asset allocation and Information Overload: The Influence of Information Display, Asset Choice, and Investor Experience', *Journal of Behavioral Finance*, 6, 57–70.

Atkinson, A. (2008). *Evidence of Impact: An Overview of Financial Education Evaluations*. London: Financial Services Authority.

Ausubel, L.M. (1999). 'Adverse Selection in the Credit Card Market'. Unpublished Manuscript, University of Maryland.

Bar-Gill, O. and Warren, E. (2008). 'Making Credit Safer', *University of Pennsylvania Law Review*, 157, 1–101.

Barber, B. and Odean, T. (2001). 'Boys Will Be Boys: Gender, Overconfidence, and Common Stock Investment', *Quarterly Journal of Economics*, 141, 261–292.

Barber, B. and Odean, T. (2002a). 'Online Investors: Do the Slow Die First?' *Review of Financial Studies*, 15, 455–487.

Barber, B. and Odean, T. (2002b). 'All that glitters: the effect of attention and news on the buying behaviour of individual and institutional investors'. Working Paper, University of California, Berkeley.

Barber, B.M., Odean, T. and Zheng, L. (2005). 'Out of Sight, Out of Mind: The Effects of Expenses on Mutual Fund Flows', *Journal of Business*, 78, 2095–2120.

Barberis, N. and Thaler, R. (2003). 'A Survey of Behavioral Finance' in Constantinides, G.M., Harris, M. and Stulz, R. (eds.), *Handbook of the Economics of Finance*, Amsterdam: North Holland.

Barr M.S., Mullainathan, S. and Shafir, E. (2008). *Behaviorally informed financial services regulation*. Washington DC: New America Foundation.

Benartzi, S. (2001). 'Excessive Extrapolation and the Allocation of 401(k) Accounts to Company Stock', *Journal of Finance*, 56, 1747–1764.

Berheim, B.D., Garrett, D.M. and Maki, D.M. (2000). 'Education and Saving: The Long-Term Effects of High School Financial Curriculum Mandates', *Journal of Public Economics*, 80, 435–465.

Bertrand, M., Karlan, D., Mullainathan, S., Shafir, E. and Zinman, J. (2010). 'What's Advertising Content Worth? Evidence from a Consumer Credit Marketing Field Experiment'. *Quarterly Journal of Economics*, 125, 263–306.

Beshears. J., Choi, J.J., Laibson, D. and Madrian, B.C. (2010). 'How Does Simplified Disclosure Affect Individuals' Mutual Fund Choices?' NBER Working Paper No. 14859.

Bhattacharya, U., Hackethal, A., Kaesler, S., Loos, B. and Meyer, S. (2012). 'Is Unbiased Financial Advice To Retail Investors Sufficient? Answers from a Large Field Study'. Forthcoming in *Review of Financial Studies*.

Brown, J.R., Ivkovic, Z., Smith, P.A. and Weisbenner, S. (2008a). 'Neighbors Matter: Causal Community Effects and Stock Market Participation,' *Journal of Finance*, 63, 1509–1531.

Brown, J.R., Kling, J.R., Mullainathan, S. and Wrobel, M.V. (2008b). 'Why Don't People Insure Late-Life Consumption? A Framing Explanation of the Under-Annuitization Puzzle', *American Economic Review*, 98, 304–309.

Carhart, M. (1997). 'On Persistence in Mutual Fund Performance', *Journal of Finance*, 52, 57–82.

Carlin, B.I. (2009). 'Strategic Price Complexity in Retail Financial Markets', *Journal of Financial Economics*, 91, 278–287.

Choi, J.J., Laibson, D. and Madrian, B.C. (2010). 'Why Does the Law of One Price Fail? An Experiment on Index Mutual Funds', *Review of Financial Studies*, 23, 1405–1432.

Clark, R.L., d'Ambrosio, M.B., McDermed, A.A. and Sawant, K. (2006). 'Retirement Plans and Savings Decisions: The Role of Information and Education', *Journal of Pension Economics and Finance*, 5, 45–67.

De Bruin, W.B., Parker, A.M. and Fischhoff, B. (2007). 'Individual Differences in Adult Decision-making Competence', *Journal of Personality and Social Psychology*, 92, 938–956.

De Meza, D., Irlenbusch, B. and Reyniers, D. (2007). *Information versus Persuasion: Experimental Evidence on Salesmanship, Mandatory Disclosure and the Purchase of*

Income and Loan Payment Protection Insurance. London: Financial Services Authority.
De Meza, D., Irlenbusch, B. and Reyniers, D. (2008). *Financial capability: A behavioural economics perspective*. London: Financial Services Authority.
DellaVigna, S. (2009). 'Psychology and Economics: Evidence from the Field', *Journal of Economic Literature*, 47, 315–372.
DellaVigna, S. and Malmendier, U. (2004). 'Contract Design and Self-Control: Theory and Evidence', *Quarterly Journal of Economics*, 119, 353–402.
Duffy, D. and Lunn, P.D. (2009). 'The Misperception of Inflation by Irish Consumers', *The Economic and Social Review*, 40, 139–163.
Duflo, E. and Saez, E. (2003). 'The Role of Information and Social Interactions in Retirement Plan Decisions: Evidence from a Randomized Experiment', *Quarterly Journal of Economics*, 118, 815–842.
European Commission (2010). *Consumer Decision-making in Retail Investment Services: A Behavioural Economics Perspective*. Brussels: European Commission.
Frederick, S., Loewenstein, G. and O'Donoghue, T. (2002). 'Time Discounting and Time Preference: A Critical Review', *Journal of Economic Literature*, 40, 351–401.
Gabaix, X. and Laibson, D. (2006). 'Shrouded Attributes and Information Suppression in Competitive Markets', *Quarterly Journal of Economics*, 121, 505–540.
Gabaix, X., Laibson, D. and Li, H. (2005). 'Extreme Value Theory and the Effects of Competition on Profits'. Working Paper, Harvard University.
Genesove, D. and Mayer, C. (2001). 'Loss Aversion and Seller Behavior: Evidence from the Housing Market', *Quarterly Journal of Economics*, 116, 1233–1260.
Grinblatt, M. and Keloharju, M. (2001). 'How distance, language, and culture influence stockholdings and trades', *Journal of Finance*, 56, 1053–1073.
Gross, D.B. and Souleles, N.S. (2002). 'Do Liquidity Constraints and Interest Rates Matter for Consumer Behavior? Evidence from Credit Card Data', *Quarterly Journal of Economics*, 117, 149–185.
Grubb, M.D. (2009). 'Selling to Overconfident Consumers', *American Economic Review*, 99, 1770–1807.
Hackethal, A., Inderst, R. and Meyer, S. (2011). 'Trading on Advice'. SSRN Working Paper, accessed at http://ssrn.com/abstract=1701777.
Hartman, R.S., Doane, M.J. and Woo, C-K. (1991). 'Consumer Rationality and the Status Quo', *Quarterly Journal of Economics*, 106, 141–162.
Hassink, H.J. and van Leuvensteijn, M. (2007). 'Measuring Transparency in the Dutch Mortgage Market', *De Economist*, 155, 23–47.
Hastopoulos, G.N. Krugman. P.R. and Poterba, J.M. (1989). *Overconsumption: The Challenge to U.S. Economic Policy*. Washington DC: American Business Conference.
Honohan, P. (2010). *The Irish Banking Crisis: Regulatory and Financial Stability Policy 2003–2008*. Accessed at: http://www.bankinginquiry.gov.ie/The%20

Irish%20Banking%20Crisis%20Regulatory%20and%20Financial%20Stability%20Policy%202003–2008.pdf

Hong, H., Kubik, J.D. and Stein, J.C. (2004). 'Social Interaction and Stock Market Participation', *Journal of Finance*, 59, 137–163.

Hortaçsu, A. and Syverson, C. (2004). 'Product Differentiation, Search Costs, and Competition in the Mutual Fund Industry: A Case Study of S&P 500 Index Funds', *Quarterly Journal of Economics*, 119, 403–456.

Huang, J.F. and Chen, Y.F. (2006). 'Herding in Online Product Choice', *Psychology & Marketing*, 23, 413–428.

Huberman, G. (2001). 'Familiarity Breeds Investment', *Review of Financial Studies*, 14, 659–680.

Huffman, D. and Barenstein, M. (2004). 'Riches to Rags Every Month? The Fall in Consumption Expenditure Between Paydays'. IZA Discussion Paper, 1430.

Iyengar, S.S., Huberman, G. and Jiang. W. (2004). 'How Much Choice Is Too Much? Contributions to 401(k) Retirement Plans' in Mitchell, O.S and Utkus, S. (eds.), *Pension Design and Structure: New Lessons from Behavioral Finance*, pp. 83–95. Oxford: Oxford University Press.

Iyengar, S. and M. Lepper (2000). 'When Choice is Demotivating: Can One Desire Too Much of a Good Thing?' *Journal of Personality and Social Psychology*, 79, 995–1006.

Kahneman, D. (2011). *Thinking, Fast and Slow*. New York and London: Penguin.

Kahneman, D. and Riepe, M.W. (1998). 'Aspects of Investor Psychology: Beliefs, Preferences, and Biases Investment Advisors Should Know About', *Journal of Portfolio Management*, 24(4).

Kooreman, P. (2000). 'The Labeling Effect of a Child Benefit System', *American Economic Review*, 90, 571–538.

Lacko, J.M. and Pappalardo, J.K. (2007). *Improving Consumer Mortgage Disclosures: An Empirical Assessment of Current and Prototype Disclosure Forms*. Federal Trade Commission Bureau of Economics Staff Report.

Larrick, R.P. (2004). 'Debiasing' in Koehler, D.K. and Harvey, N. (eds.), *Blackwell Handbook of Judgement and Decision-making*. New York: Blackwell.

Lunn, P. (2013). 'The Role of Decision-making Biases in Ireland's Banking Crisis'. Forthcoming in *Irish Political Studies*.

Lusardi, A. (2010). *Americans' Financial Capability*. Report Prepared for the Financial Crisis Inquiry Commission, February 26, 2010.

Lusardi, A. and Tufano, P. (2009). 'Debt Literacy, Financial Experiences, and Overindebtedness'. NBER Working Paper, No. 14808.

Madrian, B.C. and Shea, D.F. (2001). 'The power of suggestion: inertia in 401(k) participation and savings behaviour', *Quarterly Journal of Economics*, 116, 1149–1187.

Mandell, L. (2009). 'The Impact of Financial Education in High School and College On Financial Literacy and Subsequent Financial Decision Making'. Paper presented to the American Economic Association, January 2009.

Mandell, L. and Klein, L.S. (2009). 'The Impact of Financial Literacy Education on Subsequent Financial Behavior'. *Journal of Financial Counseling and Planning*, 20, 15–24.

Martín-Oliver, A., Salas-Fumás, V. and Saurina, J. (2007). 'A Test of the Law of One Price in Retail Banking', *Journal of Money, Credit and Banking*, 39, 2021–2040.

McCarthy, Y. (2011). 'Behavioural Characteristics and Financial Distress'. Central Bank of Ireland Research Technical paper 06/RT/11.

Miles, D. (2004). 'Incentives, Information and Efficiency in the UK Mortgage Market', *Economic Journal*, 115, C82–C98.

Monteiro, N. and Zaidi, R. (2007). *Market Impacts of MCOB*. London: Financial Services Authority.

Muellbauer, J. and Murphy, A. (1997). 'Booms and Busts in the UK Housing Market'. *Economic Journal*, 107, 1701–1727.

National Steering Group on Financial Capability (2009). 'Improving Financial capability – A Multi-Stakeholder Approach'. Accessed at: www.financial capability.ie/files/ sg.report.01jul09.ek.pdf

Nyberg, P. (2011). *Misjudging Risk: Causes of the Systemic Banking Crisis in Ireland*. Accessed at: http://www.bankinginquiry.gov.ie/Documents/Misjuding%20Risk%20-%20Causes%20of%20the%20Systemic%20Banking%20Crisis%20in%20Ireland.pdf

Odean, T. (1998). 'Are Investors Reluctant to Realize Their Losses?' *Journal of Finance*, 53, 1775–1798.

O'Donnell, N. and M. Keeney (2009). *Financial Capability: New Evidence for Ireland*. Dublin: Central Bank.

OECD (2011). 'Improving Financial Education Efficiency: OECD-Bank of Italy Symposium on Financial Literacy'. Paris: OECD.

Office of Fair Trading (2004). *Doorstep Selling: A Report on the Market Study*. London: Office of Fair Trading.

Piazzesi, M. and Schneider, M. (2009). 'Momentum Traders in the Housing Market: Survey Evidence and a Search Model', *American Economic Review*, 99, 406–411.

Regling, K. and Watson, M. (2010). *A Preliminary Report on the Sources of Ireland's Banking Crisis*. Accessed at: http://www.bankinginquiry.gov.ie/Preliminary%20Report%20into%20Ireland%27s%20Banking%20Crisis%2031%20May%202010.pdf

Samuelson, W. and Zeckhauser, R. (1988). 'Status Quo Bias in Decisions Making', *Journal of Risk and Uncertainty*, 1, 7–59.

Stanovich, K.E. and West, R.F. (2000). 'Individual Differences in Reasoning: Implications for the Rationality Debate', *Behavioural and Brain Sciences*, 23, 645–726.

Tennyson, S. and Nguyen, C.C. (2001). 'State Curriculum Mandates and Student Knowledge of Personal Finance', *Journal of Consumer Affairs*, 35, 241–263.

Thaler, R.H. and Benartzi, S. (2004). 'Save More Tomorrow: Using Behavioral Economics to Increase Employee Saving', *Journal of Political Economy*, 112, S164–S187.

Thaler, R.H. and Sunstein, C.R. (2008). *Nudge: Improving Decisions About Health, Wealth, and Happiness*. Yale University Press.

Thaler, R., Tversky, A., Kahneman, D. and Schwartz, A. (1997). 'The Effect of Myopia and Loss Aversion on Risk-Taking: An Experimental Test', *Quarterly Journal of Economics*, 112, 647–661.

Willis, L.E. (2008). 'Against Financial Literacy Education', *Iowa Law Review*, 94, 197–285.

Woodward, S. (2008). *A Study of Closing Costs for FHA Mortgages*. Washington, DC: Department of Housing and Urban Development.

Yoong, J. (2011). 'Can Behavioural Economics be Used to Make Financial Education More Effective?' in *Improving Financial Education Efficiency: OECD-Bank of Italy Symposium on Financial Literacy*, 65–101.

CHAPTER 10

Fiscal Consolidation Strategies: Evidence from the International Experience

Eddie Casey, Joseph Durkan, David Duffy

Although Ireland has done much already to reduce its government deficit, the scale of the fiscal adjustment required means that there is still some distance to go. In international terms, Ireland's fiscal consolidation will ultimately prove to be one of the largest recorded in the Organisation for Economic Co-operation and Development (OECD). In relation to the policy landscape (Figure 1.1), the extent of the policy challenge and the agreed goal of reducing the deficit have long been clear. The issue that remains is to determine which policy options to execute in order to reach that goal.

Evidence relating to previous large fiscal consolidations, in Ireland and elsewhere, has the potential to assist in this task. There is great variation in outcomes: some fiscal consolidations have been far more successful than others. If previous fiscal consolidations share common success factors, then fiscal policy in Ireland can absorb lessons from them and look to emulate the more successful programmes of adjustment. The primary research question addressed in this chapter, therefore, is: Do successful periods of fiscal consolidation share common success factors, and if so, what are they?

We employ two methods to address the issue. First, we conduct a meta-analysis of econometric studies of fiscal consolidation periods. Several existing studies have employed data from previous episodes of fiscal consolidation to build econometric models designed to identify factors associated with successful outcomes. We draw inferences from the pattern of results obtained across a group of such studies. Second, we consider in greater detail a set of case studies of fiscal consolidations that have been selected because of their similarity to the present Irish situation.

We find that there are indeed common factors associated with successful consolidations, which are defined as those that reduce the government deficit and return it to a more sustainable state. Most notably, we find that the likelihood of successful consolidation is related to the composition of the adjustment. Previous success has proved to be more likely where the bulk of the adjustment was undertaken less through increased taxation than through reduced expenditure – in particular current rather than capital expenditure. Consolidations that concentrate on reduced current expenditure tend to do less damage to economic growth and are more likely to restore stability to the public finances. A stable currency environment is also conducive to success. Our findings therefore support an ongoing balance of adjustment in Ireland that places most of the burden on reductions in current public expenditure.

Future research might uncover in more detail the mechanisms that underlie the main result, and what causes the not-insignificant variation in the relationship between the composition of the adjustment and a successful outcome.

BACKGROUND

The current need for fiscal consolidation is driven primarily by the risk that existing government debt may become unsustainable. In a situation where no budgetary correction is implemented and expenditures continue to exceed government revenues, the rise in interest costs can require further borrowings to finance repayments until such time as economic growth fails to counteract an explosive rise in government debt ratios.

It is important to remember that budgetary adjustment will inevitably have some influence on economic activity and vice versa. A principal objective of any fiscal consolidation should be to limit the costs, in terms of economic growth, given the choice of fiscal adjustment measures available. Large debt servicing payments represent a significant opportunity cost in terms of expenditure alternatives foregone. A greater degree of taxation required just to service debt also increases the likelihood of undesirable and distortionary elements being introduced into the economy. This chapter examines some of the success factors evident in previous consolidation episodes, in Ireland and elsewhere, aiming to learn lessons for the current situation in Ireland.

The context for this chapter is the current public finance problems confronting the Irish state. Ireland's envisaged consolidation, which totals over 19 per cent of GDP, is exceptionally demanding. This compares to an average of less than 5 per cent of GDP for cumulative OECD consolidation episodes recorded over the 1978 to 2009 period.

The chapter is organised as follows. The next section summarises the findings from the various existing studies based on a range of experiences of fiscal consolidation episodes internationally. The third section details individual case studies of particular relevance to the current Irish situation. Lessons from both the broader literature and the individual case studies are then drawn out in the fourth section before the final section concludes.

META-ANALYSIS[153]

This section reviews a wide but not exhaustive body of empirical research in order to ascertain a broad set of policy guidelines relating to fiscal consolidation. The research is based on the combined consolidation experiences of different economies and different governments so that the results, while quite generalisable, may not be entirely applicable as prescriptive policy frameworks for individual cases. Nevertheless, the findings do present a very useful starting point from which to investigate the preferred strategy for a successful fiscal consolidation in a country like Ireland.

We organise the meta-analysis according to a number of prominent elements found in previous consolidation processes: the pace of consolidation; the composition of consolidation in terms of expenditure cuts versus tax increases; and the types of expenditure cuts undertaken. We then explore two other elements that feed into the impact of consolidations: namely exchange-rate changes, monetary policy, and political structure.

Pace of consolidation

Larch and Turrini (2011) define fiscal consolidations as either an improvement of the cyclically adjusted primary balance (CAPB) equal to or greater than 1.5 per cent of GDP in one year, or a 1.5 per cent improvement over three years, during which there is no disimprovement in the CAPB greater than 0.5 per cent in any of those years. The first type of adjustment, indicative of a more intense consolidation, is termed a 'cold shower', the second a 'gradual consolidation'. Successful adjustments are defined in terms of tackling the current deficit, with a success involving no disimprovement in the CAPB over the following three years of greater than 0.75 per cent compared with the CAPB in the final year of adjustment. Their data set covers all 27 EU member states over the period 1971 to 2006, although data for individual country-years is not always available. Consolidation is found to take place in 146 of the 634 country-years, one-third of which were successful. Probit analysis of successful consolidations reveals that the severity of the adjustment is not the deciding factor as 'cold showers' and 'gradual adjustments' are equally successful for improving the CAPB.

More recent work by Baum *et al.* (2012), explored further by the International Monetary Fund (IMF) (2012a), emphasises how fiscal multipliers can vary across countries and time. The relative position on the business cycle is found to be a key determinant of the magnitude of the impact that fiscal policy shocks can have. Using a nonlinear threshold vector autoregressive model for G7 countries from the 1970s to the present, their results suggest that, in the short run, fiscal policy shocks can have larger negative impacts on growth if the economy is already in a downturn. This is also taken to imply that more gradual approaches

---

[153] A more detailed review is contained in Casey *et al.* (2013).

to fiscal consolidation are preferable in cases where output is below its potential so as to result in less damage to short-run growth. A 'cold shower' approach, by contrast, would be more desirable in cases where output is already above potential. Ultimately, however, their findings suggest that the differences relating to the two approaches diminish over the long run.

Composition of consolidation

A key study in the early literature is Alesina and Perotti (1995), in which adjustments are deemed successful if the debt-to-GDP ratio is 5 percentage points lower three years later. Standard measures of the fiscal position, as in the budget deficit, can change from year to year, not only because of discretionary fiscal action, but also because of the interrelationship between fiscal health and the economy.

The sample used by Alesina and Perotti (1995) consists of 20 OECD countries for the years 1960 to 1992 and contains 52 episodes of fiscal adjustment, 14 of which are classified as successful. The authors find that successful consolidations involve slightly larger adjustments on average than unsuccessful episodes and are far more focused on expenditure cuts. Indeed, 80 per cent of the adjustment in successful consolidations is found to come from changes in expenditure, the bulk of which involves cuts in the government wage bill or cuts in social transfers. In terms of the unsuccessful consolidations, tax increases typically outweighed expenditure cuts, with both direct and indirect taxes increasing substantially and a rise in the share of public employment. In contrast, successful episodes were characterised by public-sector employment shares that did not expand during the adjustment period.

While the research of Larch and Turrini (2011) suggests that the pace of consolidation may not be important, they do find that the composition of the adjustment is central, with spending cuts increasing the chances of an adjustment's success significantly. This finding is valid for all items of current expenditure, whereas spending cuts in government investment reduce the likelihood of success and are more likely to be reversed. The authors also find that fiscal consolidations accompanied by labour and product market reforms are more likely to prove successful.

Alesina and Ardagna (2012) find that, when compared with tax-based approaches, expenditure-based adjustments are more durable and less likely to be reversed, are associated with smaller recessions and, on occasion, may correspond with expansionary (or non-recessionary) outcomes if accompanied by growth-friendly policies, such as wage agreements with unions, public-sector wage restraint, accommodative monetary policies and/or exchange-rate devaluations. The IMF (2010), motivated by a desire to isolate specific fiscal measures that are taken with the expressed intent of reducing the budget deficit, arrive at similar conclusions: expenditure-based adjustments produce less contractionary outcomes relative to taxation-based adjustments.

Given the evidence, it is worth asking why fiscal consolidations that primarily target revenues rather than expenditures are so often implemented. One answer relates to how palatable expenditure measures are relative to taxation measures (Alesina and Perotti, 1995). The argument goes that risk-averse politicians may find it easier to raise certain taxes than to implement expenditure cuts. Governments are more likely to favour the easy choices of raising taxation and cutting investment, at first, before turning to areas of current expenditure that are more sensitive and take longer to implement. Another reason may be the belief that it is preferable to defer certain expenditure reductions while more palatable productivity increases are still possible in the early stages of consolidation. A final reason relates to the desire to avoid increases in income inequality, particularly those that may arise from cuts to social transfers (Alesina and Perotti, 1996). Political sensitivity may be overstated, however, as evidence from OECD countries, South America and the US fails to support the idea that adjustments generally lead to loss of office (see Alesina et al., 1998; Kraemer, 1997; Peltzman, 1992).

Although largely taxation-based consolidations tend to be discouraged in the literature, a mix of policy options is clearly a necessity in any serious consolidation of public finances. Optimal taxation measures for avoiding reductions in output can be gleaned from the OECD (2009a). The revenue-raising measures with the least impact are found to be environmental taxes (e.g., direct carbon taxes or the auction of emissions permits), consumption taxes (i.e. VAT) and property taxes.

Types of expenditure cuts

Using a dataset consisting of 20 OECD countries, Alesina and Perotti (1996) extend their definitions of fiscal tightening to allow for multi-year cases to be examined as single programmes. A disadvantage of this approach is that it risks associating favourable outcomes with other intervening factors, thus making the findings somewhat more tenuous when observed in isolation. Under the definitions of success, one-quarter of the policy implementations are found to have successful outcomes, with results reasonably resilient to alternative variations on these definitions.

The findings show that successful adjustments typically involved compositions where approximately 73 per cent was on the expenditure side. By contrast, unsuccessful cases related to compositions where just 44 per cent of the fiscal consolidation was expenditure based. The authors show that unsuccessful cases involved expenditure cuts where more than two-thirds expenditure were related to capital expenditure. Success was more likely to be found in cases where capital expenditure reductions were lower and typically in the order of 20 per cent of total expenditure cuts. Critically, the authors again find that successful adjustment strategies are characterised by large reductions in government wage bills and transfers, with these comprising almost 60 per cent of the total reduction in expenditure. Moreover, the findings also suggest that expenditure-based adjustments induce longer lasting consolidations, while taxation-based adjustments are less persistent and more likely to be contractionary.

Using the same sample of OECD countries over a slightly longer period, Alesina and Ardagna (1998) find the crucial ingredients to a successful, long lasting and even expansionary adjustment are those that involve an adjustment that emphasises expenditure reductions in the areas of transfers, welfare programmes and government wages. They highlight the importance of some form of wage agreement with unions in order to insure broader wage moderation and the beneficial role of exchange rate devaluation immediately before the adjustment. Again, the avoidance of large tax-based adjustments is also stressed, with such policies found to be more likely to result in less permanent consolidations. No example of a large tax-based adjustment is found to be expansionary in their sample.

Alesina et al. (2002) suggest that the response of private sector investment offers one explanation for why expenditure-based consolidations are typically found to be less contractionary. Taxes are more likely to deter investment, while spending reductions are less likely to have such negative impacts. Public expenditure reductions in the form of reduced government wages and reduced social transfers may actually induce increased private investment, buoyed by the downward pressure on the equilibrium wage.[154]

A vast OECD literature summarised in *Economic Outlook 2007* and presented in Sutherland et al. (2012) utilises potential output to measure the degree of consolidation. In the *OECD Economic Outlook 2007*, fiscal consolidations are identified as an improvement in the CAPB of at least 1 per cent of potential GDP in one year or over the course of two years with at least a 0.5 per cent improvement in the first of the two years. The episode continues for as long the CAPB improves, although an interruption is allowed as long as the deterioration of the CAPB does not exceed 0.3 per cent and is more than offset in the following year. Consolidations were judged successful if the fiscal adjustment was enough to stabilise the debt-to-GDP ratio within two years. Of the 85 episodes of consolidation identified across 24 counties between 1978 and 2007, slightly more than half were successful, most were short (median duration of two years) and were of limited magnitude (median underlying improvement of budget position of 2.8 per cent of GDP). Using probit analysis, the authors find that a greater weight on cuts to social spending increases the chances of successful outcomes. While expenditure-based consolidations were more likely to be successful, almost two-thirds of the episodes reviewed by the OECD involved larger contributions from revenue-based increases. Fiscal rules that focused on controlling expenditure were found to be associated with greater success, producing larger and longer adjustments – locking in gains from consolidation and maintaining debt-stabilising primary balances.

Findings from Barrios et al. (2010) lend support to earlier findings that expenditure-led consolidations tend to be more successful. The authors use probit models to link determinants of success to the initial decisions prompting consolidation episodes. These decisions may depend on the economic circumstances prior

---

154 These findings are in keeping with research elsewhere (see Finn, 1998; Daveri and Tabellini, 2000; and Ardagna, 2007).

to any adjustment and their work specifically controls for initial debt level. The definition of consolidation used is an improvement in the CAPB of at least 1.5 percentage points taking place in one year ('cold shower'), or taking place over three years if the CAPB does not deteriorate by more than 0.5 per cent of GDP in any year (gradual consolidation). Their findings suggest that repairing the financial sector, if in a state of crisis, is a necessary pre-condition for the success of any consolidation. Even after a financial sector crisis has been repaired, the presence of a financial crisis usually entails less successful consolidations (even when sample selection bias is controlled for), something which the authors note can be compensated for to some degree by 'cold shower'-style adjustments.[155] For those economies that have high initial debt levels, low growth potential and high interest rates, sharper sustained contractions are more likely to bear fruit if the 'snowball effect'[156] is positive and greater than 1 per cent of GDP, while countries in which these specific constraints are less evident are more likely to benefit from more gradual adjustment strategies.

Barrios et al. (2010) document a range of unobserved factors that may explain frequent findings that larger shares of current expenditure reductions are more likely to result in a successful consolidation of public finances. Largely expenditure-based measures are more likely to trigger a fall in private saving and in interest rates, whereas largely revenue-based consolidations are likely to have the opposite effect. An emphasis on current expenditure reductions is more likely to be successful as it reflects a stronger overall commitment to fiscal consolidation by all participants. As measures aimed at expenditure reduction are typically longer lasting, these can reassure investors of the credibility of the adjustment and result in lower interest costs on long-term debt. This can, in turn, create a positive feedback loop for the sustainability of the deficit/debt dynamics by lowering the debt-servicing costs that form a major part of their make-up (Cottarelli and Viñals, 2009). It has also been suggested that expenditure cuts are more successful because they are frequently accompanied by reforms aimed at improving public-service efficiency (European Commission, 2007).

One problem associated with the previous work on the success of fiscal consolidations is that uncertainty regarding the time frame within which consolidation would lead to an improvement in debt sustainability does not lend itself to the use of regression models using yearly data. Molnar (2012) covers the

---

[155] The authors note that in their study of EU economies success rates are about 56 per cent when consolidation is started after a financial crisis ends compared to only 9 per cent when consolidation starts during a financial crisis. This compares with a 34 per cent success rate for the benchmark case of no financial crisis.

[156] High initial debt levels here are defined as those that are above 70 per cent of GDP. The snowball effect relates to the average interest rates on the national debt less the nominal GDP growth rate. The authors note that, in high debt cases, gradual consolidations are only warranted in situations where the snowball effect is negative or in situations where it is positive, but very small.

years 1960 to 2009 and uses three specifications: (i) where debt stabilises one year after the end of the consolidation episode, (ii) two years after, or (iii) three years after. The findings show that faster growth, lower inflation and declining interest rates increase the probability of debt stabilisation. Consolidations with a greater weight on expenditure cuts were more likely to stabilise the debt-to-GDP ratio. However, for larger consolidations, debt stabilisation was more likely to be temporary for those consolidations based more on spending reductions. This implies that large cuts in spending are more prone to backsliding in future years.

Exchange rate changes

A common argument (such as those expressed by Lambertini and Tavares, 2005; IMF, 2010 and Devries et al., 2011) is that exchange rate devaluations are key features behind the success of fiscal adjustments. Alesina and Ardagna (2012) suggest this point may be overstated. A distinct lack of correlation between successful reductions in debt ratios in all the episodes of fiscal adjustments studied and the rate of growth of the nominal effective exchange rate is evident. Analysis by Barrios et al. (2010) on the role of exchange rate depreciations fails to reveal any significant bearing on the success of a fiscal consolidation, even when controlling for countries' degree of openness. The authors note that such findings do not necessarily mean that devaluations or depreciations will not help fiscal consolidations. The findings do suggest, however, that the evidence linking fiscal consolidation success with nominal devaluations is far from convincing. Even where an association is found to be significant, the relationship is often small.

Monetary policy

The interaction between monetary policy and fiscal policy is often seen as an important feature in determining the success of fiscal consolidation outcomes. Using over 100 years of data, Simon et al. (2012) examine the experiences of 26 high-debt episodes in advanced economies and combine this broad analysis with six case studies. The authors conclude that a supportive monetary environment is clearly a key ingredient in cases of successful debt reduction. Looking at episodes in Belgium, Canada, and Italy, they note that, despite implementing tight fiscal policies, each economy was unable to achieve a reduction in debt until such time as real interest rates fell and credible monetary policy frameworks were established. Earlier research by the IMF (2010) shows that interest rate reductions help to cushion the blow to domestic demand that results from fiscal consolidation measures. More recently, work by Alesina et al. (2012) and Alesina and Ardagna (2012) counters claims that differences in outcomes resulting from the type of adjustment employed might be explained away by the interaction with monetary policy. In controlling for monetary-policy decisions, they still find systematic differences associated with the composition of the adjustment.

Political structure

Although it does not lend itself to any obvious policy ramifications, it has been argued that the structure of governments can play an important role in determining the success of fiscal consolidations. Roubini and Sachs' (1988) findings suggest that weak and divided governments (with shorter average tenures in government also playing a role) are less effective in reducing budgetary deficits than stable and majority-party governments, typically taking longer to reduce these and having a tendency to oversee larger deficits. One reason posited for this feature is the veto power held by small coalition partners over policy changes.

Alesina and Perotti (1995) suggest that coalition governments show the worst performance in terms of implementing successful fiscal adjustments, when compared against single-party majority governments and even minority governments. Examining political factors relating to fiscal adjustment outcomes, the authors found that only 8.7 per cent of the coalition governments studied implemented successful consolidations, when compared with 35.7 per cent of single-party majority governments and 46.7 per cent of minority governments.

Summary

As might be expected, there is a great variety in the approaches adopted by different countries in addressing fiscal consolidation. Table 10.1 provides a summary of the key findings from each of the papers reviewed.

Table 10.1: Summary of main findings from meta-analysis

Study	Number of countries	Time period	Measure used	Definition of fiscal consolidation	Definition of success	Method of analysis	Main findings
Alesina and Ardagna (2009)	20 (OECD)	1970–2007	BFI[157]	At least 1.5 percentage points of GDP improvement in CAPB in one year.	Cumulative debt/GDP improvement is greater than 4.5 percentage points.	OLS regressions.	Composition of the fiscal adjustment matters more than its size in terms of GDP growth impact. Fiscal adjustments associated with higher GDP outcomes tend to be those involving a larger share of reduction in current spending in Government wage and non-wage components as well as subsidies.
Alesina and Perotti (1995)	20 (OECD)	1960–1992	BFI	Improvement in the CAPB of greater than 1.5% of GDP	Debt/GDP improves by 5% or more after three years.	Descriptive statistics.	Successful consolidations tend to be slightly larger and comprised mainly of expenditure cuts.
Alesina and Perotti (1996)	20 (OECD)	1960–1992	BFI	(i) A year when BFI falls by more than 1.5% of GDP. (ii) Periods of two consecutive years where BFI falls by at least 1.25% in each year.	(i) BFI is on average at least 2% of GDP lower than in the last year of tightening three years later. (ii) Debt-to-GDP ratio is 5% of GDP below level in last year of consolidation.	Descriptive statistics and case studies.	Successful adjustments typically 73% expenditure based. Capital expenditure reductions relatively lower part of expenditure-side measures relative to current expenditure and typically in the order of 20% of total expenditure cuts. Successful episodes characterised by large reductions in government wage bills and transfers, with these comprising almost 60% of total reduction in expenditure.

157 The BFI measure attempts to control for some of the problems associated with cyclicality by providing a measure of the difference between some standard measure of an actual budgetary outcome, compared with the same measure in a hypothetical case where no changes in cyclically-related developments exist (e.g., in the case of rising unemployment).

Table 10.1: Summary of main findings from meta-analysis (continued)

Study	Number of countries	Time period	Measure used	Definition of fiscal consolidation	Definition of success	Method of analysis	Main findings
Alesina and Ardagna (1998)	20 (OECD)	1960–1994	BFI	Year in which the BFI improves by at least 2% of GDP or a period of two consecutive years in which the BFI improves by at least 1.5% of GDP per year, in both years.	(i) Three years after the consolidation, the BFI is on average at least 2% of GDP below its value in the year of tight policy, or (ii) Three years after the consolidation, the debt-to-GDP ratio is 5% of GDP below its level in the year of consolidation.	Probit regression.	Composition of successful adjustments emphasises expenditure reductions in the areas of transfers, welfare programmes and government wages. Wage agreement with unions and exchange-rate devaluations immediately before adjustments are beneficial.

Table 10.1: Summary of main findings from meta-analysis (continued)

Study	Number of countries	Time period	Measure used	Definition of fiscal consolidation	Definition of success	Method of analysis	Main findings
Barrios et al. (2010)	35	1970–2008	CAPB (OECD)	(i) An improvement in the CAPB of at least 1.5 percentage points taking place in one year ('cold shower'), or (ii) Taking place over three years if each and every year the CAPB does not deteriorate by more than 0.5% of GDP (gradual consolidation).	Debt-to-GDP ratio is reduced by at least 5 percentage points of GDP in the three years following a consolidation episode.	Probit regression.	Repairing financial sector is necessary pre-condition for success of any consolidation and financial crises are more likely to entail less successful consolidations. Expenditure-based measures are more likely to trigger falls in private saving and interest rates. Revenue-based consolidations are likely to have the opposite effect. Particular emphases on current expenditure reductions are more likely to be successful because they reflect stronger overall commitment to fiscal consolidation.

Table 10.1: Summary of main findings from meta-analysis (continued)

Study	Number of countries	Time period	Measure used	Definition of fiscal consolidation	Definition of success	Method of analysis	Main findings
Guichard (2007)	24	1978–2005	CAPB (OECD)	Improvement in the CAPB of at least 1% of potential GDP in one year or over the course of two years with at least a 0.5% improvement in the first of the two years.	Adjustment large enough to stabilise Debt/GDP within two years considering the gap between the actual primary balance and debt-stabilising primary balance.	Probit regression.	Expenditure-based consolidations are important for yielding lower household savings and better growth outcomes. A greater weight on cuts to social spending increases chances of successful outcomes. Fiscal rules focusing on expenditure important for locking in gains produced during consolidation and maintaining debt-stabilising primary balance.
IMF (2010)	27 (EU)	1971–2006	CAPB (OECD)	(i) Improvement in the CAPB of greater than 1.5% over three years ('cold shower'). (ii) A 1.5% improvement over three years during which there is no disimprovement in the CAPB greater than 0.5% in any given year (gradual).	No disimprovement of the CAPB greater than 0.75% over the three years after final year of adjustment.	Probit regression.	Severity of adjustment not associated with success (i.e. 'cold shower' and gradual adjustments are equally successful). Reductions in all items of current expenditure significantly increase likelihood of success. Cuts to investment reduce likelihood of success and are more likely to be reversed. Accompanying product and labour market reforms increase likelihood of success.

Table 10.1: Summary of main findings from meta-analysis (continued)

Study	Number of countries	Time period	Measure used	Definition of fiscal consolidation	Definition of success	Method of analysis	Main findings
Larch & Turini (2011)	24	1960–2009	CAPB (OECD)	Range of definitions from any improvement in the CAPB to an improvement greater than 2%.	Debt-to-GDP ratio stabilises within (i) one year (ii) two years and (iii) three years.	Probit, duration, truncated regressions & bivariate Heckman selection model.	Spending-based consolidations more likely to be successful in stabilising debt, but also more prone to backsliding when very large. Fiscal rules (both expenditure and balance rules), higher growth, lower inflation and declining long-term interest rates also increase chances of success.
Molnar (2012)	15	1980–2009	Action-based	Introduction of policies motivated by deficit reduction.	n/a.	Impulse response functions.	Spending cuts less harmful to growth. Adjustments more painful if interest rates and exchange rates are fixed.

INDIVIDUAL CASE STUDIES

As noted in the previous section, there are many international examples of episodes of fiscal consolidation. Unfortunately, successful experiences in other economies do not provide ready models that can easily be replicated and fewer still come close to mirroring the environment that characterises the modern Irish economy. It is also difficult to arrive at specific recommendations, when much empirical work elsewhere lacks strong macroeconomic models that can capture specific features of monetary policy and labour market interactions reliably. In order to identify past experiences that may be more relevant to Irish policymakers, the following section draws from several specific case studies involving relatively similar, small, open economies operating within comparable exchange-rate regimes. For example, Denmark, Latvia, Lithuania and Estonia bear some structural similarities to Ireland in the sense that each represents a small, open economy with relatively flexible labour markets. The relative success of the Baltic States in reducing sizable fiscal deficits within a fixed-exchange rate regime has meant that these economies are uniquely interesting as case studies from an Irish perspective.

Ireland, 1983–1984 and 1987–1989

A starting point from which to draw insights is the past experience of the Irish economy itself. The fiscal consolidation between 1987 and 1989 witnessed a correction in the general government deficit of almost 8 per cent and in the CAPB of 6.3 percentage points. The adjustment was preceded by a period during which the need for substantial adjustment was well recognised. Previous efforts to correct the budget deficit had been stymied by a variety of factors, such as a succession of insecure minority or coalition governments, unfavourable external economic conditions, and higher global real interest rates earlier in the decade (see Honohan and Walsh, 2002). Moreover, growth was stunted by a significant sterling devaluation that started in mid-1985 and lasted until early 1987.

Looking at the composition of fiscal consolidation reveals a dichotomy between the initial period of adjustment (1982–1984) and the later period (1987–1989). The focus of earlier consolidation was geared more heavily towards taxation. Aside from the unfortunate timing of this adjustment given the weak external environment, the emphasis on taxation was subsequently perceived as largely counter-productive, discouraging investment and distorting labour market incentives, while encouraging tax evasion and tax avoidance behaviours (Considine and Duffy, 2007). In 1987 a revised 'Programme for National Recovery' was launched to tackle the persistent fiscal deficit and a growing national debt. The composition of the adjustment signalled a preference for deep-rooted expenditure reform over previously prioritised tax increases and, in particular, a focus on current expenditure reductions. As noted by McAleese and McCarthy (1989), most of the reduction came from lower government consumption and government investment, rather than from increases in discretionary taxes as happened in 1982. Taking all discretionary measures over the adjustment period, approximately three-quarters of the budgetary measures consisted of expenditure reductions (Perotti, 2013; Devries et al., 2011).[158]

In terms of primary expenditure, the overwhelming majority (some three-quarters) of the *ex ante* reduction ultimately came from reduced current expenditures, with the remainder due to cutbacks in capital expenditure (3 per cent of GDP). The most prominent reductions on the current side were across various forms of social spending as well as wage restraint and the reduction in public sector numbers. The reduced public sector numbers proved to be a relatively valuable source of durable savings over the decade that followed.

Capital expenditure was also subjected to cuts. On average, capital expenditures nearly halved from previous levels (1982–1986) during the 1987–1990 period. The emphasis on capital expenditure reductions has since been described as a 'mistake in retrospect' by those involved (McCarthy, 2009). This acknowledgment echoes findings in the broader literature that reductions in current expenditure are typically more successful for producing more durable adjustments that are also less likely to be reversed.

The lessons that can be drawn for the current crisis are limited somewhat by the extent of the external and non-discretionary factors that assisted the subsequent recovery. Bipartisan support for consolidation, an emergent boom in the UK economy, a coincident appreciation in sterling, a marked rise in net outward migration supported by the UK recovery, continued foreign direct investment (FDI) inflows and substantial EU aid in the form of Structural Fund allocations, all helped to create a fortuitous backdrop for the Irish consolidation. Another factor aiding in the recovery at the time, but not applicable in the current context, was the flexibility of the semi-peg.[159] While the European Exchange Rate Mechanism (ERM) was ostensibly a fixed-exchange rate regime, realignments meant that Ireland was able to devalue its currency by 8 per cent in 1986 – thus boosting competitiveness and aiding Irish exports before the implementation of renewed fiscal consolidation and before a policy of maintaining a stable exchange rate.

However, a number of lessons can be derived from the Irish experience in the 1980s. In particular, the later adjustment – with its greater emphasis on expenditure adjustments over revenue-based measures – provides some insights for the current programme of consolidation. The subsequent stability of the exchange rate after a significant early devaluation can also inform current policy, particularly given that much of the competitiveness losses during the boom have already been eroded.

---

158 Note that this composition excludes the 1988 tax amnesty that netted the equivalent of some 2.1 per cent of GDP in revenues because of its once-off nature. Including this, the estimated consolidation between 1986 and 1989 was almost equally split between revenue-based and expenditure-based measures.

159 A semi-pegged exchange rate system involves pegging currency values within specified ranges

Denmark, 1983–1986

Another remarkable adjustment episode is that of the Danish consolidation which took place early in the 1980s.[160] The correction in public finances saw the cyclically adjusted primary deficit improve by close to 11 per cent of GDP over the course of four years. The OECD (1987) estimates attribute three-quarters of the improvement in the overall balance that ensued to discretionary factors as opposed to cyclical improvements in economic activity.

Upon entering government in late 1982, a strong liberal-conservative coalition immediately commenced a medium-run fiscal stabilization programme split almost equally between expenditure-based and revenue-based measures.[161] Relative political stability was to be a feature throughout the period of adjustment: the same government coalition subsequently survived elections in 1984, 1987 and in June 1988. On the expenditure side, an emphasis on current spending was favoured, with government wages, public consumption and wide-ranging social transfer items targeted for reductions. In addition to this, numbers employed in the public sector were frozen. Similar measures targeting wage restraint elsewhere were imposed and an explicit agreement with unions was formed in 1982, wherein unions conceded to a wage freeze in addition to the suspension of wage indexation and a ceiling on public sector wage increases (Hallerberg, 2004).

Within the European Monetary System (EMS), the Danish kroner devalued four times, particularly in the 1981–1982 period. While this initially boosted competitiveness, the benefits were counteracted by wages that were still rising even as the rate of inflation had fallen substantially. Similarly, long-term nominal interest rates, having soared to just over 20 per cent in 1982, fell to 14 per cent in 1983 and 1984, before stabilising at around 10 per cent in the following seven years.

In terms of taxation measures, the largest share of tax increases related to direct taxes on households and corporations while various social security contributions were also raised. This preference for direct taxation was despite the fact that tax rates were already relatively high to begin with. A key consideration, as observed by De Bonis and Thimann (1999), is the role played by the increased stability in the external sector created when a credible commitment to a stable exchange rate was announced. Together with a credible fiscal adjustment and an easing in monetary policy, this helped to reduce the exchange rate risk premium attached

---

160 See Alesina and Ardagna (1998), Perotti (2011) for excellent summaries of the episode.

161 Perotti (2011) puts the share of revenue-based measures at 55 per cent of the total, whereas Devries et al. (2011) estimate expenditure cuts as roughly two-thirds. The difference is due to the latter classifying certain austerity measures that took place within the same time frame as other measures as being for 'countercyclical purposes'. We include the additional tax measures taken by Denmark in 1985 and 1986 as in Perotti (2011), but we also reduce this by the 1986 expansionary measures highlighted in Devries et al. (2011).

The Baltic States, 2009–2012

The experiences of Estonia, Latvia and Lithuania in the late 2000s have entered numerous discussions of the challenges facing peripheral economies in the euro area since the debt crisis began to escalate. This is due in no small part to the fact that these economies resisted the temptation of currency devaluations in favour of maintaining pegs to the euro. These decisions were motivated primarily by the anticipation of eventual accession to the euro area.

A rapid rise in current expenditures across the Baltic governments marked the pre-crisis period, with increases running far above levels of inflation. Large capital inflows (Grennes and Strazds, 2012) created wider inflationary pressure during the boom, while broadly balanced budgets masked larger underlying structural deficits. A marked reversal in the capital inflows combined with a pronounced weakening in external demand provoked a sharp downturn in 2009. Boom-related revenue buoyancy dissipated quickly. Weaknesses in tax administration were compounded by deteriorating tax compliance during this period and a simultaneous drawdown of many unclaimed VAT refunds (Purfield and Rosenberg, 2010). Despite severe double-digit declines in economic activity across the Baltic economies during 2009, a stabilisation in activity followed in 2010 and a return to strong growth was experienced in 2011.

While maintaining fixed exchange rates, the combined impact of wage declines and productivity gains in the Baltic economies was sizable enough to regain much of the competitiveness lost during the preceding expansions. This helped to promote swift macroeconomic adjustments, so that the recoveries in economic activity were initially driven by external demand and were increasingly bolstered by domestic demand thereafter.

Another factor, illustrated by Lindner (2011), relates to the role played by the structure of the banking sectors in the Baltic economies, which were dominated by foreign, particularly Scandinavian, credit institutions.[162] International lenders maintained support for subsidiaries in the region, while also providing some financial sector stability and ongoing credit lines as deep recessions ensued. Aside from the rescue of the domestically owned Parex bank in Latvia in November 2008, the costs to the Baltic economies of the crisis were relatively softened by the predominance of foreign-owned institutions. The speed at which these institutions slowed capital inflows forced the Baltic economies to adjust macroeconomic imbalances in a very short period of time.

---

162 Market shares held by such institutions typically ranged from 68 per cent in Latvia to 97 per cent in Estonia, compared to market shares in Portugal and Greece, for example, where independent domestic banks had far more dominant market shares equivalent to 80 per cent and 60 per cent, respectively.

The fiscal consolidation programmes in the Baltic economies were heavily frontloaded. The Latvian adjustment saw measures equivalent to just over 8 per cent of GDP implemented in the first year of its programme, while the total adjustment for the programme up to end-2012 is expected to be close to 16 per cent of GDP. The other economies were similarly decisive in their implementation. Lithuania enacted measures equating to around 10 per cent of GDP during 2009 and 2010, roughly three-quarters of which took place in the first year. Estonia implemented virtually all of its consolidation measures in just a single year (2009), with these measures equivalent to approximately 7.5 per cent of GDP.

In all cases, the adjustments were expenditure led, partly reflecting broad preferences for low levels of taxation in these economies. In contrast with standard findings in the literature which suggest that better outcomes are associated with reduced expenditure on social transfers, Latvia actually increased unemployment assistance. This was from a low base however, with the state still spending roughly half the EU average on social programmes.[163] Aside from the increase in social transfers, a particular emphasis on current expenditure items was apparent in each of the adjustments. All three Baltic countries introduced major public sector wage reductions in the first year of fiscal consolidation covering both regular and bonus pay. The extent of unpaid leave was increased and staff levels were reduced. Likewise, subsequent nominal wage bill freezes were extended in later budgets.

Reductions in departmental budget allocations were also steep, while a reorientation of government investment funding helped to alleviate the burden on state finances. Latvian government investment moved towards an increasing reliance on EU funding. This provided some countercyclical relief without impacting negatively on government finances. Revenue-based measures were spared for the most part, and those that were implemented primarily took the form of indirect consumption taxes.

It should be noted that the experiences of the Baltic economies were far from painless. Although unemployment rates have fallen significantly from levels in 2010, unemployment rates for 2012 are approximately more than twice those that prevailed in 2007 prior to the crisis. Notwithstanding this, living standards in 2012 are still likely to exceed their respective pre-crisis peaks as a result of the rapid recovery (see Fig 10.1). The fact that Latvian and Estonian living standards remain well below the European average (see Figure 10.2) has been cited as evidence that the economy has more scope for catch-up because of the implied distance from the technology frontier (Blanchard, 2012).

Poverty measures are also worryingly high among the Baltic economies, with severe material deprivation reportedly almost 31 per cent in Latvia, 19 per cent in Lithuania and 9 per cent in Estonia in 2011 (see Figure 10.3).[164] These have

---

163 Lithuania also introduced changes in unemployment benefits resulting in increased access for those most disadvantaged by the crisis, although reduced levels of benefits were made permanent.

164 'Severe material deprivation' measures the proportion of the total population severely burdened by a lack of material resources.

increased from record lows in 2008 for each country. Interestingly, however, they do not differ substantially from the average shares visible prior to the 2008 trough, with the share in Lithuania actually 6.3 percentage points lower in 2011 than the average during the three years that preceded its record low.

Another area worth considering in terms of the differences between the Baltic economies experiences and the Irish fiscal crisis is the role of net migration. The case studies suggest that reduced transfer costs associated with net outward migration can reduce expenditure costs, provided that this primarily arises among unemployed people. Net outward migration has been a major feature of the adjustment period in each of the economies, with Lithuanian populations seeing the largest rise in emigration rates among the Baltic economies, almost four times greater than that prior to the adjustment period (see Figure 10.4).[165] The only episode to have not witnessed this type of deterioration was the Danish experience, which was unusual in that it involved a largely domestic demand-driven recovery, albeit one that proved to be short-lived.

Figure 10.1: Unemployment

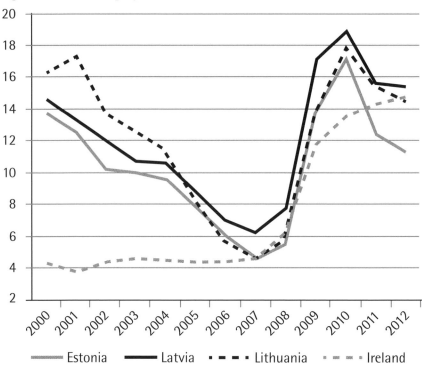

(% of total labour force)
Source: IMF and ESRI forecasts, 2012.

---

165 The IMF noted that Latvian emigration figures were likely to be much higher than official figures suggest (IMF, 2012c).

Figure 10.2: Gross national income per capita

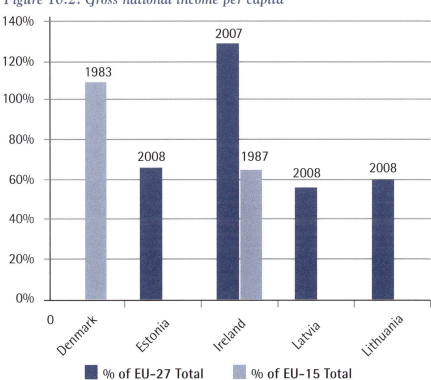

(% of EU totals based on purchasing power standard per capita before episode began)
Source: European Commission AMECO database.

Figure 10.3: Severe material deprivation rates

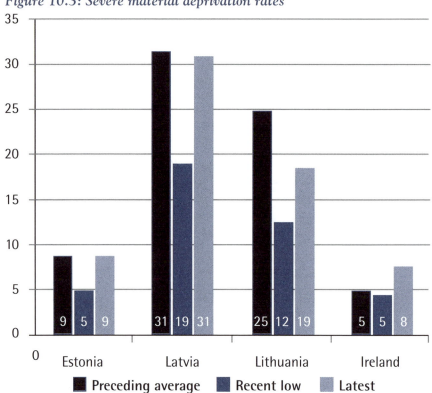

(% of total population)
Source: European Commission AMECO database.
Source: Eurostat.
Notes:
[1] Preceding averages are calculated over 2003–06 for Ireland, 2004–2007 for Estonia and 2005–2007 for others.
[2] Ireland's recent low is 2007, others are 2008.
[3] Latest data for Ireland are for 2010, the rest are for 2011.

Figure 10.4: Net migration in consolidation episodes

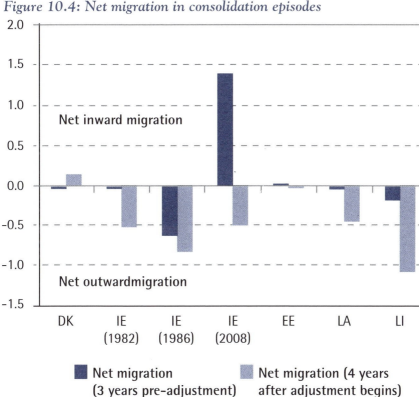

(Annual average as % of total population)
DK=Denmark, IE=Ireland, EE=Estonia, LA=Latvia, LI=Lithuania
Source: Eurostat.

LESSONS LEARNED

Some lessons can be drawn from the literature on fiscal consolidation episodes internationally and the case studies of relevance to Ireland's present situation. In particular, the evidence on the design of any fiscal consolidation appears quite conclusively to favour adjustments that focus on expenditure-based rather than taxation-based measures. Moreover, the emphasis on expenditure-based approaches in successful episodes supports reductions in current expenditure rather than capital expenditure, if the costs associated with fiscal consolidations in terms of economic growth are to be minimised.

Looking at the composition of the adjustments studied here, expenditure-led reductions were clearly a hallmark of each of the successful episodes covered. By contrast, the Irish episode of consolidation in the early 1980s, which was dominated by revenue-based measures, was notably unsuccessful. In terms of the average composition of adjustments (excluding the most recent adjustment period in

Ireland and the failed adjustment of 1982 to 1984), expenditure measures across the successful case studies examined here accounted for just over 65 per cent of the total measures implemented. The current Irish programme is expected to involve expenditure measures equivalent to 66 per cent of the total adjustment. As well as matching a broad preference in the wider literature for expenditure-led corrections, this ratio also closely matches specific compositions identified with other successful episodes. This ratio also holds regardless of the initial levels of taxation borne by the economies studied.

As identified by the broader literature, an emphasis on current expenditure items appears to be associated with better fiscal outcomes in each of the case studies – specifically, reductions in government wages and public sector numbers were key elements. Social programmes were also targeted in the successful case studies, except for some areas of Baltic economies' spending, an exception which must be seen in the light of their social programme spending lying far below the EU average at the onset of their adjustments. Ireland's social benefits, by contrast, had already risen substantially prior to the downturn and were at a relatively high level in 2008. The other item of current expenditure that was highlighted in the meta-analysis was government consumption and this was targeted in each of the successful case studies. The broad empirical research is somewhat ambiguous as to the intensity and duration of adjustment that is necessarily preferable in terms of growth outcomes. Interpretation of the case studies is also complicated by factors such as variations in the initial level of debt, the scale of the overall adjustment required, the timing of supplementary budgets, the scale of banking crises and other case-specific factors. Findings from the IMF (2012a) and Baum *et al.* (2012) suggest that upfront adjustments may be more suited in such cases where growth is above potential at the onset of the adjustment when considering the short-run impact, although growth outcomes over the long-run are estimated as being indifferent to intensity. Nevertheless, emphasis on short-run growth may be of more significance if policymakers are seeking to galvanise support for an adjustment programme in the early stages. This may be a useful avenue for further research. Similarly, it is likely that short-run considerations will be influential in relation to other factors that will determine the ultimate success of a consolidation programme.

Some authors have pointed to exchange rate devaluations as important for the success of fiscal consolidation episodes. However, in the broad literature, their association with successful fiscal consolidations is rarely statistically significant and, when it is significant, the relationship is often weak. In several cases, devaluation benefits are shown to be offset in real terms by subsequent increases in labour costs and continued price inflation. These factors are of particular relevance to highly open economies (Grennes and Strazds, 2012) and their effects were visible in the early Danish and Irish experiences.

The case studies used in this chapter seem to show that exchange rate adjustments are not necessary in order to achieve sizable annual improvements in competitiveness, although the pace of adjustment is assisted by currency depreciations. Recoveries in competitiveness are achievable under internal devaluation style approaches, although the pace is slower, on average, than in the case of exchange rate devaluations.

Arguments that the benefits of internal devaluations can be overstated by large shifts in the sectoral composition of an economy are addressed by Darvas (2012). He shows that the overall impact of compositional changes on unit labour cost based real effective exchange rates is less significant than might be expected when sectoral compositions are held constant. In addition, compositional changes in other economies may also exist. These can offset competitiveness gains measured when holding sectoral weights constant. Furthermore, downward wage flexibility was clearly visible from the sizeable peak-to-trough declines in Latvia (17 per cent), Lithuania (12 per cent) and Estonia (5 per cent).

Another factor that emerges from the case studies examined here is the importance of a stable currency as a means of anchoring inflationary pressures and of eliminating exchange rate risk premia. Both factors were relevant in the earlier episodes, with Blanchard and Fischer (1990) noting that the Irish and Danish experiences in the 1980s both availed of real devaluations in advance of their fiscal stabilisation and that both countries fixed their currencies to the Deutschmark at the time of stabilisation. The anchor provided by stable exchange rate policies and the support provided by accommodative monetary policy regimes thereafter produced an environment in which high long-term interest rates were eased, thus facilitating an expansion in investment and consumption. If competitiveness has indeed recovered sufficiently to incentivise an expansion in FDI and to sustain an expansion in export activity in the coming years, then – following the lessons from previous episodes – the next obvious target is maintaining a credible commitment to a stable currency.

Insecurity relating to the possible break-up of the currency union has also meant that monetary policy has become increasingly less accommodative, despite relatively lower short-term interest rates being targeted by the European Central Bank. As noted by Simon *et al.* (2012), countries are unlikely to experience strong improvements in their debt ratios while real rates are high and while monetary conditions remain tight.

The scope for the resumption of growth in economic activity in each of the case studies is another area influencing the success of the fiscal consolidation. Recoveries in external markets and the likely presence of convergence effects played significant roles in this respect. For example, Ireland's adjustment in the late 1980s coincided with the 'Lawson boom' in the UK. The Baltic economies, by contrast, managed to stabilise their public finances in a less benign economic environment. However, it is worth remembering that the distance of these economies from the technology frontier at the beginning of the crisis implied a greater growth potential for aiding in the recovery. Ireland's implied distance at the onset of the late-1980s' experience was of a similar magnitude. Since the Irish economy has now already converged with, and overtaken, living standards in other euro area economies, there are few potential benefits possible from reducing the gap from the productivity frontier. While experiences elsewhere show that recoveries in growth prospects do occur after episodes of fiscal adjustment, the potential for economic growth to recover on the basis of convergence effects and export demand is therefore more subdued at present (see Figure 10.5).

Figure 10.5: Gross national income per capita

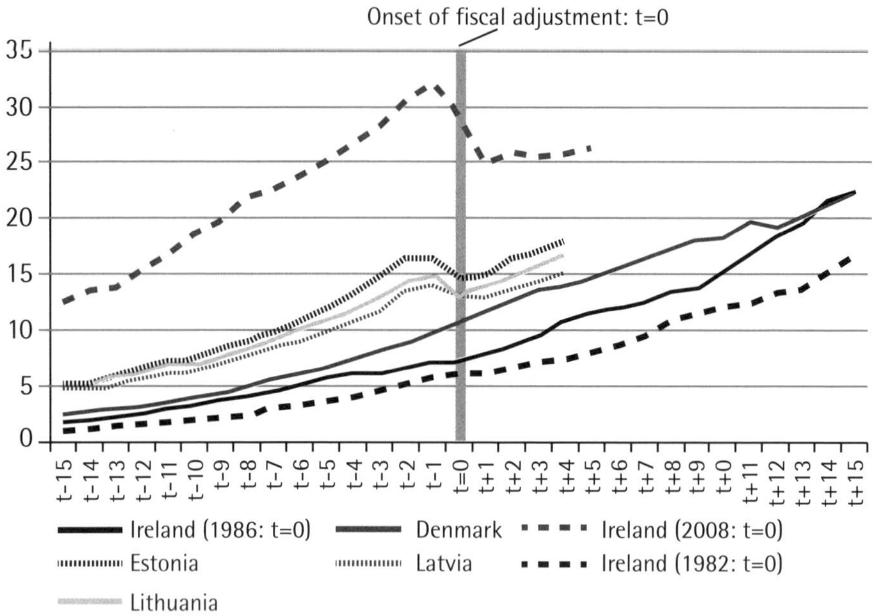

(based on purchasing power standard, where t=0 is the year that the fiscal consolidation began)
Source: AMECO.

CONCLUSIONS

The recent rise in government debt is not unique to Ireland and is a phenomenon that requires very difficult choices and a great degree of political determination both here and internationally (Tanzi, 2010). In particular, it is clear that less palatable current expenditure reductions will necessarily form a substantial part of the adjustment required. Broad empirical research on multiple fiscal consolidations and more comprehensive analyses of individual episodes, similar to those in which the Irish economy now finds itself, indicate that adjustments focusing on areas of current expenditure have proved successful in stabilising the public finances, while minimising the damage to growth. If such measures are carefully implemented, the efficient delivery of services can be preserved while facilitating a significant consolidation of the public finances, such that future growth prospects are promoted as much as possible.

REFERENCES

Alesina, A. and Ardagna, S. (2012). 'The Design of Fiscal Adjustments'. NBER Working Papers No. 18423, National Bureau of Economic Research (NBER), Inc.

Alesina, A. and Ardagna, S. (2009). 'Large Changes in Fiscal Policy: Taxes Versus Spending'. NBER Working Papers No. 15438, National Bureau of Economic Research (NBER), Inc.

Alesina, A. and Ardagna, S. (1998). 'Tales of fiscal adjustments'. *Economic Policy*, 13, 487–545.

Alesina, A., Ardagna, S., Perotti, R. and Schiantarelli, F. (2002). 'Fiscal policy, profits, and investment'. *American Economic Review*, 92, 571–589.

Alesina, A., Favero, C. and Giavazzi, F. (2012). 'The Output Effect of Fiscal Consolidations'. NBER Working Papers No. 18336, NBER, Inc.

Alesina, A. and Perotti, R. (1996). 'Fiscal Adjustments in OECD Countries: Composition and Macroeconomic Effects'. NBER Working Papers No. 5730, National Bureau of Economic Research, Inc.

Alesina, A. and Perotti, R. (1995). 'Fiscal expansions and adjustments in OECD countries'. *Economic Policy*, 21, 207–248.

Ardagna, S. (2007). 'Fiscal policy in Unionized Labor Markets'. *Journal of Economic Dynamics & Control*, 31, 1498–1534.

Barrios, S., Langedijk, S. and Pench, L. (2010). 'EU Fiscal Consolidation after the Financial Crisis – Lessons from Past Experiences'. Paper presented at the *12th Banca d'Italia Public Finance Workshop Fiscal Policy: Lessons from the crisis*, Perugia, 25–27 March.

Baum, A., Poplawski-Ribeiro, M. and Weber, A. (2012). 'Fiscal Multipliers and the State of the Economy'. International Monetary Fund (IMF) Working Paper (forthcoming; Washington: IMF).

Blanchard, O. (2012). 'Lessons from Latvia'. *VoxEU*, June.

Blanchard, O. and Fischer, S. (1990). Editorial. *NBER Macroeconomics Annual 1990*, 5, 1–10. MIT Press. Available at: http://www.nber.org/chapters/c10970.pdf (accessed 12 June 2013)

de Bonis, V. and Thimann, C. (1999). 'Expansionary effects of fiscal consolidation: The role of expectations and interest rates in the case of Denmark'. *Public Finance Review*, 27, 624–647.

Casey, E., Durkan, J. and Duffy, D. (2013). 'Fiscal Consolidation Strategies: Success Factors', ESRI Economic Renewal Series No. 12, Dublin: The Economic and Social Research Institute.

Considine, J. and Duffy, D. (2007). 'Tales of Expansionary Fiscal Contractions in Two European Countries: Hindsight and Foresight'. Working Paper No. 120,

National University of Ireland Galway, Department of Economics, revised.
Cottarelli, C. and Viñals, J. (2009). 'A Strategy for Renormalizing Fiscal and Monetary Policies in Advanced Economies'. IMF Staff Position Note 09/22.
Darvas, Z. (2012). 'Compositional effects on Productivity, Labour Cost and Export Adjustments'. Bruegel Policy Contribution 2012/11, June.
Daveri, F. and Tabellini, G. (2000). 'Unemployment growth and taxation in industrial countries'. *Economic Policy*, 15, 47–104.
Devries, P., Guajardo, J., Leigh, D. and Pescatori, A. (2011). 'A New Action-based Dataset of Fiscal Consolidation'. IMF Working Paper No. 11/128, IMF.
Duffy, D., Hore, J., MacCoille, C. and McCoy, D. (2001). 'Budget 2002: Macroeconomic context and fiscal stance'. *Budget Perspectives 2001*, Dublin: ESRI, October, 4–21.
European Commission (EC) (2010). 'Cross country study: Economic policy challenges in the Baltics'. Occasional Paper No. 58, *European Economy*. Brussels: EC.
European Commission (2007). 'Public finances in EMU – 2007'. *European Economy*, 3, Brussels: European Commission.
Finn, M. (1998). 'Cyclical effects of government's employment and goods purchases'. *International Economic Review*, 39, 635–657.
Giavazzi, F. and Pagano, M. (1990). 'Can severe fiscal contractions be expansionary? Tales of two small European countries'. *NBER Macroeconomics Annual 1990*, 5, MIT Press.
Grennes, T. and Strazds, A. (2012). 'Regaining competitiveness while maintaining a currency peg: the case of Latvia'. *Economonitor*, June 24th.
Guajardo, J., Leigh, D. and Pescatori, A. (2011). 'Expansionary Austerity: New International Evidence'. IMF Working Paper No. 11/158, July.
Guichard, S., Kennedy, M., Wurzel, E. and Andre, C. (2007). 'What Promotes Fiscal Consolidation: OECD country experiences', OECD Economics Department Working Paper No. 553.
Hallerberg, M. (2004). *Domestic Budgets in a United Europe: Fiscal governance from the end of Bretton Woods to EMU*, pp. 174–75. Ithaca: Cornell University Press
Honohan, P. (2012). 'More Europe in the Financial Arena: Good for Ireland?' Address to the Institute for International and European Affairs,' Dublin, 29 June.
Honohan, P. (2011). 'Good Times and Bad for a Globalised Economy – Macroeconomic Policy Lessons from Ireland'. Address to the Gilman Rutihinda Memorial Lecture, Bank of Tanzania, Dar es Salaam, 12 August. Available at: http://www.bis.org/review/r110818b.pdf
Honohan, P. and Walsh, B. (2002). 'Catching up with the leaders: The Irish hare'. *Brookings Papers on Economic Activity*, Economic Studies Program, The Brookings Institution, 33, 1–78.
International Monetary Fund (IMF) (2012a). *Fiscal Monitor, April 2012*. IMF World Economic and Financial Surveys, April.

IMF (2012b). *Ireland: Selected issues*. IMF Country Report No. 12/265, September.

IMF (2012c). *Republic of Latvia: Fifth review under the Stand-By Arrangement and Financing Assurances Review, request for waiver of nonobservance of a performance criterion, and proposal for post-program monitoring*. IMF Country Report No. 12/31, February.

IMF (2010). 'Will it hurt? Macroeconomic effects of fiscal consolidations' in *World Economic Outlook*, Chapter 3, October.

Kraemer, M. (1997). 'Electoral Budget Cycles in Latin America and the Caribbean: Incidence, Causes and Political Futility'. Inter-American Development Bank Working Paper. Washington: Inter-American Development Bank.

Laeven, L. and Valencia, F. (2012). 'Systemic Banking Crises Database: An Update'. IMF Working Paper No. 12/163, June.

Lagarde, C. (2012). 'Latvia and the Baltics – A Story of Recovery'. An address by Christine Lagarde, Managing Director, IMF, Riga, June. Available at: http://www.imf.org/external/np/speeches/2012/060512.htm

Lambertini, L. and Tavares, J. A. (2005). 'Exchange rates and fiscal adjustments: evidence from the OECD and implications for the EMU'. *The B.E. Journal of Macroeconomics*, De Gruyter, vol. 5(1), pages 1–30, December.

Larch, M. and Turrini, A. (2011). 'Received wisdom and beyond: lessons from fiscal consolidation in the EU'. *National Institute Economic Review*, 217, 1–18.

Lindner, A. (2011). 'Macroeconomic adjustment: the Baltic states versus euro area crisis countries'. *Intereconomics: Review of European Economic Policy*, 46, 340–345, December.

McAleese, D. and McCarthy, F. D. (1989). 'Adjustment and External Shocks in Ireland'. World Bank Policy Research Working Paper No. 262, Washington, DC.

McCarthy, C. (2009). 'Ireland's second round of cuts: A comparison with the last time' in *Dealing with Debt*, Springford, J. (ed.). London: CentreForum. Available at: http://centreforum.org/assets/pubs/dealing-with-debt.pdf

Molnar, M. (2012). 'Fiscal Consolidation: Part 5. What Factors Determine the Success of Consolidation Efforts?' OECD Economics Department Working Paper No. 936, Paris: OECD.

OECD (2009a). 'Taxation and economic growth' Prepared by Johansson, A., Heady, C. Arnold, J. Brys, B. and Vartia, L. *OECD Economic Policy Reforms: Going for Growth 2009*, Part II, Chapter 5. Paris: OECD.

OECD (2009b). 'Budgeting in Latvia'. Prepared by Kraan, D., Wehner, J., Sheppard, J., Kostyleva, V. and Duzler, B. *OECD Journal on Budgeting*, Vol. 2009/3. Paris: OECD.

OECD (2007). *Economic Outlook No. 81*, June. Paris: OECD.

OECD (1989). *Economic Survey Ireland 1988/1989*. Paris: OECD.

OECD (1987). *Economic Survey Denmark 1986/87*. Paris: OECD.

Peltzman, S. (1992). 'The voters as fiscal conservatives'. *Quarterly Journal of Economics*, 107 (May), 327–361.

Perotti, R. (2013). 'The austerity myth: gain without pain?' in Alesina, A., and F. Giavazzi (eds.), *Fiscal Policy after the Financial Crisis*. University of Chicago Press.

Purfield, C. and Rosenberg, C. (2010). 'Adjustment under a Currency Peg: Estonia, Latvia and Lithuania during the Global Financial Crisis 2008–09'. IMF Working Paper No. 10/213, September.

Roubini, N. and Sachs, J. (1988). 'Political and Economic Determinants of Budget Deficits in the Industrial Democracies'. NBER Working Paper No. 2682, August.

Simon, J., Pescatori, A. and Sandri, D. (2012). 'The good, the bad, and the ugly: 100 Years of dealing with public debt overhangs'. *IMF World Economic Outlook*, October.

Sutherland, D., Hoeller, P. and Merola, R. (2012). 'Fiscal Consolidation. Part 1. How Much is Needed and How to Reduce Debt to a Prudent Level?' OECD Economics Department Working Paper No. 932.

Tanzi, V. (2010). 'Comments on recent fiscal developments and exit strategies'. *CESifo Forum*. Ifo Institute for Economic Research at the University of Munich, vol. 2010(2), 105–110.

CHAPTER 11

Evidence on the Pattern of Earnings and Labour Costs Over the Recession

Adele Bergin, Elish Kelly, Seamus McGuinness

Ireland is currently faced with the policy challenge of having to regain competitiveness to boost growth and employment. Changes in prices and wages are arguably central to this, especially given Ireland's lack of monetary autonomy and severe fiscal constraints. This chapter offers evidence on the pattern of earnings and labour costs over the recession. The prevailing theoretical frameworks and international empirical evidence suggest that wage levels generally exhibit downward rigidity, preventing the labour market from clearing and making for high unemployment.

The key research questions addressed in this Chapter are: whether there has been any adjustment in private sector wage rates and labour costs over the crisis; the extent to which any movements were driven by compositional changes in the labour market as opposed to variations in the returns to these characteristics; and the degree to which firms have implemented strategies aimed at reducing labour costs and the relative impact of such strategies. From a policy perspective, this serves to inform on both the scale of any adjustment that has taken place and on what lies beneath any adjustment at both an individual and a firm level.

The broad methodological approach is to compare earnings as recorded in the *National Employment Survey* (NES) prior to and during the crisis, where 2006 is treated as a pre-crisis year and 2009 as a crisis year. We employ standard techniques to separate out changes in wages and labour costs over time into the components that are due to: changes in the returns to personal and job characteristics, changes in the composition of personal and job characteristics and unknown factors. The results for Ireland are then considered in the context of similar international research.

The results offer clear evidence regarding how the recession unfolded: average earnings of private sector workers and labour costs remained virtually unchanged through the worst of the recession in Ireland. This finding is consistent with international evidence. Firms that need to adjust costs try to avoid cutting wages, preferring instead to reduce staff numbers, hours worked and bonuses. The international evidence suggests that enterprises may be reluctant to cut wages because they fear productivity losses arising from lower morale, increased monitoring costs and/or higher rates of turnover, as employees resent a change in their pay relative to comparable employees elsewhere.

The authors discuss potential policy responses to the situation where private sector wages are maintained but unemployment is very high, including the possibility of negotiated wage adjustments to boost employment, drawing a parallel with what was achieved with the original social partnership model. However, several difficulties associated with such intervention in the labour market are highlighted.

BACKGROUND

Much research has been undertaken regarding the nature of wage adjustments across economies, firms and individuals over time (Babecky et al., 2009, 2010, 2012; Bertola et al., 2010; Christopoulou et al., 2010; Autor and Katz, 1999; Fuss, 2008). Most of the research has found that wage levels generally exhibit downward rigidity, with the probability of a wage cut being lower the more skilled the worker. Such downward wage rigidity during a deep recession is likely to contribute to high unemployment, prompting questions regarding whether policymakers can do anything to help the labour market to adjust.

In terms of theoretical frameworks, the finding of downward wage rigidity is consistent with a number of theoretical labour market models. For example, the efficiency wage theory (Shapiro and Stiglitz, 1984) argues that lowering wages encourages shirking, lowers levels of morale and increases monitoring costs, all of which lower productivity. According to adverse selection theory, wage reductions may also lead to higher levels of labour turnover, which are predicted to be more concentrated among higher productivity workers (Weiss, 1980). The insider-outsider theory predicts that incumbent workers will fight to maintain wage levels because they have no interest in generating new jobs (Lindbeck and Snower, 1988).

Other factors have also been found to play a role in explaining changes in the wage structure. Consistent with the predictions of efficiency wage theory, wage cuts were found to be less likely in more capital intensive firms (Layard et al., 2005) and larger firms (Oi, 1983). Institutional factors have also been found to be important, with wage rigidity associated with collective bargaining within firms and employment protection legislation (European Central Bank, 2009; Messina et al., 2010; Autor and Katz, 1999).

Evidence from recent empirical European studies is consistent with the predictions of theory. Babecky et al. (2009) examined data from a survey of over 15,300 firms employing 14.5 million people across 15 European countries, which was conducted during 2007 and 2008. They found that less than 1 per cent of workers experienced a pay cut in the previous five years. This study covers normal economic conditions. The apparent reluctance of firms to cut wages suggests that they may favour other methods of labour cost adjustment. A number of studies have found evidence in support of this. For instance Babecky *et al.*, again using the 2007/2008 European survey, found that when given the choice of six non-wage cost reduction strategies, 58 per cent of managers had implemented at least one in the previous five years. Babecky *et al.*, also found that there was substantial heterogeneity with respect to the adoption of strategies, with the chosen policy varying with the characteristics of the firm. Bertola *et al.* (2010) used a survey of 14 EU countries to examine the adjustment strategies of firms in response to shocks. They found the main channel used to cut labour costs when faced with a cost shock was employment numbers, followed by hours and flexible wage components; less than 2 per cent of firms reduced base wages.

A number of studies have focused on the adjustment strategies of firms specifically in the wake of an economic shock. Kwapil (2010) found that the main strategies employed by Austrian firms during the downturn were to reduce working hours and staff numbers, with the former being the most dominant response. Fuss (2008) explored the factors that explain wage bill adjustment under changing economic conditions in Belgium. She found that during unfavourable economic conditions employment contractions are the main source of wage bill reductions (see also Dhyne and Druant, 2010). Rõõm and Messina (2009) used a follow-up to the 2007/2008 European survey that took place in the summer of 2009 to examine changes in base wages during the crisis. They found that only 1.8 per cent of employees had experienced wage cuts since the start of the crisis, as compared to 1 per cent of employees in the earlier survey; however, there was a significant increase in the incidence of firms freezing wages, rising from 5 per cent to 32 per cent.

The evidence is somewhat limited for Ireland and tends to pre-date the current crisis. Keeney and Lawless (2010), using data from a firm-level survey of wage setting carried out in 2007/2008, found that less than 2 per cent of firms had cut wages over the previous five years. More recently, Walsh (2012), using firm-level data on average earnings, reported little change in hourly earnings between 2008 and 2011, with the majority of changes in the wage bill coming from a reduction in the number of hours worked. Walsh (2012) also exploited the longitudinal aspect to the data to demonstrate that compositional effects had little impact on earnings over the course of the downturn.

Given the findings of previous research and the underlying theoretical frameworks, we would generally expect to observe wage rigidity under normal circumstances in Ireland and this seems to have been borne out by the existing research (Keeney and Lawless, 2010 and Walsh 2012). However, the developments of recent years have been particularly severe, leaving open the possibility that more radical responses may have been implemented by firms. The rapid fall in economic activity and rise in unemployment, coupled with a lack of monetary autonomy and fiscal constraints, led many to argue that an internal devaluation was required through price and wage reductions. Furthermore, the social partnership model, which had been the dominant wage setting mechanism since 1987, effectively came to a halt; thus, potentially creating an environment more conducive to downward wage adjustments at firm level.

Given these developments, the objective of the research is to assess the extent to which private sector wage rates have adjusted and the degree to which any observed price movements were driven by compositional changes in the labour market as opposed to variations in the returns to observable characteristics. Christopoulou et al. (2010) found that over the period 1995 to 2002 changes in wages in the Irish labour market were generally driven by returns to employment and job characteristics, with compositional effects having relatively little influence. However, compositional effects are likely to be more apparent in a deep recession, particularly if employment loss is concentrated among low skilled and low paid workers, and in specific sectors.

Figure 11.1: Index of Real Unit Labour Costs (Total Economy) 1987–2009 (Base Year = 1987)

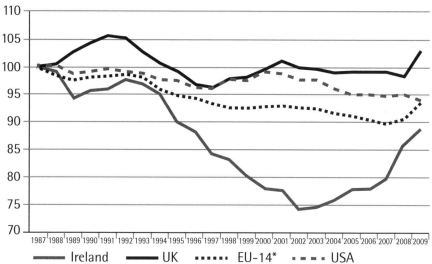

Note: * EU-15 with Luxembourg excluded.
Source: *Statistical Annex of the European Economy Spring 2011*, European Commission (2011).

We extend the analysis of individual wage rates to the level of the firm and examine how average labour costs changed following the onset of the recession. Labour costs are a key measure of competitiveness and take account of the distribution of employment across firms, which an individual-level analysis of wages cannot. We also examine the extent to which firms have implemented strategies aimed at reducing labour costs and the relative impact of such policies.

There is evidence to suggest that Ireland's competitive position, as measured by its unit labour costs, had begun to fall rapidly after 2002 following many years of gains (Figure 11.1)[166] and, as such, regaining some of that lost ground is viewed as vital for any recovery. The broad approach we adopt is to compare outcomes from before and after the crisis, where 2006 is used as an example of a pre-crisis year and 2009 to be a crisis year. It is important to note that the study is not seeking to explain individual year-on-year changes between 2006 and 2009, as the economy continued to grow in 2007.

This chapter is structured as follows: we begin by describing the macroeconomic background and deterioration in the labour market over the crisis; then we outline the dataset and methodology; we then present results of wage models and decompositions for private sector employees; outline results for the labour cost analysis; and finally we summarise the results and discuss policy implications.

THE MAGNITUDE OF THE CRISIS

The rate of contraction experienced by the Irish economy since 2007 has been truly remarkable from an international context. The bursting of a property market bubble and the overexposure of the banking system to the property sector resulted in the Irish economy losing some of what had been gained during more than a decade of strong growth. Figure 11.2 shows the quarterly profile for output and demonstrates clearly that economic activity collapsed over the period 2008 to 2010. By 2010 Q4 real GDP (GNP) was 13 (11) per cent below its 2007 Q4 level. The two vertical lines in Figure 11.2 highlight the period covered by the micro data used in this study which, we argue, encapsulates the bulk of the downturn in macroeconomic activity and, therefore, should capture most of the adjustment that took place with respect to earnings and labour costs.

From a macroeconomic perspective, one way of gauging the impact of the crisis on the labour market is to examine movements in the wage bill of the economy. Figure 11.3 shows the percentage change in the non-agricultural wage bill, and in nominal GDP and GNP. Overall, the figure shows that the decline in the wage bill started after the fall in output – the wage bill fell in 2009 whereas the contraction in output began in 2008.[167] The graph also shows that in 2010 the wage bill fell by more than GDP and GNP, so although the adjustment in the wage bill started later it may have persisted beyond any stabilisation in output. Therefore, the wage bill data provides some limited support for labour market flexibility in the form of downward wage adjustment. However, as the wage bill is a function of employment, hourly wage rates and average hours worked this is not conclusive.

---

166 See also McGuinness, Kelly and O'Connell (2010).
167 In the remainder of the paper, the focus is on comparing pre-crisis and crisis outcomes. To do this, we compare outcomes for 2006 (pre-crisis) and 2009 (during the crisis).

Figure 11.2: Quarterly GDP and GNP

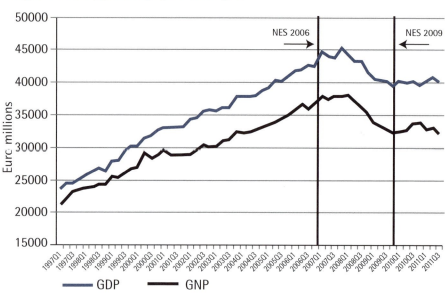

Note: Both series are seasonally adjusted and expressed at constant market prices.
Source: Quarterly National Accounts, Central Statistics Office.

Figure 11.3: Output and the Wage Bill

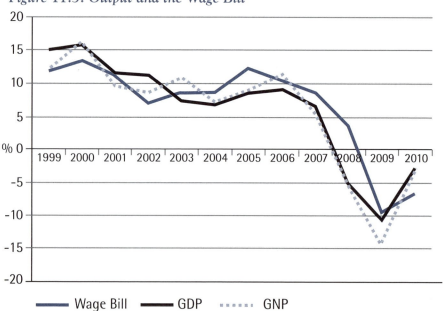

Source: National Income and Expenditure Accounts for 2010, Central Statistics Office.

Figure 11.4 shows the change in the non-agricultural wage bill and two of its components, average earnings and employment. The graph shows that the fall in employment began earlier and has been more severe than the fall in average earnings, indicating that the burden of adjustment, to date, has primarily been on employment rather than earnings.

With specific regard to the labour market, we can approximate peak to trough activity from Quarter 4 2006 through to Quarter 4 2009. There were 1.9 million people employed in 2009, which represents a 9 per cent fall on the total employed in 2006 and this decline was almost entirely concentrated in male employment. Over the same period, there was a marginal decline in the labour force, again driven by a fall in active males. Between 2009 and 2011 Q3, employment fell by another 5 per cent; however, the reduction was more evenly distributed between males and females and there was also a more marked reduction in the labour force, which has been predominately driven by a decline in the number of active males. Participation rates have also fallen over the crisis, particularly among younger people and males. The unemployment rate has more than trebled, from just 4.3 per cent in 2006 to 14.4 per cent in 2011 (See Bergin, Kelly and McGuinness, 2012 for more details).

Figure 11.4: Adjustment in Average Earnings and Employment

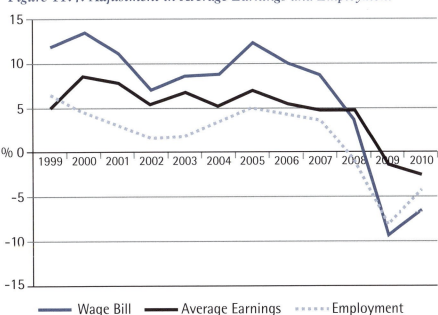

Source: Authors' calculations based on *National Income and Expenditure Accounts for 2010* and *Quarterly National Household Survey*, Central Statistics Office.

It is not clear to what extent the rapid rise in unemployment is due to business closures as opposed to downsizing. Bergin, Kelly and McGuinness (2012) present data on the number of active and birthed enterprises across various sectors between 2006 and 2009 and the number of employees in each with the aim of providing a broad indication of the degree of firm-level structural change that took place over the period. The total number of active firms fell by 1.1 per cent and this decline was driven by a fall in the number of Construction and Transport & Storage sector enterprises. All other sectors recorded an increase in the number of active enterprises. Unsurprisingly, the overall number of employees in enterprises fell between 2006 and 2009; however, there was an increase in the number of employees in wholesale & retail, information & communication and finance & insurance. The data suggest that rising unemployment has been primarily driven by firm closures within the construction sector and downsizing within other areas of the economy. In relation to enterprise births, the numbers of new firms fell each year between 2006 and 2008, but some recovery took place between 2008 and 2009. As might be expected, on average, less people are being employed in newly-created firms, and this applies across all sectors.

DATA AND METHODOLOGY

The data are from the 2006 and 2009 waves of the *National Employment Survey* (*NES*). The *NES* is a matched employer-employee workplace survey, covering both the public and private sectors, carried out by the Central Statistics Office (CSO). Approximately 6,500 private sector employers and 300 public sector bodies were surveyed across the economy. The analysis here focuses exclusively on private sector activity. Our sample sizes increase from just under 38,000 private sector employees in 2006 (over 4,000 firms) to just under 52,000 in 2009 (over 4,500 firms). Our analysis of changes in private sector wage rates is conducted at the employee level and then the dataset is reduced to the firm level for the labour costs analysis and the examination of the strategies implemented by firms to reduce labour costs.

A central objective of the chapter is to explore the drivers of wage determination over time and specifically to analyse the relative importance of factors related to compositional change, productivity growth and labour market institutions. To do this, we decompose changes in wages over time into the components that are due to (a) changes in the returns to personal and job characteristics (b) changes in the composition of personal and job characteristics and (c) unknown factors. This framework enables us to draw conclusions on the nature of wage determination, which subsequently allows us to tease out policy implications. The methodological approach adopted is referred to in the literature as an Oaxaca decomposition and details are available in Bergin, Kelly and McGuinness (2012). Using this framework we will decompose changes in both individual earnings and average labour costs which will allow us to assess the importance of changes in both the composition and returns to specific attributes in explaining movements over time.

EMPLOYEE LEVEL RESULTS

Table 11.1 shows data on earnings and hours worked for private sector workers. As the *NES* data are only available for 2006 to 2009, we also present wage data from the CSO's *Earnings, Hours and Employment Costs Survey* (*EHECS*) for 2009 to 2011, which is at firm-level.[168] What is striking from the table is the fact that hourly earnings increased annually between 2006 and 2009, while there was no change in hourly wages between 2009 and 2011 (see Walsh, 2012).[169] Both data series overlap in 2009 and present a consistent picture. As stated, the *NES* data cover the majority of the macroeconomic downturn; however, a worry relates to the possibility that wage adjustment may substantially lag output and, as such, we may not be capturing the bulk of wage movements. The *EHECS* data suggest that this is not the case. Between 2006 and 2009, real gross hourly earnings increased by 5.5 per cent, with a slightly smaller increase in male hourly earnings (5.1 per cent) and a larger increase for females (7.6 per cent).[170] Average weekly wages increased up to 2008 but have been falling since; however, this has been driven by a decline in average hours worked.

Table 11.1: Average Hourly and Weekly Earnings and Hours Worked for Private Sector Workers

	National Employment Survey					Earnings, Hours and Employment Costs Survey				
	Hourly	% Δ	Weekly	% Δ	Hours Worked	Hourly	% Δ	Weekly	% Δ	Hours Worked
2006	17.1	–	610.9	–	35.4	–	–	–	–	–
2007	18.1	5.7	639.1	4.6	35.0	–	–	–	–	–
2008	19.2	6.1	658.5	3.0	34.0	19.3	–	636.9	–	33.0
2009	19.5	1.9	645.6	–2.0	32.7	19.5	1.0	622.7	–2.2	32.0
2010	–	–	–	–	–	19.5	0.0	616.6	–1.0	31.7
2011	–	–	–	–	–	19.4	–0.5	611.5	–0.8	31.6

Source: Constructed from *National Employment Surveys*, 2006–2009, and *Earnings, Hours and Employment Costs Surveys*, 2008–2011, Central Statistics Office.

---

168 The EHECS data is a quarterly series, so the data presented in Table 10.3 is based on the average of the four quarters for each year.
169 This is consistent with the increase in average earnings derived from the National Income and Expenditure Accounts data, described in the previous section.
170 Based on the NES data, real average hourly earnings increased from €18.80 to €19.90 between 2006 and 2009.

Differences in Characteristics

Bergin, Kelly and McGuinness (2012) describe the variables used in the analysis and provide descriptive statistics for private sector employees in 2006 and 2009. There has been an increase in human capital; with a ten percentage point increase in the share of workers with degrees, while the proportion of workers with non-degree third-level qualifications and lower secondary qualifications has fallen. This would tend to support the notion that lower paid workers have fallen out of the labour market and that the observed rise in earnings is mainly due to compositional effects. However, the rise in the share of graduates appears to have been offset somewhat by a fall in average age and tenure. Similar patterns are found for males and females. In addition, there was a fall of around 4 percentage points in the proportion of male employees between 2006 and 2009, while the share of non-national workers increased by around three percentage points.

In terms of job characteristics, compared to the situation in 2006, there were much larger numbers engaged in part-time work and their share in private sector employment rose from 15 to 23 per cent. The period also saw an increase in the proportion of workers employed in large firms, a fall in union membership, a decline in the proportion of workers who were members of a professional body and a decrease in the share of workers who work fixed hours. There were only minor changes in hours worked, contract type and the proportion of employees engaged in shift work over the time period. Again, changes in characteristics by gender were broadly comparable over the time period.

In terms of changes in sectoral employment between 2006 and 2009, as expected, there was a fall in the share of workers in construction and this effect is concentrated in male employment. There was also an increase in the share of workers in health and social work in the private sector, especially in female employment. Finally, the proportion of workers in industry and business services fell, while the proportion in transport, storage and communications increased somewhat.

Differences in Returns to Characteristics

In addition to compositional impacts, average earnings will also be expected to change in response to variations in the returns to observable characteristics. To capture this, we estimate OLS log wage models (see Bergin, Kelly and McGuinness, 2012 for details).

The results indicate an increase in the returns to a degree, particularly for males. There was also a rise in the returns to sub-degree third-level qualifications for men. In addition, there was no significant change in the return to tenure for either males or females between the two years. In terms of age groups, the estimates indicate that generally most age groups earn less than those aged 40 to 49 (the reference group). However, younger workers, particularly those aged between 25 and 39, earned significantly less in 2009 than 2006 and this effect was stronger for female employees. The model for all employees indicates that the gender pay gap closed somewhat over the time period. In addition, although migrants earned lower wages than natives, the estimates imply that migrants fared relatively less badly in 2009. The fall in the migrant pay penalty could be evidence of an integration effect or alternatively it could also be due to higher levels of job loss amongst low paid migrants.

Turning to job characteristics, for males there was an increase in the loss associated with working fixed-term contracts relative to males on permanent contracts, while the penalty associated with apprentice contracts was somewhat lower in 2009. Male employees working fixed hours also experienced some reduction in the loss associated with this type of work in 2009, suggesting a rising return to regularised employment. There was an increase in the firm-size premium for females, while males and females saw an increase in the premium associated with being a member of a professional body.

Oaxaca-Blinder Decompositions

To ascertain the relative importance of these observed changes in both the distribution of endowments and the return to them in explaining the change in wages of private sector employees between 2006 and 2009, we estimate the Oaxaca-Blinder decompositions. The results are presented in Table 11.2.

Table 11.2: Decomposition of the Change in Wages Between 2006 and 2009 for All Employees

	Change
Amount attributable:	2.4
- Due to endowments (E):	0.2
- Due to coefficients (C):	2.2
Shift coefficient (U):	5.0
Raw differential (R) {E+C+U}:	7.4
Adjusted differential (D) [C＋U]:	7.1

Source: Results based on data from the 2006 and 2009 *National Employment Surveys* (NES), Central Statistics Office.

The decomposition for all employees shows the raw wage gap[171] over the two years is calculated at 7.4 per cent. The adjusted differential, which is the amount

---

171 The raw or unadjusted wage gap is the difference in wages that exists before personal or job characteristics are taken into account.

of the raw wage gap that remains unexplained by differences in endowments over time, is 7.1 per cent. This demonstrates that only a very small amount, around 3 per cent, of the rise in wages between 2006 and 2009 was attributable to differences in compositional effects. A further 30 per cent of the gap can be explained by changes in the returns to different endowments. This indicates that around two-thirds of the wage difference between 2006 and 2009 is due to influences not captured by our models.

Separate decompositions for males and females reveal that we can explain substantially more of the female raw wage differential. The male raw differential was estimated at 6.6 per cent; less than 6 per cent of the gap was due to endowment differences with only a further 3 per cent explained by changes in the returns to endowments over the two time periods. In contrast, around 12 per cent of the female gap, which was estimated at 9.6 per cent, was explained by differences in the distribution of characteristics, with a further 60 per cent explained by changes in returns (see Bergin, Kelly and McGuinness, 2012).

Nevertheless, aggregate results often conceal a good deal of movement at the individual variable level. Tables 11.3 and 11.4 describe the contribution of the individual variables to the wage gap. While only a small portion of the male raw wage differential can be explained by variations in observable characteristics, the tables reveal that some variables have strong impacts but in different directions so that, when taken together, the effects roughly cancel out. Specifically, within the male labour market, the rising shares of graduates and an increased dominance of large firm employment has tended to push wage levels upwards. Conversely, the increase in part-time work, the fall in the share of professional occupations and the decrease in tenure served to reduce male wages between 2006 and 2009. In addition, there has been an increase in the returns to education for males with third level qualifications, in the returns to tenure, to more standard employment (suggested by the positive coefficient on fixed hours) and to being a member of a professional body. With regard to the construction sector, the decline in employment in this industry, which was on the whole well paid in the pre-crisis period, resulted in a marginal decline in pay rates over time, with the fall in the return to construction-related employment proving much more important.

Table 11.4 shows that many of the endowment effects present in the male labour market were also important in explaining the movement in female wages. Nevertheless, some effects, such as the increase in the proportion of females working in larger firms are stronger than for males. In terms of coefficient effects for females, there was a big increase in the return to working in larger firms. This suggests that larger firms have gained in productivity, perhaps due to economy of scale effects or the adoption of new technologies. The large firm impacts may have been substantially more concentrated in foreign multinational enterprises. However, as we do not have information on firm ownership, we cannot confirm this hypothesis. The results for females also show a rise in the return to having a permanent contract, to being a member of a professional body and in the union premium. Finally, there was a fall in the return to working fixed hours, and younger workers did less well in 2009 relative to 2006.

It seems fair to say that the increases in both the share and the returns to graduate labour in addition to a rising return to large-firm employment are the most substantial factors driving the rise in real average earnings. Rising returns to both graduate and large-firm employment are consistent with a scenario of rising demand for labour through skill biased technological change. The pattern of results suggests that increasing rewards to productivity growth represents the most likely explanation for the continued rise in hourly pay since the downturn.

Table 11.3: Breakdown of Decomposition Results by Variable for Male Employees

Variable	Attribute	Endowment	Coefficient
Primary	0.0	0.1	-0.1
Lower Secondary	0.5	0.5	0.1
Upper Secondary	-0.6	-0.1	-0.5
Post Secondary	-0.5	0.0	-0.5
Cert/Diploma	-0.2	-0.5	0.3
Degree	3.5	2.6	0.9
Migrant	0.0	-0.3	0.3
Tenure	-0.2	-0.5	0.4
Age 15–24	0.4	-0.1	0.5
Age 25–29	-0.9	0.0	-0.8
Age 30–39	-0.7	0.1	-0.8
Age 40–49	-0.2	0.0	-0.1
Age 50–59	-0.5	-0.1	-0.3
Age 60 plus	0.3	-0.1	0.3
Permanent Contract	0.1	0.1	0.0
Fixed term Contract	-0.2	0.0	-0.2
Apprentice/trainee	0.2	0.1	0.1
Other Contract	-0.1	0.0	-0.1

Table 11.3: Breakdown of Decomposition Results by Variable for Male Employees (continued)

Variable	Attribute	Endowment	Coefficient
Fixed Hours	1.6	0.0	1.6
Shift Work	0.3	0.1	0.2
Firm Size	0.3	0.5	-0.1
Part Time	-1.1	-1.2	0.1
Professional Body	0.8	-0.5	1.3
Union Membership	-0.3	-0.1	-0.3
Industry	0.1	0.1	0.0
Construction	-1.4	-0.3	-1.1
Wholesale & Retail	-0.5	-0.1	-0.4
Hotels & Restaurants	-0.1	0.0	-0.1
Transport, Storage & Communications	-0.4	-0.2	-0.2
Finance	0.1	0.2	-0.1
Business Services	-0.4	0.1	-0.5
Education	0.1	0.0	0.1
Health & Social Work	-0.1	0.0	0.0
Other Services	0.1	0.0	0.1
Subtotal	**0.2**	**0.4**	**-0.2**

Source: Same as Table 11.2.

Table 11.4: Breakdown of Decomposition Results by Variable for Female Employees

Variable	Attribute	Endowment	Coefficient
Primary	-0.1	-0.1	0.0
Lower Secondary	0.5	0.4	0.1
Upper Secondary	-0.3	0.0	-0.3
Post Secondary	0.0	0.0	0.0
Cert/Diploma	-0.9	-0.7	-0.1
Degree	2.7	2.5	0.3
Migrant	-0.3	-0.4	0.1
Tenure	-0.5	-0.3	-0.2
Age 15–24	0.0	-0.1	0.0
Age 25–29	-0.8	0.0	-0.8
Age 30–39	-1.3	0.0	-1.3
Age 40–49	0.4	0.0	0.4
Age 50–59	0.4	0.0	0.4
Age 60 plus	0.1	0.0	0.1
Permanent Contract	1.7	0.0	1.7
Fixed term Contract	0.0	0.0	0.0
Apprentice/trainee	0.1	0.1	0.0
Other Contract	-0.2	0.0	-0.2
Fixed Hours	-0.4	0.1	-0.6
Shift Work	-0.3	0.0	-0.3
Firm Size	6.7	0.9	5.8
Part Time	-1.2	-1.0	-0.2
Professional Body	0.3	-0.5	0.8
Union Membership	0.3	0.0	0.3

Table 11.4: Breakdown of Decomposition Results by Variable for Female Employees (continued)

Variable	Attribute	Endowment	Coefficient
Industry	-0.1	0.1	-0.2
Construction	0.0	0.0	0.0
Wholesale & Retail	0.2	-0.1	0.2
Hotels & Restaurants	-0.1	-0.1	-0.1
Transport, Storage & Communications	-0.1	0.0	-0.1
Finance	-0.4	-0.1	-0.4
Business Services	0.0	0.2	-0.2
Education	0.1	0.0	0.1
Health & Social Work	0.6	0.3	0.3
Other Services	0.1	0.0	0.1
Subtotal	7.0	1.1	5.9

Source: Same as Table 11.2.

FIRM LEVEL LABOUR COST ANALYSIS

Moving on to assess the impact that the recession has had on firms' average labour costs, it is estimated that real labour costs increased by 4.3 per cent between 2006 and 2009. While the rise in labour costs is likely to reflect the rise in average earnings, this does not necessarily imply an erosion of Ireland's competitiveness as this depends on the change in costs relative to other countries.

Here we examine this finding in further detail. First, we analyse the impact that various firm-level characteristics had on average labour costs in 2006 and 2009. We then decompose the increase in average labour costs over the period to ascertain if it was being driven by compositional factors or changes in the costs associated with firm characteristics. In addition, using data for 2009, we examine the incidence and characteristics of firms implementing various changes in their employment conditions to deal with the downturn, along with the impact that these strategies had on average labour costs.

Average Labour Costs in 2006 and 2009

Bergin, Kelly and McGuinness (2012) present the results for 2006 and 2009 OLS average labour cost models. In both years average labour costs were positively correlated with the share of male workers, the share of educated workers, the share of professional body employees and firm size. On the other hand, the proportion of part-time workers, the share engaged in shift work and the percentage of migrant workers tended to reduce average labour costs. A non-linear relationship was found to exist between average labour costs and the age of the workforce: specifically, labour costs were lower in firms' with high shares of both younger (aged 15–29) and older (aged 60 and above) workers relative to firms with a large proportion of employees aged between 40 and 49.

In terms of coefficient changes between 2006 and 2009, most were in a positive direction, as one would expect given that average labour costs increased between the two time points. Specifically, there were significant increases in costs for all levels of education, the proportion of professional body workers, trade union density, the share of employees who work fixed hours and the fraction on an indefinite duration employment contract. The only significant fall related to the cost of tenured employees which suggests that there has been some reduction in the pay levels of more experienced workers. Although the proportion of migrant workers continued to reduce average labour costs in 2009, as did the shares of younger (aged 15–24) and older (aged 50 and above) employees, the magnitude of the coefficients declined between 2006 and 2009. The analysis confirms the view that migrants were a consistent factor in keeping labour costs low during the boom era; however, compared to nationals, migrants were paid relatively more in 2009 compared to 2006. Average labour costs were found to be higher in construction in both years relative to firms operating in the industrial sector; however, the scale of the difference halved during the time period. Labour costs were also higher in transport & communications; financial intermediation and business services firms in 2006, and in 2009 were significantly lower in transport & communication firms.

Oaxaca-Blinder Decompositions

As before, Oaxaca-Blinder decompositions are estimated to gauge the importance of changes in structural factors and changes in the costs to specific firm characteristics in explaining changes in average labour costs, the results for which are presented in Table 11.5.

Table 11.5: Decomposition of the 2006–2009 Average Labour Cost Gap

	Change
Amount attributable:	16.4
- Due to endowments (E):	-0.8
- Due to coefficients (C):	17.3
Shift coefficient (U):	-12.1
Raw differential (R) {E+C+U}:	4.3
Adjusted differential (D) {C+U}:	5.1

Source: Same as Table 11.2.

The raw differential tells us that average labour costs increased by 4.3 per cent between 2006 and 2009; with the growth in costs primarily due to firm level attributes. Thus, structural factors were largely unimportant in explaining rising average labour costs between 2006 and 2009, which is consistent with the employee level analysis.

Bergin, Kelly and McGuinness (2012) report the detailed decomposition results which show there were some compositional adjustments between the two time points – increases in the share of graduates and part-time workers, and a reduction in the proportion of workers from professional bodies. However, these changes effectively cancelled each other out and most of the increase in average labour costs over the time period was driven by coefficient effects. In particular, there were increasing costs to firms for a given share of standardised employees, professionally qualified workers, employees with contracts of indefinite duration and migrant workers. Costs also rose within larger firms over the period. The costs associated with a unionised workforce increased over the time period as well, even though there was a fall in trade union density. The only two attributes that firms rewarded less, and therefore reduced their labour costs, were the share of tenured workers and those with Leaving Certificate qualifications.

Changes in Employment Conditions in 2009

In the *2009 NES* questionnaire, firms were asked to indicate if they had implemented changes to various employment conditions in that year. In particular, they were asked if they had implemented cuts in i) staff numbers, ii) rates of pay/salary, iii) hours worked, iv) paid leave, v) bonuses, vi) allowances/premiums or vii) overtime. Table 11.6 illustrates the responses to these questions. Overall, almost 62 per cent of firms indicated that they had introduced some type of cut in employment conditions.[172] However, the incidence of cuts for each individual strategy is quite low, especially given the depth of the recession at that time. Reducing staff numbers was the main tool employed by firms to lower labour costs, with 34 per cent indicating they had cut employee numbers. This adjustment policy was followed by cuts in hours worked and bonuses. Anecdotal evidence at that time suggested that there were widespread cuts in private sector pay; however, Table 11.6 indicates that pay was left unchanged in three-quarters of firms. This raises the question of the differences in the characteristics of the firms that did and did not reduce pay as a method of adjusting to the crisis. This is examined later in the chapter. Thus, it would seem that in the face of falling demand, firms primarily reacted by reducing the amount of labour utilised as opposed to targeting the price of labour per se.

Table 11.6: Changes in Employment Conditions in 2009: Implementation of Cuts

	Per Cent
Overall	61.8
Type of Cut:	
Staff Numbers	34.0
Hours Worked	29.0
Bonuses	26.1
Pay	23.2
Overtime	21.6
Allowances/Premiums	15.7
Paid Leave	2.3

Source: Constructed from *2009 National Employment Survey*, Central Statistics Office.

In analysing the impact that these adjustment strategies had on firms' labour costs, there might be non-randomness in our sample of firms. It could be higher/lower labour cost firms that are more likely to have adjusted their employment conditions. If this is the case, then our adjustment strategy estimates would be biased if the strategies introduced by firms were correlated with firm-level characteristics that were in turn associated with higher/lower labour costs. We

---

[172] As discussed previously, there has been a much higher incidence of firms downsizing rather than closing over the crisis.

deal with this source of potential bias by estimating a Heckman based selection model, described in Appendix 2 in Bergin, Kelly and McGuinness (2012). The first stage of this modelling approach requires estimating the firm-level characteristics associated with the adoption of each particular strategy and these results are presented in Table 11.7.[173] No consistent pattern exists across the various strategies, apart from larger enterprises having a somewhat higher likelihood to target employment conditions which is, perhaps, unsurprising given that such firms will also have experienced the largest absolute falls in demand. It also appears that firms at the lower end of the productivity spectrum – as measured by the proportion of part-time workers in the firm, the share of shift-work employees and the proportion of the workforce with lower levels of education – were more likely to implement cuts in hours worked, bonuses and paid leave. The corollary of this is that workforce restructuring did not appear to be a major priority for firms at the higher end of the productivity distribution, despite the fact that such organisations employed higher proportions of more highly educated and costly labour.

Table 11.7: Characteristics of Firms that Implemented Cuts in Employment Conditions in 2009

	Staff	Pay	Hours Worked	Paid Leave	Bonuses	Premium/ Allow- ance	Overtime
Share of Male Workers	-	-	-0.202**	-	-	-	-
Share of Workers aged 25–29	-	-0.373**	0.585***	0.759**	-	-	0.325**
Share of Workers aged 30–39	-	-	0.236*	-	-	-	-
Share of Workers aged 50–59	-	-0.316**	-	-	-0.320**	-	-
Share of Workers aged 60 plus	-0.798***	-	-	-	-	-0.472*	-0.430*
Share of Junior Cert Workers	-	-	-	0.842*	-	-	-
Share of Leaving Cert Workers	-	-	0.323*	0.864*	0.334*	-	-
Share of Post- Leaving Cert Workers				0.962**	-	-	-
Average Tenure	0.019***	-	0.027***	-	0.011*	-	0.025***

173 Only significant coefficients included in this table.

Table 11.7: Characteristics of Firms that Implemented Cuts in Employment Conditions in 2009 (continued)

	Staff	Pay	Hours Worked	Paid Leave	Bonuses	Premium/ Allowance	Overtime
Share of Professional Body Workers	0.587***	0.775***	-	0.588**	0.474***	-	-
Firm Size	0.167***	0.057***	0.054***	0.140***	0.121***	0.046**	0.110***
Share of Fixed Term Workers	-	-	-0.231***	-	-0.162**	-	-
Share of Apprentices/ Trainees	-	-	-	1.367***	-	-	-
Average Shift Work	-0.200**	-	0.221**	-	-	-	-
Trade Union Density	-	-0.004***	-0.002*	0.009***	-	-	-
Share of Part-time Workers	-	-	0.849***	-	-	-0.177*	-

Source: Results based on data from the *2009 National Employment Survey* (NES), Central Statistics Office.
Note: *** $p<0.01$, ** $p<0.05$, * $p<0.1$.

Table 11.8 presents the results of the impact of adjustment strategies on firm's average labour costs. Our models are estimated both including and excluding controls for selection.[174] Before controlling for selection, it appears that reductions in hours worked lowered firms labour costs, while bonus cuts increased costs. This latter result seems counterintuitive; however, these results were no longer significant when selection was accounted for. In the selection consistent equation, the negative and significant hours worked term suggests that firms with lower *ex ante* labour costs were more likely to have implemented this strategy, and the

---

174 The selection terms control for the extent to which the characteristics of firms implementing adjustment strategies may themselves be correlated with labour costs and a failure to adjust for such effects can result in a biased estimate. The lamda terms can most easily be thought of as the extent to which firms' labour costs would be expected to diverge from the average ex ante given their characteristics. Thus a negative (positive) lamda would be indicative of the policy being implemented more by low cost/value added (high cost) firms. The inclusion of these lamda terms results in more reliable estimates of the policy impacts themselves.

positive and highly significant coefficient for the reduction in hours worked variable indicates that this strategy increased average labour costs within such firms. While this result might appear counterintuitive in the first instance, the stage 1 probit models shows that firms most likely to curtail the number of hours worked tended to employ a higher share of part-time workers. Thus, if firms implemented cuts in hours through part-time redundancies, this would tend to raise average labour costs as the gross weekly pay of part-time workers would be much lower than those of their full-time equivalents. Nevertheless, the overriding conclusion to be drawn from our firm level analysis is that average labour costs continued to rise over the period 2006 to 2009, largely as a consequence of price factors with compositional issues explaining only a very small proportion of the change. The vast majority of firms did not target wage rates during the period, with the evidence suggesting that the policy, when implemented, tended to be concentrated at the lower end of the productivity spectrum. Given the limited adoption of policies designed to reduce the cost of labour to firms, it is perhaps not surprising that such strategic changes were found to have little or no impact in reducing average labour costs within our sample.

Table 11.8: Impact of Individual Employment Condition Cuts on Firms' Average Labour Costs

	Individual Strategies	Lamda Adjusted
Staff Numbers	0.004 (0.011)	0.112 (0.117)
Pay	0.000 (0.012)	-0.096 (0.136)
Hours Worked	-0.034*** (0.011)	0.277*** (0.091)
Paid Leave	0.024 (0.032)	-0.064 (0.183)
Bonuses	0.055*** (0.014)	0.110 (0.177)
Allowance/Premiums	-0.024 (0.018)	0.138 (0.191)
Overtime	-0.012 (0.015)	0.027 (0.174)
Staff Numbers Lamda		-0.066 (0.071)
Pay Lamda		0.055 (0.080)

Table 11.8: Impact of Individual Employment Condition Cuts on Firms' Average Labour Costs (continued)

	Individual Strategies	Lamda Adjusted
Hours Worked Lamda		-0.189*** (0.054)
Paid Leave Lamda		0.042 (0.083)
Bonuses Lamda		-0.034 (0.106)
Allowances/Premiums Lamda		-0.091 (0.106)
Overtime Lamda		-0.023 (0.102)
Observations	4,543	4,543
R^2	0.442	0.445

Source and Notes: Same as Table 11.7.

CONCLUSIONS AND POLICY IMPLICATIONS

While high wage levels in Ireland have become a primary issue in the current environment, they were not a principal factor behind the current downturn. The Irish recession was caused by a combination of factors, including the collapse of the housing bubble, the overexposure of the banking system to the property market and the global downturn. Consequently, the fiscal deficit deteriorated and policies to reduce it have negatively impacted on domestic demand. Nevertheless, it has been widely argued that recovery should entail an adjustment in the price of labour, given our high relative costs and lack of monetary autonomy. Yet existing international research demonstrates that it is extremely unusual for firms to engage in wage cutting even in the aftermath of a shock. Historically, firms tend to use other levers, such as cutting employment, hours and non-wage remuneration to achieve reductions in labour costs. Generally, the theoretical frameworks explain such behaviour as firms seeking to avoid productivity losses, either through worker disincentive effects or higher levels of labour turnover (Shapiro and Stiglitz, 1984; Weiss, 1980; Lindbeck and Snower, 1988). The corollary of this is that wage cutting is likely to be inversely related to the average productivity levels of the workforce.

The chapter finds that private sector wage rates altered little following the onset of the recession (see also Walsh, 2012). Nevertheless, the aggregate data hide a very complex picture. Within the male labour market, wages were driven down by an increase in the share of part-time workers. However, this was more than off-set by a rising share in the proportion of graduates. There were also increased returns to membership of professional bodies, third-level qualifications and regularised employment. With respect to females, again we see compositional change with the rise of part-time employment depressing wages, but this was more than offset by an increase in the share of graduates and a substantial jump in the return to females employed in larger firms.

In relation to firm-level strategies, the results are consistent with international research in that wage cutting was a less favoured method of adjustment, with firms preferring to cut labour costs through reducing staff numbers, hours worked and bonuses. Consistent with the individual-level analysis, labour costs were held down by a rise in the share of part-time workers and a fall in the costs associated with higher tenure, but these effects were more than offset by the influences of a rising share of graduates and a rise in the average cost of labour within larger firms. The tenure result suggests that, with the onset of the recession, firms ceased to reward long service in its own right, which suggests that the pay gap between older and younger workers may have reduced during the downturn. Overall, the firm level analysis suggests that labour costs were maintained through the rising share of graduates and rising wages within foreign multinational enterprises and/or large firms.

To the extent that private sector wages reflect both worker productivity and firm-level profit maximisation, the research suggests that while some downsizing has been necessary within most sectors in response to market conditions, those firms that have survived have done so by retaining their most productive workers. While some small compositional effects have been evident, downward wage rigidity in Ireland has been a consequence of a rise in the relative share and returns to graduate employment and a rising payoff to working in a large firm, particularly for females. Given this framework, our analysis is consistent with the possibility that firms have behaved in a profit maximising way and rewarded productivity among their workforce. The demise of social partnership over the period suggests that employers were not heavily constrained by bargaining arrangements[175] and that labour market conditions were generally more flexible than they had been for quite some time. In addition, we did not find any evidence that firms faced institutional barriers to downward wage adjustment, given that there was no substantial impact on the trade union variable included in our specifications. Furthermore, given that wage costs were predominately driven by returns to rising graduate employment, our analysis also shows that wage rigidity was not a consequence of a high wage floor among low-skilled workers. In this context, the analysis suggests that there may be little to be gained from pursuing policies aimed at labour market deregulation such as, reducing the minimum wage and/or restricting bargaining arrangements within firms/industries, as such policies are unlikely to influence the wage setting behaviour of firms.

---

175 In fact, Keeney and Lawless (2010) found that Irish firms did not feel constrained by institutional factors from cutting wages even when social partnership was in operation.

Despite the rich nature of our data, the fact remains that substantial proportions of the movements in wages cannot be attributed to either coefficient or composition effects, particularly in the case of males. The international evidence and the predictions of theory suggest that the unexplained component within the data will be related to firms' reluctance to cut wages due to feared productivity losses arising from lower morale, increased monitoring costs and/or higher rates of turnover. It could be argued that there is a potential role for policy in counteracting such barriers to wage adjustment. However, the situation is far from straightforward and, consequently, the challenge for policy is considerable. Arguably, disincentive effects may follow a wage cut as a result of employee resentment relating to a change in relative pay with respect to comparable employees in other firms. If wage rates were cut in a universal fashion across all firms with, for instance a promise of future increases in take home pay through income tax relief following productivity gains, then relativities would be unaffected and disincentive effects minimised. Indeed, this would be in line with the original Irish social partnership model that was based on a system of wage restraint, with productivity growth rewarded through lower rates of income tax.

Furthermore, in 2010, the Irish government implemented blanket pay cuts across the public sector, albeit without the consent of the social partners, and a pay freeze has been agreed for public sector employees up to this year, 2013. However, even were the social partners to agree to private sector pay cuts or a freeze in nominal pay, the policy could not be implemented in a universal fashion as less than 40 per cent of private sector employees are covered by the national wage agreement (McGuinness, Kelly and O'Connell, 2010).[176] Consequently, disincentive effects are likely to persist following any intervention making such a policy unenforceable.

Given the productivity related risks arising from any attempt to reduce wage rates, as discussed above, it is clear that firms will generally tend to use other methods of achieving a reduction in labour costs. This is borne out by the results from this study, which demonstrate that strategies such as reducing staff numbers, hours worked and bonus payments are all preferred over reductions in wages.

REFERENCES

Autor, D. and Katz, L. (1999). 'Changes in the Wage Structure and Earnings Inequality' in Ashenfelter, O. and Card, D. (eds.), *Handbook of Labor Economics*, Vol. 3A, 1463–1555, Amsterdam: Elsevier.

Babecký, J., Du Caju, P., Kosma, T., Lawless, M., Messina, J. and Rõõm, T. (2009). 'The Margins of Labour Cost Adjustment: Survey Evidence from European Firms', European Central Bank, Working Paper No. 1106.

Babecký, J., Du Caju, P., Kosma, T., Lawless, M., Messina, J. and Rõõm, T. (2010).

---

[176] This is an approximation based on firm-level employees.

'Downward Nominal and Real Wage Rigidity: Survey Evidence from European Firms', *The Scandinavian Journal of Economics*, 112, 884–910.

Babecký, J., Du Caju, P., Kosma, T., Lawless, M., Messina, J. and Rõõm, T. (2012). 'Why Firms Avoid Cutting Wages: Some Evidence from European Firms', mimeo.

Bergin, A., Kelly, E. and McGuinness, S. (2012). 'Explaining Changes in Earnings and Labour Costs During the Recession', Renewal Series, Paper 9, April 2012, Dublin: ESRI.

Bertola, G., Dabusinskas, A., Hoeberichts, M., Izquierdo, M., Kwapil, C., Montornès, J. and Radowski, D. (2010). 'Price, Wage and Employment Response to Shocks: Evidence from the WDN Survey', European Central Bank, Working Paper No. 1164.

Christopoulou, R., Jimeno, J. and Lamo, A. (2010). 'Changes in the Wage Structure in EU Countries', European Central Bank, Working Paper No. 1199.

Dhyne, E. and Druant, M. (2010). 'Wages, Labor or Prices: How do Firms React to Shocks?,' European Central Bank, Working Paper No. 1224

European Central Bank (2009). 'Wage Dynamics in Europe: Final Report of the Wage Dynamics Network (WDN)', http://www.ecb.int/home/html/researcher_wdn.en.html.

Fuss, C. (2008). 'How Do Firms Adjust Their Wage Bill in Belgium. A Decomposition Along the Intensive and Extensive Margins', European Central Bank, Working Paper No. 854.

Keeney, M. and Lawless, M. (2010). 'Wage Setting and Wage Flexibility in Ireland: Results from a Firm-level Survey', Central Bank and Financial Services Authority of Ireland, Research Technical Paper 1/RT/10.

Kwapil, C. (2010). 'Firms' Reactions to the Crisis and their Consequences for the Labour Market. Results of a Company Survey Conducted in Austria', European Central Bank, Working Paper No. 1274.

Layard, R., Nickell, S. and Jackman, R. (2005). *Unemployment. Macroeconomic Performance and the Labour Market*, 2nd edition. Oxford: Oxford University Press.

Lindbeck, A. and Snower, D. (1988). 'Job Security, Work Incentives and Unemployment,' *Scandinavian Journal of Economics*, 90, 453–474.

McGuinness, S., Kelly, E. and O'Connell, P.J. (2010). 'The Impact of Wage Bargaining Regime on Firm-Level Competitiveness and Wage Inequality: The Case of Ireland', *Industrial Relations*, 49, (October 2010), 593–615.

Messina, J., Du Caju, P., Duarte, C.F., Hansen, N.L. and Izquierdo, M. (2010). 'The Incidence of Nominal and Real Wage Rigidity: An Individual-based Sectoral Approach,' European Central Bank, Working Paper No. 1213.

Oi, W. (1983). 'Heterogeneous Firms and the Organization of Production,' *Economic Inquiry*, 21, 147–171.

Rõõm, T. and Messina, J. (2009). 'Downward Wage Rigidity during the Current Financial and Economic Crisis', mimeo.

Shapiro, C. and Stiglitz, J. (1984). 'Equilibrium Unemployment as a Worker Discipline Device', *American Economic Review*, June (1984), 433–444.

Walsh, K. (2012). 'Wage Bill Change in Ireland During Recession – how have employers reacted to the downturn', paper read to The Statistical and Social Inquiry Society of Ireland, February 2012.

Weiss, Andrew W. (1980). 'Job Queues and Layoffs in Labor Markets with Flexible Wages', *Journal of Political Economy*, University of Chicago Press, 88, 526–538, June.

CHAPTER 12

Quality of Public Services: Irish Public Perceptions and Implications for Public Service Reform

Dorothy Watson

This chapter presents new evidence regarding perceptions of public service quality in Ireland, in order to draw lessons for public service reform. It focuses, in particular, on the extent to which public services are meeting the needs and expectations of those most reliant on them: vulnerable groups in the population who cannot afford the option of 'going private'. In terms of the policy landscape (Figure 1.1), this research is located at the intersection between the identification of policy challenges and the identification of policy goals. Rather than focusing on a particular policy area, the chapter provides a broad view of several key policy domains: health, education, public transport, care services for the elderly and public pension provision. As such, the chapter is less specific than many others in this volume. The chapter also differs in the type of evidence used: perceived service quality. This emphasis is appropriate, given the government commitment to a 'customer focus' in the context of public service reform.

The key research questions examined are how Ireland compares to other European countries in terms of the perceived quality of services and whether there are differences between the economically vulnerable and the well-to-do in terms of these perceptions.

The methodological approach involves an analysis of the Irish data from an existing survey (the *European Quality of Life Survey*, 2007), using multivariate statistical models to examine variations in perceived public service quality. We also develop a control for a tendency towards overly-critical or negative responding, which has the potential to distort the results.

The findings suggest that perceptions of the quality of public services tended to be more negative in Ireland than in other European countries, but with variations by service type. Another important finding was that across four of the five services, those who were economically vulnerable gave a less positive evaluation. This suggests that public services are failing those likely to be most reliant on them.

We conclude with a number of suggestions regarding how evidence on customer perceptions of quality in public sector reform might be used to improve policy. Good measures of service quality are essential if a focus on quality is to be maintained in the context of pressure to deliver budget reductions. In particular, we argue: that customers – particularly economically vulnerable groups – should be involved at the service design stage; that well designed surveys could provide important evidence for public service reform; that outcome-based performance indicators are needed; and that an ongoing flow of information between customers and service providers would contribute to the management of customer expectations.

BACKGROUND

The emphasis in public sector reform in Ireland has shifted over time. In the mid-1990s efficiency and accountability were stressed (Co-ordinating Group of Secretaries, 1996), while integration of services, performance and customer focus were emphasised by the mid to late 2000s (OECD, 2008; Task Force on the Public Service, 2008). From 2008 onwards, the national and international fiscal crisis has created a very difficult environment, leading to demand for a reduction in the cost of the public sector pay bill. In July 2011, a new Department of Public Expenditure and Reform was established to oversee the process of reform in the public sector while ensuring cost reductions. In this context, it is timely to ask how public services are perceived by their intended recipients. A focus on public perceptions is appropriate given the emphasis in the *Public Service Reform Plan* on 'placing customer service at the core of everything we do' (Department of Public Expenditure and Reform, 2011, p. 3). In addition, given the commitment in the *Programme for Government, 2011–2016* to protecting the most vulnerable (Department of the Taoiseach, 2011, p. 2 and pp. 28–43), it is worth asking whether there are differences in the perceptions of quality between those who are economically vulnerable and the general population. While the fiscal crisis has also necessarily led to an emphasis on reducing the cost of the public sector, maintaining the quality of public services is likely to be particularly important to vulnerable groups who are not in a position to purchase services in the market.

Managing the cost of the public sector in the context of increasing demand for service presents a major challenge. However, the association at the international level between spending on services and measures of quality are rather weak (Rose and Newton, 2010, p. 16). Spending on health is high in Ireland as a percentage of GNP, but it ranks second lowest of 16 countries in terms of perceived quality of health services (Watson, 2012). In contrast, when it comes to the education system, Ireland is slightly above average in terms of perceived quality but towards the middle of the distribution in terms of spending (Watson, 2012). Indeed, a focus on expenditure confuses inputs with the benefits citizens may gain (Rose and Newton, 2010, pp. 7–8). For instance, there is no clear link between spending on education and the measured performance of pupils: Finland, Austria and Portugal spend roughly the same share of GDP on education, but pupil performance at age 15 (as measured by the international PISA survey) is very different (Mandl, Dierx and Ilzkovitz, 2008, p. 21). The weak link between spending and quality is confirmed by a number of international studies that focus on the effectiveness and efficiency of public sector spending (e.g., Afonso, Schuknecht and Tanzi, 2005; Mattina and Gunnarsson, 2007; Clements, 2002; OECD, 2007). These studies show that efficiency gains are possible in the public sector (Mandl, Dierx and Ilzkovitz, 2008). The implication is that how the service is delivered is as important as how much is spent.

The quality of public services has implications for the quality of life of citizens beyond the traditional domain of particular services. Earlier analyses on the *European Quality of Life Survey* (Watson, Pichler and Wallace, 2010) showed that perceived quality of public services was significant in accounting for differences in subjective quality of life. More importantly, from the perspective of the current policy concern with protecting the most vulnerable, the impact on life satisfaction was stronger for those who were facing material deprivation.

The importance of public services to quality of life is also found where analysis is conducted at the small-area level and using objective measures of public service quality. Castelli *et al.* (2009) find that differences between local areas in the quality of public services (measured using objective performance indicators) can have an impact on variations between areas in general measures of quality of life.

In this chapter, data from the 2007 *European Quality of Life Survey* (EQLS, Anderson *et al.*, 2009) are used to examine variations in the perceived quality of public services in Ireland. The key questions addressed are:

- How does Ireland compare with other European countries in terms of the perceived quality of public services?
- Are there differences between the economically deprived and the well-to-do in terms of how the quality of public services is assessed?
- What are the implications for policy on public sector reform?

Five different public services are distinguished in this chapter: the health services, public education, public transport, care services for older adults and the state pension. In the context of subjective evaluations of public service quality, the analysis incorporates a control for any impact of a tendency to give negative or critical survey responses.

PUBLIC SERVICE QUALITY

Three aspects of quality are particularly relevant to public services. Two of these centre on 'whose quality' (Gaster and Squires, 2003) and the third aspect is related to the cost of service provision. In terms of 'whose quality', we can distinguish between approaches that emphasise the perspective of 'experts' and those that emphasise the perspective of users or customers. The expert definition – what Garvin (1984) calls the 'manufacturing' approach – is based on specifications and criteria derived from an 'expert' view of the content of the service (Garvin, 1984; Moullin, 2002). This emphasises the perspective of service designers and providers – often professionals with a distinct set of priorities and concepts of what constitutes 'good service'. In the context of health services, for instance, the professional perspective would emphasise correct diagnosis, treatment and outcomes, and place less emphasis on difficulties in accessing the service – physical or financial. In the educational setting, professionals may emphasise academic and learning outcomes rather than social, health or contextual criteria.

An alternative perspective, and one which is more prominent in the private sector where services are purchased, is to emphasise the perspective of the 'customers' or service users (Garvin, 1984; Moullin, 2002). From the 'customer' perspective, accessibility, convenience and cost are likely to enter into the calculus. In the educational setting, parents and students, while sharing a concern with the quality of education as defined by professionals, are likely to have other concerns as well, including things like proximity of the school or college; affordability; the integration of class times and break periods with work and family commitments; the pleasantness of the environment, and so on. Current controversies over the closure of regional hospitals highlight this difference in perspective in the context of health services, particularly differences in the importance assigned to proximity by professionals and service users. This implies that an important source of variation in the evaluation of public services in the population will be the degree to which the service meets the needs and priorities of particular groups. We may, therefore, find different evaluations of the same public service by age, gender, family circumstances, education, health status and economic status.

In the context of public services, however, there is a third set of interests besides those of providers and users: the interests of those who pay for the services through taxation. In this sense, the general public is a stakeholder with a legitimate interest in the quality of public services since they pay for these services through direct and indirect taxation.

This chapter emphasises the perspective of the users and paymasters. Their perspective may be based on first-hand knowledge of the service, on the experience of family and friends or on media reports. The EQLS data on perceived quality of public services allows us to look directly at how these services are evaluated by their intended recipients and the general public. Such perceptions are also important in that they will affect the level of demand for privately-produced substitutes, including health insurance, private schools, private modes of transport and private pensions, and the legitimacy of taxation to pay for the services.

DATA AND MEASUREMENT

The data used in this analysis come from the *European Quality of Life Survey* (EQLS), 2007. The EQLS 2007 round covered 31 countries (the EU-27, the three candidate countries and Norway). The sample of about 1,000 individuals in each country was based on a random route methodology. In this chapter, we focus on the data for Ireland (N=1,000).

Measuring Perceived Quality of Public Services

As well as detailed background information, the EQLS includes a set of items where respondents rate on a 10-point scale the quality of five public services (health, education, public transport, care for older adults and pensions). Service quality is rated by respondents on a scale ranging from 1 (lowest quality) to 10 (highest quality). Cases where the rating is missing are excluded for the analysis of perceptions of a particular service.[177]

Evaluations across different public services tend to be correlated (Rose and Newton, 2010). In the present chapter, we are interested in evaluations of particular services, so we do not adopt the strategy of constructing a general 'quality of public services' scale. Analysing the services separately is possible in Ireland because the ratings of different services are only modestly correlated.[178]

Figure 12.1 shows the ratings of these five public services in each of the EU15 countries and Norway. The countries are sorted according to the average rating across the five services. Ratings of public services tend to be higher in the Scandinavian countries, particularly Finland, and in Luxembourg, Belgium, Austria and the Netherlands. Typical ratings are lower than average in Ireland and are lowest in Greece, Portugal and Italy. There is a marked contrast in Ireland between the public evaluations of the health services, which are among the lowest across this group of countries (4.9 versus 6.6 on average), and education services, which are evaluated more favourably than average (7.3 versus 6.7 on average). Irish evaluations of the quality of public transport, care services for the elderly and the state pension are between these two extremes (5.6 to 5.7).

The difference in Ireland between the evaluation of the health and education systems is not unique to 2007. A similar pattern was found in the 2003 data: Ireland rated the health services lower than education (Fahey, Whelan and Maître, 2004, pp. 60, 73). Compared to the 2003 EQLS data for Ireland, there was a decline in the perceived quality of health services (from 5.3 to 4.9) and of the

---

[177] There is a high proportion of missing information on the items dealing with the state pension system and care services for the elderly (29–31 per cent), compared to 2–5 per cent for the other three services.

[178] Most of the correlations in Ireland are in the range .29 to .42, but with a higher correlation of 0.63 between evaluations of care services for older adults and evaluations of the state pension (Watson, 2012).

pensions system (6.1 to 5.7) (Fahey, Whelan and Maître, 2004, p. 60). On the other hand, the perceived quality of the education system had increased from 6.9 to 7.3 (Fahey, Whelan and Maître, 2004. p. 73). Thus, despite the increase in spending on public services in the period (Watson, 2012), there was a disappointing lack of improvement in the perceived quality of many services. This may be partly due to rising expectations in the context of the extended period of economic growth.

Figure 12.1: Rating of Public Services in Europe (EU15 Countries and Norway)

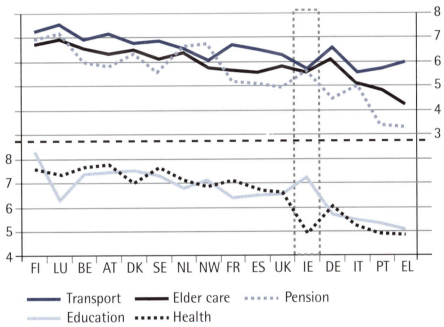

Note: Countries shown, in order, are Finland, Luxembourg, Belgium, Austria, Denmark, Sweden, The Netherlands, Norway, France, Spain, United Kingdom, Ireland, Germany, Italy, Portugal and Greece.

A different ranking of countries might be obtained if alternative measures of service quality were used. For example, Afonso, Schuknecht and Tanzi (2003) use 'performance indicators' to rank public services across countries based on outcomes. For the education system they used school enrolment and educational achievement, while infant mortality and life expectancy are used to rank the health services. Using data from 2000, Ireland ranks lowest of the EU15 in terms of the quality of the health services and in the lower third of the distribution in terms of the quality of the education system (Afonso, Schuknecht and Tanzi, 2003, p. 12). These attempts to measure quality based on outputs are not without their own problems, however. One issue is that the results are very sensitive to the choice of indicators. In the context of education, for instance, studies on the efficiency of spending on education vary according to the methodology, with some finding that Ireland can make no efficiency gains and others that substantial improvement is possible (see overview by Mandl, Dierx and Ilzkovitz, 2008 p. 23; see also Kuhry, Pommer and de Kam, 2006). Another problem is that the use of 'output' indicators without any control for inputs such as the level of demand, age distribution and other factors which may affect the health or educational status of the population ultimately attributes to public service organisations credit (or blame) for outcomes over which they have limited control (Boyle, 2006).

Characteristics of Individuals and Households

In examining perceived public service quality in Ireland, we focus on a range of characteristics of the individuals and their households which might be expected to have an impact on their perceptions of public services. These include age, gender, marital status and a number of other characteristics, as shown in Table 12.1. We identify those living in cities (self-defined) to check for differences between urban and rural locations. Self-rated health is also examined. The item is coded to identify those whose health is not good. We also identify those who have a disability: a person with a chronic physical or mental health problem, illness or disability that hampers them in their daily activities.

Economic vulnerability refers to an inability to afford the kinds of basic goods and services that would allow someone to participate fully in the normal standard of living in a society (Whelan and Maître, 2010). Economic vulnerability is here measured as an additive scale comprised of level of difficulty in making ends meet (0='very easily' – 5 = 'with great difficulty') and the number of basic items (as shown in Table 12.2) which the household lacks because it cannot afford them (0=none, 5=5 or six).[179] Both scales are standardised before summing the scores and the resulting index is re-scaled to range from 0 (not vulnerable) to 1 (high level of vulnerability).

Another aspect of vulnerability is social isolation. As a proxy for social isolation we use an item capturing the availability of someone to provide practical support if the person were ill, distinguishing those who could receive such help from family, non-family or from nobody. People who lack such practical support are likely to be particularly reliant on public services in adverse circumstances.

As the state pension is likely to be particularly important to households receiving pension income, a control for receipt of pension income is also included in the model. Note that such households may also receive other sources of income,

---

179 The correlation between the two scales is 0.52. Although Whelan and Maître (2010) measure economic vulnerability using three indicators (income, subjective economic stress and deprivation), the measure based on the EQLS uses two indicators because of a high level of missing data for income.

from employment or other types of social welfare, and that the pension may be a private or occupational pension (rather than the state pension).

Table 12.1: Characteristics of Individuals and Households

Variable	Items	Coding
Health not good	In general, would you say your health is …(1=very good to 5=very bad)	Fair, bad or very bad=1
Has disability	Do you have any chronic (long-standing) physical or mental health problem, illness or disability? (1=Yes; 2=No) [If yes] Are you hampered in your daily activities by this physical or mental health problem, illness or disability? (1=Yes severely; 2=Yes, to some extent; 3=No)	Limited severely or to some extent = 1
Economic Vulnerability (scale, 1–10)	A household may have different sources of income and more than one household member may contribute to it. Thinking of your household's total monthly income: is your household able to make ends meet….? (1=very easily to 6=with great difficulty) There are some things that many people cannot afford, even if they would like them. For each of the following things on this card, can I just check whether your household can afford it if you want it? – Keeping your home adequately warm – Paying for a week's annual holiday away from home (not staying with relatives) – Replacing any worn-out furniture – A meal with meat, chicken or fish every second day if you wanted it – Buying new, rather than second-hand, clothes – Having friends or family for a drink or meal at least once a month	Sum of economic strain (1–5) and number of items lacked (1–5, 5=5 or more of 6) (Standardised before summing; rescaled to range from 0 = not vulnerable to 1 = highest vulnerability)
Practical support	From whom would you get support if you needed help around the house when ill (Partner/spouse; Other family member; Work colleague; Friend; Neighbour; Someone else; Nobody)	Family Non-family None (from nobody)
Pension income	Have you or someone else in your household received any of the following types of income over the past 12 months? Pension	Household received income from pension

Table 12.1: Characteristics of Individuals and Households (continued)

Variable	Items	Coding
Other services in area	Still thinking about your immediate neighbourhood, are there any of the following facilities available within walking distance? (1=Yes; 2=No) Food store or supermarket Post office Banking facilities	Count of number of these services available in the area
Access to public transport	Public transport facilities (bus, metro, tram, etc.)	Access to public transport
Access to medical services Distance Delay Cost	On the last occasion you needed to see a doctor or medical specialist, to what extent did each of the following factors make it difficult for you to do so? (1=very difficult to 4=not applicable) Distance to doctor's office/hospital/medical centre Delay in getting appointment Cost of seeing the doctor	Recoded – 0=no difficulty/NA 1=a little difficulty 2=very difficult
Negative Responding	Included as a control for a tendency to give negative or critical responses (see Watson, 2012, for details)	Range 0 (low) to 1 (high negative responding)

We include controls for general availability of services in the area. We distinguish public transport separately. Three other types of private services – post office, banking and food store or supermarket – capture aspects of the availability of general services within walking distance. This is correlated with city-dwelling, but the correlation is rather low (only 0.17). Three-quarters of the population has access to all three types of service within walking distance, 89 per cent of city-dwellers and 69 per cent of non city-dwellers. Thus, it captures aspects of service provision in the immediate area apart from the differences between urban and rural locations.

For health services, we have direct measures of the experience of service use. Three measures are included in the model, capturing the level of difficulty experienced in accessing a doctor or medical specialist due to the distance, delay in getting an appointment and cost. Table 12.2 shows the correlation between these measures and economic vulnerability. Those who are economically vulnerable are more likely to experience difficulty in accessing health services, although the correlations are not strong. The correlation between economic vulnerability and difficulties associated with cost is lower than those associated with distance or waiting lists, because people with the lowest incomes (approximately one-third of the population) would qualify for free doctor visits and prescriptions under the

General Medical System. There is no significant relationship between economic vulnerability and access to public transport or the number of general services (banking, post office, food store) in the area, however.

Table 12.2: Correlations between Economic Vulnerability, Problems in Accessing Health Services and Public Transport and Number of General Services in Area

	Correlations					
	A	B	C	D	E	F
A. Economic Vulnerability	1					
B. Difficulty – distance to medical services	0.22**	1				
C. Difficulty – wait for medical appointment	0.25**	0.47**	1			
D. Difficulty – cost of medical services	0.18**	0.33**	0.37**	1		
E. No public transport in area	-0.01	0.14**	0.08**	0.04	1	
F. Num. general services in area	0.06+	-0.07*	-0.02	-0.04	-0.50**	1

Note: ** p<=.01; * p<=.05; + p<=.10.

Critical Response Pattern

In analysing subjective indicators it is important to be aware of the potential of response patterns to bias the results. In this analysis, we are particularly concerned that a tendency to give critical evaluations may influence the measure of perceived quality of public services and the pattern of differences between groups. The final variable in the model, then, represents an attempt to control for any tendency to give negative or critical responses to survey items. It is constructed as the number of extremely negative responses given to 6 items taken from different scales, dealing with trust in others, trust in the legal system and the press and with views on general compliance in terms of showing consideration for others, paying taxes and obeying traffic laws (see Watson, 2012, for further details). A tendency towards negative responding is higher among those with lower levels of education, the economically vulnerable and those living in cities (Watson, 2012). Controlling for negative responding, then, results in a somewhat weaker (but less biased) association between these characteristics and the evaluation of public services.

FINDINGS FROM THE ANALYSIS

A set of regression models was estimated, one for the perceived quality of each service. The results are shown in Table 12.3. Where respondents were unable to rate the quality of a particular service, the case was excluded from the analysis. The fit statistics indicate well-fitting models.[180]

All of the coefficients in the models are unstandardised. Recall that the scales measuring perceived quality of services run from 1 to 10 and all of the independent variables are dichotomies, with the exception of economic vulnerability (which has been scaled to range from 0 to 1) and number of services in the area (ranges from 0 to 3). The coefficients can be interpreted as the amount of change in the service evaluation resulting from a one unit change in the independent variable.

The models control for a tendency to give negative or critical responses. We can see from the table a pattern of negative responding is associated with a lower evaluation of some services, but not of others. The largest effect is on the perceived quality of health services (–6.28), followed by the quality of the state pension (–3.89) and care services for the elderly (–3.49). There is no impact of negative responding on the perceived quality of the education system or of public transport, when other factors are controlled. In the following, we will discuss the findings with a particular emphasis on the perceptions of vulnerable groups.

Vulnerable groups

Those who are economically vulnerable have a more negative perception of four of the five services (the association with public education does not reach statistical significance, p=.089). The difference between the most vulnerable group and the least vulnerable group is substantial for the remaining services: about one point for the health services, public transport, care services for the elderly and about two points for the state pension system. This is disturbing, as the economically vulnerable are likely to be most reliant on public services. It is worth recalling that we have controlled for difficulties in gaining access to the health services and to public transport, and for a tendency to give negative or critical responses. The negative association, then, must reflect differences in the extent to which economically vulnerable people see these services as meeting their needs.

People with health problems or a disability comprise another vulnerable group. Health status, rather than having a disability, seems to be the important factor in predicting differences in perceived quality of services. Those who rate their health as fair, bad or very bad give a lower rating to the health services, education system and public transport. We have controlled for a tendency to respond negatively or critically (which may also influence self-reported health status), and for difficulties in accessing health services, such as cost, distance travelled, and waiting lists.

---

[180] The root mean square error of approximation (RMSEA) ranges from 0.022 to 0.026. The Tucker-Lewis Index ranges from 0.927 to 0.940.

There is no significant association between self-rated health and the perceived quality of either the state pension or care services for older adults, however.

People who do not have a family member to rely on in the event of illness are another vulnerable group. Once we control for economic vulnerability and health problems, this group has a substantially more positive view of the health services (by 1.6 points). This is a very small group (less than 1 per cent of the population), but one for whom primary care services from the GP or community health nurse is likely to be particularly important.

Other Characteristics

Since other characteristics are not the main focus of this chapter, their impact on perceived service quality will be briefly summarised here. There are no significant differences between men and women in the perceived quality of any of the five services when we control for other characteristics and few age differences. The only significant age difference is that adults in their thirties have a slightly more negative perception of the quality of health services. If retirement is omitted from the model, we find a positive association between older age and perceptions of the public transport system, which probably reflects the fact that older adults are entitled to free public transport services.[181]

City-dwellers have a more negative view of the quality of the education system (by two-thirds of a point on the ten point scale), care services for the elderly and the state pension. On the other hand, access to public transport and to general services is somewhat higher in cities. The number of services in the area is associated with a more positive perception of the quality of health services (by about 0.3 for each of the three – food store, bank and post office) and having public transport within walking distance is associated with a very substantial increase in the rating of public transport services (1.3 points on the ten point scale). The number of general services in the area is associated with an increase in the perceived quality of the state pension.

There are no differences by marital status in perceptions of the quality of health services, the education system or care services for older adults. However, single and separated/divorced people have a more positive view of the quality of public transport. These groups are less likely to own a car and may be more reliant on public transport. Single (never married) adults also have a more positive view of the state pension system, by about half a point on the ten point scale.

Adults with children tend to have a more positive view of the health services and also of public transport and care services for the elderly. There is no significant difference between adults with children and those without children in their view

---

181 The positive association between household receipt of pension income and evaluation of the health services and care services for the elderly, however, appears to be driven by the perceptions of other adults living with the pensioner rather than the pensioner himself or herself (see below).

of the education system or of the quality of state pensions, however. Taken together with the absence of a significant effect of age on the perceived quality of the education system, this suggests that the fairly positive perception of the education system pertains across levels of the system: parents are likely to be thinking mainly of the primary and secondary levels while young childless adults are likely to be thinking mainly of the second and third levels.

Table 12.3: Model of Ratings of Quality of Public Services (Maximum Likelihood, Unstandardized Coefficients)

Models ----->		Health	Education	Transport	Elder Care	Pension
Economic vulnerability	Scale, 0–1	-1.06*	-0.58 +	-1.19**	-1.11*	-2.03**
Health	Fair/(V) Bad	-0.48*	-0.45**	-0.64**	-0.32	0.13
Disability	A little/Severe	0.17	0.00	0.45 +	0.52	0.13
Practical support	From others	0.17	-0.05	-0.20	0.00	-0.45 +
(Ref=from family)	None	1.60*	0.16	0.90	0.44	1.33
Gender	Female	-0.07	-0.18	0.09	0.14	0.25
Age (Ref:18–29)	30–39	-0.52*	0.32 +	0.11	-0.34	-0.20
	40–49	-0.26	0.15	0.17	-0.31	0.03
	50–64	-0.23	0.37 +	-0.15	-0.09	0.15
	65 and over	0.01	0.15	-0.32	-0.15	0.43
Location	City	-0.19	-0.67**	-0.01	-0.55**	-0.44*
Marital status	Separated	-0.34	0.03	0.62*	0.47	0.35
(Ref: married)	Widowed	0.41	0.34	0.45	0.25	-0.03
	Never married	0.22	0.30 +	0.40*	0.31	0.53*
Has children?	Yes	0.47*	0.24	0.36*	0.49*	0.45 +
Education	Upper 2nd	0.01	0.17	-0.23	-0.29	0.10
(Ref=< Lower 2nd)	3rd level	0.07	0.27 +	-0.21	-0.03	0.03
Economic situation	Unemployed	-0.08	-0.54	0.25	-0.49	-0.07

Table 12.3: *Model of Ratings of Quality of Public Services (Maximum Likelihood, Unstandardized Coefficients)* (continued)

Models ----->		Health	Education	Transport	Elder Care	Pension
(Ref=at work)	Retired	0.36	0.42	0.95**	0.31	0.48
	Other inactive	-0.10	0.20	0.37*	-0.21	0.01
Income sources	Pension	0.54*	0.28	0.33	0.74*	0.55 +
Difficulty in accessing health services	Distance	-0.29	-0.33*	-0.73**	-0.55*	-0.27
	Wait for appt.	-0.16	-0.17	0.02	-0.23	-0.45*
	Cost	-0.37**	-0.06	0.10	-0.14	-0.24 +
Services in area	No pub. transport	-0.17	-0.07	-1.30**	-0.24	0.08
	N. serv. in area	0.29**	-0.07	-0.06	0.13	0.27**
Response pattern	Negative	-6.28**	-0.64	0.01	-3.49*	-3.89**
Model information	N cases	984	927	944	717	700
	R-square	0.151	0.112	0.149	0.106	0.163
	CFI	0.942	0.943	0.944	0.951	0.950
	TLI	0.927	0.929	0.931	0.940	0.938
	RMSEA	0.026	0.025	0.025	0.022	0.022

Source: EQLS 2007, analysis by author.
Note: ** p<=.01; * p<=.05; + p<=.10.

There is no association between education and perceived quality of services when we control for other characteristics. The only significant differences by economic status are between the retired and those in employment, with retired people giving a substantially more positive evaluation to the public transport system. This probably reflects their entitlement to free transport services. The 'other economically inactive' group (caring for home and family, student, unable to work because of illness or disability) also give positive evaluation to public transport.

We have a number of measures of service use or difficulties in accessing services in the model. Those in households with income from a pension, as noted above, tend to give a more positive rating to healthcare and care services for the elderly. Additional checks by age group suggested that these positive evaluations are mainly driven by people under 50 years who live with a pensioner rather than by people over age 50 who may be the beneficiaries of pension income in their own right.

The findings suggest that negative experiences in accessing one type of service may well be associated with negative experiences in accessing other services as well. For instance, those who have had difficulty in accessing a doctor or medical services because of the distance they had to travel give a lower rating to public transport (–.73), the education system (–.33) and care services for the elderly (–.55). It is the cost of healthcare services that is significantly associated with a lower evaluation of health services in the model, however (–.37), rather than distance travelled or waiting time. The different difficulties encountered in accessing health services (distance, wait and cost) are correlated (Table 12.2). Each would be significantly associated with a reduced evaluation of the quality of the health services if entered singly into the model. Cost emerged as the strongest effect as it may be capturing problems encountered by those who are not economically vulnerable (which is controlled in the model) and who do not qualify for the free medical services covered by the GMS. It is likely that the impact of costs on perceived quality of the health services is driven by those with middle incomes who experience the costs of primary care (GP visits and prescriptions) as burdensome.

DISCUSSION

To return to the questions posed at the outset, the overall evaluation of the quality of public services in Ireland in 2007 was below the EU15 average. Nonetheless, there are important variations across type of service. There is a contrast, in particular, between perceived quality of public health services and of public education. Ratings of the quality of the health services are particularly low in Ireland while ratings of the quality of the education system are above the EU15 average. It is difficult to say how that might have changed in the interim, with the onset of the recession. At the time of writing, the results from the 2011 survey are not yet available. There is only a weak association across countries between public spending on particular services and the perceived quality of these services (Afonso, Schuknecht and Tanzi, 2005). However, cuts in spending implemented on an emergency basis, without the time required to reorganise service delivery to enhance efficiency, may well have resulted in a drop in service quality. The impact on public perceptions, however, may also be conditioned by a general adjustment of expectations.

The second major question was whether there were differences between those who are economically vulnerable and those who are better-off in terms of how services are perceived. The findings in this regard from the model were very striking. Those who are economically vulnerable – the group most likely to be reliant on public services – give less positive ratings across four of the five types of public service (all except education). The strongest association was found for the state pension. Those with poor health, another vulnerable group, also gave a lower rating to health services, the education system and public transport. In contrast, our third vulnerable group, the small number of people who do not have a family member to rely on in the event of illness gave a substantially more positive view of the health services (by 1.6 points). These patterns persist even when we control for a number of measures of personally experienced difficulties in accessing health services, for non-availability of public transport in the area and for a pattern of negative responding.

In terms of the experience of service use and perceived quality of health services, cost emerged as a significant factor. The significance of the cost of health services, when economic vulnerability is controlled, may arise because those who do not qualify for the GMS, face substantial doctor fees for each visit and charges for prescriptions.

Difficulty in accessing medical services due to the distance the person needed to travel was negatively associated with perceived quality of several of the services, including education, public transport and elder care. Since we have no specific measure of difficulties in accessing these services, this variable is likely to be capturing elements of a more general problem in accessing services in some areas or for some service users.

Apart from the measures of difficulty in accessing health services, we did not have measures of actual service use. However, there was some evidence of more positive evaluations on the part of groups likely to be users of other services: parents were more positive in their evaluation of health services and public transport; households with pension income gave more positive evaluations of the state pension; retired people (who are entitled to free travel) and single and separated adults (who are less likely to have access to a car) give more positive evaluations of public transport.

The analysis in this chapter had a number of limitations. In particular, there was limited information on the use of specific services (apart from difficulties in accessing health services) and on services entitlements (such as GMS membership, private health insurance). As a result, we are not in a position to draw conclusions regarding differences in perspective between users and non-users of services. The absence of information on why people were reporting positive and negative evaluations of particular services means we are not able to draw conclusions about specific service deficits. Nevertheless, the broad patterns in the data do point to a number of implications for policy at a general level.

POLICY IMPLICATIONS

The customer perspective is a legitimate and important element of the quality of a service, alongside the criteria emphasised by professionals involved in service design. The findings here show that vulnerable groups tend to evaluate public services less positively. This suggests that particular attention needs to be paid to understanding precisely how public services are failing them.

While the Government's *Public Service Reform Plan* expresses a strong commitment to 'placing customer service at the core of everything we do' (Department of Public Expenditure and Reform, 2011, p.3), this commitment needs to be given real content. There are some specific strategies that could ensure that a commitment to quality and customer focus is grounded in evidence.

Survey of Public Perceptions of Service Quality

The establishment in 2011 of the Department of Public Expenditure and Reform provides an opportunity to consider public service quality and the issue of the customer perspective at the broadest level. The fact that this Department is at a remove from the concerns and interests of particular service-oriented departments puts it in a good position to direct this exercise with objectivity. This would involve a survey of the general population based on a robust statistical sample, large enough to provide breakdowns at the level of broad regions. The target group for this exercise should be the general population – users and non-users of public services – and the scope should be the main public services (health, education, long-term care services and community services, income protection, roads and public transport). The aim would be to obtain an overview of public perceptions of the quality of services. In this process, particular attention should be paid to the perspective of economically vulnerable service users (and potential users), as this is the group most reliant on public services. The use of subjective indicators provides a metric which allows a comparison across types of service and with results from other countries. It would also give real content to the commitment to place customer service at the centre of public sector reform.

The survey should go beyond what was possible here with the EQLS data by (a) collecting general information on the use of different services by the respondent and other household members; (b) collecting general information on the reasons for choosing privately provided services in each domain, where applicable; (c) collect information on the socio-demographic characteristics and, especially, the income position of the household and (d) collect high level information on barriers to access, particularly cost, overcrowding/waiting lists and distance.

Like the analysis here, for the reasons outlined in more detail in Watson (2012), attention should be paid to controlling for a pattern of negative responding which may distort the results and bias the comparisons across groups in the population. When the risk of this kind of bias is anticipated at the survey design stage, improved methods of correcting for it can be built into the survey.

Incorporating into this survey the items on perceptions of the quality of services used in the EQLS would allow trends over time and across services to be compared as well as permitting a comparison with the position in other European countries. The survey should be conducted on a regular basis (every 2–3 years) with a standardised content to allow monitoring of trends and of Ireland's position in a European context.

Performance Indicators

The *Public Service Reform Plan* also commits to the development of performance indicators, although these appear under a number of different headings, at a number of different levels[182] and their precise role in ensuring improved quality of public services is not clear. While there are many problems with the broad measures of public sector performance that have been used in international studies (see review by Boyle, 2006), this is often because of limitations in the data available, because of the level of generality of the indicators or the failure to take account of 'inputs' such as differing levels of demand or need for services. Other less tractable difficulties include the challenge involved in measuring quality, as opposed to quantity. The general survey of perceptions of the quality of public services, described above, could potentially play a role in providing broad indicators of quality from the customer perspective.

The ideal performance indicator would be (a) closely tied to the core mission of the public service organisation (b) flexible enough to take account of changes in the 'inputs' – the socio-demographic characteristics of the population served, changing needs and opportunities and (c) used by the organisation on a continuous basis to assess how well it is meeting its goals so that corrections and improvements can be implemented. Because of the need for flexibility and the need for indicators that are useful to the organisation, a case can be made that these should be established at the level of the public service organisation rather than being imposed externally. The parent department and the Department of Public Expenditure and Reform would have a role in assessing the adequacy of the indicators and in ensuring a balance between the professional standards of the provider and the legitimate concerns of customers.

Nevertheless, given commitment in the *Public Service Reform Plan* to 'radically reducing our costs to drive better value for money' (p. 4), there is also a need for high-level public service performance indicators to ensure that service quality is maintained, while costs are being reduced. In the context of our present economic crisis, there is a danger that the focus will be directed to the easily measured cost of the public sector, or numbers employed, at the expense of measures of quality. Further, without broad measures of performance, it will be impossible to detect or quantify improvements in the efficiency of public sector delivery. High level measures of outputs and outcomes are required to support a budgetary process that emphasises performance and accountability (Boyle and MacCarthaigh, 2011). Suggesting the form of such performance indicators goes beyond the scope of this

---

182 Performance indicators are mentioned five times in the Plan: in the context of rationalising the number of state agencies on p. 9; in the context of communicating the level of cross-government initiatives on p. 6; in the context of back-office functions within departments on p. 13; in the context of communicating information on public service delivery to the public on p. 29; in the context of the activities of state agencies on p. 30.

chapter, but a good beginning could be made by assessing the usefulness of approaches adopted elsewhere (see reviews by Boyle, 2006; Mandl, Dierx, and Ilzkovitz, 2008; Prendergast, 2010).

Customer Focus and Service Design

As well as the survey of perceptions of public services, outlined above, proactive strategies could be adopted to involve service recipients in the design of services. The *Programme for Government*, for instance, emphasises the inclusion of representatives of local communities as well as staff on hospital boards (Department of the Taoiseach, 2011, p. 5). As well as involvement at the level of delivery (where the location, size and scope of the hospital, school, care home or bus route has already been decided), service users and potential service users could be involved at the design stage. Particular care should be taken to ensure that vulnerable service users are represented in this context. A proactive strategy is needed here, rather than a passive request for submissions. The latter is likely to attract inputs mainly from groups that are already organised and who might not represent the interests of service users more generally.

Organisation-level Customer Satisfaction Surveys and Staff Climate Surveys

Customer satisfaction and staff climate surveys would be most useful as a means of monitoring service quality by the service-delivery organisation where the results are relevant to the specific service and available in a timely fashion. Ideally, customer satisfaction surveys would be conducted on an ongoing basis and staff climate surveys would be conducted annually.

Customer satisfaction surveys could be implemented relatively inexpensively by having the questionnaire administered at the point of service contact. This serves an important dual function. It provides feedback to service providers and it affirms to service-users that their opinion matters. A carefully designed customer satisfaction survey, administered at the point of contact in a manner that ensures the anonymity of the respondent, could yield important information that is immediately useful to the organisation in assessing its approach to service delivery on an ongoing basis. This would allow problems to be detected relatively quickly and, where possible, remedial action to be taken. If the survey could be completed electronically, this would obviate the need for a separate data entry exercise. Surveys completed at the point of contact have a further advantage in that they generally have a higher response rate, and are more representative as they do not rely on people feeling strongly (positively or negatively) enough to take the trouble to complete a questionnaire afterwards.

In designing the survey, information must be collected in enough detail to allow for the identification of unsuccessful applications for service due to eligibility criteria. Specific questions are likely to be more useful than general ones: such as items on accessibility of information on entitlements prior to the application, gaining access to the building, waiting time, courtesy of the official, clarity of the explanations provided, outcome of the application, whether a follow-up call or return visit is needed, and so on.

Regular anonymous staff climate surveys have the potential to provide information important to effectively managing an organisation. When these surveys focus on problems or challenges emerging in the workplace – either in interpersonal relationships, in interactions with customers or in executing tasks – they have the potential to provide information that facilitates timely management intervention to address issues before they become problems in service delivery. They are likely to be most useful in this regard when they are designed with the specific needs of the organisation in mind. Staff surveys are likely to be most useful in large organisations. Even in relatively small organisations, however, where management-staff relationships are positive, they have a role in bringing to light issues that individual staff members may be reluctant to raise directly with management.

Communicating with customers and the public

It may not always be feasible to deliver services in the way customers would prefer, either for reasons of cost or because there is a trade-off between different aspects of the quality of the service (such as between proximity of service and quality advantages associated with scale of operation). The response of service providers and service designers should be one of respect for the legitimate concerns of the customers and the public; managing expectations while working with the customers to find alternative solutions. This involves rethinking where the responsibility of the public service provider begins and ends: at the door of the school or hospital or at the point where the service need is first identified. Issues of access must necessarily enter into the evaluation of public services.

When the expectations of service recipients and the public cannot be met, there is a need for clear communication and dialogue. A continual flow of information, through customer and staff surveys is important to this process. The general survey of public perceptions, considered alongside high-level performance indicators specific to each service, could play an important part in identifying areas where communication gaps need to be addressed.

REFERENCES

Afonso, A., Schuknecht, L. and Tanzi, V. (2003). 'Public sector efficiency: an international comparison', ECB Working Paper No. 242. Frankfurt: European Central Bank.

Afonso, A., Schuknecht, L. and Tanzi, V. (2005). 'Public sector efficiency: an international comparison', *Public Choice*, 123 (3–4), pp. 321ff.

Anderson, R., Mikulic, B., Vermeylen, G., Lyly-Yrjänäinen, M., Zigante, V. (2009). *Second European Quality of Life Survey: Overview*. Dublin: European

Foundation for the Improvement of Living and Working Conditions.

Boyle, R. (2006). 'Measuring Public Sector Productivity: Lessons from International Experience', (CPMR Discussion Paper Series), Dublin: Institute of Public Administration.

Boyle, R. and MacCarthaigh, M. (2011). *Fit for Purpose? Challenges for Irish Public Administration and Priorities for Public Service Reform*. (IPA State of the Public Service Series, Research Paper No. 4), Dublin: Institute of Public Administration.

Castelli, A., Jacobs, R., Goddard, M. and Smith, P.C. (2009). 'Exploring the Impact of Public Services on Quality of Life Indicators', University of York Centre for Health Economics, Research Paper 46.

Central Statistics Office (2011). *Statistical Yearbook*. Dublin: Government Publications Office.

Clements, B. (2002). 'How Efficient is Education Spending in Europe?' *European Review of Economics and Finance*, 1, 3ff.

Co-ordinating Group of Secretaries (1996). *Delivering Better Government: Second Report to Government of the Co-ordinating Group of Secretaries – A Programme of Change for the Irish Civil Service*, May 1996. Dublin: Department of the Taoiseach. (available at: http://www.taoiseach.gov.ie/ eng/Publications/ Publications_Archive/Publications_2006/Publications_pre_1997/Delivering BetterGov1.pdf)

Department of Public Expenditure and Reform (2011). *Public Service Reform Plan*, (17 November 2011). Dublin: Department of Public Expenditure and Reform (http://per.gov.ie/wp-content/uploads/Public-Service-Reform-181120111.pdf)

Department of the Taoiseach (2011). *Programme for Government*, (11 March 2011; available at http://www.taoiseach.gov.ie/eng/Publications/ Publications_ 2011/Programme_for_Government_2011.pdf)

Fahey, T., Whelan, C., Maître, B. (2004). *Quality of life in Europe – First European Quality of Life Survey 2003*, Eurofound, Office for Official Publications of the European Communities, Luxembourg.

Garvin, D.A. (1984). 'What Does 'Product Quality' Really Mean?' *MIT The Sloan Management Review*, October 15, 1984, 26, 25–43.

Gaster, L. and Squires, A. (2003). 'The conceptual framework: stakeholders, values, objectives and definitions' pp. 39–62 in Gaster, L., Squires, A., Crawley, J., Greenwood, M., Harding, T., Hayden, C. and Scrutton, P. (eds.), *Providing Quality in the Public Sector: A Practical Approach to Improving Public Services*, Philadelphia: Open University Press, 42, Questia, Web, 30 Sept. 2011.

Kuhry, B., Pommer, E. and De Kam, F. (2006). 'Public Sector Performance, An International Comparison', paper presented at the National Institute of Economic and Social Research (NIESR), Fourth Public Sector Performance Conference, London, 20 January.

Mandl, U., Dierx, A., Ilzkovitz, F. (2008). *The Effectiveness and Efficiency of Public Spending*. Brussels: European Commission (doi: 10.2765/22776)

Mattina, T.D. and Gunarsson, V. (2007). 'Budget Rigidity and Expenditure Efficiency in Slovenia'. IMF Working Paper WP/07/131.

Moullin, M. (2002). *Delivering Excellence in Health and Social Care: Quality, Excellence, and Performance Measurement*, Philadelphia: Open University Press, 13, Questia, Web, 30 Sept. 2011.

OECD (2007). 'Public spending efficiency: institutional indicators in primary and secondary education', OECD: Economic Department Working Paper No 543.

OECD (2008). *Ireland: Towards An Integrated Public Service*, OECD Public Management Reviews, Paris: OECD Publishing.

Prendergast, C. (2010). 'What Have We Learnt About Pay For Performance?' (Geary Lecture Winter 2010) *The Economic and Social Review*, 42, Summer, 2011, 113–134

Rose, R. and Newton, K. (2010). *Second European Quality of Life Survey: Evaluating the Quality of Society and Public Services*. Dublin: European Foundation for the Improvement of Living and Working Conditions.

Task Force on the Public Service (2008). *Transforming Public Service: Report of the Task Force on the Public Service*. Dublin: The Stationery Office. (http://per.gov.ie/wp-content/uploads/Transforming_Public_Services_Report.pdf)

Watson, D. (2012) 'Quality of Public Services: Irish Public Perceptions and Implications for Renewal', Dublin: Economic and Social Research Institute, Renewal Series, Paper 6.

Watson, D., Pichler, F. and Wallace, C. (2010). *Subjective Well-being in Europe* (Second European Quality of Life Survey). Dublin: European Foundation for the Improvement of Living and Working Conditions.

Whelan, C.T. and Maître, B. (2010). 'Identifying Economically Vulnerable Groups as the Economic Crisis Emerged'. *The Economic and Social Review*, 41, Winter, 2010, 501–525.

CHAPTER 13

Increasing the Contribution of Evidence to Policy

Frances Ruane, Pete Lunn

> *'A wise man proportions his belief to the evidence.'*
> David Hume

INTRODUCTION

The opening chapter of this volume stressed that the relationship between researchers and policymakers is crucial to the exploitation of evidence for policy. We outlined a specific understanding of what research evidence can contribute to policy and what it cannot – an understanding that researchers and policymakers can hopefully share. In the light of the international movement towards evidence-based policymaking, we argued that even very good evidence is only part of what a policymaker must consider when determining policy. Fairness, priorities, risks and uncertainty all add important and largely subjective elements to any policy decision, even before one considers the financial and political context. Yet we also argued that the potential to use evidence to inform policy is much greater than is often appreciated. High quality research can contribute to the evaluation of specific policies, but good evidence can do much more than that. It can identify new policy challenges, improve predictions of the likely outcomes associated with different policy options, give insights into important causal mechanisms, and prompt the creation of new policy designs.

In this chapter, we return to these two dominant themes: the contribution of evidence to policy and the relationship between researchers and policymakers. We draw on the intervening chapters and our knowledge of policymaking in Ireland to explore how research in Ireland could be used more effectively in policymaking. The analysis is forward looking, offering arguments and propositions intended to improve the way that evidence for policy is generated by researchers and used by Irish policymakers.

REFLECTING ON WHAT EVIDENCE CAN DO

The chapters in this book provided case studies that, when considered together, substantiate the view expressed in Chapter 1 that the potential contribution of research to policy is much broader than its role in the evaluation of specific policies. Some chapters did focus on the evaluation of specific policies: for example, Chapter 2 looked at evidence on how to improve the present method of cost-benefit analysis used for major infrastructure investments; Chapter 3 collated international evidence for and against the introduction of loan-to-value limits for mortgages as a means for reducing the risk of housing bubbles; Chapter 4 performed a similar exercise in relation to pay-for-performance in healthcare, a proposition often mooted as a means to increase efficiency and accountability in that area.

Nevertheless, most of the chapters offered evidence that is relevant to other parts of the policy landscape identified in Figure 1.1 of Chapter 1. Chapters 5 and 6 considered potential improvements to particular interventions within broad policy areas – second-level education and innovation respectively. The analysis in the next two chapters focused more on policy options, where the primary goal of policy was not a matter of much dispute but where evidence could be used to inform the choice of options. Substantial bodies of international evidence were employed to assess the likely outcomes of different options: Chapter 7 considered which of four options was likely to be most effective in getting unemployed people back into work; Chapter 8 weighed up the economic impact of relaxing competition and regulatory policy against perceived potential benefits for insecure workers. The following two chapters combined evidence on the nature of a policy challenge, in both cases associated with the Great Recession, with available evidence on potential options for addressing the challenge. In the case of Chapter 9, the focus was on consumer decision-making in financial services, where relatively recent international evidence raises the question of what policymakers might do to improve consumer decisions; options for addressing the challenge were considered against a much thinner evidence base. Chapter 10 then looked at evidence on the comparative scale of Ireland's fiscal adjustment and at common themes associated with previous fiscal consolidations in Ireland and elsewhere, in search of more successful strategies.

The remaining two chapters both involved new data analysis, the results of which pose fresh policy challenges. Chapter 11 revealed that average earnings and labour costs in the private sector did not fall as the recession took hold, despite very high unemployment, raising the issue of whether policymakers can do anything to help the labour market to clear. Lastly, Chapter 12 found the perceived quality of some public services in Ireland to be lower among the more economically vulnerable, leading naturally to the question of whether these services can be improved for this most disadvantaged group.

LIMITATIONS OF EVIDENCE FOR POLICY

Thus, looking across the whole set of chapters, the role played by evidence varies substantially and, in all cases, has significant policy implications. Yet in no case can good policy be deduced solely from the evidence provided – there are always other considerations. The research adds to the evidence base, but policy must ultimately be based on more. This is the case even where the evidence is clear and strong. One such example is the negative impact on outcomes of streaming[183] in second-level education, as documented in Chapter 5. Any response by policymakers requires not only consideration of this evidence but also a view regarding school autonomy and, by extension, parental choice, because 'policy' is in large measure implemented by schools themselves rather than by central direction. Policy towards and funding for continuing professional development for teachers with respect to teaching mixed-ability groups is also relevant. For policymakers, each of these factors involves a determination of priorities and the taking on of some risks and uncertainties, not to mention potential resource issues. Nonetheless, the evidence to be taken on board is strong and highly informative.

Sometimes the research itself is specifically relevant to the priorities of policymakers. Chapter 4 on pay-for-performance (P4P) in healthcare provides a nice example of this. It concludes that there is insufficient international evidence to support the view that P4P increases the efficiency and/or quality of healthcare. Of itself, this may not be a reason to rule out P4P entirely, but other parts of the research have identified damaging incentives in the Irish health system, the tackling of which ought therefore to take priority over introducing a new payments system. Institutional factors may be important in drawing policy implications too. Any policy response to the main result presented in Chapter 11, which shows that private sector earnings and labour costs did not fall when the recession struck, is likely to take account of the recent political context of social partnership and national wage bargaining. Similarly, in most chapters, the institutional context and recent history of the given policy area are important to the policy implications drawn.

Although the evidence presented in this volume is primarily empirical, the role of theoretical reasoning deserves some discussion. Theories and theoretical models are often valuable tools for selecting the research questions, including the design of data collection systems and priorities for analysis. Theory can play an important role in clarifying assumptions and understanding mechanisms. These assumptions can then be scrutinised and tested for validity in the particular context. Likewise, the mechanisms can be explored, often using micro-data, ideally from longitudinal data, to test their validity. This type of analysis is important to policy design as it heightens policymakers' awareness to the dangers

---

183 'Streaming' is the term used to indicate the grouping of students on the basis of ability for all subjects; 'setting' is the term used to describe ability grouping for individual subjects.

of perverse incentives, resulting in behaviour that is opposite to stated policy objectives. Examples of important theoretical insights include the discussion in Chapter 6 of how externalities are likely to lead to underinvestment in innovation in the private sector and the examination in Chapter 11 of the rationales for firms cutting jobs rather than wages. Sometimes, however, the empirical findings question predominant and influential theoretical models, as when behavioural research on financial decision-making exposes the limits of orthodox competitive market models for understanding the likely impact of competition in retail financial services (Chapter 9).

Theoretical insight can be necessary not only with respect to understanding theories and models of social and economic mechanisms, but also in relation to the validity of inferences. Coherent and sometimes statistically sophisticated theoretical frameworks are essential for estimating the effectiveness of potential interventions. The structural model of innovation in Chapter 6 is a case in point. Understanding such frameworks requires expertise, which is often essential for distinguishing causal relationships from correlations or for ensuring that the evidence presented is unbiased.

Where policymakers are exploring new initiatives, researchers can provide independent critical reviews of empirical evidence – both national and international. This collation of published evidence is common to the majority of the studies in this book. Such reviews may simplify the policymaker's decision or, contrastingly, complicate it, by drawing out elements that could otherwise have been ignored. In such cases, the relatively small investment in research is likely to prove worthwhile, as these elements may have a crucial bearing on managing the risk of policy interventions or non-interventions. An example of the latter is the consistent finding of optimism bias in the *ex ante* evaluation of proposed capital projects, described in Chapter 2.

In relation to the evaluation of specific projects or programmes more generally, either before or after implementation, researchers can assist with ensuring that the methodology incorporates best practice and with assessing the rigour of the process/analysis followed.[184] Many evaluation exercises are straightforward and can be conducted by policy analysts within the civil/public service;[185] the exceptions are where the specific context is very complex from a conceptual, methodological or econometric perspective, or requires the stamp of having been independently analysed.[186] In contributing to evaluation exercises, researchers are

---

[184] Where the institutional or legal setting is complex, researchers from several different disciplines (law, accounting, etc.) may be needed to ensure that the approach is holistic.

[185] Good practice is that such evaluations are either undertaken outside the relevant line department or, if undertaken within the department, are reviewed by the relevant central government department, i.e., Public Expenditure and Reform.

[186] Sometimes external analysts are required to undertake the evaluations to guarantee independence, and where these are very complex, researcher inputs are required, e.g., EU Structural Fund programmes.

well placed to help identify additional data sources or robust programme indicators that will capture programme impact objectively.

Whether undertaken by researchers or by analysts within the public sector, best practice is that policy evaluations should be published. A similar approach is needed for regulatory impact assessments. Sometimes market confidentiality is used as an argument for not publishing – in such cases, confidential peer reviews should be undertaken by researchers who can ensure that the quality of the underlying analysis is appropriate and adequate.

The previous chapters make use of a range of techniques for generating high quality evidence, but there are methods that do not feature. Chapters 6, 11 and 12 each employ original analysis of new or very recent data, but researchers can also generate good evidence from existing or even quite old data. For example, in designing tax changes, response rates (elasticities) based on data from earlier periods can be used to measure likely responses to a specific tax change. Policy changes sometimes generate instructive 'natural experiments' that can inform policy design: for example, the change in smoking behaviour that accompanied the ban on smoking in public places, or the impact of the introduction of divorce on marital breakdown rates. In some cases, specific policy proposals can be tested via policy experiments or randomised controlled trials. Examples include alternative interventions in childhood learning or methods of seeking tax compliance.

Both researchers and policymakers need to appreciate from the outset that any given piece of research is unlikely to provide a 'silver bullet' solution, although on occasion it may suggest a possible course of action to be explored further. Nevertheless, good research can provide evidence that alters the balance of an argument. Many of the policy implications of the previous chapters are of this sort. Although the findings are not, in and of themselves, decisive, policymakers are likely to find them helpful in taking a balanced view ahead of making a decision. As Hume's quote at the opening of this chapter suggests, the wise policymaker will be swayed in proportion to the strength of the evidence. In altering the balance of argument, research challenges some perspectives, supports others, and thus helps to identify the most promising options rather than providing solutions. Even when the volume of research is large and the evidence base broad, the policymaker is still likely to face hard choices and their consequences. High quality research illuminates the context and provides policymakers with the best evidence to inform and, potentially, to justify tough decisions.

THE RESEARCHER–POLICYMAKER RELATIONSHIP[187]

Relationships are likely to be successful where they are based on mutual self-interest and trust – where both parties see benefits to the association and recognise each other's perspective. Researchers are more likely to engage in policy-relevant research if it is compatible with publication in academic journals, if undertaking

---

[187] This section draws on the discussion in Ruane (2012).

policy-related research is recognised and rewarded by their institutions through increased likelihood of promotion, and if they believe that the work will have an influence on policy. Although there are instances where these three criteria are met, more generally there may be grounds for doubting the widespread applicability of all three conditions in Ireland at present. An important question is whether there is a need to improve the incentives for researchers to undertake policy-related work. In addition to these criteria, the relationship is also more likely to be successful where the research questions are interesting, the policy engagement is wide-ranging and the researcher's involvement promises access to data that would not otherwise be available.[188] The researcher is also more likely to be positively engaged when the timeframe for the research is realistic and compatible with other commitments.

Unlike researchers, who act autonomously or quasi-autonomously, the individual policymaker is likely to have limited opportunities to promote greater engagement with the research community without institutional support. Consequently, the culture towards research established by senior officials within a department or agency has a major influence on the behaviour of policymakers within that organisation. Typically, senior officials are likely to be disposed positively towards research if they can see clearly what it can offer. This may depend on several factors. First, given the demands of accountability, the attitude to research is likely to be affected by how policymakers in an area articulate the reason why engagement with research will be productive. A more positive outlook is likely where the department or agency already has analysts with relevant expertise. Second, senior officials are more likely to engage if the output of the relevant researchers is accessible to non-specialists. This accessibility is enhanced where researchers routinely produce non-technical summaries of findings, via research bulletins, policy briefs, web-pages, and so on. Third, engagement is more likely when the relevant researchers are known to be capable of delivering agreed research outputs in a timely way.

From the point of view of increasing the use of evidence in policymaking, there may be much to be gained by fostering more intimate engagement between researchers and policymakers. Based on Best and Holmes (2010), Chapter 1 outlined three models of increasing effectiveness to characterise the researcher-policymaker relationship: linear models, relationship models and systems models. The latter, which involves research and researchers being embedded within the network of stakeholders in a given policy area, represents a potential ideal form of 'engaged scholarship' to aim for. Within such a system, researchers should be able to bring a questioning and technical mind to the issues, while the policymakers and other stakeholders contribute the bulk of institutional and contextual knowledge. This would help to reduce the risk of 'groupthink' and enlarge the options canvassed in a particular policy domain. Working closer together on a

---

188 This is also more likely if institutional accounting systems and intellectual property contracts do not hinder the development of policy research and teaching.

meaningful research agenda would help to establish a clearer understanding of roles, interests and requirements and to reduce potential tensions. At the centre of the relationship is the sharing of robust evidence prepared by the researcher for serious consideration by the policymaker. If the evidence is not robust, or the policymaker is not willing to give it serious consideration, the relationship is doomed.

This level of engagement is not without potential risks. The most obvious is the danger that embedded researchers lose their independence and cease to question or challenge prevailing views: that they promote rather than protect against groupthink. This risk is high if those involved are only comfortable with consensus. This can be mitigated by having open dialogue events, under the Chatham House Rule,[189] and greater acceptance of the value of critical thinking on both sides.[190] To be of value, the debate cannot be one-sided – so those engaging must be in a position to question the researchers effectively. The development of a culture of internal debate within the public service, using 'devil's advocate' processes might also help policymakers to engage with research more effectively. A related proposal was made by the Commission for Investigation into the Banking Sector in Ireland, which diagnosed groupthink within the relevant authorities as a major cause of Ireland's banking crisis (Nyberg, 2011). The independence of researchers can be assisted by active engagement with international networks where they present their research to their peers.

This is not the only available proposal for fostering a culture within the policymaking process that values critical thinking, open discussion and debate. Serious consideration might also be given to a recent proposal intended to improve the quality of all commissioned research by government. The idea is that any researchers, analysts or consultants who are commissioned to produce such research must present their methodology and preliminary findings to a seminar of peers as part of their contractual requirements. This proposal has clear merits. It is not costly, creates good incentives to produce high quality research, and would be likely to increase the overall level of engagement between researchers and policymakers.[191]

PROGRESS

Recent developments do suggest the possibility of more fruitful engagement between researchers and policymakers in the future, and there are healthy signs

---

189 When a meeting, or part thereof, is held under the Chatham House Rule, participants are free to use the information received, but neither the identity nor the affiliation of a speaker, nor that of any other participant, may be revealed.

190 Such events were relatively limited in the past decade, and meetings of the Statistical and Social Inquiry Society of Ireland, which have provided a forum for policy debates for over 150 years, have been poorly attended by policymakers in recent years.

191 This suggestion was made by Frank Barry (Trinity College Dublin) at a meeting at the Royal Irish Academy in 2010.

that this has both political and leadership support within the public sector. While Ireland clearly has some distance to go in relation to the more systematic use of evidence in policymaking, it is important to recognise some developments of note. One is the greater investment in data, which has been coupled with a readiness to make more data accessible for use by researchers. A second is the greater availability of information on websites of many government departments and agencies, which provide much easier access than in the past to information about policies and outcomes, via reports, statistical data, information on management structures, and so on.

A third notable development is the establishment in 2012 of the Irish Government Economic and Evaluation Service (IGEES). It is intended to create 'government economists', who combine high levels of economic skills with institutional knowledge. How the service will work has yet to be clarified, but it would make sense for consideration to be given to the current model being used in Scotland. These economists belong formally to the *Government Economic Service*, which is led by the Chief Economist in Scotland. However, they work alongside statisticians and social policy analysts (who have their own professional groups led by the Chief Statistician and Chief Policy Analyst respectively) in units in different government departments. The professionals in these units work collectively to build evidence bases for use in policymaking, and provide a natural interface with the broader research community.

From where we now stand, the challenge of building a Scottish-style system should not be underestimated. The creation of such analytical units within the civil service departments, and the closer relationships between policymakers and research communities that would likely ensue, would be a step-change for policymaking in Ireland. Ideally, the IGEES should incorporate the whole of the public service and not just the civil service. It is an opportune time to do this, given the major investments in data infrastructure in recent decades and increased numbers of well-trained M.Sc. and Ph.D. graduates. What is required is that the approach to research becomes more systematic, more questioning, and with a greater focus on the important policy issues facing Ireland now and over the coming decades. The time horizon for good policy research is long. Policymakers should see it as investment in infrastructure and not simply as current expenditure.

The research landscape, no more than the policy landscape, does not remain static. The greater availability of data sets and software to analyse them has already had a major impact on policy research internationally as well as nationally, and is linked to the heightened interest in having an evidence base for policy. In Ireland, research and policy have already reaped the benefits of decisions made more than a decade ago, when we began to build what is now described as the National Data Infrastructure. We are now on the cusp of realising the benefits of the investments in the longitudinal studies of children (*Growing up in Ireland*) and of elderly people (*TILDA*), as researchers see the advantage of these high quality surveys to both academic papers and policy research, and policymakers see the potential to ask and have answered complex questions about the life course.[192] Yet further changes that are likely to make the opportunities for more policy relevant research much greater are under way. These changes are being driven by EUROSTAT, which sees the building of longitudinal data sets from administrative records in departments and agencies as a key direction for statistics over the coming decades. This will dramatically increase the amount of data available for policy research, thereby increasing the opportunities for closer collaboration between the research and policymaking communities.

The interaction of evidence and policy, just like the relationship between researchers and policymakers, is dynamic. Evidence needs to be generated on an ongoing basis, if it is to be used effectively. This implies that a successful policy-making system, one that exploits evidence well, will display continual tension between evidence and policy, as new findings change understanding. The trick must be to ensure that this tension is not troublesome or damaging, but creative.

REFERENCES

Best, A. and Holmes, B. (2010). 'Systems Thinking, Knowledge and Action: Towards Better Models and Methods.' *Evidence & Policy*, 6, 145–159.

Nyberg, P. (2011). *Misjudging Risk: Causes of the Systemic Banking Crisis in Ireland*. Accessed at: http://www.bankinginquiry.gov.ie.

Ruane, F. (2012). 'Research Evidence and Policymaking in Ireland'. *Administration*, 60, 119–38.

---

192 An example of the usefulness of such longitudinal data is evident in the redesign of the second-level curriculum, which has been heavily informed by the ESRI Post-Primary Longitudinal Study.

Index

A
active labour market policies 118–39
  and activation strategies 119–21
  conclusion 131–2
  direct employment schemes in Ireland 128
  direct job creation in public sector 124
  effectiveness of programmes 124–31
  incentives to create jobs in private sector 124
  institutional reforms in Ireland 133
  instruments used to activate the unemployed 121–3
  internship programmes 129
  Intreo 125–6, 133
  job search assistance 118–19, 123–6, 131, 132
  job search requirements 122
  Jobseekers Benefit and Jobseekers Allowance 119–21
  market links 132
  National Employment Action Plan 125–6, 133
  private sector incentive schemes 128–9, 131
  programmes 123–4
  Public Employment Services 118–19, 120, 121, 132
  public sector job creation programmes 127–8, 131
  referrals to ALMPs 122
  SOLAS 133
  training 119, 123–4, 126–7, 131–3
  what works? 130–1
  youth measures 129–30, 132
  see also unemployment
aims of book 4–5
Asia 144
Australia 23, 31, 35, 60, 61–2
Austria 104, 107, 219, 246, 248, 249

B
Baltic States 201, 204–12
banking
  crisis 44
  legislation 148, 165
  system 221
Belgium 104, 194, 219, 248, 249
Benefit to Cost Ratio 29
Best, Allan 18
Britain *see* UK

C
Canada 48, 50, 149, 194
capital investment 23–8
cartels 144–5
Central Bank 44–5, 165
Central Statistics Office 108, 224
Centres for Science, Engineering and Technology 113
China 48, 52
Coalition for Evidence-Based Policy 7
Commission for Aviation Regulation 148
Commission for Investigation into the Banking Sector in Ireland 272
Committee on the Global Financial System 40, 43, 51
Community Employment Scheme 119
Community Innovation Surveys 103, 104, 113
Competence/Technology Centres 113
competition 96, 97, 140–61, 217, 221
  codes of fair 147
  Competition Act 152–3
  Competition Authority 153
  conclusions 156–7
  and employment 147
  excessive or destructive 141–2, 149, 150, 154
  exemptions from 146–7, 156

in financial services 167–74
reduced enforcement of competition law 142–3, 144–6, 156–7
standards and tests for 152–6
see also economic security; regulatory policy
Comptroller and Auditor General 34
Consumer Protection Code 176–7, 180

D
Denmark 104, 130, 201, 203–4, 206, 210, 249
Department of Education and Skills 133
Department of the Environment 44
Department of Finance 23
Department of Public Expenditure and Reform 245, 261
Department of Social Protection 125

E
earnings and labour costs over the recession 217–43
  adjustment strategies of firms 219
  average labour costs in 2006 and 2009 233
  background 218–21
  banking system 221
  changes in employment conditions in 2009 234–5
  conclusions and policy implications 239–41
  data and methodology 224
  difference in characteristics 226
  difference in returns to characteristics 226–7
  Earnings, Hours and Employment Costs Survey 225
  employee level results 225–39
  enterprise births 224
  European survey 219
  Figure 11.1 index of real unit labour costs 220
  Figure 11.2 quarterly GDP and GNP 222
  Figure 11.3 output and the wage bill 222
  Figure 11.4 adjustment in average earnings and employment 223
  firm level labour cost analysis 232–9
  larger firms 228–9
  magnitude of crisis 221–4
  male and female workers 226–8, 240, 241
  migrant workers 227
  Oaxaca-Blinder decompositions 227, 233
  part-time workers 226, 228, 238, 239–40
  pay cuts across public sector 241
  property market 221
  return to education 226, 228
  social partnership model 220, 240
  Table 11.1 average hourly and weekly earnings 225
  Table 11.2 decomposition of change in wages 227
  Table 11.3 breakdown of decomposition results for male employees 229–30
  Table 11.4 breakdown of decomposition results for female employees 231–2
  Table 11.5 decomposition of 2006–09 average labour cost gap 234
  Table 11.6 changes in employment conditions in 2009 235
  Table 11.7 characteristics of firms that implemented cuts in employment conditions 236–7
  Table 11.8 impact of individual employment condition cuts on firms' average labour costs 238–9
  unemployment 218–19, 223–4
  wages 217–20, 221, 224, 227, 239–41
  younger workers 226, 229
Economic Outlook 2007 192
Economic Research Institute 2
economic security 140–61
  background 141–3
  competition and regulatory policy intervention to promote 151–2
  conclusions 156–7
  and consumer welfare 141, 151, 153
  and fair tax system 141
  see also competition; regulatory policy
Economic and Social Research Council 7
Economic and Social Research Institute 4, 77

educational research 77–95
  ability grouping 77–8, 82–4, 90
  challenges for second-level education
    80–1
  conclusions and implications for policy
    89–90
  curriculum assessment 88
  differences between schools 82
  differentiation in teaching methods 4
  early school leaving 80, 82, 85, 129
  Educational Research Centre 77
  exam-focused system 81, 87–9
  expenditure on second-level education 80
  inequality in educational outcomes
    80–1, 85
  international benchmarks 80
  literacy and numeracy 80
  mathematics 80, 85, 87
  mixed ability grouping 82–4
  outcomes 79–80
  pace of instruction 81, 83–4, 90
  PISA study 84
  Post-Primary Longitudinal Study 88
  rates of attainment 80
  ratio of students to teachers 80
  reform of junior cycle 78, 88, 90
  school effects 81–2
  setting 82, 83
  social class and ethnicity 83, 90
  social climate of school 84–5
  streaming 77–8, 82–3
  teacher characteristics 85–6
  teacher-student relations 82–4, 88, 90
  Teaching and Learning International
    Survey 87
  teaching methods 80–1, 86–9
  Transition Year 88
  work experience 88
employment 128, 147, 217, 225–39
  Intreo 125–6, 133
  National Employment Action Plan
    125–6, 133
  National Employment Survey 217, 224
  Public Employment Services 118–19,
    120, 121, 132
  public sector job creation programmes
    127–8, 131
  see also unemployment
enterprise innovation surveys 96–7
Enterprise Ireland 109, 110, 111, 112, 114
Estonia 201, 204–5, 211
European Central Bank 211
European Commission 140–1, 143, 153,
  177
European Monetary System 203
European Quality of Life Survey 246
European Union 13, 140, 153
  Consumer Survey 165
  EU-IMF Programme of Financial Support
    for Ireland 142
  Key Investor Information Documents 177
EUROSTAT 274
evaluation methods for public
  infrastructure 23–8
  methodologies 25–7
Expert Group on Resource Allocation and
  Financing in the Health Sector 58

F
FÁS 125–6
Financial Regulator 44, 166
financial services, protecting consumers of
  162–86
  advertising 165–6
  background 163
  behavioural biases 167–74, 176
  Central Bank Reform Act 165
  competition, information and
    behavioural biases 167–74
  conclusions 179–80
  consumer perceptions of inflation 165
  consumers and Ireland's crisis 163–7
  credit cards 164–5, 173, 178
  decision-making 163–5, 167–79
  Figure 9.1 savings ratio 164
  Figure 9.2 consumers in Ireland who
    switched provider 168
  financial advice 176
  financial capability survey 164
  financial education 174–6

homeowners and mortgages 163, 164, 166, 173, 178
impact of biases at market level 172–4
investments 165, 173
post-crisis policy context 165–7
retirement and pensions 172
safety tests for finanacial products 178–9
saving and borrowing 172–3
soft paternalism 177–8
Table 9.1 behavioural biases in decision-making 170–1
Finland 44, 104, 246, 248, 249
fiscal consolidation strategies 187–216
  Baltic States 204–12
  CAPB 192, 193, 201
  common factors 187–8
  composition of consolidation 190–1
  conclusions 212–13
  Denmark 203–4
  European Exchange Rate Mechanism 202
  exchange rate changes 194
  expenditure measures 209–10
  expenditure reform 201–2
  Figure 10.1 unemployment 206
  Figure 10.2 gross national income per capita 207
  Figure 10.3 severe material deprivation rates 208
  Figure 10.4 net migration in consolidation episodes 209
  Figure 10.5 gross national income per capita 212
  individual case studies 201–9
  Ireland 1983–84 and 1987–89 201–2
  lessons learned 209–12
  meta-analysis 189–95
  monetary policy 194
  pace of consolidation 189–90
  political structure 195
  Programme for National Recovery 201
  social benefits in Ireland 210
  summary 195
  Table 10.1 main findings from meta-analysis 196–200
  taxation 201–2
  types of expenditure cuts 191–4
France 104, 249

G
General Medical System 253, 259
Germany 31, 63, 85, 104, 126, 249
Government Economic Service 273
Greece 248, 249

H
Harvard University 177
healthcare 1–2, 6, 56–76
  background 57–8
  conclusions 68–9
  and decreases in public expenditure 68
  financial incentives 58, 67–8
  gaming 61
  General Medical System 253, 259
  hospital care 62–3
  integrated care 63–4, 67–8
  interaction between public and private sectors 58
  pay for performance in 59–61, 64–6
  policy implications and lessons 66–8
  primary care 60–2, 67
  Public Service Agreement 57–8
  public services 245, 247, 248, 249, 250, 252–3
  quality of care for chronic disease 60
  recommendations 66–8
Higher Education Institute 112
homeownership 49–52, 163, 164, 166, 173, 178
Hong Kong 46–8, 50–1, 53
Honohan report into Irish banking crisis 44
housing 39–55
  boom and crash 40–1
  and homeownership 49–52, 163, 164, 166, 173, 178
  house price volatility 41, 45–6, 52
  mortgages 40–50, 163–4, 166, 173, 178
  see also loan-to-value ratios
Hume, David 266

I
IMF 46, 142, 189, 190, 194, 210
increasing the contribution of evidence to policy 266–74
  limitations of evidence for policy 268–70
  progress 272–4
  reflecting what evidence can do 267
  researcher–policymaker relationship 270–2
innovation and productivity in enterprises 96–117
  analytical framework 100–3
  background 97–100
  building research excellence 99
  Community Innovation Surveys 103
  conclusions 112–14
  empirical evidence 103–5
  enterprise size 100–1
  framework conditions 97–8
  High Potential Start-Ups 110
  indigenous enterprises 108–9, 111–12
  innovation expenditure per employee 106, 110
  innovation systems 101
  international trade 102
  key issues for policy 112
  key policy messages 108–12, 114
  link between innovation and productivity 105, 108–9
  market power 100–1
  market and systemic failures 98
  measurement and data 102–3
  R&D 100, 101, 102, 103, 109, 111, 113
  small and medium-size enterprises 98–9
  which enterprises innovate successfully? 106–8, 110
  which enterprises invest in R&D? 105–6, 109–10
Intreo 125–6, 133
Irish Financial Services Regulatory Authority 165
Irish Government Economic and Evaluation Service 273
Italy 194, 248, 249

J
Japan 146

K
Knowledge-to-Action framework 18
Korea 47, 48–9, 51, 52, 53

L
labour market policies *see* active labour market policies
Latvia 201, 204–5, 211
Lind, James 1–2
Lithuania 201, 204–6, 211
loan-to-value ratios 39–55
  background 40–1
  conclusions 52–3
  evidence on limits on 46–7
  Figure 3.1 average loan-to-value ratio 42
  Figure 3.2 average house price 42
  Figures 3.3 and 3.3b mortgages 43
  and homeownership 49–52
  house price volatility 41, 45–6, 52–3
  international evidence 39–40
  issues surrounding implementation of 50–2
  LTV limits and debt-to-income limits 48–9
  macroprudential policy 40, 48, 51–2
  mortgages 40–50
  multiple loans and debt problems 51
  and risks 44
  role in housing booms 45–6
  what happened in Ireland? 41–5
Luxembourg 104, 107, 248, 249

M
Making Credit Safer 179
mortgages 40–50, 163–4, 166, 173, 178
movement towards evidence-based policy-making 5–15
multidisciplinary approaches 6

N
National Consumer Agency 165, 167, 178
National Data Infrastructure 273

National Development Plan 24
National Economic and Social Forum 7
National Employment Action Plan 125–6
National Employment Survey 217, 224
Netherlands, The 104, 107, 168, 248, 249
Norway 104, 248, 249
Nudge 177

O
OECD 121, 140–1, 143, 149, 154, 155, 157
  Economic Outlook 2007 192
  and fiscal consolidation strategies 187, 191–2, 203
  Jobs Strategy 120, 122
Office of Fair Trading 166
optimism bias 24, 28–9
Oslo Manual 103

P
policy areas 10–13
policy challenges 8–9
policy landscape 14–15
policy options 10
Portugal 246, 248, 249
Programme for Government 58, 68, 245
Programme for National Recovery 201
project evaluation 23
Public Employment Services 118–19, 120, 121, 132
public infrastructure 23–38
  assessment of likely future needs 35–6
  background 24–5
  climate change impacts 32
  conclusions 34–6
  consumption approach 31
  cost overruns 27–9
  cost-benefit analysis 24–35
  decision-making 27
  discount rates 29–36
  evaluation methodologies 25–7
  Figure 2.1 comparison 33
  macroeconomic return 24
  maintenance of existing 36
  and optimism bias 24, 28–9

project evaluation and cost-benefit analysis 23
project risks 27–9, 35
and reduced budget 24
Table 2.1 discount rate 30
public services 241, 244–74
  background 245
  care services for the elderly 248, 249, 254, 257–8
  characteristics of individuals and households 250–1
  communicating with customers and the public 263
  critical response pattern 253
  customer focus and service design 262
  data and measurement 248–59
  Department of Public Expenditure and Reform 245
  discussion 258–9
  and economic vulnerability 250, 252, 254–5
  education 245–6, 247, 249, 250, 255, 256, 258
  European Quality of Life Survey 246–8, 260
  Figure 12.1 rating of public services in Europe 249
  findings from the analysis 254
  health 245–50, 252–3, 254–5, 257–8, 259
  measuring perceived quality of 248–9
  organisation-level customer satisfaction surveys 262–3
  organisation-level staff climate surveys 262–3
  other characteristics 255–6
  perceptions of quality 244–5
  performance indicators 261–2
  policy implications 259–63
  Programme for Government 245
  Public Service Reform Plan 245, 259–61
  quality 246–7
  and social isolation 250
  state pension 248–9, 250–1, 254–5, 256, 258, 259
  survey of public perceptions of service quality 260

Table 12.1 characteristics of individuals and households 251–2
Table 12.2 economic vulnerability, health and transport 253
Table 12.3 model of ratings of quality of 256–7
taxation 247
transport 248–9, 252–5, 257–8
vulnerable groups 254–5, 259
see also educational research; healthcare

R
regulatory policy 140–61
  Better Regulation Unit 154–5
  changing rules 147–9
  conclusions 156–7
  dual objectives 148
  and economic rents 149–50, 251
  and the European Union 140, 142
  independence of regulators 148
  intervention 152–6
  and licences 149–50, 151
  and regulated enterprises 148
  Regulatory Impact Analysis 154
  restrictive sector-specific entry and price regulation 149–51
  screening new regulations 154–6
  standards and tests for intervention 156
  and vital services 148
  see also competition; economic security
researcher–policymaker relationship 4–5, 18–19
Russell, Bertrand 1

S
Scotland 61, 273
Singapore 47, 52
Solesbury, William 17
South America 191
Spain 104, 168, 249
specific policies 13–14
Statistical and Social Inquiry Society of Ireland 2
structure of book 19–21
Sunstein, Cass 177

Sweden 44, 127, 249
Switzerland 104, 107

T
transport 1, 248–9, 252–5, 257–8

U
UK 6, 13–14, 17, 144, 148, 177
  boom in economy 202, 211
  Economic and Social Research Council 7, 17
  education 81
  healthcare 56, 60, 61, 63, 65
  House of Commons Science and Technology Committee 17
  infrastructure 31, 34
  innovation 104
  mortgages 173
  public services 249
  unemployment 130
unemployment 19, 118–39, 147, 151, 206, 218–19, 223–4
  background 119
  Community Employment Scheme 119
  and early school leaving 129
  instruments used to activate the unemployed 121–3
  Intreo 125–6, 133
  job search assistance 118–19, 123–6, 131, 132
  job search requirements 122
  Jobseekers Benefit and Jobseekers Allowance 119–21
  long-term during recessions 130
  National Employment Action Plan 125–6, 133
  private sector incentive schemes 128–9
  Public Employment Services 118–19, 120, 121–3, 132
  public sector job creation programmes 127–8, 131
  publicly subsidised employment schemes 122
  referrals to ALMPs 122
  scale of Irish crisis 133

SOLAS 133
training 119, 123–4, 126–7, 131–3
youth measures 129–30
see also active labour market policies; employment
United States 12, 168–9, 172, 174, 175–6, 178
   cartels 144–5
   Coalition for Evidence-Based Policy 7, 14
   Consumer Financial Protection Bureau 181
   education 81, 86
   fiscal consolidation strategies 191
   Great Depression 140, 143, 149
   healthcare 56, 62–3, 64
   housing loans 44, 51
   infrastructure 28, 31
   LTV ratios 45, 49
   Making Credit Safer 179
   New Deal 146–7
   Office of Information and Regulatory Affairs 177
   Physician Group Practice 60
   Securities and Exchange Commission 177

W

what evidence can do 8
what evidence cannot do 15–17
when and how can evidence inform policy? 1–22
   Figure 1.1 the policy landscape 9
   introduction 1–5
   movement towards evidence-based policy-making 5–15
   policy areas 10–13
   policy challenges 8
   policy landscape 9, 14–15
   policy options 10
   researcher-policymaker relationship 18
   specific policies 13–14
   structure of book 19–21
   what evidence can do 8
   what evidence cannot do 15–17
Whitaker, T.K. 2